NOTICE TO SUBSCRIBERS.

MESSRS. CLARK have much pleasure in issuing to their Subscribers: Tatian, Theophilus, and the Clementine Recognitions, in one volume, and the first volume of Clement of Alexandria, completing the first year's subscription.

The very great favour with which this series has been received, assures the Publishers, not only that it was needed, but that the public are satisfied with the learning and impartiality with which the Editors and Translators have so far executed their task ; and all care is being taken in carrying out the arrangements for the future.

The first issue (of two volumes) for the second year will be ready about October ; it will consist of one volume of Irenæus, and probably of the Clementine Homilies and the Apostolic Constitutions. The Publishers endeavour to adhere as nearly as possible to chronological order ; but, as formerly stated, this is not always practicable.

The success of such an enterprise depends very much on the kindness of Subscribers in making the series known among their friends, and the Publishers have been already very much indebted in this matter.

The subscription for second year may be remitted as soon as convenient after the issue of the present volumes.

EDINBURGH, 38, GEORGE STREET,
May 1867.

ANTE-NICENE

CHRISTIAN LIBRARY:

TRANSLATIONS OF
THE WRITINGS OF THE FATHERS

DOWN TO A.D. 325.

EDITED BY THE

REV. ALEXANDER ROBERTS, D.D.,

AND

JAMES DONALDSON, LL.D.

VOL. III.

TATIAN, THEOPHILUS, AND THE CLEMENTINE
RECOGNITIONS.

EDINBURGH:
T. AND T. CLARK, 38, GEORGE STREET.

MDCCCLXVIII.

MURRAY AND GIBB, EDINBURGH,
PRINTERS TO HER MAJESTY'S STATIONERY OFFICE.

THE WRITINGS OF TATIAN

AND THEOPHILUS;

AND

THE CLEMENTINE RECOGNITIONS.

TRANSLATED BY

REV. B. P. PRATTEN, REV. MARCUS DODS, A.M.,

AND

REV. THOMAS SMITH, D.D.

EDINBURGH:

T. & T. CLARK, 38, GEORGE STREET.

LONDON: HAMILTON & CO.   DUBLIN: JOHN ROBERTSON & CO.

MDCCCLXVIII.

CONTENTS.

TATIAN.

TRANSLATED BY REV. B. P. PRATTEN.

THEOPHILUS.

TRANSLATED BY REV. MARCUS DODS, A.M.

CLEMENT.

TRANSLATED BY REV. THOMAS SMITH, D.D.

TATIAN'S ADDRESS TO THE GREEKS.

A

INTRODUCTORY NOTICE.

E learn from several sources that Tatian was an Assyrian, but know nothing very definite either as to the time or place of his birth. Epiphanius (*Hær.* xlvi.) declares that he was a native of Mesopotamia; and we infer from other ascertained facts regarding him, that he flourished about the middle of the second century. He was at first an eager student of heathen literature, and seems to have been especially devoted to researches in philosophy. But he found no satisfaction in the bewildering mazes of Greek speculation, while he became utterly disgusted with what heathenism presented to him under the name of religion. In these circumstances, he happily met with the sacred books of the Christians, and was powerfully attracted by the purity of morals which these inculcated, and by the means of deliverance from the bondage of sin which they revealed. He seems to have embraced Christianity at Rome, where he became acquainted with Justin Martyr, and enjoyed the instructions of that eminent teacher of the gospel. After the death of Justin, Tatian unfortunately fell under the influence of the Gnostic heresy, and founded an ascetic sect, which, from the rigid principles it professed, was called that of the Encratites, that is, "*The self-controlled,*" or, "*The masters of themselves.*" Tatian latterly established himself at Antioch, and acquired a considerable number of disciples, who continued after his death to be distinguished by the practice of those austerities which he had enjoined. The sect of the Encratites is supposed to have been established about A.D. 166, and Tatian appears to have died some few years afterwards.

The only extant work of Tatian is his "Address to the Greeks." It is a most unsparing and direct exposure of the enormities of heathenism. Several other works are said to have been composed by Tatian; and of these, a *Diatessaron*, or *Harmony of the Four Gospels*, is specially mentioned. His Gnostic views led him to exclude from the continuous narrative of our Lord's life, given in this work, all those passages which bear upon the incarnation and true humanity of Christ. Notwithstanding this defect, we cannot but regret the loss of this earliest gospel harmony; but the very title it bore is important, as showing that the four Gospels, and these only, were deemed authoritative about the middle of the second century.

ADDRESS OF TATIAN TO THE GREEKS.

——◆——

CHAP. I.—*The Greeks claim, without reason, the invention of the arts.*

BE not, O Greeks, so very hostilely disposed towards the Barbarians, nor look with ill will on their opinions. For which of your institutions has not been derived from the Barbarians? The most eminent of the Telmessians invented the art of divining by dreams; the Carians, that of prognosticating by the stars; the Phrygians and the most ancient Isaurians, augury by the flight of birds; the Cyprians, the art of inspecting victims. To the Babylonians you owe astronomy; to the Persians, magic; to the Egyptians, geometry; to the Phœnicians, instruction by alphabetic writing. Cease, then, to miscall these imitations inventions of your own. Orpheus, again, taught you poetry and song; from him, too, you learned the mysteries. The Tuscans taught you the plastic art; from the annals of the Egyptians you learned to write history; you acquired the art of playing the flute from Marsyas and Olympus,—these two rustic Phrygians constructed the harmony of the shepherd's pipe. The Tyrrhenians invented the trumpet; the Cyclops, the smith's art; and a woman who was formerly a queen of the Persians, as Hellanicus tells us, the method of joining together epistolary tablets :[1] her name was Atossa. Wherefore lay aside this conceit, and be not ever boasting of your elegance of diction; for, while you applaud yourselves, your own people will of course side with you. But it becomes a man of sense to wait for the testimony of others, and it becomes men to be

[1] ἐπιστολὰς συντάττειν, *i.e.* for transmission by letter-carriers.—*Otto.*

5

of one accord also in the pronunciation of their language.
But, as matters stand, to you alone it has happened not
to speak alike even in common intercourse; for the way
of speaking among the Dorians is not the same as that of
the inhabitants of Attica, nor do the Æolians speak like
the Ionians. And, since such a discrepancy exists where it
ought not to be, I am at a loss whom to call a Greek. And,
what is strangest of all, you hold in honour expressions not
of native growth, and by the intermixture of barbaric words
have made your language a medley. On this account we
have renounced your wisdom, though I was once a great pro-
ficient in it; for, as the comic poet[1] says—

> These are gleaners' grapes and small talk,—
> Twittering places of swallows, corrupters of art;

Yet those who eagerly pursue it shout lustily, and croak like
so many ravens. You have, too, contrived the art of rhetoric
to serve injustice and slander, selling the free power of your
speech for hire, and often representing the same thing at one
time as right, at another time as not good. The poetic art,
again, you employ to describe battles, and the amours of the
gods, and the corruption of the soul.

CHAP. II.—*The vices and errors of the philosophers.*

What noble thing have you produced by your pursuit of
philosophy? Who of your most eminent men has been free
from vain boasting? Diogenes, who made such a parade of
his independence with his tub, was seized with a bowel com-
plaint through eating a raw polypus, and so lost his life by
gluttony. Aristippus, walking about in a purple robe, led a
profligate life, in accordance with his professed opinions.
Plato, a philosopher, was sold by Dionysius for his gorman-
dizing propensities. And Aristotle, who absurdly placed a
limit to Providence and made happiness to consist in the
things which give pleasure, quite contrary to his duty as a
preceptor flattered Alexander, forgetful that he was but a
youth; and he, showing how well he had learned the lessons
of his master, because his friend would not worship him

[1] Aristoph. *Ranæ*, 92, 93.

shut him up and carried him about like a bear or a leopard. He in fact obeyed strictly the precepts of his teacher in displaying manliness and courage by feasting, and transfixing with his spear his intimate and most beloved friend, and then, under a semblance of grief, weeping and starving himself, that he might not incur the hatred of his friends. I could laugh at those also who in the present day adhere to his tenets,—people who say that sublunary things are not under the care of Providence; and so, being nearer the earth than the moon, and below its orbit, they themselves look after what is thus left uncared for; and as for those who have neither beauty, nor wealth, nor bodily strength, nor high birth, they have no happiness, according to Aristotle. Let such men philosophize, for me!

CHAP. III.—*Ridicule of the philosophers.*

I cannot approve of Heraclitus, who, being self-taught and arrogant, said, "I have explored myself." Nor can I praise him for hiding his poem[1] in the temple of Artemis, in order that it might be published afterwards as a mystery; and those who take an interest in such things say that Euripides the tragic poet came there and read it, and, gradually learning it by heart, carefully handed down to posterity this darkness[2] of Heraclitus. Death, however, demonstrated the stupidity of this man; for, being attacked by dropsy, as he had studied the art of medicine as well as philosophy, he plastered himself with cow-dung, which, as it hardened, contracted the flesh of his whole body, so that he was pulled in pieces, and thus died. Then, one cannot listen to Zeno, who declares that at the conflagration the same men will rise again to perform the same actions as before; for instance, Anytus and Miletus to accuse, Busiris to murder his guests, and Hercules to repeat his labours; and in this doctrine of the conflagration he introduces more wicked than just persons—one Socrates and a Hercules, and a few more of the same class, but not many, for the bad will be found far more numerous than the good. And according to him the

---

[1] περὶ φύσεως. [2] He was called ὁ σκοτεινός for his obscurity.

Deity will manifestly be the author of evil, dwelling in sewers and worms, and in the perpetrators of impiety. The eruptions of fire in Sicily, moreover, confute the empty boasting of Empedocles, in that, though he was no god, he falsely almost gave himself out for one. I laugh, too, at the old wife's talk of Pherecydes, and the doctrine inherited from him by Pythagoras, and that of Plato, an imitation of his, though some think otherwise. And who would give his approval to the cynogamy of Crates, and not rather, repudiating the wild and tumid speech of those who resemble him, turn to the investigation of what truly deserves attention? Wherefore be not led away by the solemn assemblies of philosophers who are no philosophers, who dogmatize one against the other, though each one vents but the crude fancies of the moment. They have, moreover, many collisions among themselves; each one hates the other; they indulge in conflicting opinions, and their arrogance makes them eager for the highest places. It would better become them, moreover, not to pay court to kings unbidden, nor to flatter men at the head of affairs, but to wait till the great ones come to them.

CHAP. IV.—*The Christians worship God alone.*

For what reason, men of Greece, do you wish to bring the civil powers, as in a pugilistic encounter, into collision with us? And, if I am not disposed to comply with the usages of some of them, why am I to be abhorred as a vile miscreant? Does the sovereign order the payment of tribute, I am ready to render it. Does my master command me to act as a bondsman and to serve, I acknowledge the serfdom. Man is to be honoured as a fellow-man; God alone is to be feared,—He who is not visible to human eyes, nor comes within the compass of human art. Only when I am commanded to deny Him, will I not obey, but will rather die than show myself false and ungrateful. Our God did not begin to be in time: He alone is without beginning, and He Himself is the beginning of all things. God is a Spirit,[1] not

[1] John iv. 24.

pervading matter, but the Maker of material spirits, and of the forms that are in matter; He is invisible, impalpable, being Himself the Father of both sensible and invisible things. Him we know from His creation, and apprehend His invisible power by His works.[1] I refuse to adore that workmanship which He has made for our sakes. The sun and moon were made for us: how, then, can I adore my own servants? How can I speak of stocks and stones as gods? For the spirit that pervades matter is inferior to the more divine spirit; and this, even when assimilated to the soul, is not to be honoured equally with the perfect God. Nor even ought the ineffable God to be presented with gifts; for He who is in want of nothing is not to be misrepresented by us as though He were indigent. But I will set forth our views more distinctly.

CHAP. v.—*The doctrine of the Christians as to the creation of the world.*

God was in the beginning; but the beginning, we have been taught, is the power of the Logos. For the Lord of the universe, who is Himself the necessary ground (ὑπόστα-σις) of all being, inasmuch as no creature was yet in existence was alone; but inasmuch as He was all power, Himself the necessary ground of things visible and invisible, with Him were all things; with Him, by Logos-power (διὰ λογικῆς δυνάμεως), the Logos Himself also, who was in Him, subsists. And by His simple will the Logos springs forth; and the Logos, not coming forth in vain, becomes the first-begotten work of the Father. Him (the Logos) we know to be the beginning of the world. But He came into being by partici-pation,[2] not by abscission; for what is cut off is separated from the original substance, but that which comes by partici-

---

[1] Rom. i. 20.

[2] κατὰ μερισμόν. Some translate, "by division," but the above is preferable. The sense, according to Otto, is that the Logos, having received a peculiar nature, shares in the *rational power* of the Father as a lighted torch partakes of the light of the torch from which it is kindled. Comp. Just. Mar. *Dial. c. T.*, chap. lxi.

pation, making its choice of function,[1] does not render him deficient from whom it is taken. For just as from one torch many fires are lighted, but the light of the first torch is not lessened by the kindling of many torches, so the Logos, coming forth from the Logos-power of the Father, has not divested of the Logos-power Him who begat Him. I myself, for instance, talk, and you hear ; yet, certainly, I who converse do not become destitute of speech (λόγος) by the transmission of speech, but by the utterance of my voice I endeavour to reduce to order the unarranged matter in your minds. And as the Logos, begotten in the beginning, begat in turn our world, having first created for Himself the necessary matter, so also I, in imitation of the Logos, being begotten again, and having become possessed of the truth, am trying to reduce to order the confused matter which is kindred with myself. For matter is not, like God, without beginning, nor, as having no beginning, is of equal power with God ; it is begotten, and not produced by any other being, but brought into existence by the Framer of all things alone.

Chap. vi.—*Christians' belief in the resurrection.*

And on this account we believe that there will be a resurrection of bodies after the consummation of all things ; not, as the Stoics affirm, according to the return of certain cycles, the same things being produced and destroyed for no useful purpose, but a resurrection once for all, when our periods of existence are completed, and in consequence solely of the constitution of things under which men alone live, for the purpose of passing judgment upon them. Nor is sentence upon us passed by Minos or Rhadamanthus, before whose decease not a single soul, according to the mythic tales, was judged ; but the Creator, God Himself, becomes the arbiter. And, although you regard us as mere triflers and babblers, it troubles us not, since we have faith in this doctrine. For just as, not existing before I was born, I knew not who I was, and only existed in the potentiality (ὑπόστασις) of fleshly

---

[1] οἰκονομίας τὴν αἵρεσιν προσλαβόν. The above seems the simplest rendering of this difficult passage, but several others have been proposed.

matter, but being born, after a former state of nothingness, I have obtained through my birth a certainty of my existence; in the same way, having been born, and through death existing no longer, and seen no longer, I shall exist again, just as before I was not, but was afterwards born. Even though fire destroy all traces of my flesh, the world receives the vaporized matter; and though dispersed through rivers and seas, or torn in pieces by wild beasts, I am laid up in the storehouses of a wealthy Lord. And, although the poor and the godless know not what is stored up, yet God the Sovereign, when He pleases, will restore the substance that is visible to Him alone to its pristine condition.

CHAP. VII.—*Concerning the fall of man.*

For the heavenly Logos, a spirit emanating from the Father and a Logos from the Logos-power, in imitation of the Father who begat Him made man an image of immortality, so that, as incorruption is with God, in like manner, man, sharing in a part of God, might have the immortal principle also. The Logos, too, before the creation of men, was the Framer of angels. And each of these two orders of creatures was made free to act as it pleased, not having the nature of good, which again is with God alone, but is brought to perfection in men through their freedom of choice, in order that the bad man may be justly punished, having become depraved through his own fault, but the just man be deservedly praised for his virtuous deeds, since in the exercise of his free choice he refrained from transgressing the will of God. Such is the constitution of things in reference to angels and men. And the power of the Logos, having in itself a faculty to foresee future events, not as fated, but as taking place by the choice of free agents, foretold from time to time the issues of things to come; it also became a forbidder of wickedness by means of prohibitions, and the encomiast of those who remained good. And, when men attached themselves to one who was more subtle than the rest,[1] having regard to his being the first-born, and declared him to be

---

[1] Gen. iii. 1.

God, though he was resisting the law of God, then the power of the Logos excluded the beginner of the folly and his adherents from all fellowship with Himself. And so he who was made in the likeness of God, since the more powerful spirit is separated from him, becomes mortal; but that first-begotten one through his transgression and ignorance becomes a demon; and they who imitated him, that is his illusions, are become a host of demons, and through their freedom of choice have been given up to their own infatuation.

CHAP. VIII.—The demons sin among mankind.

But men form the material (ὑπόθεσις) of their apostasy. For, having shown them a plan of the position of the stars, like dice-players, they introduced Fate, a flagrant injustice. For the judge and the judged are made so by Fate; the murderers and the murdered, the wealthy and the needy, are the offspring of the same Fate; and every nativity is regarded as a theatrical entertainment by those beings of whom Homer says :

> " Among the gods
> Rose laughter irrepressible."[1]

But must not those who are spectators of single combats and are partisans on one side or the other, and he who marries and is a pæderast and an adulterer, who laughs and is angry, who flees and is wounded, be regarded as mortals? For, by whatever actions they manifest to men their characters, by these they prompt their hearers to copy their example. And are not the demons themselves, with Zeus at their head, subjected to Fate, being overpowered by the same passions as men? And, besides, how are those beings to be worshipped among whom there exists such a great contrariety of opinions? For Rhea, whom the inhabitants of the Phrygian mountains call Cybele, enacted emasculation on account of Attis, of whom she was enamoured; but Aphrodite is delighted with conjugal embraces. Artemis is a poisoner; Apollo heals diseases. And after the decapitation of the Gorgon, the beloved of Poseidon, whence sprang the horse Pegasus and Chrysaor,

[1] *Il.* i. 599 ; *Od.* viii. 326.

Athené and Asclepios divided between them the drops of blood; and, while he saved men's lives by means of them, she, by the same blood, became a homicide and the instigator of wars. From regard to her reputation, as it appears to me, the Athenians attributed to the earth the son born of her connection with Hephæstos, that Athené might not be thought to be deprived of her virility by Hephæstos, as Atalanta by Meleager. This limping manufacturer of buckles and ear-rings, as is likely, deceived the motherless child and orphan with these girlish ornaments. Poseidon frequents the seas; Ares delights in wars; Apollo is a player on the cithara; Dionysus is absolute sovereign of the Thebans; Kronos is a tyrannicide; Zeus has intercourse with his own daughter, who becomes pregnant by him. I may instance, too, Eleusis, and the mystic Dragon, and Orpheus, who says,

" Close the gates against the profane!"

Aïdoneus carries off Koré, and his deeds have been made into mysteries; Demeter bewails her daughter, and some persons are deceived by the Athenians. In the precincts of the temple of the son of Leto is a spot called Omphalos; but Omphalos is the burial-place of Dionysus. You now I laud, O Daphne!—by conquering the incontinence of Apollo, you disproved his power of vaticination; for, not foreseeing what would occur to you,[1] he derived no advantage from his art. Let the far-shooting god tell me how Zephyrus slew Hyacinthus. Zephyrus conquered him; and, in accordance with the saying of the tragic poet :

" A breeze is the most honourable chariot of the gods,"[2]

conquered by a slight breeze Apollo lost his beloved.

CHAP. IX.—*They give rise to superstitions.*

Such are the demons; these are they who laid down the doctrine of Fate. Their fundamental principle was the placing of animals in the heavens. For the creeping things on the earth, and those that swim in the waters, and the

---

[1] On fleeing from Apollo, she became a bay-tree.
[2] It is uncertain from whom this line is quoted.

quadrupeds on the mountains, with which they lived when expelled from heaven,—these they dignified with celestial honour, in order that they might themselves be thought to remain in heaven, and, by placing the constellations there, might make to appear rational the irrational course of life on earth.[1] Thus the high-spirited and he who is crushed with toil, the temperate and the intemperate, the indigent and the wealthy, are what they are simply from the controllers of their nativity. For the delineation of the zodiacal circle is the work of gods. And, when the light of one of them predominates, as they express it, it deprives all the rest of their honour; and he who now is conquered, at another time gains the predominance. And the seven planets are well pleased with them,[2] as if they were amusing themselves with dice. But we are superior to Fate, and instead of wandering ($\pi\lambda\alpha\nu\eta\tau\tilde{\omega}\nu$) demons, we have learned to know one Lord who wanders not; and, as we do not follow the guidance of Fate, we reject its lawgivers. Tell me, I adjure you,[3] did Triptolemus sow wheat and prove a benefactor to the Athenians after their sorrow? And why was not Demeter, before she lost her daughter, a benefactress to men? The Dog of Erigone is shown in the heavens, and the Scorpion the helper of Artemis, and Chiron the Centaur, and the divided Argo, and the Bear of Callisto. Yet how, before these performed the aforesaid deeds, were the heavens unadorned? And to whom will it not appear ridiculous that the Deltotum[4] should be placed among the stars, according to some, on account of Sicily, or, as others say, on account of the first letter in the name of Zeus ($\Delta\iota\acute{o}\varsigma$)? For why are not Sardinia and Cyprus honoured in heaven? And why have not the letters of the names of the brothers of Zeus, who shared the kingdom with him, been fixed there too? And how is it that Kronos, who was put in chains and ejected from his kingdom, is constituted a manager of Fate? How, too, can he give kingdoms who no longer reigns himself?

---

[1] Comp. ch. viii. init.   [2] The signs of the Zodiac (Gesner).

[3] Literally, " Tell me by God," or, " in the name of God."

[4] The Deltotum was a star of the shape of a triangle.—*Otto.*

Reject, then, these absurdities, and do not become transgressors by hating us unjustly.

CHAP. X.—*Ridicule of the heathen divinities.*

There are legends of the metamorphosis of men: with you the gods also are metamorphosed. Rhea becomes a tree; Zeus a dragon, on account of Persephone; the sisters of Phaëthon are changed into poplars, and Leto into a bird of little value, on whose account what is now Delos was called Ortygia. A god, forsooth, becomes a swan, or takes the form of an eagle, and, making Ganymede his cupbearer, glories in a vile affection. How can I reverence gods who are eager for presents, and angry if they do not receive them? Let them have their Fate! I am not willing to adore wandering stars. What is that hair of Berenicé? Where were her stars before her death? And how was the dead Antinoüs fixed as a beautiful youth in the moon? Who carried him thither: unless perchance, as men, perjuring themselves for hire, are credited when they say in ridicule of the gods that kings have ascended into heaven, so some one, in like manner, has put this man also among the gods, and been recompensed with honour and reward? Why have you robbed God? Why do you dishonour His workmanship? You sacrifice a sheep, and you adore the same animal. The Bull is in the heavens, and you slaughter its image. The Kneeler[1] crushes a noxious animal; and the eagle that devours the man-maker Prometheus is honoured. The swan is noble, forsooth, because it was an adulterer; and the Dioscuri, living on alternate days, the ravishers of the daughters of Leucippus, are also noble! Better still is Helen, who forsook the flaxen-haired Menelaus, and followed the turbaned and gold-adorned Paris. A just man also is Sophron,[2] who transported this adulteress to the Elysian fields! But even the daughter of Tyndarus is not gifted with immortality, and Euripides has wisely represented this woman as put to death by Orestes.

[1] Hercules—a sign in the sky. Leaning on his right knee, he tries to crush with his left foot the right side of the dragon's head.

[2] A writer of mimes.

CHAP. XI.—*The sin of men due not to Fate, but to free-will.*

How, then, shall I admit this nativity according to Fate, when I see such managers of Fate? I do not wish to be a king; I am not anxious to be rich; I decline military command; I detest fornication; I am not impelled by an insatiable love of gain to go to sea; I do not contend for chaplets; I am free from a mad thirst for fame; I despise death; I am superior to every kind of disease; grief does not consume my soul. Am I a slave, I endure servitude. Am I free, I do not make a vaunt of my good birth. I see that the same sun is for all, and one death for all, whether they live in pleasure or destitution. The rich man sows, and the poor man partakes of the same sowing. The wealthiest die, and beggars have the same limits to their life. The rich lack many things, and are glorious only through the estimation they are held in;[1] but the poor man and he who has very moderate desires, seeking as he does only the things suited to his lot, more easily obtains his purpose. How is it that you are fated to be sleepless through avarice? Why are you fated to grasp at things often, and often to die? Die to the world, repudiating the madness that is in it. Live to God, and by apprehending Him lay aside your old nature. We were not created to die, but we die by our own fault. Our free-will has destroyed us; we who were free have become slaves; we have been sold through sin. Nothing evil has been created by God; we ourselves have manifested wickedness; but we, who have manifested it, are able again to reject it.

CHAP. XII.—*The two kinds of spirits.*

We recognise two varieties of spirit, one of which is called the soul (ψυχή), but the other is greater than the soul, an image and likeness of God: both existed in the first men, that in one sense they might be material (ὑλικοί), and in another superior to matter. The case stands thus: we can see that the whole structure of the world, and the whole crea-

[1] Or, reading with Maranus, κἂν . . . γεν., " even though," etc.

tion, has been produced from matter, and the matter itself
brought into existence[1] by God; so that on the one hand it
may be regarded as rude and unformed before it was separated into parts, and on the other as arranged in beauty and
order after the separation was made. Therefore in that
separation the heavens were made of matter, and the stars
that are in them ; and the earth and all that is upon it has a
similar constitution : so that there is a common origin of all
things. But, while such is the case, there yet are certain
differences in the things made of matter, so that one is more
beautiful, and another is beautiful but surpassed by something better. For as the constitution of the body is under one
management, and is engaged in doing that which is the cause
of its having been made,[2] yet though this is the case, there are
certain differences of dignity in it, and the eye is one thing,
and another the ear, and another the arrangement of the hair
and the distribution of the intestines, and the compacting together of the marrow and the bones and the tendons ; and
though one part differs from another, there is yet all the
harmony of a concert of music in their arrangement ;—in
like manner the world, according to the power of its Maker
containing some things of superior splendour, but some unlike
these, received by the will of the Creator a material spirit.
And these things severally it is possible for him to perceive
who does not conceitedly reject those most divine explanations
which in the course of time have been consigned to writing,
and make those who study them great lovers of God. Therefore the demons, as you call them, having received their
structure from matter and obtained the spirit which inheres
in it, became intemperate and greedy; some few, indeed,

[1] Literally, " brought forth " or " forward." The word does not
imply that matter was created by God.

[2] Tatian's words are somewhat obscure. We have given substantially
the opinion of Worth, as expressed in his translation. The sense is :
The body is evidently a unity in its organization and its activity, and the
ultimate end which it serves in creation is that with which it is occupied,
yet there are differences in respect of the parts. Otto renders : " For as
the constitution of the body is of one plan, and in reference to the body
the cause of its origin is occupied."

turning to what was purer, but others choosing what was inferior in matter, and conforming their manner of life to it. These beings, produced from matter, but very remote from right conduct, you, O Greeks, worship. For, being turned by their own folly to vaingloriousness, and shaking off the reins [of authority], they have been forward to become robbers of Deity ; and the Lord of all has suffered them to besport themselves, till the world, coming to an end, be dissolved, and the Judge appear, and all those men who, while assailed by the demons, strive after the knowledge of the perfect God obtain as the result of their conflicts a more perfect testimony in the day of judgment. There is, then, a spirit in the stars, a spirit in angels, a spirit in plants and the waters, a spirit in men, a spirit in animals ; but, though one and the same, it has differences in itself. And while we say these things not from mere hearsay, nor from probable conjectures and sophistical reasoning, but using words of a certain diviner speech, do you who are willing hasten to learn. And you who do not reject with contempt the Scythian Anacharsis, do not disdain to be taught by those who follow a barbaric code of laws. Give at least as favourable a reception to our tenets as you would to the prognostications of the Babylonians. Hearken to us when we speak, if only as you would to an oracular oak. And yet the things just referred to are the trickeries of frenzied demons, while the doctrines we inculcate are far beyond the apprehension of the world.

CHAP. XIII.—*Theory of the soul's immortality.*

The soul is not in itself immortal, O Greeks, but mortal. Yet it is possible for it not to die. If, indeed, it knows not the truth, it dies, and is dissolved with the body, but rises again at last at the end of the world with the body, receiving death by punishment in immortality. But, again, if it acquires the knowledge of God, it dies not, although for a time it be dissolved. In itself it is darkness, and there is nothing luminous in it. And this is the meaning of the saying, " The darkness comprehendeth not the light."[1] For

---

[1] John i. 5.

the soul does not preserve the spirit, but is preserved by it, and the light comprehends the darkness. The Logos, in truth, is the light of God, but the ignorant soul is darkness. On this account, if it continues solitary, it tends downward towards matter, and dies with the flesh; but, if it enters into union with the Divine Spirit, it is no longer helpless, but ascends to the regions whither the Spirit guides it : for the dwelling-place of the spirit is above, but the origin of the soul is from beneath. Now, in the beginning the spirit was a constant companion of the soul, but the spirit forsook it because it was not willing to follow. Yet, retaining as it were a spark of its power, though unable by reason of the separation to discern the perfect, while seeking for God it fashioned to itself in its wandering many gods, following the sophistries of the demons. But the Spirit of God is not with all, but, taking up its abode with those who live justly, and intimately combining with the soul, by prophecies it announced hidden things to other souls. And the souls that are obedient to wisdom have attracted to themselves the cognate spirit ; but the disobedient, rejecting the minister of the suffering God, have shown themselves to be fighters against God, rather than His worshippers.

CHAP. XIV.—*The demons shall be punished more severely than men.*

And such are you also, O Greeks,—profuse in words, but with minds strangely warped ; and you acknowledge the dominion of many rather than the rule of one, accustoming yourselves to follow demons as if they were mighty. For, as the inhuman robber is wont to overpower those like himself by daring ; so the demons, going to great lengths in wickedness, have utterly deceived the souls among you which are left to themselves by ignorance and false appearances. These beings do not indeed die easily, for they do not partake of flesh ; but while living they practise the ways of death, and die themselves as often as they teach their followers to sin. Therefore, what is now their chief distinction, that they do not die like men, they will retain when about to suffer punishment : they will not partake of everlasting life, so as to receive this instead of death in a blessed immortality. And as we, to whom it now easily happens to die, afterwards receive the immortal with enjoyment, or the painful with immortality, so the demons, who abuse the present life to purposes of wrong-doing, dying continually even while they live, will have hereafter the same immortality, like that which they had during the time they lived, but in its nature like that of men, who voluntarily performed what the demons prescribed to them during their lifetime. And do not fewer kinds of sin break out among men owing to the brevity of their lives, while on the part of these demons transgression is more abundant owing to their boundless existence ?

CHAP. XV.—*Necessity of a union with the Holy Spirit.*

But further, it becomes us now to seek for what we once had, but have lost, to unite the soul with the Holy Spirit, and to strive after union with God. The human soul consists of many parts, and is not simple ; it is composite, so as to manifest itself through the body ; for neither could it ever appear by itself without the body, nor does the flesh rise again without the soul. Man is not, as the croaking philosophers say, merely a rational animal, capable of understanding and knowledge ; for, according to them, even irrational creatures appear possessed of understanding and knowledge. But man alone is the image and likeness of God ; and I mean by man, not one who performs actions similar to those of animals, but one who has advanced far beyond mere humanity—to God Himself. This question we have discussed more minutely in the treatise concerning animals. But the principal point to be spoken of now is, what is intended by the image and likeness of God. That which cannot be compared is no other than abstract being ; but that which is compared is no other than that which is like. The perfect God is without flesh ; but man is flesh. The bond of the flesh is the soul ; that which encloses the soul is the flesh. Such is the nature of man's constitution ; and, if it be like a temple, God is pleased to dwell in it by the spirit, His representative ; but, if it be not such a habitation, man excels the wild beasts in articulate language only,—in other respects his manner of life is like theirs, as one who is not a likeness of God. But none of the demons possess flesh ; their structure is spiritual, like that of fire or air. And only by those whom the Spirit of God dwells in and fortifies are the bodies of the demons easily seen, not at all by others,—I mean those who possess only soul ;[1] for the inferior has not the ability to apprehend the superior. On this account the nature of the demons has no place for repentance ; for they are the reflection of matter and of wickedness. But matter desired to exercise lordship over the soul ; and according to their free-will these gave laws of death to men ; but men, after the loss of immortality, have conquered death by submitting to death in faith ; and by repentance a call has been given to them, according to the word which says, " Since they were made a little lower than the angels."[2] And, for every one who has been conquered, it is possible again to conquer, if he rejects the condition which brings death. And what that is, may be easily seen by men who long for immortality.

Chap. XVI.—*Vain display of power by the demons.*

But the demons who rule over men are not the souls of men ; for how should these be capable of action after death ? unless man, who while living was void of understanding and power, should be believed when dead to be endowed with more of active power. But neither could this be the case, as we have shown elsewhere.[3] And it is difficult to conceive that the immortal soul, which is impeded by the members of the body, should become more intelligent when it has migrated from it. For the demons, inspired with frenzy against men by reason of their own wickedness, pervert their minds, which already incline downwards, by various deceptive scenic representations, that they may be disabled from rising to the path that leads to heaven. But from us the things which are in the world are not hidden, and the divine is easily

---

[1] Comp. 1 Cor. ii. 14, 15. [2] Ps. viii. 5.
[3] Perhaps in his treatise " on Animals."

apprehended by us if the power that makes souls immortal
visits us. The demons are seen also by the men possessed
of soul, when, as sometimes, they exhibit themselves to men,
either that they may be thought to be something, or as evil-
disposed friends may do harm to them as to enemies, or afford
occasions of doing them honour to those who resemble them.
For, if it were possible, they would without doubt pull down
heaven itself with the rest of creation. But now this they
can by no means effect, for they have not the power; but
they make war by means of the lower matter against the
matter that is like themselves. Should any one wish to
conquer them, let him repudiate matter. Being armed with
the breastplate[1] of the celestial Spirit, he will be able to
preserve all that is encompassed by it. There are, indeed,
diseases and disturbances of the matter that is in us; but,
when such things happen, the demons ascribe the causes of
them to themselves, and approach a man whenever disease
lays hold of him. Sometimes they themselves disturb the
habit of the body by a tempest of folly; but, being smitten by
the word of God, they depart in terror, and the sick man is
healed.

CHAP. XVII.—*They falsely promise health to their votaries.*

Concerning the sympathies and antipathies of Democritus
what can we say but this, that, according to the common
saying, the man of Abdera is Abderiloquent? But, as he
who gave the name to the city, a friend of Hercules as it is
said, was devoured by the horses of Diomedes, so he who
boasted of the Magian Ostanes[2] will be delivered up in the
day of consummation as fuel for the eternal fire. And you,
if you do not cease from your laughter, will gain the same
punishment as the jugglers. Wherefore, O Greeks, hearken
to me, addressing you as from an eminence, nor in mockery
transfer your own want of reason to the herald of the truth.
A diseased affection ($\pi\acute{a}\theta o\varsigma$) is not destroyed by a counter-
affection ($\grave{a}\nu\tau\iota\pi\acute{a}\theta\epsilon\iota a$), nor is a maniac cured by hanging
little amulets of leather upon him. There are visitations of

---

[1] Comp. Eph. vi. 13, 14, 17.   [2] Democritus.

demons; and he who is sick, and he who says he is in love, and he who hates, and he who wishes to be revenged, accept them as helpers. And this is the method of their operation: just as the forms of alphabetic letters and the lines composed of them cannot of themselves indicate what is meant, but men have invented for themselves signs of their thoughts, knowing by their peculiar combination what the order of the letters was intended to express; so, in like manner, the various kinds of roots and the mutual relation of the sinews and bones can effect nothing of themselves, but are the elemental matter with which the depravity of the demons works, who have determined for what purpose each of them is available. And, when they see that men consent to be served by means of such things, they take them and make them their slaves. But how can it be honourable to minister to adulteries? How can it be noble to stimulate men in hating one another? Or how is it becoming to ascribe to matter the relief of the insane, and not to God? For by their art they turn men aside from the pious acknowledgment of God, leading them to place confidence in herbs and roots. But God, if He had prepared these things to effect just what men wish, would be a Producer of evil things; whereas He Himself produced everything which has good qualities, but the profligacy of the demons has made use of the productions of nature for evil purposes, and the appearance of evil which these wear is from them, and not from the perfect God. For how comes it to pass that when alive I was in no wise evil, but that now I am dead and can do nothing, my remains, which are incapable of motion or even sense, should effect something cognizable by the senses? And how shall he who has died by the most miserable death be able to assist in avenging any one? If this were possible, much more might he defend himself from his own enemy; being able to assist others, much more might he constitute himself his own avenger.

CHAP. XVIII.—*They deceive, instead of healing.*

But medicine and everything included in it is an invention

of the same kind. If any one is healed by matter, through trusting to it, much more will he be healed by having recourse to the power of God. As noxious preparations are material compounds, so are curatives of the same nature. If, however, we reject the baser matter, some persons often endeavour to heal by a union of one of these bad things with some other, and will make use of the bad to attain the good. But, just as he who dines with a robber, though he may not be a robber himself, partakes of the punishment on account of his intimacy with him, so he who is not bad but associates with the bad, having dealings with them for some supposed good, will be punished by God the Judge for partnership in the same object. Why is he who trusts in the system of matter not willing to trust in God? For what reason do you not approach the more powerful Lord, but rather seek to cure yourself, like the dog with grass, or the stag with a viper, or the hog with river-crabs, or the lion with apes? Why do you deify the objects of nature? And why, when you cure your neighbour, are you called a benefactor? Yield to the power of the Logos! The demons do not cure, but by their art make men their captives. And the most admirable Justin has rightly denounced them as robbers. For, as it is the practice of some to capture persons and then to restore them to their friends for a ransom, so those who are esteemed gods, invading the bodies of certain persons, and producing a sense of their presence by dreams, command them to come forth into public, and in the sight of all, when they have taken their fill of the things of this world, fly away from the sick, and, destroying the disease which they had produced, restore men to their former state.

CHAP. XIX.—*Depravity lies at the bottom of demon-worship.*

But do you, who have not the perception of these things, be instructed by us who know them: though you do profess to despise death, and to be sufficient of yourselves for everything. But this is a discipline in which your philosophers are so greatly deficient, that some of them receive from the king of the Romans 600 aurei yearly, for no useful service they perform, but that they may not even wear a long beard without being paid for it! Crescens, who made his nest in the great city, surpassed all men in unnatural love (παιδεραστία), and was strongly addicted to the love of money. Yet this man, who professed to despise death, was so afraid of death, that he endeavoured to inflict on Justin, and indeed on me, the punishment of death, as being an evil, because by proclaiming the truth he convicted the philosophers of being gluttons and cheats. But whom of the philosophers, save you only, was he accustomed to inveigh against? If you say, in agreement with our tenets, that death is not to be dreaded, do not court death from an insane love of fame among men, like Anaxagoras, but become despisers of death by reason of the knowledge of God. The construction of the world is excellent, but the life men live in it is bad; and we may see those greeted with applause as in a solemn assembly who know not God. For what is divination? and why are ye deceived by it? It is a minister to thee of worldly lusts. You wish to make war, and you take Apollo as a counsellor of slaughter. You want to carry off a maiden by force, and you select a divinity to be your accomplice. You are ill by your own fault; and, as Agamemnon[1] wished for ten councillors, so you wish to have gods with you. Some woman by drinking water gets into a frenzy, and loses her senses by the fumes of frankincense, and you say that she has the gift of prophecy. Apollo was a prognosticator and a teacher of soothsayers: in the matter of Daphne he deceived himself. An oak, forsooth, is oracular, and birds utter presages! And so you are inferior to animals and plants! It would surely be a fine thing for you to become a divining rod, or to assume the wings of a bird! He who makes you fond of money also foretells your getting rich; he who excites to seditions and wars also predicts victory in war. If you are superior to the passions, you will despise all worldly things. Do not abhor us who have made this attainment, but, repudiating the demons, follow the one God. "All things[2] were made by Him, and without Him not one

[1] Comp. Hom. *Il.* ii. 372.   [2] John i. 3.

thing was made." If there is poison in natural productions, this has supervened through our sinfulness. I am able to show the perfect truth of these things; only do you hearken, and he who believes will understand.

Chap. xx.—*Thanks are ever due to God.*

Even if you be healed by drugs (I grant you that point by courtesy), yet it behoves you to give testimony of the cure to God. For the world still draws us down, and through weakness I incline towards matter. For the wings of the soul were the perfect spirit, but, having cast this off through sin, it flutters like a nestling and falls to the ground. Having left the heavenly companionship, it hankers after communion with inferior things. The demons were driven forth to another abode; the first created human beings were expelled from their place: the one, indeed, were cast down from heaven; but the other were driven from earth, yet not out of this earth, but from a more excellent order of things than exists here now. And now it behoves us, yearning after that pristine state, to put aside everything that proves a hindrance. The heavens are not infinite, O man, but finite and bounded; and beyond them are the superior worlds which have not a change of seasons, by which various diseases are produced, but, partaking of every happy temperature, have perpetual day, and light unapproachable by men below. Those who have composed elaborate descriptions of the earth have given an account of its various regions so far as this was possible to man; but, being unable to speak of that which is beyond, because of the impossibility of personal observation, they have assigned as the cause the existence of tides; and that one sea is filled with weed, and another with mud; and that some localities are burnt up with heat, and others cold and frozen. We, however, have learned things which were unknown to us, through the teaching of the prophets, who, being fully persuaded that the heavenly spirit along with the soul will acquire a clothing of mortality, foretold things which other minds were unacquainted with. But it is pos-

sible for every one who is naked to obtain this apparel, and
to return to its ancient kindred.

CHAP. XXI.—*Doctrines of the Christians and Greeks respecting God compared.*

We do not act as fools, O Greeks, nor utter idle tales,
when we announce that God was born in the form of a man.
I call on you who reproach us to compare your mythical
accounts with our narrations. Athené, as they say, took the
form of Deïphobus for the sake of Hector,[1] and the unshorn
Phœbus for the sake of Admetus fed the trailing-footed oxen,
and the spouse of Zeus came as an old woman to Semelé.
But, while you treat seriously such things, how can you
deride us? Your Asclepios died, and he who ravished fifty
virgins in one night at Thespiæ lost his life by delivering himself to the devouring flame. Prometheus, fastened to Caucasus,
suffered punishment for his good deeds to men. According
to you, Zeus is envious, and hides the dream[2] from men,
wishing their destruction. Wherefore, looking at your own
memorials, vouchsafe us your approval, though it were only
as dealing in legends similar to your own. We, however,
do not deal in folly, but your legends are only idle tales. If
you speak of the origin of the gods, you also declare them to
be mortal. For what reason is Hera now never pregnant?
Has she grown old? or is there no one to give you information? Believe me now, O Greeks, and do not resolve your
myths and gods into allegory. If you attempt to do this, the
divine nature as held by you is overthrown by your own selves;
for, if the demons with you are such as they are said to be, they
are worthless as to character; or, if regarded as symbols of
the powers of nature, they are not what they are called. But
I cannot be persuaded to pay religious homage to the natural
elements, nor can I undertake to persuade my neighbour.
And Metrodorus of Lampsacus, in his treatise concerning
Homer, has argued very foolishly, turning everything into
allegory. For he says that neither Hera, nor Athené, nor
Zeus are what those persons suppose who consecrate to

[1] *Il.* xxii. 227.   [2] *Il.* ii. init.

them sacred enclosures and groves, but parts of nature and
certain arrangements of the elements. Hector also, and
Achilles, and Agamemnon, and all the Greeks in general,
and the Barbarians with Helen and Paris, being of the same
nature, you will of course say are introduced merely for the
sake of the machinery of the poem, not one of these personages
having really existed. But these things we have put forth
only for argument's sake; for it is not allowable even to compare our notion of God with those who are wallowing in
matter and mud.

Chap. XXII.—*Ridicule of the solemnities of the Greeks.*

And of what sort are your teachings? Who must not treat
with contempt your solemn festivals, which, being held in
honour of wicked demons, cover men with infamy? I have
often seen a man [1]—and have been amazed to see, and the
amazement has ended in contempt, to think how he is one
thing internally, but outwardly counterfeits what he is not—
giving himself excessive airs of daintiness and indulging in
all sorts of effeminacy; sometimes darting his eyes about;
sometimes throwing his hands hither and thither, and raving
with his face smeared with mud ; sometimes personating
Aphrodité, sometimes Apollo ; a solitary accuser of all the
gods, an epitome of superstition, a vituperator of heroic
deeds, an actor of murders, a chronicler of adultery, a
storehouse of madness, a teacher of cynædi, an instigator
of capital sentences ;—and yet such a man is praised by
all. But I have rejected all his falsehoods, his impiety,
his practices,—in short, the man altogether. But you are
led captive by such men, while you revile those who do not
take a part in your pursuits. I have no mind to stand agape
at a number of singers, nor do I desire to be affected in
sympathy with a man when he is winking and gesticulating
in an unnatural manner. What wonderful or extraordinary
thing is performed among you? They utter ribaldry in
affected tones, and go through indecent movements ; your
daughters and your sons behold them giving lessons in

[1] Tatian here describes an actor.

adultery on the stage. Admirable places, forsooth, are your lecture-rooms, where every base action perpetrated by night is proclaimed aloud, and the hearers are regaled with the utterance of infamous discourses! Admirable, too, are your mendacious poets, who by their fictions beguile their hearers from the truth!

CHAP. XXIII.—*Of the pugilists and gladiators.*

I have seen men weighed down by bodily exercise, and carrying about the burden of their flesh, before whom rewards and chaplets are set, while the adjudicators cheer them on, not to deeds of virtue, but to rivalry in violence and discord; and he who excels in giving blows is crowned. These are the lesser evils; as for the greater, who would not shrink from telling them? Some, giving themselves up to idleness for the sake of profligacy, sell themselves to be killed; and the indigent barters himself away, while the rich man buys others to kill him. And for these the witnesses take their seats, and the boxers meet in single combat, for no reason whatever, nor does any one come down into the arena to succour. Do such exhibitions as these redound to your credit? He who is chief among you collects a legion of blood-stained murderers, engaging to maintain them; and these ruffians are sent forth by him, and you assemble at the spectacle to be judges, partly of the wickedness of the adjudicator, and partly of that of the men who engage in the combat. And he who misses the murderous exhibition is grieved, because he was not doomed to be a spectator of wicked and impious and abominable deeds. You slaughter animals for the purpose of eating their flesh, and you purchase men to supply a cannibal banquet for the soul, nourishing it by the most impious bloodshedding. The robber commits murder for the sake of plunder, but the rich man purchases gladiators for the sake of their being killed.

CHAP. XXIV.—*Of the other public amusements.*

What advantage should I gain from him who is brought on the stage by Euripides raving mad, and acting the matricide of Alcmæon; who does not even retain his natural behaviour, but with his mouth wide open goes about sword in hand, and, screaming aloud, is burned to death, habited in a robe unfit for man? Away, too, with the mythical tales of Acusilaus, and Menander, a versifier of the same class! And why should I admire the mythic piper? Why should I busy myself about the Theban Antigenides,[1] like Aristoxenus? We leave to you these worthless things; and do you either believe our doctrines, or, like us, give up yours.

CHAP. XXV.—*Boastings and quarrels of the philosophers.*

What great and wonderful things have your philosophers effected? They leave uncovered one of their shoulders; they let their hair grow long; they cultivate their beards; their nails are like the claws of wild beasts. Though they say that they want nothing, yet, like Proteus,[2] they need a currier for their wallet, and a weaver for their mantle, and a wood-cutter for their staff, and the rich,[3] and a cook also for their gluttony. O man competing with the dog,[4] you know not God, and so have turned to the imitation of an irrational animal. You cry out in public with an assumption of authority, and take upon you to avenge your own self; and if you receive nothing, you indulge in abuse, and philosophy is with you the art of getting money. You follow the doctrines of Plato, and a disciple of Epicurus lifts up his voice to oppose you. Again, you wish to be a disciple of Aristotle, and a follower of Democritus rails at you. Pythagoras says that he was Euphorbus, and he is the heir of the doctrine of Pherecydes; but Aristotle impugns the immortality of the soul. You who receive from your predecessors doctrines which clash with one another, you the inharmonious, are fighting against the harmonious. One of you asserts that God is body, but I assert that He is without body; that the world is indestructible, but I say that it is to be destroyed; that a

---

[1] Antigenides was a flute-player, and Aristoxenus a writer on music and musical instruments.

[2] The Cynic Peregrinus is meant.

[3] They need the rich to invite them to banquets.

[4] The Cynic.

conflagration will take place at various times, but I say that
it will come to pass once for all; that Minos and Rhadamanthus are judges, but I say that God Himself is Judge; that
the soul alone is endowed with immortality, but I say that
the flesh also is endowed with it. What injury do we inflict
upon you, O Greeks? Why do you hate those who follow
the word of God, as if they were the vilest of mankind? It
is not we who eat human flesh—they among you who assert
such a thing have been suborned as false witnesses; it is
among you that Pelops is made a supper for the gods, although
beloved by Poseidon, and Kronos devours his children, and
Zeus swallows Metis.

CHAP. XXVI.—*Ridicule of the studies of the Greeks.*

Cease to make a parade of sayings which you have derived
from others, and to deck yourselves like the daw in borrowed
plumes. If each state were to take away its contribution to
your speech, your fallacies would lose their power. While
inquiring what God is, you are ignorant of what is in yourselves; and, while staring all agape at the sky, you stumble
into pitfalls. The reading of your books is like walking
through a labyrinth, and their readers resemble the cask of the
Danaïds. Why do you divide time, saying that one part is
past, and another present, and another future? For how
can the future be passing when the present exists? As
those who are sailing imagine in their ignorance, as the ship
is borne along, that the hills are in motion, so you do not
know that it is you who are passing along, but that time
(ὁ αἰών) remains present as long as the Creator wills it to
exist. Why am I called to account for uttering my opinions,
and why are you in such haste to put them all down? Were
not you born in the same manner as ourselves, and placed
under the same government of the world? Why say that
wisdom is with you alone, who have not another sun, nor
other risings of the stars, nor a more distinguished origin, nor
a death preferable to that of other men? The grammarians
have been the beginning of this idle talk; and you who parcel
out wisdom are cut off from the wisdom that is according to

truth, and assign the names of the several parts to particular men; and you know not God, but in your fierce contentions destroy one another. And on this account you are all nothing worth. While you arrogate to yourselves the sole right of discussion, you discourse like the blind man with the deaf. Why do you handle the builder's tools without knowing how to build? Why do you busy yourselves with words, while you keep aloof from deeds, puffed up with praise, but cast down by misfortunes? Your modes of acting are contrary to reason, for you make a pompous appearance in public, but hide your teaching in corners. Finding you to be such men as these, we have abandoned you, and no longer concern ourselves with your tenets, but follow the word of God. Why, O man, do you set the letters of the alphabet at war with one another? Why do you, as in a boxing match, make their sounds clash together with your mincing Attic way of speaking, whereas you ought to speak more according to nature? For if you adopt the Attic dialect though not an Athenian, pray why do you not speak like the Dorians? How is it that one appears to you more rugged, the other more pleasant for intercourse?

CHAP. XXVII.—*The Christians are hated unjustly.*

And if you adhere to *their* teaching, why do you fight against me for choosing such views of doctrine as I approve? Is it not unreasonable that, while the robber is not to be punished for the name he bears, but only when the truth about him has been clearly ascertained, yet we are to be assailed with abuse on a judgment formed without examination? Diagoras was an Athenian, but you punished him for divulging the Athenian mysteries; yet you who read his Phrygian discourses hate us. You possess the commentaries of Leo, and are displeased with our refutations of them; and having in your hands the opinions of Apion concerning the Egyptian gods, you denounce us as most impious. The tomb of Olympian Zeus is shown among you,[1] though some one

[1] In Crete.

says that the Cretans are liars.[1] Your assembly of many gods is nothing. Though their despiser Epicurus acts as a torch-bearer,[2] I do not any the more conceal from the rulers that view of God which I hold in relation to His government of the universe. Why do you advise me to be false to my principles? Why do you who say that you despise death exhort us to use art in order to escape it? I have not the heart of a deer; but your zeal for dialectics resembles the loquacity of Thersites. How can I believe one who tells me that the sun is a red-hot mass and the moon an earth? Such assertions are mere logomachies, and not a sober exposition of truth. How can it be otherwise than foolish to credit the books of Herodotus relating to the history of Hercules, which tell of an upper earth from which the lion came down that was killed by Hercules? And what avails the Attic style, the sorites of philosophers, the plausibilities of syllogisms, the measurements of the earth, the positions of the stars, and the course of the sun? To be occupied in such inquiries is the work of one who imposes opinions on himself as if they were laws.

CHAP. XXVIII.—*Condemnation of the Greek legislation.*

On this account I reject your legislation also; for there ought to be one common polity for all; but now there are as many different codes as there are states, so that things held disgraceful in some are honourable in others. The Greeks consider intercourse with a mother as unlawful, but this practice is esteemed most becoming by the Persian Magi; pæderasty is condemned by the Barbarians, but by the Romans, who endeavour to collect herds of boys like grazing horses, it is honoured with certain privileges.

CHAP. XXIX.—*Account of Tatian's conversion.*

Wherefore, having seen these things, and moreover also having been admitted to the mysteries, and having everywhere

---

[1] Comp. Tit. i. 12. Callimachus is probably the author referred to, though others express the same opinion respecting the Cretans.

[2] Accommodating himself to the popular opinions, through fear.

C

examined the religious rites performed by the effeminate and the pathic, and having found among the Romans their Latiarian Jupiter delighting in human gore and the blood of slaughtered men, and Artemis not far from the great city[1] sanctioning acts of the same kind, and one demon here and another there instigating to the perpetration of evil,—retiring by myself, I sought how I might be able to discover the truth. And, while I was giving my most earnest attention to the matter, I happened to meet with certain barbaric writings, too old to be compared with the opinions of the Greeks, and too divine to be compared with their errors; and I was led to put faith in these by the unpretending cast of the language, the inartificial character of the writers, the foreknowledge displayed of future events, the excellent quality of the precepts, and the declaration of the government of the universe as centred in one Being. And, my soul being taught of God, I discerned that the former class of writings lead to condemnation, but that these put an end to the slavery that is in the world, and rescue us from a multiplicity of rulers and ten thousand tyrants, while they give us, not indeed what we had not before received, but what we had received but were prevented by error from retaining.

CHAP. XXX.—*How he resolved to resist the devil.*

Therefore, being initiated and instructed in these things, I wish to put away my former errors as the follies of childhood. For we know that the nature of wickedness is like that of the smallest seeds; since it has waxed strong from a small beginning, but will again be destroyed if we obey the words of God and do not scatter ourselves. For He has become master of all we have by means of a certain "hidden treasure,"[2] which while we are digging for we are indeed covered with dust, but we secure it as our fixed possession. He who receives the whole of this treasure has obtained command of the most precious wealth. Let these things, then, be said to our friends. But to you Greeks what can I say, except to request you not to rail at those who are better than yourselves, nor if they

[1] At Aricia, near Rome.   [2] Comp. Matt. xiii. 44.

are called Barbarians to make that an occasion of banter? For, if you are willing, you will be able to find out the cause of men's not being able to understand one another's language; for to those who wish to examine our principles I will give a simple and copious account of them.

CHAP. XXXI.—*The philosophy of the Christians more ancient than that of the Greeks.*

But now it seems proper for me to demonstrate that our philosophy is older than the systems of the Greeks. Moses and Homer shall be our limits, each of them being of great antiquity; the one being the oldest of poets and historians, and the other the founder of all barbaric wisdom. Let us, then, institute a comparison between them; and we shall find that our doctrines are older, not only than those of the Greeks, but than the invention of letters. And I will not bring forward witnesses from among ourselves, but rather have recourse to Greeks. To do the former would be foolish, because it would not be allowed by you; but the other will surprise you, when, by contending against you with your own weapons, I adduce arguments of which you had no suspicion. Now the poetry of Homer, his parentage, and the time in which he flourished have been investigated by the most ancient writers,—by Theagenes of Rhegium, who lived in the time of Cambyses, Stesimbrotus of Thasos and Antimachus of Colophon, Herodotus of Halicarnassus, and Dionysius the Olynthian; after them, by Ephorus of Cumæ, and Philochorus the Athenian, Megaclides and Chamæleon the Peripatetics; afterwards by the grammarians, Zenodotus, Aristophanes, Callimachus, Crates, Eratosthenes, Aristarchus, and Apollodorus. Of these, Crates says that he flourished before the return of the Heraclidæ, and within 80 years after the Trojan war; Eratosthenes says that it was after the 100th year from the taking of Ilium; Artistarchus, that it was about the time of the Ionian migration, which was 140 years after that event; but, according to Philochorus, after the Ionian migration, in the archonship of Archippus at Athens, 180 years after the Trojan war; Apollodorus says it was 100 years after the

Ionian migration, which would be 240 years after the Trojan war. Some say that he lived 90 years before the Olympiads, which would be 317 years after the taking of Troy. Others carry it down to a later date, and say that Homer was a contemporary of Archilochus; but Archilochus flourished about the 23d Olympiad, in the time of Gyges the Lydian, 500 years after Troy. Thus, concerning the age of the aforesaid poet, I mean Homer, and the discrepancies of those who have spoken of him, we have said enough in a summary manner for those who are able to investigate with accuracy. For it is possible to show that the opinions held about the facts themselves also are false. For, where the assigned dates do not agree together, it is impossible that the history should be true. For what is the cause of error in writing, but the narrating of things that are not true?

CHAP. XXXII.—*The doctrine of the Christians is opposed to dissensions, and fitted for all.*

But with us there is no desire of vainglory, nor do we indulge in a variety of opinions. For, having renounced the popular and earthly, and obeying the commands of God, and following the law of the Father of immortality, we reject everything which rests upon human opinion. Not only do the rich among us pursue our philosophy, but the poor enjoy instruction gratuitously; for the things which come from God surpass the requital of worldly gifts. Thus we admit all who desire to hear, even old women and striplings; and, in short, persons of every age are treated by us with respect, but every kind of licentiousness is kept at a distance. And in speaking we do not utter falsehood. It would be an excellent thing if your continuance in unbelief should receive a check; but, however that may be, let our cause remain confirmed by the judgment pronounced by God. Laugh, if you please; but you will have to weep hereafter. Is it not absurd that Nestor,[1] who was slow at cutting his horses' reins owing to his weak and sluggish old age, is, according to you, to be admired for attempting to rival the young men

[1] *Il.* ix.

in fighting, while you deride those among us who struggle against old age and occupy themselves with the things pertaining to God? Who would not laugh when you tell us that the Amazons, and Semiramis, and certain other warlike women existed, while you cast reproaches on our maidens? Achilles was a youth, yet is believed to have been very magnanimous; and Neoptolemus was younger, but strong; Philoctetes was weak, but the divinity had need of him against Troy. What sort of man was Thersites? yet he held a command in the army, and, if he had not through doltishness had such an unbridled tongue, he would not have been reproached for being peak-headed and bald. As for those who wish to learn our philosophy, we do not test them by their looks, nor do we judge of those who come to us by their outward appearance; for we argue that there may be strength of mind in all, though they may be weak in body. But your proceedings are full of envy and abundant stupidity.

CHAP. XXXIII.—*Vindication of Christian women.*

Therefore I have been desirous to prove from the things which are esteemed honourable among you, that our institutions are marked by sober-mindedness, but that yours are in close affinity with madness. You who say that we talk nonsense among women and boys, among maidens and old women, and scoff at us for not being with you, hear what silliness prevails among the Greeks. For their works of art are devoted to worthless objects, while they are held in higher estimation by you than even your gods; and you behave yourselves unbecomingly in what relates to woman. For Lysippus cast a statue of Praxilla, whose poems contain nothing useful, and Menestratus one of Learchis, and Selanion one of Sappho the courtezan, and Naucydes one of Erinna the Lesbian, and Boiscus one of Myrtis, and Cephisodotus one of Myro of Byzantium, and Gomphus one of Praxigoris, and Amphistratus one of Clito. And what shall I say about Anyta, Telesilla, and Mystis? Of the first Euthycrates and Cephisodotus made a statue, and of the second Niceratus, and of the third

Aristodotus; Euthycrates made one of Mnesiarchis the Ephesian, Selanion one of Corinna, and Euthycrates one of Thalarchis the Argive. My object in referring to these women is, that you may not regard as something strange what you find among us, and that, comparing the statues which are before your eyes, you may not treat the women with scorn who among us pursue philosophy. This Sappho is a lewd, love-sick female, and sings her own wantonness; but all our women are chaste, and the maidens at their distaffs sing of divine things more nobly than that damsel of yours. Wherefore be ashamed, you who are professed disciples of women yet scoff at those of the sex who hold our doctrine, as well as at the solemn assemblies they frequent. What a noble infant did Glaucippé present to you, who brought forth a prodigy, as is shown by her statue cast by Niceratus, the son of Euctemon the Athenian! But, if Glaucippé brought forth an elephant, was that a reason why she should enjoy public honours? Praxiteles and Herodotus made for you Phryné the courtezan, and Euthycrates cast a brazen statue of Panteuchis, who was pregnant by a whoremonger; and Dinomenes, because Besantis queen of the Pæonians gave birth to a black infant, took pains to preserve her memory by his art. I condemn Pythagoras too, who made a figure of Europa on the bull; and you also, who honour the accuser of Zeus on account of his artistic skill. And I ridicule the skill of Myron, who made a heifer and upon it a Victory because by carrying off the daughter of Agenor it had borne away the prize for adultery and lewdness. The Olynthian Herodotus made statues of Glycera the courtezan and Argeia the harper. Bryaxis made a statue of Pasiphaë; and, by having a memorial of her lewdness, it seems to have been almost your desire that the women of the present time should be like her. A certain Melanippë was a wise woman, and for that reason Lysistratus made her statue. But, forsooth, you will not believe that among us there are wise women!

Chap. XXXIV.—*Ridicule of the statues erected by the Greeks.*

Worthy of very great honour, certainly, was the tyrant Phalaris, who devoured sucklings, and accordingly is exhibited by the workmanship of Polystratus the Ambraciot, even to this day, as a very wonderful man! The Agrigentines dreaded to look on that countenance of his, because of his cannibalism; but people of culture now make it their boast that they behold him in his statue! Is it not shameful that fratricide is honoured by you who look on the statues of Polynices and Eteocles, and that you have not rather buried them with their maker Pythagoras? Destroy these memorials of iniquity! Why should I contemplate with admiration the figure of the woman who bore thirty children, merely for the sake of the artist Periclymenus? One ought to turn away with disgust from one who bore off the fruits of great incontinence, and whom the Romans compared to a sow, which also on a like account, they say, was deemed worthy of a mystic worship. Ares committed adultery with Aphrodité, and Andron made an image of their offspring Harmonia. Sophron, who committed to writing trifles and absurdities, was more celebrated for his skill in casting metals, of which specimens exist even now. And not only have his tales kept the fabulist Æsop in everlasting remembrance, but also the plastic art of Aristodemus has increased his celebrity. How is it then that you, who have so many poetesses whose productions are mere trash, and innumerable courtezans, and worthless men, are not ashamed to slander the reputation of our women? What care I to know that Euanthé gave birth to an infant in the Peripatus, or to gape with wonder at the art of Callistratus, or to fix my gaze on the Neæra of Calliades? For she was a courtezan. Laïs was a prostitute, and Turnus made her a monument of prostitution. Why are you not ashamed of the fornication of Hephæstion, even though Philo has represented him very artistically? And for what reason do you honour the hermaphrodite Ganymede by Leochares, as if you possessed something admirable? Praxiteles even made a statue of a woman with the stain of impurity upon it. It behoved you, repudiating everything of this kind, to seek what is truly worthy of attention, and not to turn with disgust from our mode of life while receiving with approval the shameful productions of Philænis and Elephantis.

CHAP. XXXV.—*Tatian speaks as an eye-witness.*

The things which I have thus set before you I have not learned at second hand. I have visited many lands; I have followed rhetoric, like yourselves; I have fallen in with many arts and inventions; and finally, when sojourning in the city of the Romans, I inspected the multiplicity of statues brought thither by you: for I do not attempt, as is the custom with many, to strengthen my own views by the opinions of others, but I wish to give you a distinct account of what I myself have seen and felt. So, bidding farewell to the arrogance of Romans and the idle talk of Athenians, and all their ill-connected opinions, I embraced our barbaric philosophy. I began to show how this was more ancient than your institutions,[1] but left my task unfinished, in order to discuss a matter which demanded more immediate attention; but now it is time I should attempt to speak concerning its doctrines. Be not offended with our teaching, nor undertake an elaborate reply filled with trifling and ribaldry, saying, "Tatian, aspiring to be above the Greeks, above the infinite number of philosophic inquirers, has struck out a new path, and embraced the doctrines of Barbarians." For what grievance is it, that men manifestly ignorant should be reasoned with by a man of like nature with themselves? Or how can it be irrational, according to your own sophist,[2] to grow old always learning something?

CHAP. XXXVI.—*Testimony of the Chaldeans to the antiquity of Moses.*

But let Homer be not later than the Trojan war; let it be granted that he was contemporary with it, or even that he was in the army of Agamemnon, and, if any so please, that

---

[1] Chap. xxxi.   [2] Solon. Bergh. *Poetæ Græc. Lyr.* fr. 18.

he lived before the invention of letters. The Moses before mentioned will be shown to have been many years older than the taking of Troy, and far more ancient than the building of Troy, or than Tros and Dardanus. To demonstrate this I will call in as witnesses the Chaldeans, the Phœnicians, and the Egyptians. And what more need I say? For it behoves one who professes to persuade his hearers to make his narrative of events very concise. Berosus, a Babylonian, a priest of their god Belus, born in the time of Alexander, composed for Antiochus, the third after him, the history of the Chaldeans in three books; and, narrating the acts of the kings, he mentions one of them, Nabuchodonosor by name, who made war against the Phœnicians and the Jews,—events which we know were announced by our prophets, and which happened much later than the age of Moses, seventy years before the Persian empire. But Berosus is a very trustworthy man, and of this Juba is a witness, who, writing concerning the Assyrians, says that he learned the history from Berosus: there are two books of his concerning the Assyrians.

CHAP. XXXVII.—*Testimony of the Phœnicians.*

After the Chaldeans, the testimony of the Phœnicians is as follows. There were among them three men, Theodotus, Hypsicrates, and Mochus; Chaitus translated their books into Greek, and also composed with exactness the lives of the philosophers. Now, in the histories of the aforesaid writers it is shown that the abduction of Europa happened under one of the kings, and an account is given of the coming of Menelaus into Phœnicia, and of the matters relating to Chiramus,[1] who gave his daughter in marriage to Solomon the king of the Jews, and supplied wood of all kind of trees for the building of the temple. Menander of Pergamus composed a history concerning the same things. But the age of Chiramus is somewhere about the Trojan war; but Solomon, the contemporary of Chiramus, lived much later than the age of Moses.

[1] Called Hiram in our authorized translation.

CHAP. XXXVIII.—*The Egyptians place Moses in the reign*
of Inachus

Of the Egyptians also there are accurate chronicles.
Ptolemy, not the king, but a priest of Mendes, is the inter-
preter of their affairs. This writer, narrating the acts of
the kings, says that the departure of the Jews from Egypt to
the places whither they went occurred in the time of king
Amosis, under the leadership of Moses. He thus speaks:
" Amosis lived in the time of king Inachus." After him,
Apion the grammarian, a man most highly esteemed, in
the fourth book of his Ægyptiaca (there are five books of
his), besides many other things, says that Amosis destroyed
Avaris in the time of the Argive Inachus, as the Mendesian
Ptolemy wrote in his annals. But the time from Inachus to
the taking of Troy occupies twenty generations. The steps
of the demonstration are the following :—

CHAP. XXXIX.—*Catalogue of the Argive kings.*

The kings of the Argives were these : Inachus, Phoroneus,
Apis, Criasis, Triopas, Argeius, Phorbas, Crotopas, Sthenelaus, Danaus, Lynceus, Prœtus, Abas, Acrisius, Perseus,
Sthenelaus, Eurystheus, Atreus, Thyestes, and Agamemnon,
in the eighteenth year of whose reign Troy was taken. And
every intelligent person will most carefully observe that,
according to the tradition of the Greeks, they possessed no
historical composition ; for Cadmus, who taught them letters,
came into Bœotia many generations later. But after Inachus,
under Phoroneus, a check was with difficulty given to their
savage and nomadic life, and they entered upon a new order
of things. Wherefore, if Moses is shown to be contemporary with Inachus, he is four hundred years older than the
Trojan war. But this is demonstrated from the succession
of the Attic, [and of the Macedonian, the Ptolemaic, and
the Antiochian][1] kings. Hence, if the most illustrious deeds
among the Greeks were recorded and made known after

---

[1] The words within brackets, though they occur in the MSS. and in
Eusebius, are supposed by some scholars to be a very old interpolation.

Inachus, it is manifest that this must have been after Moses. In the time of Phoroneus, who was after Inachus, Ogygus is mentioned among the Athenians, in whose time was the first deluge; and in the time of Phorbas was Actæus, from whom Attica was called Actæa; and in the time of Triopas were Prometheus, and Epimetheus, and Atlas, and Cecrops of double nature, and Io; in the time of Crotopas was the burning of Phaëthon and the flood of Deucalion; in the time of Sthenelus was the reign of Amphiction and the coming of Danaus into Peloponnesus, and the founding of Dardania by Dardanus, and the return of Europa from Phœnicia to Crete; in the time of Lynceus was the abduction of Koré, and the founding of the temple in Eleusis, and the husbandry of Triptolemus, and the coming of Cadmus to Thebes, and the reign of Minos; in the time of Prœtus was the war of Eumolpus against the Athenians; in the time of Acrisius was the coming over of Pelops from Phrygia, and the coming of Ion to Athens, and the second Cecrops, and the deeds of Perseus and Dionysus, and Musæus, the disciple of Orpheus; and in the reign of Agamemnon Troy was taken.

CHAP. XL.—*Moses more ancient and credible than the heathen heroes.*

Therefore, from what has been said it is evident that Moses was older than the ancient heroes, wars, and demons. And we ought rather to believe him, who stands before them in point of age, than the Greeks, who, without being aware of it,[1] drew his doctrines [as] from a fountain. For many of the sophists among them, stimulated by curiosity, endeavoured to adulterate whatever they learned from Moses, and from those who have philosophized like him, first that they might be considered as having something of their own, and secondly, that covering up by a certain rhetorical artifice whatever things they did not understand, they might misrepresent

---

[1] This expression admits of several meanings: "Without properly understanding them"—*Worth*; "not with a proper sense of gratitude" —*Maranus.*

the truth as if it were a fable. But what the learned among the Greeks have said concerning our polity and the history of our laws, and how many and what kind of men have written of these things, will be shown in the treatise against those who have discoursed of divine things.

CHAP. XLI.

But the matter of principal importance is to endeavour with all accuracy to make it clear that Moses is not only older than Homer, but than all the writers that were before him—older than Linus, Philammon, Thamyris, Amphion, Musæus, Orpheus, Demodocus, Phemius, Sybilla, Epimenides of Crete, who came to Sparta, Aristæus of Proconnesus, who wrote the Arimaspia, Asbolus the Centaur, Isatis, Drymon, Euclus the Cyprian, Horus the Samian, and Pronapis the Athenian. Now, Linus was the teacher of Hercules, but Hercules preceded the Trojan war by one generation; and this is manifest from his son Tlepolemus, who served in the army against Troy. And Orpheus lived at the same time as Hercules; moreover, it is said that all the works attributed to him were composed by Onomacritus the Athenian, who lived during the reign of the Pisistratids, about the fiftieth Olympiad. Musæus was a disciple of Orpheus. Amphion, since he preceded the siege of Troy by two generations, forbids our collecting further particulars about him for those who are desirous of information. Demodocus and Phemius lived at the very time of the Trojan war; for the one resided with the suitors, and the other with the Phæacians. Thamyris and Philammon were not much earlier than these. Thus, concerning their several performances in each kind, and their times and the record of them, we have written very fully, and, as I think, with all exactness. But, that we may complete what is still wanting, I will give my explanation respecting the men who are esteemed wise. Minos, who has been thought to excel in every kind of wisdom, and mental acuteness, and legislative capacity, lived in the time of Lynceus, who reigned after Danaus in the eleventh generation after Inachus. Lycurgus, who was born

long after the taking of Troy, gave laws to the Lacede-
monians. Draco is found to have lived about the thirty-ninth
Olympiad, Solon about the forty-sixth, and Pythagoras about
the sixty-second. We have shown that the Olympiads com-
menced 407 years after the taking of Troy. These facts
being demonstrated, we shall briefly remark concerning the
age of the seven wise men. The oldest of these, Thales,
lived about the fiftieth Olympiad; and I have already spoken
briefly of those who came after him.

CHAP. XLII.—*Concluding statement as to the author.*

These things, O Greeks, I Tatian, a disciple of the barbaric philosophy, have composed for you. I was born in the
land of the Assyrians, having been first instructed in your
doctrines, and afterwards in those which I now undertake to
proclaim. Henceforward, knowing who God is and what is
His work, I present myself to you prepared for an examination concerning my doctrines, while I adhere immoveably to
that mode of life which is according to God.

FRAGMENTS OF THE LOST WORKS OF TATIAN.[1]

I.

N his treatise, *Concerning Perfection according to the Saviour*, he writes, "Consent indeed fits for prayer, but fellowship in corruption weakens supplication. At any rate, by the permission he certainly, though delicately, forbids ; for while he permits them to return to the same on account of Satan and incontinence, he exhibits a man who will attempt to serve two masters—God by the 'consent' (1 Cor. vii. 5), but by want of consent, incontinence, fornication, and the devil."

(Clem. Alex. Strom. iii. c. 12.)

II.

A certain person inveighs against generation, calling it corruptible and destructive ; and some one does violence [to Scripture], applying to procreation the Saviour's words, "Lay not up treasure on earth, where moth and rust corrupt;" and he is not ashamed to add to these the words of the prophet: "You all shall grow old as a garment, and the moth shall devour you."

And, in like manner, they adduce the saying concerning the resurrection of the dead, "The sons of that world neither marry nor are given in marriage."

(Clem. Alex. iii. c. 12, § 86.)

III.

Tatian, who maintaining the imaginary flesh of Christ, pronounces all sexual connection impure, who was also the

<hr>

[1] From the appendix to Otto's edition.

very violent heresiarch of the Encratites, employs an argument of this sort: "If any one sows to the flesh, of the flesh he shall reap corruption;" but he sows to the flesh who is joined to a woman; therefore he who takes a wife and sows in the flesh, of the flesh he shall reap corruption.

(Hieron. Com. in Ep. ad Gal.)

IV.

Seceding from the church, and being elated and puffed up by a conceit of his teacher,[1] as if he were superior to the rest, he formed his own peculiar type of doctrine. Imagining certain invisible Æons like those of Valentinus, and denouncing marriage as defilement and fornication in the same way as Marcion and Saturninus, and denying the salvation of Adam as an opinion of his own.

(Irenæus, adv. Hær. i. 28.)

V.

Tatian attempting from time to time to make use of Paul's language, that in Adam all die, but ignoring that "where sin abounded, grace has much more abounded."

(Irenæus, adv. Heres. iii. 37.)

VI.

Against Tatian, who says that the words, "Let there be light," are to be taken as a prayer. If He who uttered it knew a superior God, how is it that He says, "I am God, and there is none beside me?"

He said that there are punishments for blasphemies, foolish talking, and licentious words, which are punished and chastised by the Logos. And he said that women were punished on account of their hair and ornaments by a power placed over those things, which also gave strength to Samson by his hair, and punishes those who by the ornament of their hair are urged on to fornication.

(Clem. Alex. Frag.)

---

[1] *i.e.* Justin.

VII.

But Tatian, not understanding that the expression "Let there be" is not always precative but sometimes imperative, most impiously imagined concerning God, who said "Let there be light," that He prayed rather than commanded light to be, as if, as he impiously thought, God was in darkness.

(Origen, *de Orat.*)

VIII.

Tatian separates the old man and the new, but not, as we say, understanding the old man to be the law, and the new man to be the gospel. We agree with him in saying the same thing, but not in the sense he wishes, abrogating the law as if it belonged to another God.

(Clem. Alex. *Strom.* iii. 12.)

IX.

Tatian condemns and rejects not only marriage, but also meats which God has created for use.

(Hieron. *adv. Jovin.* i. 3.)

X.

"But ye gave the Nazarites wine to drink, and commanded the prophets, saying, Prophesy not." On this, perhaps, Tatian the chief of the Encratites endeavours to build his heresy, asserting that wine is not to be drunk, since it was commanded in the law that the Nazarites were not to drink wine, and now those who give the Nazarite wine are accused by the prophet. (Hieron. *Com. in Amos.*)

XI.

Tatian, the patriarch of the Encratites, who himself rejected some of Paul's epistles, believed this especially, that is [addressed] to Titus, ought to be declared to be the apostle's, thinking little of the assertion of Marcion and others, who agree with him on this point.

(Hieron. *Præf. in Com. ad Tit.*)

THE THREE BOOKS OF

THEOPHILUS OF ANTIOCH TO AUTOLYCUS.

D

INTRODUCTORY NOTICE.

ITTLE is known of the personal history of Theophilus of Antioch. We gather from the following treatise that he was born a pagan (i. 14), and owed his conversion to Christianity to the careful study of the Holy Scriptures. Eusebius (*Hist. Eccl.* iv. 20) declares that he was the sixth bishop of Antioch in Syria from the apostles, the names of his supposed predecessors being Eros, Cornelius, Hero, Ignatius, and Euodius. We also learn from the same writer that Theophilus succeeded to the bishopric of Antioch in the eighth year of the reign of Marcus Aurelius, that is, in A.D. 168. He is related to have died either in A.D. 181, or in A.D. 188; some assigning him an episcopate of thirteen, and others of twenty-one, years.

Theophilus is said by Eusebius, Jerome, and others, to have written several works against the heresies which prevailed in his day. He himself refers in the following treatise (ii. 30) to another of his compositions. Commentaries on the Gospels, arranged in the form of a harmony, and on the book of Proverbs, are also ascribed to him by Jerome; but the sole remaining specimen of his writings consists of the three books that follow, addressed to his friend Autolycus. The occasion which called these forth is somewhat doubtful. It has been thought that they were written in refutation of a work which Autolycus had published against Christianity; but the more probable opinion is, that they were drawn forth by disparaging remarks made in conversation. The language of the writer (ii. 1) leads to this conclusion.

In handling his subject, Theophilus goes over much the same ground as Justin Martyr and the rest of the early apologists. He is somewhat fond of fanciful interpretations of Scripture; but he evidently had a profound acquaintance with the inspired writings, and he powerfully exhibits their immense superiority in every respect over the heathen poetry and philosophy. The whole treatise was well fitted to lead on an intelligent pagan to the cordial acceptance of Christianity.

THEOPHILUS TO AUTOLYCUS.

BOOK I.

Chap. i.—Autolycus an idolater and scorner of Christians.

A FLUENT tongue and an elegant style afford pleasure and such praise as vainglory delights in, to wretched men who have been corrupted in mind; the lover of truth does not give heed to ornamented speeches, but examines the real matter of the speech, what it is, and what kind it is. Since, then, my friend, you have assailed me with empty words, boasting of your gods of wood and stone, hammered and cast, carved and graven, which neither see nor hear, for they are idols, and the works of men's hands; and since, besides, you call me a Christian, as if this were a damning name to bear, I, for my part, avow that I am a Christian, and bear this name beloved of God, hoping to be serviceable[1] to God. For it is not the case, as you suppose, that the name of God is hard to bear; but possibly you entertain this opinion of God, because you are yourself yet unserviceable to Him.

Chap. ii.—That the eyes of the soul must be purged ere God can be seen.

But if you say, "Show me thy God," I would reply, "Show me yourself,[2] and I will show you my God." Show, then, that the eyes of your soul are capable of seeing, and the ears of your heart able to hear; for as those who look with the eyes of the body perceive earthly objects and what concerns

[1] Εὔχρηστος, punning on the name *Christian.*
[2] Literally, "your man;" the invisible soul, as the noblest part of man, being probably intended.

this life, and discriminate at the same time between things that differ, whether light or darkness, white or black, deformed or beautiful, well-proportioned and symmetrical or dispropor- tioned and awkward, or monstrous or mutilated; and as in like manner also, by the sense of hearing, we discriminate either sharp, or deep, or sweet sounds; so the same holds good regarding the eyes of the soul and the ears of the heart, that it is by them we are able to behold God. For God is seen by those who are enabled to see Him when they have the eyes of their soul opened : for all have eyes; but in some they are overspread,[1] and do not see the light of the sun. Yet it does not follow, because the blind do not see, that the light of the sun does not shine ; but let the blind blame themselves and their own eyes. So also thou, O man, hast the eyes of thy soul overspread by thy sins and evil deeds. As a burnished mirror, so ought man to have his soul pure. When there is rust on the mirror, it is not possible that a man's face be seen in the mirror ; so also when there is sin in a man, such a man cannot behold God. Do you, therefore, show me yourself, whether you are not an adulterer, or a fornicator, or a thief, or a robber, or a purloiner ; whether you do not corrupt boys ; whether you are not insolent, or a slanderer, or passionate, or envious, or proud, or supercilious; whether you are not a brawler, or covetous, or disobedient to parents ; and whether you do not sell your children ; for to those who do these things God is not manifest, unless they have first cleansed themselves from all impurity. All these things, then, involve you in darkness, as when a filmy de- fluxion on the eyes prevents one from beholding the light of the sun : thus also do iniquities, O man, involve you in darkness, so that you cannot see God.

Chap. III.—*Nature of God.*

You will say, then, to me, " Do you, who see God, explain to me the appearance of God." Hear, O man. The appear- ance of God is ineffable and indescribable, and cannot be seen by eyes of flesh. For in glory He is incomprehensible,

---

[1] The technical word for a disease of the eye, like cataract.

in greatness unfathomable, in height inconceivable, in power incomparable, in wisdom unrivalled, in goodness inimitable, in kindness unutterable. For if I say He is Light, I name but His own work; if I call Him Word, I name but His sovereignty; if I call Him Mind, I speak but of His wisdom; if I say He is Spirit, I speak of His breath; if I call Him Wisdom, I speak of His offspring; if I call Him Strength, I speak of His sway; if I call Him Power, I am mentioning His activity; if Providence, I but mention His goodness; if I call Him Kingdom, I but mention His glory; if I call Him Lord, I mention His being judge; if I call Him Judge, I speak of Him as being just; if I call Him Father, I speak of all things as being from Him;[1] if I call Him Fire, I but mention His anger. You will say, then, to me, "Is God angry?" Yes; He is angry with those who act wickedly, but He is good, and kind, and merciful, to those who love and fear Him; for He is a chastener[2] of the godly, and father of the righteous; but he is a judge and punisher of the impious.

CHAP. IV.—*Attributes of God.*

And He is without beginning, because He is unbegotten; and He is unchangeable, because He is immortal. And He is called God [Θεὸς] on account of His having placed [τεθει-κέναι] all things on security afforded by Himself; and on account of [θέειν], for θέειν means running, and moving, and being active, and nourishing, and foreseeing, and governing, and making all things alive. But he is Lord, because He rules over the universe; Father, because he is before all things; Fashioner and Maker, because He is creator and maker of the universe; the Highest, because of His being above all; and Almighty, because He Himself rules and embraces all. For the heights of heaven, and the depths of

---

[1] The translation here follows the Hamburg editor; others read, "If Father, I say everything."

[2] Maranus observes that Theophilus means to indicate the difference between God's chastisement of the righteous and His punishment of the wicked.

the abysses, and the ends of the earth, are in His hand, and there is no place of His rest. For the heavens are His work, the earth is His creation, the sea is His handiwork; man is His formation and His image; sun, moon, and stars are His elements, made for signs, and seasons, and days, and years, that they may serve and be slaves to man; and all things God has made out of things that were not into things that are, in order that through His works His greatness may be known and understood.

CHAP. V.—*The invisible God perceived through His works.*

For as the soul in man is not seen, being invisible to men, but is perceived through the motion of the body, so God cannot indeed be seen by human eyes, but is beheld and perceived through His providence and works. For, in like manner, as any person, when he sees a ship on the sea rigged and in sail, and making for the harbour, will no doubt infer that there is a pilot in her who is steering her; so we must perceive that God is the governor [pilot] of the whole universe, though He be not visible to eyes of flesh, since He is incomprehensible. For if a man cannot look upon the sun, though it be a very small heavenly body, on account of its exceeding heat and power, how shall not a mortal man be much more unable to face the glory of God, which is unutterable? For as the pomegranate, with the rind containing it, has within it many cells and compartments which are separated by tissues, and has also many seeds dwelling in it, so the whole creation is contained by the spirit[1] of God, and the containing spirit is along with the creation contained by the hand of God. As, therefore, the seed of the pomegranate, dwelling inside, cannot see what is outside the rind, itself being within; so neither can man, who along with the whole creation is enclosed by the hand of God, behold God. Then again, an earthly king is believed to exist, even though he be not seen by all, for he is recognised by his laws and ordinances, and authorities, and

[1] The reference here is not to the Holy Spirit, but to that vital power which is supposed to be diffused throughout the universe. Comp. Book ii. 4.

forces, and statues ; and are you unwilling that God should be recognised by His works and mighty deeds ?

Chap. vi.—*God is known by His works.*

Consider, O man, His works,—the timely rotation of the seasons, and the changes of temperature ; the regular march of the stars ; the well-ordered course of days and nights, and months, and years; the various beauty of seeds, and plants, and fruits ; and the divers species[1] of quadrupeds, and birds, and reptiles, and fishes, both of the rivers and of the sea ; or consider the instinct implanted in these animals to beget and rear offspring, not for their own profit, but for the use of man ; and the providence with which God provides nourishment for all flesh, or the subjection in which He has ordained that all things subserve mankind. Consider, too, the flowing of sweet fountains and never-failing rivers, and the seasonable supply of dews, and showers, and rains ; the manifold movement of the heavenly bodies, the morning star rising and heralding the approach of the perfect luminary ; and the constellation of Pleiades, and Orion, and Arcturus, and the orbit of the other stars that circle through the heavens, all of which the manifold wisdom of God has called by names of their own. He is God alone who made light out of darkness, and brought forth light from His treasures, and formed the chambers of the south wind,[2] and the treasure-houses of the deep, and the bounds of the seas, and the treasuries of snows and hail-storms, collecting the waters in the storehouses of the deep, and the darkness in His treasures, and bringing forth the sweet, and desirable, and pleasant light out of His treasures ; " who causeth the vapours to ascend from the ends of the earth : He maketh lightnings for the rain ;"[3] who sends forth His thunder to terrify, and foretells by the lightning the peal of the thunder, that no soul may faint with the sudden shock ; and who so moderates the violence of the lightning as it flashes out of heaven, that it does not consume the earth ; for, if the lightning were allowed all its power, it would burn up the earth ; and were the thunder

[1] Literally, " propagation."   [2] Job ix. 9.   [3] Ps. cxxxv. 7.

allowed all its power, it would overthrow all the works that are therein.

CHAP. VII.—*We shall see God when we put on immortality.*

This is my God, the Lord of all, who alone stretched out the heaven, and established the breadth of the earth under it; who stirs the deep recesses of the sea, and makes its waves roar; who rules its power, and stills the tumult of its waves; who founded the earth upon the waters, and gave a spirit to nourish it; whose breath giveth life to the whole, who, if He withdraw His breath, the whole will utterly fail. By Him you speak, O man; His breath you breathe, yet Him you know not. And this is your condition, because of the blindness of your soul, and the hardness of your heart. But, if you will, you may be healed. Entrust yourself to the Physician, and He will couch the eyes of your soul and of your heart. Who is the Physician? God, who heals and makes alive through His word and wisdom. God by His own word and wisdom made all things; for "by His word were the heavens made, and all the host of them by the breath of His mouth."[1] Most excellent is His wisdom. By His wisdom God founded the earth; and by knowledge He prepared the heavens; and by understanding were the fountains of the great deep broken up, and the clouds poured out their dews. If thou perceivest these things, O man, living chastely, and holily, and righteously, thou canst see God. But before all let faith and the fear of God have rule in thy heart, and then shalt thou understand these things. When thou shalt have put off the mortal, and put on incorruption, then shalt thou see God worthily. For God will raise thy flesh immortal with thy soul; and then, having become immortal, thou shalt see the Immortal, if now you believe on Him; and then you shall know that you have spoken unjustly against Him.

[1] Ps. xxxiii. 6.

Chap. VIII.—*Faith required in all matters.*

But you do not believe that the dead are raised. When the resurrection shall take place, then you will believe, whether you will or no; and your faith shall be reckoned for unbelief, unless you believe now. And why do you not believe? Do you not know that faith is the leading principle in all matters? For what husbandman can reap, unless he first trust his seed to the earth? Or who can cross the sea, unless he first entrust himself to the boat and the pilot? And what sick person can be healed, unless first he trust himself to the care of the physician? And what art or knowledge can any one learn, unless he first apply and entrust himself to the teacher? If, then, the husbandman trusts the earth, and the sailor the boat, and the sick the physician, will you not place confidence in God, even when you hold so many pledges at His hand? For first He created you out of nothing, and brought you into existence (for if your father was not, nor your mother, much more were you yourself at one time not in being), and formed you out of a small and moist substance, even out of the least drop, which at one time had itself no being; and God introduced you into this life. Moreover, you believe that the images made by men are gods, and do great things; and can you not believe that the God who made you is able also to make you afterwards?[1]

Chap. IX.—*Immoralities of the gods.*

And, indeed, the names of those whom you say you worship, are the names of dead men. And these, too, who and what kind of men were they? Is not Saturn found to be a cannibal, destroying and devouring his own children? And if you name his son Jupiter, hear also his deeds and conduct —first, how he was suckled by a goat on Mount Ida, and having slain it, according to the myths, and flayed it, he made himself a coat of the hide. And his other deeds,—his incest, and adultery, and lust,—will be better recounted by

[1] *i.e.* in the resurrection.

Homer and the rest of the poets. Why should I further speak of his sons? How Hercules burnt himself; and about the drunk and raging Bacchus; and of Apollo fearing and fleeing from Achilles, and falling in love with Daphne, and being unaware of the fate of Hyacinthus; and of Venus wounded, and of Mars, the pest of mortals; and of the ichor flowing from the so-called gods. And these, indeed, are the milder kinds of legends; since the god who is called Osiris is found to have been torn limb from limb, whose mysteries are celebrated annually, as if he had perished, and were being found, and sought for limb by limb. For neither is it known whether he perished, nor is it shown whether he is found. And why should I speak of Atys mutilated, or of Adonis wandering in the wood, and wounded by a boar while hunting; or of Æsculapius struck by a thunderbolt; or of the fugitive Serapis chased from Sinope to Alexandria; or of the Scythian Diana, herself, too, a fugitive, and a homicide, and a huntress, and a passionate lover of Endymion? Now, it is not we who publish these things, but your own writers and poets.

Chap. x.—*Absurdities of idolatry.*

Why should I further recount the multitude of animals worshipped by the Egyptians, both reptiles, and cattle, and wild beasts, and birds, and river-fishes; and even wash-pots and disgraceful noises? But if you cite the Greeks and the other nations, they worship stones and wood, and other kinds of material substances,—the images, as we have just been saying, of dead men. For Phidias is found in Pisa making for the Eleians the Olympian Jupiter, and at Athens the Minerva of the Acropolis. And I will inquire of you, my friend, how many Jupiters exist. For there is, firstly, Jupiter surnamed Olympian, then Jupiter Latiaris, and Jupiter Cassius, and Jupiter Tonans, and Jupiter Propator, and Jupiter Pannychius, and Jupiter Poliuchus, and Jupiter Capitolinus; and that Jupiter, the son of Saturn, who is king of the Cretans, has a tomb in Crete, but the rest, possibly, were not thought worthy of tombs. And if you speak of

the mother of those who are called gods, far be it from me
to utter with my lips her deeds, or the deeds of those by
whom she is worshipped (for it is unlawful for us so much
as to name such things), and what vast taxes and revenues
she and her sons furnish to the king. For these are not
gods, but idols, as we have already said, the works of men's
hands and unclean demons. And such may all those become
who make them and put their trust in them!

CHAP. XI.—*The king to be honoured, God to be worshipped.*

Wherefore I will rather honour the king [than your
gods], not, indeed, worshipping him, but praying for him.
But God, the living and true God, I worship, knowing that
the king is made by Him. You will say, then, to me,
"Why do you not worship the king?" Because he is not
made to be worshipped, but to be reverenced with lawful
honour, for he is not a god, but a man appointed by God,
not to be worshipped, but to judge justly. For in a kind of
way his government is committed to him by God: as He will
not have those called kings whom He has appointed under
Himself; for "king" is his title, and it is not lawful for
another to use it; so neither is it lawful for any to be worshipped but God only. Wherefore, O man, you are wholly
in error. Accordingly, honour the king, be subject to him,
and pray for him with loyal mind; for if you do this,
you do the will of God. For the law that is of God, says,
"My son, fear thou the Lord and the king, and be not
disobedient to them; for suddenly they shall take vengeance on their enemies."[1]

CHAP. XII.—*Meaning of the name Christian.*

And about your laughing at me and calling me "Christian," you know not what you are saying. First, because that
which is anointed[2] is sweet and serviceable, and far from con-

---

[1] Prov. xxiv. 21, 22. The Greek of Theophilus has "honour" instead
of "fear."

[2] "The argumentation of this chapter depends on the literal meaning
which Theophilus attaches to Christos, the anointed One; and he plays

temptible. For what ship can be serviceable and seaworthy, unless it be first caulked [anointed]? Or what castle or house is beautiful and serviceable when it has not been anointed? And what man, when he enters into this life or into the gymnasium, is not anointed with oil? And what work has either ornament or beauty unless it be anointed and burnished? Then the air and all that is under heaven is in a certain sort anointed by light and spirit; and are you unwilling to be anointed with the oil of God? Wherefore we are called Christians on this account, because we are anointed with the oil of God.

CHAP. XIII.—*The resurrection proved by examples.*

Then, as to your denying that the dead are raised—for you say, "Show me even one who has been raised from the dead, that seeing I may believe,"—first, what great thing is it if you believe when you have seen the thing done? Then, again, you believe that Hercules, who burned himself, lives; and that Æsculapius, who was struck with lightning, was raised; and do you disbelieve the things that are told you by God? But, suppose I should show you a dead man raised and alive, even this you would disbelieve. God indeed exhibits to you many proofs that you may believe Him. For consider, if you please, the dying of seasons, and days, and nights, how these also die and rise again. And what? Is there not a resurrection going on of seeds and fruits, and this, too, for the use of men? A seed of wheat, for example, or of the other grains, when it is cast into the earth, first dies and rots away, then is raised, and becomes a stalk of corn. And the nature of trees and fruit-trees,—is it not that according to the appointment of God they produce their fruits in their seasons out of what has been unseen and invisible? Moreover, sometimes also a sparrow or some of the other birds, when in drinking it has swallowed a seed of apple or fig, or something else, has come to some rocky hillock or tomb, and has left the seed in its droppings, and the seed, on this meaning, and also on the similarity of pronunciation between χρηστός, 'useful,' and χριστός, 'anointed.'"—DONALDSON.

which was once swallowed, and has passed through so great a heat, now striking root, a tree has grown up. And all these things does the wisdom of God effect, in order to manifest even by these things, that God is able to effect the general resurrection of all men. And if you would witness a more wonderful sight, which may prove a resurrection not only of earthly but of heavenly bodies, consider the resurrection of the moon, which occurs monthly; how it wanes, dies, and rises again. Hear further, O man, of the work of resurrection going on in yourself, even though you are unaware of it. For perhaps you have sometimes fallen sick, and lost flesh, and strength, and beauty; but when you received again from God mercy and healing, you picked up again in flesh and appearance, and recovered also your strength. And as you do not know where your flesh went away and disappeared to, so neither do you know whence it grew, or whence it came again. But you will say, " From meats and drinks changed into blood." Quite so; but this, too, is the work of God, who thus operates, and not of any other.

CHAP. XIV.—*Theophilus an example of conversion.*

Therefore, do not be sceptical, but believe; for I myself also used to disbelieve that this would take place, but now, having taken these things into consideration, I believe. At the same time, I met with the sacred Scriptures of the holy prophets, who also by the Spirit of God foretold the things that have already happened, just as they came to pass, and the things now occurring as they are now happening, and things future in the order in which they shall be accomplished. Admitting, therefore, the proof which events happening as predicted afford, I do not disbelieve, but I believe, obedient to God, whom, if you please, do you also submit to, believing Him, lest if now you continue unbelieving, you be convinced hereafter, when you are tormented with eternal punishments; which punishments, when they had been foretold by the prophets, the later-born poets and philosophers stole from the holy Scriptures, to make their doctrines worthy of credit. Yet these also have spoken beforehand of the punishments that are to light upon the profane and unbelieving, in order that none be left without a witness, or be able to say, " We have not heard, neither have we known." But do you also, if you please, give reverential attention to the prophetic Scriptures, and they will make your way plainer for escaping the eternal punishments, and obtaining the eternal prizes of God. For He who gave the mouth for speech, and formed the ear to hear, and made the eye to see, will examine all things, and will judge righteous judgment, rendering merited awards to each. To those who by patient continuance in well-doing[1] seek immortality, He will give life everlasting, joy, peace, rest, and abundance of good things, which neither hath eye seen, nor ear heard, nor hath it entered into the heart of man to conceive.[2] But to the unbelieving and despisers, who obey not the truth, but are obedient to unrighteousness, when they shall have been filled with adulteries and fornications, and filthiness, and covetousness, and unlawful idolatries, there shall be anger and wrath, tribulation and anguish,[3] and at the last everlasting fire shall possess such men. Since you said, " Show me thy God," this is my God, and I counsel you to fear Him and to trust Him.

[1] Rom. ii. 6.   [2] 1 Cor. xi. 9.   [3] Rom. ii. 8.

THEOPHILUS TO AUTOLYCUS.

BOOK II.

CHAP. I.—*Occasion of writing this book.*

When we had formerly some conversation, my very good friend Autolycus, and when you inquired who was my God, and for a little paid attention to my discourse, I made some explanations to you concerning my religion ; and then having bid one another adieu, we went with much mutual friendliness each to his own house, although at first you had borne somewhat hard upon me. For you know and remember that you supposed our doctrine was foolishness. As you then afterwards urged me to do, I am desirous, though not educated to the art of speaking, of more accurately demonstrating, by means of this tractate, the vain labour and empty worship in which you are held ; and I wish also, from a few of your own histories which you read, and perhaps do not yet quite understand, to make the truth plain to you.

CHAP. II.—*The gods are despised when they are made ; but become valuable when bought.*

And in truth it does seem to me absurd that statuaries and carvers, or painters, or moulders, should both design and paint, and carve, and mould, and prepare gods, who, when they are produced by the artificers, are reckoned of no value ; but as soon as they are purchased [1] by some and placed in some so-called temple, or in some house, not only do those who bought them sacrifice to them, but also those who made and sold them come with much devotion, and apparatus of sacrifice, and libations, to worship them ; and they reckon them gods, not seeing that they are just such as when they were made by themselves,

---

[1] The words "by some and placed in" are omitted in some editions, but occur in the best MSS.

E

whether stone, or brass, or wood, or colour, or some other material. And this is your case, too, when you read the histories and genealogies of the so-called gods. For when you read of their births, you think of them as men, but afterwards you call them gods, and worship them, not reflecting nor understanding that, when born, they are exactly such beings as ye read of before.

CHAP. III.—*What has become of the gods?*

And of the gods of former times, if indeed they were begotten, the generation was sufficiently prolific. But now, where is their generation exhibited? For if of old they begot and were begotten, it is plain that even to the present time there should be gods begotten and born; or at least if it be not so, such a race will be reckoned impotent. For either they have waxed old, and on that account no longer beget, or they have died out and no longer exist. For if the gods were begotten, they ought to be born even until now, as men, too, are born; yea, much more numerous should the gods be than men, as the Sibyl says:—

> "For if the gods beget, and each remains
> Immortal, then the race of gods must be
> More numerous than mortals, and the throng
> So great that mortals find no room to stand."

For if the children begotten of men who are mortal and short-lived make an appearance even until now, and men have not ceased to be born, so that cities and villages are full, and even the country places also are inhabited, how ought not the gods, who, according to your poets, do not die, much rather to beget and be begotten, since you say that the gods were produced by generation? And why was the mount which is called Olympus formerly inhabited by the gods, but now lies deserted? Or why did Jupiter, in days of yore, dwell on Ida, and was known to dwell there, according to Homer and other poets, but now is beyond ken? And why was he found only in one part of the earth, and not everywhere? For either he neglected the other parts, or was not able to be present everywhere and provide for all. For if he were, *e.g.*

in an eastern place, he was not in the western; and if, on
the other hand, he were present in the western parts, he was
not in the eastern. But this is the attribute of God, the
Highest and Almighty, and the living God, not only to be
everywhere present, but also to see all things and to hear all,
and by no means to be confined in a place; for if He were,
then the place containing Him would be greater than He;
for that which contains is greater than that which is contained.
For God is not contained, but is Himself the place of all.
But why has Jupiter left Ida? Was it because he died, or
did that mountain no longer please him? And where has
he gone? To heaven? No. But you will perhaps say, To
Crete? Yes, for there, too, his tomb is shown to this day.
Again, you will say, To Pisa, where he reflects glory on the
hands of Phidias to this day. Let us, then, proceed to the
writings of the philosophers and poets.

CHAP. IV.—*Absurd opinions of the philosophers concerning
God.*

Some of the philosophers of the Porch say that there is no
God at all; or, if there is, they say that He cares for none
but Himself; and these views the folly of Epicurus and
Chrysippus has set forth at large. And others say that all
things are produced without external agency, and that the
world is uncreated, and that nature is eternal;[1] and have dared
to give out that there is no providence of God at all, but
maintain that God is only each man's conscience. And others
again maintain that the spirit which pervades all things is
God. But Plato and those of his school acknowledge indeed
that God is uncreated, and the Father and Maker of all
things; but then they maintain that matter as well as God is
uncreated, and aver that it is coeval with God. But if God
is uncreated and matter uncreated, God is no longer, according to the Platonists, the Creator of all things, nor, so far as
their opinions hold, is the monarchy[2] of God established. And

[1] This is according to the Benedictine reading: the reading of Wolf,
"nature is left to itself," is also worthy of consideration.

[2] That is, the existence of God as sole first principle.

further, as God, because He is uncreated, is also unalterable , so if matter, too, were uncreated, it also would be unalterable, and equal to God; for that which is created is mutable and alterable, but that which is uncreated is immutable and unalterable. And what great thing is it if God made the world out of existent materials?[1] For even a human artist, when he gets material from some one, makes of it what he pleases. But the power of God is manifested in this, that out of things that are not He makes whatever He pleases; just as the bestowal of life and motion is the prerogative of no other than God alone. For even man makes indeed an image, but reason and breath, or feeling, he cannot give to what he has made. But God has this property in excess of what man can do, in that He makes a work, endowed with reason, life, sensation. As, therefore, in all these respects God is more powerful than man, so also in this; that out of things that are not He creates and has created things that are, and whatever He pleases, as He pleases.

CHAP. V.—*Opinions of Homer and Hesiod concerning the gods.*

So that the opinion of your philosophers and authors is discordant; for while the former have propounded the foregoing opinions, the poet Homer is found explaining the origin not only of the world, but also of the gods, on quite another hypothesis. For he says somewhere:[2]

> "Father of Gods, Oceanus, and she
> Who bare the gods, their mother Tethys, too,
> From whom all rivers spring, and every sea."

In saying which, however, he does not present God to us. For who does not know that the ocean is water? But if water, then not God. God indeed, if He is the creator of all things, as He certainly is, is the creator both of the water and of the seas. And Hesiod himself also declared the origin, not only of the gods, but also of the world itself. And though he said that the world was created, he showed no inclination to tell us by whom it was created. Besides, he said that Saturn, and his sons Jupiter, Neptune,

---

[1] Literally, "subject-matter."   [2] *Il.* xiv. 201.

and Pluto, were gods, though we find that they are later born than the world. And he also relates how Saturn was assailed in war by his own son Jupiter; for he says :[1]

> " His father Saturn he by might o'ercame,
> And 'mong th' immortals ruled with justice wise,
> And honours fit distributed to each."

Then he introduces in his poem the daughters of Jupiter, whom he names Muses, and as whose suppliant he appears, desiring to ascertain from them how all things were made; for he says :[2]

> " Daughters of Jove, all hail! Grant me your aid
> That I in numbers sweet and well-arrayed,
> Of the immortal gods may sing the birth;
> Who of the starry heav'ns were born, and earth;
> Who, springing from the murky night at first,
> Were by the briny ocean reared and nursed.
> Tell, too, who form unto the earth first gave,
> And rivers, and the boundless sea whose wave
> Unwearied sinks, then rears its crest on high;
> And how was spread yon glittering canopy
> Of glistening stars that stud the wide-spread heaven.
> Whence sprang the gods by whom all good is given?
> Tell from their hands what varied gifts there came,
> Riches to some, to others wealth, or fame;
> How they have dwelt from the remotest time
> In many-nooked Olympus' sunny clime.
> These things, ye Muses, say, who ever dwell
> Among Olympian shades—since ye can tell :
> From the beginning there thy feet have strayed;
> Then tell us which of all things first was made."

But how could the Muses, who are younger than the world, know these things? Or how could they relate to Hesiod [what was happening], when their father was not yet born ?

CHAP. VI.—*Hesiod on the origin of the world.*

And in a certain way he indeed admits matter [as self-existent] and the creation of the world [without a creator], saying :

> "First of all things was chaos made, and next
> Broad-bosom'd earth's foundations firm were fixed,

---

[1] Hesiod, *Theog.* 74.   [2] *Theog.* 104.

Where safely the immortals dwell for aye,
Who in the snowy-peak'd Olympus stay.
Afterwards gloomy Tartarus had birth
In the recesses of broad-pathwayed earth,
And Love, ev'n among gods most beauteous still,
Who comes all-conquering, bending mind and will,
Delivering from care, and giving then
Wise counsel in the breasts of gods and men.
From chaos Erebus and night were born,
From night and Erebus sprung air and morn.
Earth in her likeness made the starry heaven,
That unto all things shelter might be given,
And that the blessed gods might there repose.
The lofty mountains by her power arose,
For the wood-nymphs she made the pleasant caves,
Begot the sterile sea with all his waves,
Loveless ; but when by heaven her love was sought,
Then the deep-eddying ocean forth she brought."

And saying this, he has not yet explained by whom all this
was made.   For if chaos existed in the beginning, and matter
of some sort, being uncreated, was previously existing, who
was it that effected the change on its condition, and gave it a
different order and shape ?   Did matter itself alter its own
form and arrange itself into a world (for Jupiter was born,
not only long after matter, but long after the world and many
men ; and so, too, was his father Saturn), or was there some
ruling power which made it ; I mean, of course, God, who also
fashioned it into a world ?   Besides, he is found in every way
to talk nonsense, and to contradict himself.   For when he
mentions earth, and sky, and sea, he gives us to understand
that from these the gods were produced ; and from these
again [the gods] he declares that certain very dreadful men
were sprung,—the race of the Titans and the Cyclopes, and a
crowd of giants, and of the Egyptian gods,—or, rather, vain
men, as Apollonides, surnamed Horapius, mentions in the
book entitled *Semenouthi*, and in his other histories concerning the worship of the Egyptians and their kings, and the
vain labours in which they engaged.[1]

---

[1] The Benedictine editor proposes to read these words after the first
clause of c. 7.   We follow the reading of Wolf and Fell, who understand
the pyramids to be referred to.

CHAP. VII.—*Fabulous heathen genealogies.*

Why need I recount the Greek fables,—of Pluto, king of darkness, of Neptune descending beneath the sea, and embracing Melanippe and begetting a cannibal son,—or the many tales your writers have woven into their tragedies concerning the sons of Jupiter, and whose pedigree they register because they were born men, and not gods? And the comic poet Aristophanes, in the play called "The Birds," having taken upon him to handle the subject of the Creation, said that in the beginning the world was produced from an egg, saying:[1]

> " A windy egg was laid by black-winged night
> At first."

But Satyrus, also giving a history of the Alexandrine families, beginning from Philopator, who was also named Ptolemy, gives out that Bacchus was his progenitor; wherefore also Ptolemy was the founder of this[2] family. Satyrus then speaks thus: That Dejanira was born of Bacchus and Althea, the daughter of Thestius; and from her and Hercules the son of Jupiter there sprang, as I suppose, Hyllus; and from him Cleodemus, and from him Aristomachus, and from him Temenus, and from him Ceisus, and from him Maron, and from him Thestius, and from him Acous, and from him Aristomidas, and from him Caranus, and from him Cœnus, and from him Tyrimmas, and from him Perdiccas, and from him Philip, and from him Æropus, and from him Alcetas, and from him Amyntas, and from him Bocrus, and from him Meleager, and from him Arsinoe, and from her and Lagus Ptolemy Soter, and from him and Arsinoe Ptolemy Euergetes, and from him and Berenice, daughter of Maga, king of Cyrene, Ptolemy Philopator. Thus, then, stands the relationship of the Alexandrine kings to Bacchus. And therefore in the Dionysian tribe there are distinct families: the Althean from Althea, who was the wife of Dionysus and daughter of Thestius; the family of Dejanira also, from her who was the

---

[1] Aristoph. *Av.* 695. A wind-egg being one produced without impregnation, and coming to nothing.

[2] The Dionysian family taking its name from Dionysus or Bacchus.

daughter of Dionysus and Althea, and wife of Hercules; —whence, too, the families have their names: the family of Ariadne, from Ariadne, daughter of Minos and wife of Dionysus, a dutiful daughter, who had intercourse with Dionysus in another form; the Thestian, from Thestius, the father of Althea; the Thoantian, from Thoas, son of Dionysus; the Staphylian, from Staphylus, son of Dionysus; the Euænian, from Eunous, son of Dionysus; the Maronian, from Maron, son of Ariadne and Dionysus;—for all these are sons of Dionysus. And, indeed, many other names were thus originated, and exist to this day; as the Heraclidæ from Hercules, and the Apollonidæ from Apollo, and the Poseidonii from Poseidon, and from Zeus the Dii and Diogenæ.

CHAP. VIII.—*Opinions concerning Providence.*

And why should I recount further the vast array of such names and genealogies? So that all the authors and poets, and those called philosophers, are wholly deceived; and so, too, are they who give heed to them. For they plentifully composed fables and foolish stories about their gods, and did not exhibit them as gods, but as men, and men, too, of whom some were drunken, and others fornicators and murderers. But also concerning the origin of the world, they uttered contradictory and absurd opinions. First, some of them, as we before explained, maintained that the world is uncreated. And those who said it was uncreated and self-producing contradicted those who propounded that it was created. For by conjecture and human conception they spoke, and not knowing the truth. And others, again, said that there was a providence, and destroyed the positions of the former writers. Aratus, indeed, says:[1]

> " From Jove begin my song; nor ever be
> The name unuttered: all are full of thee;
> The ways and haunts of men; the heavens and sea:
> On thee our being hangs; in thee we move;
> All are thy offspring and the seed of Jove.

---

[1] The following lines are partly from the translation of Hughes.

> Benevolent, he warns mankind to good,
> Urges to toil and prompts the hope of food.
> He tells where cattle best may graze, and where
> The soil, deep-furrowed, yellow grain will bear.
> What time the husbandman should plant or sow,
> 'Tis his to tell, 'tis his alone to know."

Who, then, shall we believe: Aratus as here quoted, or Sophocles, when he says:[1]

> "And foresight of the future there is none;
> 'Tis best to live at random, as one can"?

And Homer, again, does not agree with this, for he says[2] that virtue

> "Waxes or wanes in men as Jove decrees."

And Simonides says:

> "No man nor state has virtue save from God;
> Counsel resides in God; and wretched man
> Has in himself nought but his wretchedness."

So, too, Euripides:

> "Apart from God, there's nothing owned by men."

And Menander:

> "Save God alone, there's none for us provides."

And Euripides again:

> "For when God wills to save, all things He'll bend
> To serve as instruments to work His end."

And Thestius:

> "If God design to save you, safe you are,
> Though sailing in mid-ocean on a mat."[3]

And saying numberless things of a like kind, they contradicted themselves. At least Sophocles, who in another place denied Providence, says:

> "No mortal can evade the stroke of God."

Besides, they both introduced a multitude of gods, and yet spoke of a Unity; and against those who affirmed a Providence they maintained in opposition that there was no Providence. Wherefore Euripides says:

> "We labour much and spend our strength in vain,
> For empty hope, not foresight, is our guide."

---

[1] *Œdipus Rex.* line 978.   [2] *Il.* xx. 242.

[3] This verse is by Plutarch hesitatingly attributed to Pindar. The expression, "Though you swim in a wicker basket," was proverbial.

And without meaning to do so, they acknowledge that they know not the truth ; but being inspired by demons and puffed up by them, they spoke at their instance whatever they said. For indeed the poets,—Homer, to wit, and Hesiod, being, as they say, inspired by the Muses,—spoke from a deceptive fancy,[1] and not with a pure but an erring spirit. And this, indeed, clearly appears from the fact, that even to this day the possessed are sometimes exorcised in the name of the living and true God ; and these spirits of error themselves confess that they are demons who also formerly inspired these writers. But sometimes some of them wakened up in soul, and, that they might be for a witness both to themselves and to all men, spoke things in harmony with the prophets regarding the monarchy of God, and the judgment and such like.

Chap. ix.—*The prophets inspired by the Holy Ghost.*

But men of God carrying in them a holy spirit[2] and becoming prophets, being inspired and made wise by God, became God-taught, and holy, and righteous. Wherefore they were also deemed worthy of receiving this reward, that they should become instruments of God, and contain the wisdom that is from Him, through which wisdom they uttered both what regarded the creation of the world and all other things. For they predicted also pestilences, and famines, and wars. And there was not one or two, but many, at various times and seasons among the Hebrews ; and also among the Greeks there was the Sibyl ; and they all have spoken things consistent and harmonious with each other, both what happened before them and what happened in their own time, and what things are now being fulfilled in our own day : wherefore we are persuaded also concerning the future things that they will fall out, as also the first have been accomplished.

Chap. x.—*The world created by God through the Word.*

And first, they taught us with one consent that God made all things out of nothing ; for nothing was coeval with God :

---

[1] Literally, " in fancy and error."

[2] Wolf prefers πνευματόφοροι, carried or borne along by the Spirit.

but He being His own place, and wanting nothing, and
existing before the ages, willed to make man by whom He
might be known ; for him, therefore, He prepared the world.
For he that is created is also needy ; but he that is uncreated
stands in need of nothing. God, then, having His own Word
internal[1] within His own bowels, begat Him, emitting[2] Him
along with His own wisdom before all things. He had this
Word as a helper in the things that were created by Him, and
by Him He made all things. He is called "governing principle" [ἀρχή], because He rules, and is Lord of all things
fashioned by Him. He, then, being Spirit of God, and
governing principle, and wisdom, and power of the highest,
came down upon the prophets, and through them spake of the
creation of the world and of all other things. For the prophets were not when the world came into existence, but the
wisdom of God which was in Him, and His holy Word which
was always present with Him. Wherefore He speaks thus
by the prophet Solomon : " When He prepared the heavens I
was there, and when He appointed the foundations of the
earth I was by Him as one brought up with Him."[3] And
Moses, who lived many years before Solomon, or, rather, the
Word of God by him as by an instrument, says, " In the beginning God created the heavens and the earth." First he
named the " beginning,"[4] and " creation,"[5] then he thus introduced God; for not lightly and on slight occasion is it
right to name God. For the divine wisdom foreknew that
some would trifle and name a multitude of gods that do not
exist. In order, therefore, that the living God might be
known by His works, and that [it might be known that] by
His Word God created the heavens and the earth, and all
that is therein, he said, " In the beginning God created the
heavens and the earth." Then having spoken of their creation,

---

[1] ἐνδιάθετον.　　　　　　[2] Literally, belching or vomiting.

[3] Prov. viii. 27. Theophilus reads with the Septuagint, " I was with
Him, putting things into order," instead of " I was by Him as one brought
up with Him."

[4] That is, the first principle, whom he has just shown to be the Word.

[5] In the Greek version of Gen. i. 1, the word " created" stands before
" God."

he explains to us: "And the earth was without form, and void, and darkness was upon the face of the deep; and the Spirit of God moved upon the water." This, sacred Scripture teaches at the outset, to show that matter, from which God made and fashioned the world, was in some manner created, being produced by God.[1]

CHAP. XI.—*The six days' work described.*

Now, the beginning of the creation is light; since light manifests the things that are created. Wherefore it is said: "And God said, Let light be, [2]and light was; and God saw the light, that it was good," manifestly made good for man. "And God divided the light from the darkness; and God called the light Day, and the darkness He called Night. And the evening and the morning were the first day. And God said, Let there be a firmament in the midst of the waters, and let it divide the waters from the waters: and it was so. And God made the firmament, and divided the waters which were under the firmament from the waters which were above the firmament. And God called the firmament Heaven: and God saw that it was good. And the evening and the morning were the second day. And God said, Let the water under the heaven be gathered into one place, and let the dry land appear: and it was so. And the waters were gathered together into their places, and the dry land appeared. And God called the dry land Earth, and the gathering together of the waters He called Seas: and God saw that it was good. And God said, Let the earth bring forth grass, the herb yielding seed after his kind and in his likeness, and the fruit-tree yielding fruit after his kind, whose seed is in itself, in his likeness: and it was so. And the earth brought forth grass, the herb yielding seed after his kind, and the

---

[1] Theophilus, therefore, understands that when in the first verse it is said that God created the earth, it is meant that He created the matter of which the earth is formed.

[2] The words, "and light was; and God saw the light, that it was good," are omitted in the two best MSS. and in some editions; but they seem to be necessary, and to have fallen out by the mistake of transcribers.

fruit-tree yielding fruit, whose seed was in itself, after his kind, on the earth : and God saw that it was good. And the evening and the morning were the third day. And God said, Let there be lights in the firmament of the heaven, to give light on earth, to divide the day from the night; and let them be for signs, and for seasons, and for days, and for years ; and let them be for lights in the firmament of the heaven, to give light upon the earth : and it was so. And God made two great lights; the greater light to rule the day, and the lesser light to rule the night : He made the stars also. And God set them in the firmament of the heaven to give light upon the earth, and to rule over the day and over the night, and to divide the light from the darkness : and God saw that it was good. And the evening and the morning were the fourth day. And God said, Let the waters bring forth the creeping things that have life, and fowl flying over the earth in the firmament of heaven : and it was so. And God created great whales, and every living creature that creepeth, which the waters brought forth after their kind, and every winged fowl after his kind : and God saw that it was good. And God blessed them, saying, Increase and multiply, and fill the waters of the sea, and let fowl multiply in the earth. And the evening and the morning were the fifth day. And God said, Let the earth bring forth the living creature after his kind, cattle, and creeping thing, and beast of the earth after his kind : and it was so. And God made the beasts of the earth after their kind, and the cattle after their kind, and all the creeping things of the earth. And God said, Let us make man in our image, after our likeness ; and let them have dominion over the fish of the sea, and over the fowl of the heaven, and over the cattle, and over all the earth, and over every creeping thing that creepeth upon the earth. And God created man : in the image of God created He him ; male and female created He them. And God blessed them, saying, Be fruitful, and multiply, and replenish the earth, and subdue it, and have dominion over the fish of the sea, and over the fowl of the heaven, and over all cattle, and over all the earth,

and over all the creeping things that creep upon the earth.
And God said, Behold I have given you every herb bearing
seed, which is upon the face of all the earth, and every tree
in the which is the fruit of a tree yielding seed; to you it
shall be for meat, and to all the beasts of the earth, and to all
the fowls of heaven, and to every creeping thing that creepeth
upon the earth, which has in it the breath of life; every green
herb for meat: and it was so. And God saw everything that
He had made, and, behold, it was very good. And the evening and the morning were the sixth day. And the heaven and
the earth were finished, and all the host of them. And on the
sixth day God finished His works which He made, and rested
on the seventh day from all His works which He made. And
God blessed the seventh day, and sanctified it; because in it
He rested from all His works which God began to create."

CHAP. XII.—*The glory of the six days' work.*

Of this six days' work no man can give a worthy explanation and description of all its parts, not though he had
ten thousand tongues and ten thousand mouths; nay, though
he were to live ten thousand years, sojourning in this life,
not even so could he utter anything worthy of these things,
on account of the exceeding greatness and riches of the
wisdom of God which there is in the six days' work above
narrated. Many writers indeed have imitated [the narration],
and essayed to give an explanation of these things; yet,
though they thence derived some suggestions, both concerning
the creation of the world and the nature of man, they have
emitted no slightest spark of truth. And the utterances of
the philosophers, and writers, and poets have an appearance
of trustworthiness, on account of the beauty of their diction;
but their discourse is proved to be foolish and idle, because
the multitude of their nonsensical frivolities is very great;
and not a stray morsel of truth is found in them. For even
if any truth seems to have been uttered by them, it has a
mixture of error. And as a deleterious drug, when mixed
with honey or wine, or some other thing, makes the whole
[mixture] hurtful and profitless; so also eloquence is in their

case found to be labour in vain; yea, rather an injurious thing to those who credit it. Moreover, [they spoke] concerning the seventh day, which all men acknowledge; but the most know not that what among the Hebrews is called the "Sabbath," is translated into Greek the "Seventh" (ἑβδομὰς), a name which is adopted by every nation, although they know not the reason of the appellation. And as for what the poet Hesiod says of Erebus being produced from chaos, as well as the earth and love which lords it over *his* [Hesiod's] gods and men, his dictum is shown to be idle and frigid, and quite foreign to the truth. For it is not meet that God be conquered by pleasure; since even men of temperance abstain from all base pleasure and wicked lust.

CHAP. XIII.—*Remarks on the creation of the world.*

Moreover, his [Hesiod's] human, and mean, and very weak conception, so far as regards God, is discovered in his beginning to relate the creation of all things from the earthly things here below. For man, being below, begins to build from the earth, and cannot in order make the roof, unless he has first laid the foundation. But the power of God is shown in this, that, first of all, He creates out of nothing, according to His will, the things that are made. "For the things which are impossible with men are possible with God."[1] Wherefore, also, the prophet mentioned that the creation of the heavens first of all took place, as a kind of roof, saying: "At the first God created the heavens"—that is, that by means of the "first" principle the heavens were made, as we have already shown. And by "earth" he means the ground and foundation, as by "the deep" he means the multitude of waters; and "darkness" he speaks of, on account of the heaven which God made covering the waters and the earth like a lid. And by the Spirit which is borne above the waters, he means that which God gave for animating the creation, as he gave life to man, mixing what is fine with what is fine. For the Spirit is fine, and the water is fine, that the Spirit may nourish the water, and the

[1] Luke xviii. 27.

water penetrating everywhere along with the Spirit, may nourish creation. For the Spirit being one, and holding the place of light,[1] was between the water and the heaven, in order that the darkness might not in any way communicate with the heaven, which was nearer God, before God said, "Let there be light." The heaven, therefore, being like a dome-shaped covering, comprehended matter which was like a clod. And so another prophet, Isaiah by name, spoke in these words : "It is God who made the heavens as a vault, and stretched them as a tent to dwell in."[2] The command, then, of God, that is, His Word, shining as a lamp in an enclosed chamber, lit up all that was under heaven, when He had made light apart from the world.[3] And the light God called Day, and the darkness Night. Since man would not have been able to call the light Day, or the darkness Night, nor, indeed, to have given names to the other things, had not he received the nomenclature from God, who made the things themselves. In the very beginning, therefore, of the history and genesis of the world, the holy Scripture spoke not concerning this firmament [which we see], but concerning another heaven, which is to us invisible, after which this heaven which we see has been called "firmament," and to which half the water was taken up that it might serve for rains, and showers, and dews to mankind. And half the water was left on earth for rivers, and fountains, and seas. The water, then, covering all the earth, and specially its hollow places, God, through His Word, next caused the waters to be collected into one collection, and the dry land to become visible, which formerly had been invisible. The earth thus becoming visible, was yet without form. God therefore formed and adorned it[4] with all kinds of herbs, and seeds and plants.

[1] This follows the Benedictine reading. Other editors, as Humphry, read τύπον, "resembling light."

[2] Isa. xl. 22.   [3] Following Wolf's rendering.

[4] Or, suitably arranged and appointed it.

CHAP. XIV.—*The world compared to the sea.*

Consider, further, their variety, and diverse beauty, and multitude, and how through them resurrection is exhibited, for a pattern of the resurrection of all men which is to be. For who that considers it will not marvel that a fig-tree is produced from a fig-seed, or that very huge trees grow from the other very little seeds? And we say that the world resembles the sea. For as the sea, if it had not had the influx and supply of the rivers and fountains to nourish it, would long since have been parched by reason of its saltness; so also the world, if it had not had the law of God and the prophets flowing and welling up sweetness, and compassion, and righteousness, and the doctrine of the holy commandments of God, would long ere now have come to ruin, by reason of the wickedness and sin which abound in it. And as in the sea there are islands, some of them habitable, and well-watered, and fruitful, with havens and harbours in which the storm-tossed may find refuge,—so God has given to the world which is driven and tempest-tossed by sins, assemblies[1]—we mean holy churches—in which survive the doctrines of the truth, as in the island-harbours of good anchorage; and into these run those who desire to be saved, being lovers of the truth, and wishing to escape the wrath and judgment of God. And as, again, there are other islands, rocky and without water, and barren, and infested by wild beasts, and uninhabitable, and serving only to injure navigators and the storm-tossed, on which ships are wrecked, and those driven among them perish,—so there are doctrines of error—I mean heresies—which destroy those who approach them. For they are not guided by the word of truth; but as pirates, when they have filled their vessels,[2] drive them on the fore-mentioned places, that they may spoil them : so also it happens in the case of those who err from the truth, that they are all totally ruined by their error.

[1] Literally, synagogues.
[2] That is, as the Benedictine edition suggests, when they have filled them with unsuspecting passengers.

Chap. xv.—*Of the fourth day.*

On the fourth day the luminaries were made; because God, who possesses foreknowledge, knew the follies of the vain philosophers, that they were going to say, that the things which grow on the earth are produced from the heavenly bodies, so as to exclude God. In order, therefore, that the truth might be obvious, the plants and seeds were produced prior to the heavenly bodies, for what is posterior cannot produce that which is prior. And these contain the pattern and type of a great mystery. For the sun is a type of God, and the moon of man. And as the sun far surpasses the moon in power and glory, so far does God surpass man. And as the sun remains ever full, never becoming less, so does God always abide perfect, being full of all power, and understanding, and wisdom, and immortality, and all good. But the moon wanes monthly, and in a manner dies, being a type of man; then it is born again, and is crescent, for a pattern of the future resurrection. In like manner also the three days which were before the luminaries,[1] are types of the Trinity,[2] of God, and His Word, and His wisdom. And the fourth is the type of man, who needs light, that so there may be God, the Word, wisdom, man. Wherefore also on the fourth day the lights were made. The disposition of the stars, too, contains a type of the arrangement and order of the righteous and pious, and of those who keep the law and commandments of God. For the brilliant and bright stars are an imitation of the prophets, and therefore they remain fixed, not declining, nor passing from place to place. And those which hold the second place in brightness, are types of the people of the righteous. And those, again, which change their position, and flee from place to place, which also are called planets,[3] they too are a type of the men who have wandered from God, abandoning His law and commandments.

Chap. xvi.—*Of the fifth day.*

On the fifth day the living creatures which proceed from

---

[1] Following Wolf's reading.   [2] Τριάδος.   [3] *i.e.* wandering stars.

the waters were produced, through which also is revealed the manifold wisdom of God in these things; for who could count their multitude and very various kinds? Moreover, the things proceeding from the waters were blessed by God, that this also might be a sign of men's being destined to receive repentance and remission of sins, through the water and laver of regeneration,—as many as come to the truth, and are born again, and receive blessing from God. But the monsters of the deep and the birds of prey are a similitude of covetous men and transgressors. For as the fish and the fowls are of one nature,—some indeed abide in their natural state, and do no harm to those weaker than themselves, but keep the law of God, and eat of the seeds of the earth; others of them, again, transgress the law of God, and eat flesh, and injure those weaker than themselves: thus, too, the righteous, keeping the law of God, bite and injure none, but live holily and righteously. But robbers, and murderers, and godless persons are like monsters of the deep, and wild beasts, and birds of prey; for they virtually devour those weaker than themselves. The race, then, of fishes and of creeping things, though partaking of God's blessing, received no very distinguishing property.

Chap. XVII.—*Of the sixth day.*

And on the sixth day, God having made the quadrupeds, and wild beasts, and the land reptiles, pronounced no blessing upon them, reserving His blessing for man, whom He was about to create on the sixth day. The quadrupeds, too, and wild beasts, were made for a type of some men, who neither know nor worship God, but mind earthly things, and repent not. For those who turn from their iniquities and live righteously, in spirit fly upwards like birds, and mind the things that are above, and are well-pleasing to the will of God. But those who do not know nor worship God, are like birds which have wings, but cannot fly nor soar to the high things of God. Thus, too, though such persons are called men, yet being pressed down with sins, they mind grovelling and earthly things. And the animals are named wild beasts [θηρία], from their being hunted [θηρεύεσθαι], not as if they had been made evil or venomous from the first—for nothing was made evil by God, but all things good, yea, very good,—but the sin in which man was concerned brought evil upon them. For when man transgressed, they also transgressed with him. For as, if the master of the house himself acts rightly, the domestics also of necessity conduct themselves well; but if the master sins, the servants also sin with him; so in like manner it came to pass, that in the case of man's sin, he being master, all that was subject to him sinned with him. When, therefore, man again shall have made his way back to his natural condition, and no longer does evil, those also shall be restored to their original gentleness.

Chap. xviii.—*The creation of man.*

But as to what relates to the creation of man, his own creation cannot be explained by man, though it is a succinct account of it which holy Scripture gives. For when God said, " Let us make man in our image, after our likeness," He first intimates the dignity of man. For God having made all things by His Word, and having reckoned them all mere bye-works, reckons the creation of man to be the only work worthy of His own hands. Moreover, God is found, as if needing help, to say, "Let us make man in our image, after our likeness." But to no one else than to His own Word and wisdom did He say, " Let us make." And when He had made and blessed him, that he might increase and replenish the earth, He put all things under his dominion, and at his service; and He appointed from the first that he should find nutriment from the fruits of the earth, and from seeds, and herbs, and acorns, having at the same time appointed that the animals be of habits similar to man's, that they also might eat of all the seeds of the earth.

Chap. xix.—*Man is placed in Paradise.*

God having thus completed the heavens, and the earth, and the sea, and all that are in them, on the sixth day, rested on the seventh day from all His works which He made.

Then holy Scripture gives a summary in these words: "This is the book of the generation of the heavens and the earth, when they were created, in the day that the Lord made the heavens and the earth, and every green thing of the field, before it was made, and every herb of the field before it grew. For God had not caused it to rain' upon the earth, and there was not a man to till the ground."[1] By this He signifies to us, that the whole earth was at that time watered by a divine fountain, and had no need that man should till it; but the earth produced all things spontaneously by the command of God, that man might not be wearied by tilling it. But that the creation of man might be made plain, so that there should not seem to be an insoluble problem existing among men, since God had said, "Let us make man;" and since His creation was not yet plainly related, Scripture teaches us, saying: "And a fountain went up out of the earth, and watered the face of the whole earth; and God made man of the dust of the earth, and breathed into his face the breath of life, and man became a living soul."[2] Whence also by most persons the soul is called immortal. And after the formation of man, God chose out for him a region among the places of the East, excellent for light, brilliant with a very bright atmosphere, [abundant] in the finest plants; and in this He placed man.

CHAP. XX.—*The scriptural account of Paradise.*

Scripture thus relates the words of the sacred history: "And God planted Paradise, eastward, in Eden; and there He put the man whom He had formed. And out of the ground made God to grow every tree that is pleasant to the sight, and good for food; the tree of life also in the midst of Paradise, and the tree of the knowledge of good and evil. And a river flows out of Eden, to water the garden; thence it is parted into four heads. The name of the first is Pison: that is it which compasseth the whole land of Havilah, where there is gold; and the gold of that land is good, and there is bdellium and the onyx stone. And the name of the second

[1] Gen. ii. 4, 5.   [2] Gen. ii. 6.

river is Gihon : the same is it that compasseth the whole
land of Ethiopia. And the third river is Tigris : this is it
which goeth toward Syria. And the fourth river is Euphrates. And the Lord God took the man whom He had
made, and put him in the garden, to till and to keep it. And
God commanded Adam, saying, Of every tree that is in the
garden thou mayest freely eat; but of the tree of the knowledge of good and evil, ye shall not eat of it; for in the day
ye eat of it ye shall surely die. And the Lord God said, It
is not good that the man should be alone; let us make him
an helpmeet for him. And out of the ground God formed
all the beasts of the field, and all the fowls of heaven, and
brought them to Adam. And whatsoever Adam called every
living creature, that was the name thereof. And Adam gave
names to all cattle, and to the fowls of the air, and to all the
beasts of the field. But for Adam there was not found an
helpmeet for him. And God caused an ecstasy to fall upon
Adam, and he slept ; and He took one of his ribs, and closed
up the flesh instead thereof. And the rib, which the Lord
God had taken from man, made He a woman, and brought
her unto Adam. And Adam said, This is now bone of my
bones, and flesh of my flesh; she shall be called Woman,
because she was taken out of man. Therefore shall a man
leave his father and his mother, and shall cleave unto his
wife, and they two shall be one flesh. And they were both
naked, Adam and his wife, and were not ashamed.

CHAP. XXI.—*Of the fall of man.*

" Now the serpent was more subtile than any beast of the
field which the Lord God had made. And the serpent said
to the woman, Why hath God said, Ye shall not eat of every
tree of the garden ? And the woman said unto the serpent,
We eat of every tree of the garden, but of the fruit of the
tree which is in the midst of the garden God hath said,
Ye shall not eat of it, neither shall ye touch it, lest ye die.
And the serpent said unto the woman, Ye shall not surely
die. For God doth know that in the day ye eat thereof,
then your eyes shall be opened, and ye shall be as gods,

knowing good and evil. And the woman saw that the tree was good for food, and that it was pleasant to the eyes, and a tree to be desired to make one wise; and having taken of the fruit thereof, she did eat, and gave also unto her husband with her: and they did eat. And the eyes of them both were opened, and they knew that they were naked; and they sewed fig leaves together, and made themselves aprons. And they heard the voice of the Lord God walking in the garden in the cool of the day, and Adam and his wife hid themselves from the presence of the Lord God amongst the trees of the garden. And the Lord God called unto Adam, and said unto him, Where art thou? And he said unto Him, I heard Thy voice in the garden, and I was afraid, because I was naked, and I hid myself. And He said unto him, Who told thee that thou wast naked, unless thou hast eaten of the tree whereof I commanded thee that thou shouldest not eat? And Adam said, The woman whom Thou gavest to be with me, she gave me of the tree, and I did eat. And God said to the woman, What is this that thou hast done? And the woman said, The serpent beguiled me, and I did eat. And the Lord God said unto the serpent, Because thou hast done this, thou art accursed above all the beasts of the earth; on thy breast and belly shalt thou go, and dust shalt thou eat all the days of thy life: and I will put enmity between thee and the woman, and between thy seed and her seed; it shall bruise thy head, and thou shalt bruise his heel.[1] And to the woman He said, I will greatly multiply thy sorrow and thy travail: in sorrow shalt thou bring forth children; and thy desire shall be to thy husband, and he shall rule over thee. And unto Adam He said, Because thou hast hearkened unto the voice of thy wife, and hast eaten of the tree of which I commanded thee, saying, Thou shalt not eat of it; cursed is the ground in[2] thy works: in sorrow shalt thou eat of it all the days of thy life; thorns and thistles shall it bring forth to thee; and thou shalt eat the herb of the field. In the

---

[1] Theophilus reads, "it shall watch thy head, and thou shalt watch his heel."

[2] Or, "by thy works."

sweat of thy face shalt thou eat thy bread, till thou return
unto the ground ; for out of it wast thou taken : for dust thou
art, and unto dust shalt thou return."[1]   Such is the account
given by holy Scripture of the history of man and of Paradise.

Chap. XXII.—*Why God is said to have walked.*

You will say, then, to me : " You said that God ought not
to be contained in a place, and how do you now say that He
walked in Paradise ? "   Hear what I say. The God and
Father, indeed, of all cannot be contained, and is not found
in a place, for there is no place of His rest ; but His Word,
through whom He made all things, being His power and His
wisdom, assuming the person[2] of the Father and Lord of all,
went to the garden in the person of God, and conversed with
Adam. For the divine writing itself teaches us that Adam
said that he had heard the voice. But what else is this voice
but the Word of God, who is also His Son? Not as the poets
and writers of myths talk of the sons of gods begotten from
intercourse [with women], but as truth expounds, the Word,
that always exists, residing within the heart of God. For
before anything came into being He had Him as a counsellor, being His own mind and thought. But when God
wished to make all that He determined on, He begot this
Word, uttered,[3] the first-born of all creation, not Himself
being emptied of the Word [Reason], but having begotten
Reason, and always conversing with His Reason.   And
hence the holy writings teach us, and all the spirit-bearing
[inspired] men, one of whom, John, says, " In the beginning
was the Word, and the Word was with God,"[4] showing that
at first God was alone, and the Word in Him. Then he

[1] Gen. ii. 8–iii. 19.

[2] The annotators here warn us against supposing that "person" is used
as it was afterwards employed in discussing the doctrine of the Trinity,
and show that the word is used in its original meaning, and with reference to an actor taking up a mask and personating a character.

[3] Προφορικός, the term used of the Logos as manifested ; the Word as
uttered by the Father, in distinction from the Word immanent in Him.

[4] John i. 1.

says, "The Word was God; all things came into existence through Him; and apart from Him not one thing came into existence." The Word, then, being God, and being naturally[1] produced from God, whenever the Father of the universe wills, He sends Him to any place; and He, coming, is both heard and seen, being sent by Him, and is found in a place.

CHAP. XXIII.—*The truth of the account in Genesis.*

Man, therefore, God made on the sixth day, and made known this creation after the seventh day, when also He made Paradise, that he might be in a better and distinctly superior place. And that this is true, the fact itself proves. For how can one miss seeing that the pains which women suffer in childbed, and the oblivion of their labours which they afterwards enjoy, are sent in order that the word of God may be fulfilled, and that the race of men may increase and multiply?[2] And do we not see also the judgment of the serpent,—how hatefully he crawls on his belly and eats the dust,—that we may have this, too, for a proof of the things which were said aforetime?

CHAP. XXIV.—*The beauty of Paradise.*

God, then, caused to spring out of the earth every tree that is beautiful in appearance, or good for food. For at first there were only those things which were produced on the third day,—plants, and seeds, and herbs; but the things which were in Paradise were made of a superior loveliness and beauty, since in it the plants were said to have been planted by God. As to the rest of the plants, indeed, the world contained plants like them; but the two trees,—the tree of life and the tree of knowledge,—the rest of the earth possessed not, but only Paradise. And that Paradise is earth, and is planted on the earth, the Scripture states, saying:[3] "And the

---

[1] That is, being produced by generation, not by creation.

[2] The Benedictine editor remarks: "Women bring forth with labour and pain as the punishment awarded to sin: they forget the pain, that the propagation of the race may not be hindered."

[3] Gen. ii. 8.

Lord God planted Paradise in Eden eastwards, and placed man there ; and out of the ground made the Lord God to grow every tree that is pleasant to the sight and good for food." By the expressions, therefore, " out of the ground," and " eastwards," the holy writing clearly teaches us that Paradise is under this heaven, under which the east and the earth are. And the Hebrew word Eden signifies " delight." And it was signified that a river flowed out of Eden to water Paradise, and after that divides into four heads; of which the two called Pison and Gihon water the eastern parts, especially Gihon, which encompasses the whole land of Ethiopia, and which, they say, reappears in Egypt under the name of Nile. And the other two rivers are manifestly recognisable by us— those called Tigris and Euphrates—for these border on our own regions. And God having placed man in Paradise, as has been said, to till and keep it, commanded him to eat of all the trees,—manifestly of the tree of life also ; but only of the tree of knowledge He commanded him not to taste. And God transferred him from the earth, out of which he had been produced, into Paradise, giving him means of advancement, in order that, maturing and becoming perfect, and being even declared a god, he might thus ascend into heaven in possession of immortality. For man had been made a middle nature, neither wholly mortal, nor altogether immortal, but capable of either; so also the place, Paradise, was made in respect of beauty intermediate between earth and heaven. And by the expression, " till it,"[1] no other kind of labour is implied than the observance of God's command, lest, disobeying, he should destroy himself, as indeed he did destroy himself, by sin.

CHAP. XXV.—*God was justified in forbidding man to eat of the tree of knowledge.*

The tree of knowledge itself was good, and its fruit was good. For it was not the tree, as some think, but the disobedience, which had death in it. For there was nothing else in the fruit than only knowledge ; but knowledge is good

[1] In the Greek the word is, " work" or " labour," as we also speak of working land.

when one uses it discreetly. But Adam, being yet an infant in age, was on this account as yet unable to receive knowledge worthily. For now, also, when a child is born it is not at once able to eat bread, but is nourished first with milk, and then, with the increment of years, it advances to solid food. Thus, too, would it have been with Adam; for not as one who grudged him, as some suppose, did God command him not to eat of knowledge. But He wished also to make proof of him, whether he was submissive to His commandment. And at the same time He wished man, infant as he was, to remain for some time longer simple and sincere. For this is holy, not only with God, but also with men, that in simplicity and guilelessness subjection be yielded to parents. But if it is right that children be subject to parents, how much more to the God and Father of all things? Besides, it is unseemly that children in infancy be wise beyond their years; for as in stature one increases in an orderly progress, so also in wisdom. But as when a law has commanded abstinence from anything, and some one has not obeyed, it is obviously not the law which causes punishment, but the disobedience and transgression;— for a father sometimes enjoins on his own child abstinence from certain things, and when he does not obey the paternal order, he is flogged and punished on account of the disobedience; and in this case the actions themselves are not the [cause of] stripes, but the disobedience procures punishment for him who disobeys;—so also for the first man, disobedience procured his expulsion from Paradise. Not, therefore, as if there were any evil in the tree of knowledge; but from his disobedience did man draw, as from a fountain, labour, pain, grief, and at last fall a prey to death.

CHAP. XXVI.—*God's goodness in expelling man from Paradise.*

And God showed great kindness to man in this, that He did not suffer him to remain in sin for ever; but, as it were, by a kind of banishment, cast him out of Paradise, in order that, having by punishment expiated, within an appointed time, the sin, and having been disciplined, he should afterwards be restored. Wherefore also, when man had been formed in this world, it is mystically written in Genesis, as if he had been twice placed in Paradise; so that the one was fulfilled when he was placed there, and the second will be fulfilled after the resurrection and judgment. For just as a vessel, when on being fashioned it has some flaw, is remoulded or remade, that it may become new and entire; so also it happens to man by death. For somehow or other he is broken up, that he may rise in the resurrection whole; I mean spotless, and righteous, and immortal. And as to God's calling, and saying, Where art thou, Adam? God did this, not as if ignorant of this; but, being long-suffering, He gave him an opportunity of repentance and confession.

Chap. XXVII.—*The nature of man.*

But some one will say to us, Was man made by nature mortal? Certainly not. Was he, then, immortal? Neither do we affirm this. But one will say, Was he, then, nothing? Not even this hits the mark. He was by nature neither mortal nor immortal. For if He had made him immortal from the beginning, He would have made him God. Again, if He had made him mortal, God would seem to be the cause of his death. Neither, then, immortal nor yet mortal did He make him, but, as we have said above, capable of both; so that if he should incline to the things of immortality, keeping the commandment of God, he should receive as reward from Him immortality, and should become God; but if, on the other hand, he should turn to the things of death, disobeying God, he should himself be the cause of death to himself. For God made man free, and with power over himself. That, then, which man brought upon himself through carelessness and disobedience, this God now vouchsafes to him as a gift through His own philanthropy and pity, when men obey Him.[1] For as man, disobeying, drew death upon himself; so, obeying the will of God, he who desires is able to procure for himself life everlasting. For God has given us a law and holy

---

[1] Apparently meaning, that God turns death, which man brought on himself by disobedience, into a blessing.

commandments; and every one who keeps these can be saved, and, obtaining the resurrection, can inherit incorruption.

CHAP. XXVIII.—*Why Eve was formed of Adam's rib.*

And Adam having been cast out of Paradise, in this condition knew Eve his wife, whom God had formed into a wife for him out of his rib. And this He did, not as if He were unable to make his wife separately, but God foreknew that men would call upon a number of gods. And having this prescience, and knowing that through the serpent error would introduce a number of gods which had no existence,—for there being but one God, even then error was striving to disseminate a multitude of gods, saying, "Ye shall be as gods;"—lest, then, it should be supposed that one God made the man and another the woman, therefore He made them both; and God made the woman together with the man, not only that thus the mystery of God's sole government might be exhibited, but also that their mutual affection might be greater. Therefore said Adam to Eve, "This is now bone of my bones, and flesh of my flesh." And besides, he prophesied, saying, "For this cause shall a man leave his father and his mother, and shall cleave unto his wife; and they two shall be one flesh;"[1] which also itself has its fulfilment in ourselves. For who that marries lawfully does not despise mother and father, and his whole family connection, and all his household, cleaving to and becoming one with his own wife, fondly preferring her? So that often, for the sake of their wives, some submit even to death. This Eve, on account of her having been in the beginning deceived by the serpent, and become the author of sin, the wicked demon, who also is called Satan, who then spoke to her through the serpent, and who works even to this day in those men that are possessed by him, invokes as Eve.[2] And he is called "demon" and "dragon," on account of his [ἀποδεδρακέναι] revolting from God. For at first he was an

---

[1] Gen. ii. 24.

[2] Referring to the bacchanalian orgies in which "Eva" was shouted, and which the fathers professed to believe was an unintentional invocation of Eve, the authoress of all sin.

angel. And concerning his history there is a great deal to be said; wherefore I at present omit the relation of it, for I have also given an account of him in another place.

CHAP. XXIX.—*Cain's crime.*

When, then, Adam knew Eve his wife, she conceived and bare a son, whose name was Cain; and she said, "I have gotten a man from God." And yet again she bore a second son, whose name was Abel, "who began to be a keeper of sheep, but Cain tilled the ground."[1] Their history receives a very full narration, yea, even a detailed explanation : wherefore the book itself, which is entitled "The Genesis of the World," can more accurately inform those who are anxious to learn their story. When, then, Satan saw Adam and his wife not only still living, but also begetting children—being carried away with spite because he had not succeeded in putting them to death,—when he saw that Abel was well-pleasing to God, he wrought upon the heart of his brother called Cain, and caused him to kill his brother Abel. And thus did death get a beginning in this world, to find its way into every race of man, even to this day. But God, being pitiful, and wishing to afford to Cain, as to Adam, an opportunity of repentance and confession, said, "Where is Abel thy brother?" But Cain answered God contumaciously, saying, "I know not; am I my brother's keeper?" God, being thus made angry with him, said, "What hast thou done? The voice of thy brother's blood crieth to me from the earth, which opened her mouth to receive thy brother's blood from thy hand. Groaning and trembling shalt thou be on the earth." From that time the earth, through fear, no longer receives human blood,[2] no, nor the blood of any animal; by which it appears that it is not the cause [of death], but man, who transgressed.

[1] Gen. iv. 1, 2.

[2] Fell remarks, "Blood shed at once coagulates, and does not easily enter the earth."

CHAP. XXX.—*Cain's family and their inventions.*

Cain also himself had a son, whose name was Enoch; and he built a city, which he called by the name of his son, Enoch. From that time was there made a beginning of the building of cities, and this before the flood; not as Homer falsely says : [1]

"Not yet had men a city built."

And to Enoch was born a son, by name Gaidad; who begat a son called Meel; and Meel begat Mathusala; and Mathusala, Lamech. And Lamech took unto him two wives, whose names were Adah and Zillah. At that time there was made a beginning of polygamy, and also of music. For Lamech had three sons : Jabal, Jubal, Tubal. And Jabal became a keeper of cattle, and dwelt in tents ; but Jubal is he who made known the psaltery and the harp; and Tubal became a smith, a forger in brass and iron. So far the seed of Cain is registered; and for the rest, the seed of his line has sunk into oblivion, on account of his fratricide of his brother. And, in place of Abel, God granted to Eve to conceive and bear a son, who was called Seth; from whom the remainder of the human race proceeds until now. And to those who desire to be informed regarding all generations, it is easy to give explanations by means of the holy Scriptures. For, as we have already mentioned, this subject, the order of the genealogy of man, has been partly handled by us in another discourse, in the first book of *The History.* And all these things the Holy Spirit teaches us, who speaks through Moses and the rest of the prophets, so that the writings which belong to us godly people are more ancient, yea, and are shown to be more truthful, than all writers and poets. But also, concerning music, some have fabled that Apollo was the inventor, and others say that Orpheus discovered the art of music from the sweet voices of the birds. Their story is shown to be empty and vain, for these inventors lived many years after the flood. And what relates to Noah, who is called by some Deucalion, has been explained by us in the book before mentioned, and which, if you wish it, you are at liberty to read.

[1] *Il.* xx. 216. But Homer refers only to Troy.

CHAP. XXXI.—*The history after the flood.*

After the flood was there again a beginning of cities and kings, in the following manner:—The first city was Babylon, and Erech, and Accad, and Calneh, in the land of Shinar. And their king was called Nebroth [Nimrod]. From these came Asshur, from whom also the Assyrians receive their name. And Nimrod built the cities Nineveh and Rehoboth, and Calah, and Resen, between Nineveh and Calah; and Nineveh became a very great city. And another son of Shem, the son of Noah, by name Mizraim, begat Ludim, and those called Anamim, and Lehabim, and Naphtuhim, and Pathrusim, and Casluhim, out of whom came Philistim. Of the three sons of Noah, however, and of their death and genealogy, we have given a compendious register in the above-mentioned book. But now we will mention the remaining facts both concerning cities and kings, and the things that happened when there was one speech and one language. Before the dividing of the languages these fore-mentioned cities existed. But when men were about to be dispersed, they took counsel of their own judgment, and not at the instigation of God, to build a city, a tower whose top might reach into heaven, that they might make a glorious name to themselves. Since, therefore, they had dared, contrary to the will of God, to attempt a grand work, God destroyed their city, and overthrew their tower. From that time He confounded the languages of men, giving to each a different dialect. And similarly did the Sibyl speak, when she declared that wrath would come on the world. She says:

"When are fulfilled the threats of the great God,
　With which He threatened men, when formerly
　In the Assyrian land they built a tower,
　And all were of one speech, and wished to rise
　Even till they climbed unto the starry heaven,
　Then the Immortal raised a mighty wind
　And laid upon them strong necessity;
　For when the wind threw down the mighty tower,
　Then rose among mankind fierce strife and hate.
　One speech was changed to many dialects,
　And earth was filled with divers tribes and kings."

And so on. These things, then, happened in the land of the Chaldæans. And in the land of Canaan there was a city, by name Haran. And in these days, Pharaoh, who by the Egyptians was also called Nechaoth, was first king of Egypt, and thus the kings followed in succession.[1] And in the land of Shinar, among those called Chaldæans, the first king was Arioch, and next after him Ellasar, and after him Chedorlaomer, king of Elam, and after him Tidal, king of the nations called Assyrians. And there were five other cities in the territory of Ham, the son of Noah; the first called Sodom, then Gomorrah, Admah, Zeboiim, and Balah, which was also called Zoar. And the names of their kings are these: Bera, king of Sodom; Birsha, king of Gomorrah; Shinab, king of Admah; Shemeber, king of Zeboiim; Bela, king of Zoar, which is also called Kephalac.[2] These served Chedorlaomer, the king of the Assyrians, for twelve years, and in the thirteenth year they revolted from Chedorlaomer; and thus it came to pass at that time that the four Assyrian kings waged war upon the five kings. This was the first commencement of making war on the earth; and they destroyed the giants Karnaim, and the strong nations that were with them in their city, and the Horites of the mountains called Seir, as far as the plain of Paran, which is by the wilderness. And at that time there was a righteous king called Melchisedek, in the city of Salem, which now is Jerusalem. This was the first priest of all priests of the Most High God; and from him the above-named city Hierosolyma was called Jerusalem. And from his time priests were found in all the earth. And after him reigned Abimelech in Gerar; and after him another Abimelech. Then reigned Ephron, surnamed the Hittite. Such are the names of the kings that were in former times. And the rest of the kings of the Assyrians, during an interval of

[1] But the Benedictine editor understands the words to mean, that the succeeding kings were in like manner called Pharaoh.

[2] Theophilus spells some of the names differently from what they are given in our text. For Tidal he has Thargal; for Bera, Ballas; for Birsha, Barsas; for Shinab, Senaar; for Shemeber, Hymoor. Kephalac is taken to be a corruption for Balak, which in the previous sentence is inserted by many editors, though it is not in the best MSS.

many years, have been passed over in silence unrecorded, all writers narrating the events of our own recent days. There were these kings of Assyria : Tiglath-Pileser, and after him Shalmaneser, then Sennacherib; and Adrammelech the Ethiopian, who also reigned over Egypt, was his triarch ;— though these things, in comparison with our books, are quite recent.

CHAP. XXXII.—*How the human race was dispersed.*

Hence, therefore, may the lovers of learning and of antiquity understand the history, and see that those things are recent which are told by us apart from the holy prophets.[1] For though at first there were few men in the land of Arabia and Chaldæa, yet, after their languages were divided, they gradually began to multiply and spread over all the earth ; and some of them tended towards the east to dwell there, and others to the parts of the great continent, and others northwards, so as to extend as far as Britain, in the Arctic regions. And others went to the land of Canaan, which is called Judæa, and Phœnicia, and the region of Ethiopia, and Egypt, and Lybia, and the country called torrid, and the parts stretching towards the west ; and the rest went to places by the sea, and Pamphylia, and Asia, and Greece, and Macedonia, and, besides, to Italy, and the whole country called Gaul, and Spain, and Germany ; so that now the whole world is thus filled with inhabitants. Since then the occupation of the world by men was at first in three divisions,—in the east, and south, and west : afterwards, the remaining parts of the earth were inhabited, when men became very numerous. And the writers, not knowing these things, are forward to maintain that the world is shaped like a sphere, and to compare it to a cube. But how can they say what is true regarding these things, when they do not know about the creation of the world and its population ? Men gradually increasing in number and

---

[1] Proving the antiquity of Scripture, by showing that no recent occurrences are mentioned in it. Wolf, however, gives another reading, which would be rendered, " understand whether those things are recent which we utter on the authority of the holy prophets."

multiplying on the earth, as we have already said, the islands also of the sea and the rest of the countries were inhabited.

Chap. xxxiii.—*Profane history gives no account of these matters.*

Who, then, of those called sages, and poets, and historians, could tell us truly of these things, themselves being much later born, and introducing a multitude of gods, who were born so many years after the cities, and are more modern than kings, and nations, and wars? For they should have made mention of all events, even those which happened before the flood; both of the creation of the world and the formation of man, and the whole succession of events. The Egyptian or Chaldæan prophets, and the other writers, should have been able accurately to tell, if at least they spoke by a divine and pure spirit, and spoke truth in all that was uttered by them; and they should have announced not only things past or present, but also those that were to come upon the world. And therefore it is proved that all others have been in error; and that we Christians alone have possessed the truth, inasmuch as we are taught by the Holy Spirit, who spoke in the holy prophets, and foretold all things.

Chap. xxxiv.—*The prophets enjoined holiness of life.*

And, for the rest, would that in a kindly spirit you would investigate divine things—I mean the things that are spoken by the prophets—in order that, by comparing what is said by us with the utterances of the others, you may be able to discover the truth. We[1] have shown from their own histories, which they have compiled, that the names of those who are called gods, are found to be the names of men who lived among them, as we have shown above. And to this day their images are daily fashioned, idols, " the works of men's hands." And these the mass of foolish men serve, whilst they reject the maker and fashioner of all things and the nourisher of all breath of life, giving credit to vain doctrines through the deceitfulness of the senseless tradition received

[1] Benedictine editor proposes " they."

from their fathers. But God at least, the Father and Creator of the universe, did not abandon mankind, but gave a law, and sent holy prophets to declare and teach the race of men, that each one of us might awake and understand that there is one God. And they also taught us to refrain from unlawful idolatry, and adultery, and murder, fornication, theft, avarice, false swearing, wrath, and every incontinence and uncleanness; and that whatever a man would not wish to be done to himself, he should not do to another; and thus he who acts righteously shall escape the eternal punishments, and be thought worthy of the eternal life from God.

CHAP. XXXV.—*Precepts from the prophetic books.*

The divine law, then, not only forbids the worshipping of idols, but also of the heavenly bodies, the sun, the moon, or the other stars; yea, not heaven, nor earth, nor the sea, nor fountains, nor rivers, must be worshipped, but we must serve in holiness of heart and sincerity of purpose only the living and true God, who also is Maker of the universe. Wherefore saith the holy law: "Thou shalt not commit adultery; thou shalt not steal; thou shalt not bear false witness; thou shalt not desire thy neighbour's wife." So also the prophets. Solomon indeed teaches us that we must not sin with so much as a turn of the eye,[1] saying, "Let thine eyes look right on, and let thy eyelids look straight before thee."[2] And Moses, who himself also was a prophet, says, concerning the sole government of God: "Your God is He who establishes the heaven, and forms the earth, whose hands have brought forth all the host of heaven; and He has not set these things before you that you should go after them."[3] And Isaiah himself also says: "Thus saith the Lord God who established the heavens, and founded the earth and all that is therein, and giveth breath unto the people upon it, and spirit to them that walk therein. This is the Lord your God."[4] And again, through him He says: "I have made the earth, and man upon it. I by my hand have established the

---

[1] Literally, "a nod." [2] Prov. iv. 25.
[3] Cf. Deut. iv. 19. [4] Isa. xlii. 5.

heavens."[1] And in another chapter, "This is your God, who created the ends of the earth; He hungereth not, neither is weary, and there is no searching of His understanding."[2] So, too, Jeremiah says : "Who hath made the earth by His power, and established the world by His wisdom, and by His discretion hath stretched out the heavens, and a mass of water in the heavens, and He caused the clouds to ascend from the ends of the earth; He made lightnings with rain, and brought forth winds out of His treasures."[3] One can see how consistently and harmoniously all the prophets spoke, having given utterance through one and the same spirit concerning the unity of God, and the creation of the world, and the formation of man. Moreover, they were in sore travail, bewailing the godless race of men, and they reproached those, who seemed to be wise, for their error and hardness of heart. Jeremiah, indeed, said: "Every man is brutishly gone astray from the knowledge of Him; every founder is confounded by his graven images; in vain the silversmith makes his molten images; there is no breath in them: in the day of their visitation they shall perish."[4] The same, too, says David : "They are corrupt, they have done abominable works; there is none that doeth good, no, not one; they have all gone aside, they have together become profitless."[5] So also Habakkuk : "What profiteth the graven image that he has graven it a lying image? Woe to him that saith to the stone, Awake; and to the wood, Arise."[6] Likewise spoke the other prophets of the truth. And why should I recount the multitude of prophets, who are numerous, and said ten thousand things consistently and harmoniously? For those who desire it, can, by reading what they uttered, accurately understand the truth, and no longer be carried away by opinion and profitless labour. These, then, whom we have already mentioned, were prophets among the Hebrews,—illiterate, and shepherds, and uneducated.

[1] Isa. xlv. 12.   [2] Isa. xl. 28.   [3] Jer. x. 12, 13.
[4] Jer. li. 17, 18.   [5] Ps. xiv. 1, 3.   [6] Hab. ii. 18.

CHAP. XXXVI.—*Prophecies of the Sibyl.*

And the Sibyl, who was a prophetess among the Greeks and the other nations, in the beginning of her prophecy, reproaches the race of men, saying :—

" How are ye still so quickly lifted up,
And how so thoughtless of the end of life,
Ye mortal men of flesh, who are but nought?
Do ye not tremble, nor fear God most high?
Your overseer, the knower, seer of all,
Who ever keeps those whom His hand first made,
Puts His sweet Spirit into all His works,
And gives Him for a guide to mortal men.
There is one only uncreated God,
Who reigns alone, all-powerful, very great,
From whom is nothing hid.   He sees all things,
Himself unseen by any mortal eye.
Can mortal man see the immortal God,
Or fleshly eyes, which shun the noontide beams,
Look upon Him who dwells beyond the heavens?
Worship Him, then, the self-existent God,
The unbegotten Ruler of the world,
Who only was from everlasting time,
And shall to everlasting still abide.
Of evil counsels ye shall reap the fruit,
Because ye have not honoured the true God,
Nor offered to Him sacred hecatombs.
To those who dwell in Hades ye make gifts,
And unto demons offer sacrifice.
In madness and in pride ye have your walk;
And leaving the right way, ye wander wide,
And lose yourselves in pitfalls and in thorns.
Why do ye wander thus, O foolish men?
Cease your vain wanderings in the black, dark night;
Why follow darkness and perpetual gloom
When, see, there shines for you the blessed light?
Lo, He is clear—in Him there is no spot.
Turn, then, from darkness, and behold the day;
Be wise, and treasure wisdom in your breasts.
There is one God who sends the winds and rains,
The earthquakes, and the lightnings, and the plagues,
The famines, and the snow-storms, and the ice,
And all the woes that visit our sad race.
Nor these alone, but all things else He gives,

Ruling omnipotent in heaven and earth,
And self-existent from eternity."

And regarding those [gods] that are said to have been born,
she said :—

"If all things that are born must also die,
God cannot be produced by mortal man.
But there is only One, the All-Supreme,
Who made the heavens, with all their starry host,
The sun and moon ; likewise the fruitful earth,
With all the waves of ocean, and the hills,
The fountains, and the ever flowing streams ;
He also made the countless multitude
Of ocean creatures, and He keeps alive
All creeping things, both of the earth and sea ;
And all the tuneful choir of birds He made,
Which cleave the air with wings, and with shrill pipe
Trill forth at morn their tender, clear-voiced song.
Within the deep glades of the hills He placed
A savage race of beasts ; and unto men
He made all cattle subject, making man
The God-formed image, ruler over all,
And putting in subjection to his sway
Things many and incomprehensible.
For who of mortals can know all these things ?
He only knows who made them at the first,
He the Creator, incorruptible,
Who dwells in upper air eternally ;
Who proffers to the good most rich rewards,
And against evil and unrighteous men
Rouses revenge, and wrath, and bloody wars,
And pestilence, and many a tearful grief.
O man exalted vainly—say why thus
Hast thou so utterly destroyed thyself ?
Have ye no shame worshipping beasts for gods ?
And to believe the gods should steal your beasts,
Or that they need your vessels—is it not
Frenzy's most profitless and foolish thought ?
Instead of dwelling in the golden heavens,
Ye see your gods become the prey of worms,
And hosts of creatures noisome and unclean.
O fools ! ye worship serpents, dogs, and cats,
Birds, and the creeping things of earth and sea,
Images made with hands, statues of stone,
And heaps of rubbish by the wayside placed.

All these, and many more vain things, ye serve,
Worshipping things disgraceful even to name :
These are the gods who lead vain men astray,
From whose mouth streams of deadly poison flow.
But unto Him in whom alone is life,
Life, and undying, everlasting light ;
Who pours into man's cup of life a joy
Sweeter than sweetest honey to his taste,—
Unto Him bow the head, to Him alone,
And walk in ways of everlasting peace.
Forsaking Him, ye all have turned aside,
And, in your raving folly, drained the cup
Of justice quite unmixed, pure, mastering, strong ;
And ye will not again be sober men,
Ye will not come unto a sober mind,
And know your God and King, who looks on all :
Therefore, upon you burning fire shall come,
And ever ye shall daily burn in flames,
Ashamed for ever of your useless gods.
But those who worship the eternal God,
They shall inherit everlasting life,
Inhabiting the blooming realms of bliss,
And feasting on sweet food from starry heaven."

That these things are true, and useful, and just, and profitable to all men, is obvious. Even the poets have spoken of the punishments of the wicked.

CHAP. XXXVII.—*The testimonies of the poets.*

And that evil-doers must necessarily be punished in proportion to their deeds, has already been, as it were, oracularly uttered by some of the poets, as a witness both against themselves and against the wicked, declaring that they shall be punished. Æschylus said :

"He who has done must also suffer."

And Pindar himself said :

"It is fit that suffering follow doing."

So, too, Euripides :

"The deed rejoiced you—suffering endure ;
The taken enemy must needs be pain'd."

And again:

> "The foe's pain is the hero's meed."

And, similarly, Archilochus:

> "One thing I know, I hold it ever true,
> The evil-doer evil shall endure."

And that God sees all, and that nothing escapes His notice, but that, being long-suffering, He refrains until the time when He is to judge—concerning this, too, Dionysius said:

> "The eye of Justice seeing all,
> Yet seemeth not to see."

And that God's judgment is to be, and that evils will suddenly overtake the wicked,—this, too, Æschylus declared, saying:

> "Swift-footed is the approach of fate,
> And none can justice violate,
> But feels its stern hand soon or late.
>
> 'Tis with you, though unheard, unseen;
> You draw night's curtain in between,
> But even sleep affords no screen.
>
> 'Tis with you if you sleep or wake;
> And if abroad your way you take,
> Its still, stern watch you cannot break.
>
> 'Twill follow you, or cross your path;
> And even night no virtue hath
> To hide you from th' Avenger's wrath.
>
> To show the ill the darkness flees;
> Then, if sin offers joy or ease,
> Oh stop, and think that some one sees!"

And may we not cite Simonides also?

> "To men no evil comes unheralded;
> But God with sudden hand transforms all things."

Euripides again:

> "The wicked and proud man's prosperity
> Is based on sand: his race abideth not;
> And time proclaims the wickedness of men."

Once more Euripides:

> "Not without judgment is the Deity,
> But sees when oaths are struck unrighteously,
> And when from men unwilling they are wrung."

And Sophocles:

"If ills you do, ills also you must bear."

That God will make inquiry both concerning false swearing
and concerning every other wickedness, they themselves have
well-nigh predicted. And concerning the conflagration of
the world, they have, willingly or unwillingly, spoken in
conformity with the prophets, though they were much more
recent, and stole these things from the law and the prophets.
The poets corroborate the testimony of the prophets.

CHAP. XXXVIII.—*The teachings of the Greek poets and philosophers confirmatory of those of the Hebrew prophets.*

But what matters it whether they were before or after
them? Certainly they did at all events utter things confirmatory of the prophets. Concerning the burning up of
the world, Malachi the prophet foretold: "The day of the
Lord cometh as a burning oven, and shall consume all the
wicked."[1]   And Isaiah: "For the wrath of God is as a
violent hail-storm, and as a rushing mountain torrent."[2] The
Sibyl, then, and the other prophets, yea, and the poets and
philosophers, have clearly taught both concerning righteousness, and judgment, and punishment; and also concerning
providence, that God cares for us, not only for the living
among us, but also for those that are dead: though, indeed,
they said this unwillingly, for they were convinced by the
truth.   And among the prophets indeed, Solomon said of the
dead, "There shall be healing to thy flesh, and care taken
of thy bones."[3]   And the same says David, "The bones
which Thou hast broken shall rejoice."[4]   And in agreement
with these sayings was that of Timocles:

"The dead are pitied by the loving God."

And the writers who spoke of a multiplicity of gods came
at length to the doctrine of the unity of God, and those who
asserted chance spoke also of providence; and the advocates
of impunity confessed there would be a judgment, and those

[1] Mal. iv. 1.   [2] Isa. xxx. 30.
[3] Prov. iii. 8.   [4] Ps. li. 8.

who denied that there is sensation after death acknowledged
that there is. Homer, accordingly, though he had said,

" Like fleeting vision passed the soul away,"[1]

says in another place :

" To Hades went the disembodied soul ;"[2]

And again :

"That I may quickly pass through Hades' gates,
    Me bury." [3]

And as regards the others whom you have read, I think
you know with sufficient accuracy how they have expressed
themselves. But all these things will every one understand
who seeks the wisdom of God, and is well pleasing to Him
through faith and righteousness and the doing of good works.
For one of the prophets whom we already mentioned, Hosea
by name, said, " Who is wise, and he shall understand these
things? prudent, and he shall know them? for the ways of
the Lord are right, and the just shall walk in them : but the
transgressors shall fall therein."[4] He, then, who is desirous of
learning, should learn much.[5] Endeavour therefore to meet
[with me] more frequently, that, by hearing the living voice,
you may accurately ascertain the truth.

[1] *Od.* xi. 221.   [2] *Il.* xvi. 856.   [3] xxiii. 71.   [4] Hos. xiv. 9.

[5] We have adopted the reading of Wolf in the text. The reading of
the MSS. is, " He who desires to learn should desire to learn." Perhaps
the most satisfactory emendation is that of Heumann, who reads φιλομυ-
θεῖν instead of φιλομαθεῖν: "He who desires to learn should also desire to
discuss subjects, and hold conversations on them." In this case, Theophilus most probably borrows his remark from Aristotle, *Metaphysic.* i.
c. 2.

THEOPHILUS TO AUTOLYCUS.

BOOK III.

CHAP. I.—*Autolycus not yet convinced.*

HEOPHILUS to Autolycus, greeting : Seeing that writers are fond of composing a multitude of books for vainglory,—some concerning gods, and wars, and chronology, and some, too, concerning useless legends, and other such labour in vain, in which you also have been used to employ yourself until now, and do not grudge to endure that toil; but though you conversed with me, are still of opinion that the word of truth is an idle tale, and suppose that our writings are recent and modern ;—on this account I also will not grudge the labour of compendiously setting forth to you, God helping me, the antiquity of our books, reminding you of it in few words, that you may not grudge the labour of reading it, but may recognise the folly of the other authors.

CHAP. II.—*Profane authors had no means of knowing the truth.*

For it was fit that they who wrote should themselves have been eye-witnesses of those things concerning which they made assertions, or should accurately have ascertained them from those who had seen them ; for they who write of things unascertained beat the air. For what did it profit Homer to have composed the Trojan war, and to have deceived many ; or Hesiod, the register of the theogony of those whom he calls gods; or Orpheus, the three hundred and sixty-five gods, whom in the end of his life he rejects, maintaining in his precepts that there is one God? What profit did the sphærography of the world's circle confer on Aratus, or those who held the same doctrine as he, except glory among men? And not even that did they reap as they deserved. And what truth did they utter? Or what good did their tragedies do to Euripides and Sophocles, or the other tragedians? Or their comedies to Menander and Aristophanes, and the other comedians? Or their histories to Herodotus and Thucydides? Or the shrines [1] and the pillars of Hercules to Pythagoras, or the Cynic philosophy to Diogenes? What good did it do Epicurus to maintain that there is no providence; or Empedocles to teach atheism; or Socrates to swear by the dog, and the goose, and the plane-tree, and Æsculapius struck by lightning, and the demons whom he invoked? And why did he willingly die? What reward, or of what kind, did he expect to receive after death? What did Plato's system of culture profit him? Or what benefit did the *rest* of the philosophers derive from their doctrines, not to enumerate the whole of them, since they are numerous? But these things we say, for the purpose of exhibiting their useless and godless opinions.

CHAP. III.—*Their contradictions.*

For all these, having fallen in love with vain and empty reputation, neither themselves knew the truth, nor guided others to the truth: for the things which they said themselves convict them of speaking inconsistently; and most of them demolished their own doctrines. For not only did they refute one another, but some, too, even stultified their own teachings; so that their reputation has issued in shame and folly, for they are condemned by men of understanding. For either they made assertions concerning the gods, and afterwards taught that there was no god; or if they spoke even of the creation of the world, they finally said that all things were produced spontaneously. Yea, and even speaking of

---

[1] While in Egypt, Pythagoras was admitted to the penetralia of the temples and the arcana of religion.

providence, they taught again that the world was not ruled
by providence. But what? Did they not, when they essayed
to write even of honourable conduct, teach the perpetration
of lasciviousness, and fornication, and adultery; and did they
not introduce hateful and unutterable wickedness? And
they proclaim that their gods took the lead in committing
unutterable acts of adultery, and in monstrous banquets.
For who does not sing Saturn devouring his own children,
and Jove his son gulping down Metis, and preparing for the
gods a horrible feast, at which also they say that Vulcan, a
lame blacksmith, did the waiting; and how Jove not only
married Juno, his own sister, but also with foul mouth did
abominable wickedness? And the rest of his deeds, as many
as the poets sing, it is likely you are acquainted with. Why
need I further recount the deeds of Neptune and Apollo, or
Bacchus and Hercules, of the bosom-loving Minerva, and the
shameless Venus, since in another place[1] we have given a
more accurate account of these?

CHAP. IV.—*How Autolycus had been misled by false accusa-
tions against the Christians.*

Nor indeed was there any necessity for my refuting these,
except that I see you still in dubiety about the word of the
truth. For though yourself prudent, you endure fools gladly.
Otherwise you would not have been moved by senseless men
to yield yourself to empty words, and to give credit to the
prevalent rumour wherewith godless lips falsely accuse us,
who are worshippers of God, and are called Christians,
alleging that the wives of us all are held in common and
made promiscuous use of; and that we even commit incest
with our own sisters, and, what is most impious and barbarous
of all, that we eat human flesh. But further, they say that
our doctrine has but recently come to light, and that we have
nothing to allege in proof of what we receive as truth, nor of
our teaching, but that our doctrine is foolishness. I wonder,
then, chiefly that you, who in other matters are studious, and
a scrutinizer of all things, give but a careless hearing to us.

[1] Viz. in the first book to Autolycus.

For, if it were possible for you, you would not grudge to spend the night in the libraries.

CHAP. V.—*Philosophers inculcate cannibalism.*

Since, then, you have read much, what is your opinion of the precepts of Zeno, and Diogenes, and Cleanthes, which their books contain, inculcating the eating of human flesh : that fathers be cooked and eaten by their own children ; and that if any one refuse or reject a part of this infamous food, he himself be devoured who will not eat? An utterance even more godless than these is found,—that, namely, of Diogenes, who teaches children to bring their own parents in sacrifice, and devour them. And does not the historian Herodotus narrate that Cambyses,[1] when he had slaughtered the children of Harpagus, cooked them also, and set them as a meal before their father? And, still further, he narrates that among the Indians the parents are eaten by their own children. Oh! the godless teaching of those who recorded, yea, rather, inculcated such things! Oh! their wickedness and godlessness! Oh! the conception of those who thus accurately philosophized, and profess philosophy! For they who taught these doctrines have filled the world with iniquity.

CHAP. VI.— *Other opinions of the philosophers.*

And regarding lawless conduct, those who have blindly wandered into the choir of philosophy have, almost to a man, spoken with one voice. Certainly Plato, to mention him first who seems to have been the most respectable philosopher among them, expressly, as it were, legislates in his first book,[2] entitled *The Republic,* that the wives of all be common, using the precedent of the son[3] of Jupiter and the lawgiver of the Cretans, in order that under this pretext there might be an abundant offspring from the best persons, and that those who were worn with toil might be comforted by such intercourse.[4]

---

[1] It was not Cambyses, but Astyages, who did this ; see Herod. i. 119.
[2] Not in the first, but the fifth book of the *Republic.*   [3] Minos.
[4] As this sentence cannot be intelligibly rendered without its original in Plato, we subjoin the latter : " As for those youths who excel either

And Epicurus himself, too, as well as teaching atheism, teaches along with it incest with mothers and sisters, and this in transgression of the laws which forbid it; for Solon distinctly legislated regarding this, in order that from a married parent children might lawfully spring, that they might not be born of adultery, so that no one should honour as his father him who was not his father, or dishonour him who was really his father, through ignorance that he was so. And these things the other laws of the Romans and Greeks also prohibit. Why, then, do Epicurus and the Stoics teach incest and sodomy, with which doctrines they have filled libraries, so that from boyhood this lawless intercourse is learned? And why should I further spend time on them, since even of those they call gods they relate similar things?

CHAP. VII.—*Varying doctrine concerning the gods.*

For after they had said that these are gods, they again made them of no account. For some said that they were composed of atoms; and others, again, that they eventuate in atoms; and they say that the gods have no more power than men. Plato, too, though he says these are gods, would have them composed of matter. And Pythagoras, after he had made such a toil and moil about the gods, and travelled up and down [for information], at last determines that all things are produced naturally and spontaneously, and that the gods care nothing for men. And how many atheistic opinions Clitomachus the academician introduced, [I need not recount.] And did not Critias and Protagoras of Abdera say, "For whether the gods exist, I am not able to affirm concerning them, nor to explain of what nature they are; for there are many things would prevent me"? And to speak of the opinions of the most atheistical, Euhemerus, is superfluous. For having made many daring assertions concerning the gods, he at last would absolutely deny their existence, and have all

in war or other pursuits, they ought both to have other rewards and prizes given them; and specially this, of being allowed the freest intercourse with women, that, at the same time, under this pretext the greatest number of children may spring from such parents."

things to be governed by self-regulated action.[1] And Plato,
who spoke so much of the unity of God and of the soul of
man, asserting that the soul is immortal, is not he himself
afterwards found, inconsistently with himself, to maintain that
some souls pass into other men, and that others take their
departure into irrational animals? How can his doctrine fail
to seem dreadful and monstrous—to those at least who have
any judgment—that he who was once a man shall afterwards be a wolf, or a dog, or an ass, or some other irrational
brute? Pythagoras, too, is found venting similar nonsense,
besides his demolishing providence. Which of them, then,
shall we believe? Philemon, the comic poet, who says,

    " Good hope have they who praise and serve the gods;"

or those whom we have mentioned—Euhemerus, and Epicurus, and Pythagoras, and the others who deny that the
gods are to be worshipped, and who abolish providence?
Concerning God and providence, Ariston said:

    " Be of good courage: God will still preserve
     And greatly help all those who so deserve.
     If no promotion waits on faithful men,
     Say what advantage goodness offers then.
     'Tis granted—yet I often see the just
     Faring but ill, from ev'ry honour thrust;
     While they whose own advancement is their aim,
     Oft in this present life have all they claim.
     But we must look beyond, and wait the end,
     That consummation to which all things tend.
     'Tis not, as vain and wicked men have said,
     By an unbridled destiny we're led:
     It is not blinded chance that rules the world,
     Nor uncontrolled are all things onward hurled.
     The wicked blinds himself with this belief;
     But be ye sure, of all rewards, the chief
     Is still reserved for those who holy live;
     And Providence to wicked men will give
     Only the just reward which is their meed,
     And fitting punishment for each bad deed."

And one can see how inconsistent with each other are the
things which others, and indeed almost the majority, have said
about God and providence. For some have absolutely can-

    [1] αὐτοματισμῷ.

celled God and providence; and others, again, have affirmed God, and have avowed that all things are governed by providence. The intelligent hearer and reader must therefore give minute attention to their expressions; as also Simylus said: "It is the custom of the poets to name by a common designation the surpassingly wicked and the excellent; we therefore must discriminate." As also Philemon says: "A senseless man who sits and merely hears is a troublesome feature; for he does not blame himself, so foolish is he." We must then give attention, and consider what is said, critically inquiring into what has been uttered by the philosophers and the poets.

CHAP. VIII.—*Wickedness attributed to the gods by heathen writers.*

For, denying that there are gods, they again acknowledge their existence, and they said they committed grossly wicked deeds. And, first, of Jove the poets euphoniously sing the wicked actions. And Chrysippus, who talked a deal of nonsense, is he not found publishing that Juno had the foulest intercourse with Jupiter? For why should I recount the impurities of the so-called mother of the gods, or of Jupiter Latiaris thirsting for human blood, or the castrated Attis; or of Jupiter, surnamed Tragedian, and how he defiled himself, as they say, and now is worshipped among the Romans as a god? I am silent about the temples of Antinous, and of the others whom you call gods. For when related to sensible persons, they excite laughter. They who elaborated such a philosophy regarding either the non-existence of God, or promiscuous intercourse and beastly concubinage, are themselves condemned by their own teachings. Moreover, we find from the writings they composed that the eating of human flesh was received among them; and they record that those whom they honour as gods were the first to do these things.

CHAP. IX.—*Christian doctrine of God and His law.*

Now we also confess that God exists, but that He is one, the creator, and maker, and fashioner of this universe; and we know that all things are arranged by His providence, but by Him alone. And we have learned a holy law; but we have as lawgiver Him who is really God, who teaches us to act righteously, and to be pious, and to do good. And concerning piety[1] He says, "Thou shalt have no other gods before me. Thou shalt not make unto thee any graven image, or any likeness of anything that is in heaven above, or that is in the earth beneath, or that is in the water under the earth: thou shalt not bow down thyself to them, nor serve them: for I am the Lord thy God."[2] And of doing good He said: "Honour thy father and thy mother; that it may be well with thee, and that thy days may be long in the land which I the Lord God give thee." Again, concerning righteousness: "Thou shalt not commit adultery. Thou shalt not kill. Thou shalt not steal. Thou shalt not bear false witness against thy neighbour. Thou shalt not covet thy neighbour's wife, thou shalt not covet thy neighbour's house, nor his land, nor his man-servant, nor his maidservant, nor his ox, nor his beast of burden, nor any of his cattle, nor anything that is thy neighbour's. Thou shalt not wrest the judgment of the poor in his cause.[3] From every unjust matter keep thee far. The innocent and righteous thou shalt not slay; thou shalt not justify the wicked; and thou shalt not take a gift, for gifts blind the eyes of them that see and pervert righteous words." Of this divine law, then, Moses, who also was God's servant, was made the minister both to all the world, and chiefly to the Hebrews, who were also called Jews, whom an Egyptian king had in ancient days enslaved, and who were the righteous seed of godly and holy men—Abraham, and Isaac, and Jacob. God, being mindful of them, and doing marvellous and strange miracles by the hand of Moses, delivered them, and led them out of Egypt, leading them through what is called the desert; whom He also settled again in the land of Canaan, which afterwards was called Judæa, and gave them a law, and taught them these things. Of this great and wonderful law, which tends to all righteousness, the ten heads are such as we have already rehearsed.

[1] Or, right worship.   [2] Ex. xx. 3.   [3] Ex. xxiii. 6.

Chap. x.—*Of humanity to strangers.*

Since therefore they were strangers in the land of Egypt, being by birth Hebrews from the land of Chaldæa,—for at that time, there being a famine, they were obliged to migrate to Egypt for the sake of buying food there, where also for a time they sojourned; and these things befell them in accordance with a prediction of God,—having sojourned, then, in Egypt for 430 years, when Moses was about to lead them out into the desert, God taught them by the law, saying, "Ye shall not afflict a stranger; for ye know the heart of a stranger: for yourselves were strangers in the land of Egypt."

Chap. xi.—*Of repentance.*

And when the people transgressed the law which had been given to them by God, God being good and pitiful, unwilling to destroy them, in addition to His giving them the law, afterwards sent forth also prophets to them from among their brethren, to teach and remind them of the contents of the law, and to turn them to repentance, that they might sin no more. But if they persisted in their wicked deeds, He forewarned them that they should be delivered into subjection to all the kingdoms of the earth; and that this has already happened them, is manifest. Concerning repentance, then, Isaiah the prophet, generally indeed to all, but expressly to the people, says: "Seek ye the Lord while He may be found, call ye upon Him while He is near: let the wicked forsake his ways, and the unrighteous man his thoughts: and let him return unto the Lord his God, and he will find mercy, for He will abundantly pardon."[1] And another prophet, Ezekiel, says: "If the wicked will turn from all his sins that he hath committed, and keep all my statutes, and do that which is right in my sight, he shall surely live, he shall not die. All his transgressions that he hath committed, they shall not be mentioned unto him; but in his righteousness that he hath done he shall live: for I desire not the death of the sinner,

[1] Isa. lv. 6.

saith the Lord, but that he turn from his wicked way, and live."[1] Again Isaiah: "Ye who take deep and wicked counsel, turn ye, that ye may be saved."[2] And another prophet, Jeremiah: "Turn to the Lord your God, as a grape-gatherer to his basket, and ye shall find mercy."[3] Many therefore, yea rather, countless are the sayings in the Holy Scriptures regarding repentance, God being always desirous that the race of men turn from all their sins.

CHAP. XII.—*Of righteousness.*

Moreover, concerning the righteousness which the law enjoined, confirmatory utterances are found both with the prophets and in the Gospels, because they all spoke inspired by one Spirit of God. Isaiah accordingly spoke thus: "Put away the evil of your doings from your souls; learn to do well, seek judgment, relieve the oppressed, judge the fatherless, plead for the widow."[4] And again the same prophet said: "Loose every band of wickedness, dissolve every oppressive contract, let the oppressed go free, and tear up every unrighteous bond. Deal out thy bread to the hungry, and bring the houseless poor to thy home. When thou seest the naked, cover him, and hide not thyself from thine own flesh. Then shall thy light break forth as the morning, and thine health shall spring forth speedily, and thy righteousness shall go before thee."[5] In like manner also Jeremiah says: "Stand in the ways, and see, and ask which is the good way of the Lord your God, and walk in it, and ye shall find rest for your souls. Judge just judgment, for in this is the will of the Lord your God."[6] So also says Hosea: "Keep judgment, and draw near to your God, who established the heavens and created the earth."[7] And another, Joel, spoke in agreement with these: "Gather the people, sanctify the congregation, assemble the elders, gather the children that are in arms; let the bridegroom go forth of his chamber, and the bride out of her closet, and pray to the Lord thy God urgently that He may have mercy upon you, and blot out your sins."[8] In like

[1] Ezek. xviii. 21.   [2] Isa. xxxi. 6.   [3] Jer. vi. 9.   [4] Isa. i. 16, 17.
[5] Isa. lviii. 6.   [6] Jer. vi. 16.   [7] Hos. xii. 6.   [8] Joel ii. 16.

manner also another, Zachariah: "Thus saith the Lord
Almighty, Execute true judgment, and show mercy and compassion every man to his brother; and oppress not the widow,
nor the fatherless, nor the stranger; and let none of you
imagine evil against his brother in your heart, saith the Lord
Almighty."[1]

Chap. xiii.—*Of chastity.*

And concerning chastity, the holy word teaches us not only
not to sin in act, but not even in thought, not even in the
heart to think of any evil, nor looking on another man's wife
with our eyes to lust after her. Solomon, accordingly, who
was a king and a prophet, said: "Let thine eyes look right
on, and let thine eyelids look straight before thee: make
straight paths for your feet."[2] And the voice of the gospel
teaches still more urgently concerning chastity, saying:
"Whosoever looketh on a woman who is not his own wife, to
lust after her, hath committed adultery with her already in
his heart."[3] "And he that marrieth," says [the gospel], "her
that is divorced from her husband, committeth adultery;
and whosoever putteth away his wife, saving for the cause
of fornication, causeth her to commit adultery."[4] Because
Solomon says: "Can a man take fire in his bosom, and his
clothes not be burned? Or can one walk upon hot coals, and
his feet not be burned? So he that goeth in to a married
woman shall not be innocent."[5]

Chap. xiv.—*Of loving our enemies.*

And that we should be kindly disposed, not only towards
those of our own stock, as some suppose, Isaiah the prophet
said: "Say to those that hate you, and that cast you out,
Ye are our brethren, that the name of the Lord may be
glorified, and be apparent in their joy."[6] And the gospel
says: "Love your enemies, and pray for them that despite-
fully use you. For if ye love them who love you, what
reward have ye? This do also the robbers and the publicans."[7]

[1] Zech. vii. 9, 10.   [2] Prov. iv. 25.   [3] Matt. v. 28.   [4] Matt. v. 32.
[5] Prov. vi. 27-29.   [6] Isa. lxvi. 5.   [7] Matt. v. 44.

And those that do good it teaches not to boast, lest they become men-pleasers. For it says: "Let not your left hand know what your right hand doeth."[1] Moreover, concerning subjection to authorities and powers, and prayer for them, the divine word gives us instructions, in order that "we may lead a quiet and peaceable life."[2] And it teaches us to render all things to all,[3] "honour to whom honour, fear to whom fear, tribute to whom tribute; to owe no man anything, but to love all."

Chap. xv.—*The innocence of the Christians defended.*

Consider, therefore, whether those who teach such things can possibly live indifferently, and be commingled in unlawful intercourse, or, most impious of all, eat human flesh, especially when we are forbidden so much as to witness shows of gladiators, lest we become partakers and abettors of murders. But neither may we see the other spectacles,[4] lest our eyes and ears be defiled, participating in the utterances there sung. For if one should speak of cannibalism, in these spectacles the children of Thyestes and Tereus are eaten; and as for adultery, both in the case of men and of gods, whom they celebrate in elegant language for honours and prizes, this is made the subject of their dramas. But far be it from Christians to conceive any such deeds; for with them temperance dwells, self-restraint is practised, monogamy is observed, chastity is guarded, iniquity exterminated, sin extirpated, righteousness exercised, law administered, worship performed, God acknowledged: truth governs, grace guards, peace screens them; the holy word guides, wisdom teaches, life directs, God reigns. Therefore, though we have much to say regarding our manner of life, and the ordinances of God, the maker of all creation, we yet consider that we have for the present reminded you of enough to induce you to study these things, especially since you can now read [our writings] for yourself, that as you have been fond of acquiring information, you may still be studious in this direction also.

[1] Matt. vi. 3.
[2] 1 Tim. ii. 2.
[3] Rom. xiii. 7, 8.
[4] At the theatres.

CHAP. XVI.— *Uncertain conjectures of the philosophers.*

But I wish now to give you a more accurate demonstration, God helping me, of the historical periods, that you may see that our doctrine is not modern nor fabulous, but more ancient and true than all poets and authors who have written in uncertainty. For some, maintaining that the world was uncreated, went into infinity;[1] and others, asserting that it was created, said that already 153,075 years had passed. This is stated by Apollonius the Egyptian. And Plato, who is esteemed to have been the wisest of the Greeks, into what nonsense did he run? For in his book entitled *The Republic*,[2] we find him expressly saying: "For if things had in all time remained in their present arrangement, when ever could any new thing be discovered? For ten thousand times ten thousand years elapsed without record, and one thousand or twice as many years have gone by since some things were discovered by Dædalus, and some by Orpheus, and some by Palamedes." And when he says that these things happened, he implies that ten thousand times ten thousand years elapsed from the flood to Dædalus. And after he has said a great deal about the cities of the world, and the settlements, and the nations, he owns that he has said these things conjecturally. For he says, "If then, my friend, some god should promise us, that if we attempted to make a survey of legislation, the things now said,"[3] etc., which shows that he was speaking by guess; and if by guess, then what he says is not true.

CHAP. XVII.— *Accurate information of the Christians.*

It behoved, therefore, that he should the rather become a scholar of God in this matter of legislation, as he himself confessed that in no other way could he gain accurate

---

[1] *i.e.* tracing back its history through an infinite duration.

[2] The following quotation is not from the *Republic*, but from the third book of the *Laws*.

[3] Plato goes on to say, that if he had this pledge of divine assistance, he would go further in his speculation; and therefore Theophilus argues that what he said without this assistance he felt to be unsafe.

information than by God's teaching him through the law.
And did not the poets Homer and Hesiod and Orpheus
profess that they themselves had been instructed by Divine
Providence? Moreover, it is said that among your writers
there were prophets and prognosticators, and that those wrote
accurately who were informed by them. How much more,
then, shall *we* know the truth who are instructed by the holy
prophets, who were possessed by[1] the Holy Spirit of God!
On this account all the prophets spoke harmoniously and in
agreement with one another, and foretold the things that
would come to pass in all the world. For the very accomplishment of predicted and already consummated events
should demonstrate to those who are fond of information,
yea rather, who are lovers of truth, that those things are
really true which they declared concerning the epochs and
eras before the deluge: to wit, how the years have run on
since the world was created until now, so as to manifest the
ridiculous mendacity of your authors, and show that their
statements are not true.

CHAP. XVIII.—*Errors of the Greeks about the deluge.*

For Plato, as we said above, when he had demonstrated
that a deluge had happened, said that it extended not over
the whole earth, but only over the plains, and that those who
fled to the highest hills saved themselves. But others say
that there existed Deucalion and Pyrrha, and that they were
preserved in a chest; and that Deucalion, after he came out
of the chest, flung stones behind him, and that men were
produced from the stones; from which circumstance they say
that men in the mass are named "people."[2] Others, again,
say that Clymenus existed in a second flood. From what has
already been said, it is evident that they who wrote such
things and philosophized to so little purpose are miserable,
and very profane and senseless persons. But Moses, our
prophet and the servant of God, in giving an account of the
genesis of the world, related in what manner the flood came

[1] Literally, "contained."
[2] λαός, from λᾶας, stone.

upon the earth, telling us, besides, how the details of the flood
came about, and relating no fable of Pyrrha nor of Deucalion
or Clymenus; nor, forsooth, that only the plains were sub-
merged, and that those only who escaped to the mountains
were saved.

CHAP. XIX.—*Accurate account of the deluge.*

And neither does he make out that there was a second
flood : on the contrary, he said that never again would there
be a flood of water on the world; as neither indeed has there
been, nor ever shall be.   And he says that eight human
beings were preserved in the ark, in that which had been
prepared by God's direction, not by Deucalion, but by Noah;
which Hebrew word means in English[1] " rest," as we have
elsewhere shown that Noah, when he announced to the men
then alive that there was a flood coming, prophesied to them,
saying, Come hither, God calls you to repentance.   On this
account he was fitly called Deucalion.[2]   And this Noah had
three sons (as we mentioned in the second book), whose
names were Shem, and Ham, and Japheth; and these had
three wives, one wife each ; each man and his wife.   This
man some have surnamed Eunuchus.   All the eight persons,
therefore, who were found in the ark were preserved.   And
Moses showed that the flood lasted forty days and forty
nights, torrents pouring from heaven, and from the fountains
of the deep breaking up, so that the water overtopped every
high hill 15 cubits.   And thus the race of all the men that
then were was destroyed, and those only who were protected
in the ark were saved; and these, we have already said, were
eight.   And of the ark, the remains are to this day to be seen
in the Arabian mountains.   This, then, is in sum the history
of the deluge.

CHAP. XX.—*Antiquity of Moses.*

And Moses, becoming the leader of the Jews, as we have
already stated, was expelled from the land of Egypt by the

---

[1] Literally, in Greek, ἀνάπαυσις.
[2] Deucalion, from Δεῦτε, come, and καλέω, I call.

king, Pharaoh, whose name was Amasis, and who, they say, reigned after the expulsion of the people 25 years and 4 months, as Manetho assumes. And after him [reigned] Chebron, 13 years. And after him Amenophis, 20 years 7 months. And after him his sister Amessa, 21 years 1 month. And after her Mephres, 12 years 9 months. And after him Methramuthosis, 20 years and 10 months. And after him Tythmoses, 9 years 8 months. And after him Damphenophis, 30 years 10 months. And after him Orus, 35 years 5 months. And after him his daughter, 10 years 3 months. After her Mercheres, 12 years 3 months. And after him his son Armais, 30 years 1 month. After him Messes, son of Miammus, 6 years 2 months. After him Rameses, 1 year 4 months. After him Amenophis, 19 years 6 months. After him his sons Thoessus and Rameses, 10 years, who, it is said, had a large cavalry force and naval equipment. The Hebrews, indeed, after their own separate history, having at that time migrated into the land of Egypt, and been enslaved by the king Tethmosis, as already said, built for him strong cities, Peitho, and Rameses, and On, which is Heliopolis; so that the Hebrews, who also are our ancestors, and from whom we have those sacred books which are older than all authors, as already said, are proved to be more ancient than the cities which were at that time renowned among the Egyptians. And the country was called Egypt from the king Sethos. For the word Sethos, they say, is pronounced "Egypt."[1] And Sethos had a brother, by name Armais. He is called Danaus, the same who passed from Egypt to Argos, whom the other authors mention as being of very ancient date.

CHAP. XXI.—*Of Manetho's inaccuracy.*

And Manetho, who among the Egyptians gave out a great deal of nonsense, and even impiously charged Moses and the Hebrews who accompanied him with being banished from Egypt on account of leprosy, could give no accurate chronological statement. For when he said they were shepherds,

[1] Or, reading ὁ γὰρ Σέθως, "Sethos is also called Egyptus."

and enemies of the Egyptians, he uttered truth indeed, because he was forced to do so. For our forefathers who sojourned in Egypt were truly shepherds, but not lepers. For when they came into the land called Jerusalem, where also they afterwards abode, it is well known how their priests, in pursuance of the appointment of God, continued in the temple, and there healed every disease, so that they cured lepers and every unsoundness. The temple was built by Solomon the king of Judæa. And from Manetho's own statements his chronological error is manifest. (As it is also in respect of the king who expelled them, Pharaoh by name. For he no longer ruled them. For having pursued the Hebrews, he and his army were engulphed in the Red Sea. And he is in error still further, in saying that shepherds made war against the Egyptians.) For they went out of Egypt, and thenceforth dwelt in the country now called Judæa, 313[1] years before Danaus came to Argos. And that most people consider him older than any other of the Greeks is manifest. So that Manetho has unwillingly declared to us, by his own writings, two particulars of the truth : first, avowing that they were shepherds; secondly, saying that they went out of the land of Egypt. So that even from these writings Moses and his followers are proved to be 900 or even 1000 years prior to the Trojan war.[2]

Chap. XXII.—*Antiquity of the temple.*

Then concerning the building of the temple in Judæa, which Solomon the king built 566 years after the exodus of the Jews from Egypt, there is among the Tyrians a record how the temple was built; and in their archives writings have been preserved, in which the temple is proved to have existed 143[3] years 8 months before the Tyrians founded Carthage (and this record was made by Hiram[4] (that is the name of the king of the Tyrians), the son of Abimalus, on account of the hereditary friendship which existed between Hiram and

---

[1] The Bened. editor shows that this should be 393 years.
[2] The correct date would be about 400 years.
[3] Others read 134 years.   [4] Literally, Hieromus.

Solomon, and at the same time on account of the surpassing wisdom possessed by Solomon. For they continually engaged with each other in discussing difficult problems. And proof of this exists in their correspondence, which to this day is preserved among the Tyrians, and the writings that passed between them); as Menander the Ephesian, while narrating the history of the Tyrian kingdom, records, speaking thus: " For when Abimalus the king of the Tyrians died, his son Hiram succeeded to the kingdom. He lived 53 years. And Bazorus succeeded him, who lived 43, and reigned 17 years. And after him followed Methuastartus, who lived 54 years, and reigned 12. And after him succeeded his brother Atharymus, who lived 58 years, and reigned 9. He was slain by his brother of the name of Helles, who lived 50 years, and reigned 8 months. He was killed by Juthobalus, priest of Astarte, who lived 40 years, and reigned 12. He was succeeded by his son Bazorus, who lived 45 years, and reigned 7. And to him his son Metten succeeded, who lived 32 years, and reigned 29. Pygmalion, son of Pygmalius, succeeded him, who lived 56 years, and reigned 7.[1] And in the 7th year of his reign, his sister, fleeing to Libya, built the city which to this day is called Carthage." The whole period, therefore, from the reign of Hiram to the founding of Carthage, amounts to 155 years and 8 months. And in the 12th year of the reign of Hiram the temple in Jerusalem was built. So that the entire time from the building of the temple to the founding of Carthage was 143 years and 8 months.

CHAP. XXIII.—*Prophets more ancient than Greek writers.*

So then let what has been said suffice for the testimony of the Phœnicians and Egyptians, and for the account of our chronology given by the writers Manetho the Egyptian, and Menander the Ephesian, and also Josephus, who wrote the Jewish war, which they waged with the Romans. For from these very old records it is proved that the writings of the

---

[1] In this register it seems that the number of years during which each person lived does not include the years of his reign.

rest are more recent than the writings given to us through Moses, yes, and than the subsequent prophets. For the last of the prophets, who was called Zechariah, was contemporary with the reign of Darius. But even the lawgivers themselves are all found to have legislated subsequently to that period. For if one were to mention Solon the Athenian, he lived in the days of the kings Cyrus and Darius, in the time of the prophet Zechariah first mentioned, who was by many years the last of the prophets.[1] Or if you mention the lawgivers Lycurgus, or Draco, or Minos, Josephus tells us in his writings that the sacred books take precedence of them in antiquity, since even before the reign of Jupiter over the Cretans, and before the Trojan war, the writings of the divine law which has been given to us through Moses were in existence. And that we may give a more accurate exhibition of eras and dates, we will, God helping us, now give an account not only of the dates after the deluge, but also of those before it, so as to reckon the whole number of all the years, as far as possible ; tracing up to the very beginning of the creation of the world, which Moses the servant of God recorded through the Holy Spirit. For having first spoken of what concerned the creation and genesis of the world, and of the first man, and all that happened after in the order of events, he signified also the years that elapsed before the deluge. And I pray for favour from the only God, that I may accurately speak the whole truth according to His will, that you and every one who reads this work may be guided by His truth and favour. I will then begin first with the recorded genealogies, and I begin my narration with the first man.

CHAP. XXIV.—*Chronology from Adam.*

Adam lived till he begat a son,[2] 230 years. And his son Seth, 205. And his son Enos, 190. And his son Cainan, 170. And his son Mahaleel, 165. And his son Jared, 162. And his son Enoch, 165. And his son Methuselah, 167. And

---

[1] But the meaning here is obscure in the original. Malachi was much later than Zechariah.

[2] *i.e.* till he begat Seth.

his son Lamech, 188. And Lamech's son was Noah, of whom we have spoken above, who begat Shem when 500 years old. During Noah's life, in his 600th year, the flood came. The total number of years, therefore, till the flood, was 2242. And immediately after the flood, Shem, who was 100 years old, begat Arphaxad. And Arphaxad, when 135 years old, begat Salah. And Salah begat a son when 130. And his son Eber, when 134. And from him the Hebrews name their race. And his son Phaleg begat a son when 130. And his son Reu, when 132. And his son Serug, when 130. And his son Nahor, when 75. And his son Terah, when 70. And his son Abraham, our patriarch, begat Isaac when he was 100 years old. Until Abraham, therefore, there are 3278 years. The fore-mentioned Isaac lived until he begat a son, 60 years, and begat Jacob. Jacob, till the migration into Egypt, of which we have spoken above, lived 130 years. And the sojourning of the Hebrews in Egypt lasted 430 years; and after their departure from the land of Egypt they spent 40 years in the wilderness, as it is called. All these years, therefore, amount to 3938. And at that time, Moses having died, Jesus the son of Nun succeeded to his rule, and governed them 27 years. And after Jesus, when the people had transgressed the commandments of God, they served the king of Mesopotamia, by name Chusarathon, 8 years. Then, on the repentance of the people, they had judges : Gothonoel, 40 years ; Eglon, 18 years ; Aoth, 8 years. Then having sinned, they were subdued by strangers for 20 years. Then Deborah judged them 40 years. Then they served the Midianites 7 years. Then Gideon judged them 40 years ; Abimelech, 3 years ; Thola, 22 years ; Jair, 22 years. Then the Philistines and Ammonites ruled them 18 years. After that Jephthah judged them 6 years; Esbon, 7 years ; Ailon, 10 years ; Abdon, 8 years. Then strangers ruled them 40 years. Then Samson judged them 20 years. Then there was peace among them for 40 years. Then Samera judged them one year ; Eli, 20 years ; Samuel, 12 years.

CHAP. XXV.—*From Saul to the captivity.*

And after the judges they had kings, the first named Saul, who reigned 20 years; then David, our forefather, who reigned 40 years. Accordingly, there are to the reign of David [from Isaac] 496 years. And after these kings Solomon reigned, who also, by the will of God, was the first to build the temple in Jerusalem; he reigned 40 years. And after him Rehoboam, 17 years; and after him Abias, 7 years; and after him Asa, 41 years; and after him Jehoshaphat, 25 years; and after him Joram, 8 years; and after him Ahaziah, 1 year; and after him Athaliah, 6 years; and after her Josiah, 40 years; and after him Amaziah, 39 years; and after him Uzziah, 52 years; and after him Jotham, 16 years; and after him Ahaz, 17 years; and after him Hezekiah, 29 years; and after him Manasseh, 55 years; and after him Amon, 2 years; and after him Josiah, 31 years; and after him Jehoahaz, 3 months; and after him Jehoiakim, 11 years. Then another Jehoiakim, 3 months 10 days; and after him Zedekiah, 11 years. And after these kings, the people, continuing in their sins, and not repenting, the king of Babylon, named Nebuchadnezzar, came up into Judæa, according to the prophecy of Jeremiah. He transferred the people of the Jews to Babylon, and destroyed the temple which Solomon had built. And in the Babylonian banishment the people passed 70 years. Until the sojourning in the land of Babylon, there are therefore, in all, 4954 years 6 months and 10 days. And according as God had, by the prophet Jeremiah, foretold that the people should be led captive to Babylon, in like manner He signified beforehand that they should also return into their own land after 70 years. These 70 years then being accomplished, Cyrus becomes king of the Persians, who, according to the prophecy of Jeremiah, issued a decree in the second year of his reign, enjoining by his edict that all Jews who were in his kingdom should return to their own country, and rebuild their temple to God, which the fore-mentioned king of Babylon had demolished. Moreover, Cyrus, in compliance with the instructions of God, gave orders to his own body-guards, Sabessar and Mithridates, that the vessels which had been taken out of the temple of Judæa by Nebuchadnezzar should be restored, and placed again in the temple. In the second year, therefore, of Darius are fulfilled the 70 years which were foretold by Jeremiah.

CHAP. XXVI.—*Contrast between Hebrew and Greek writings.*

Hence one can see how our sacred writings are shown to be more ancient and true than those of the Greeks and Egyptians, or any other historians. For Herodotus and Thucydides, as also Xenophon, and most other historians, began their relations from about the reign of Cyrus and Darius, not being able to speak with accuracy of prior and ancient times. For what great matters did they disclose if they spoke of Darius and Cyrus, barbarian kings, or of the Greeks Zopyrus and Hippias, or of the wars of the Athenians and Lacedæmonians, or the deeds of Xerxes or of Pausanias, who ran the risk of starving to death in the temple of Minerva, or the history of Themistocles and the Peloponnesian war, or of Alcibiades and Thrasybulus? For my purpose is not to furnish mere matter of much talk, but to throw light upon the number of years from the foundation of the world, and to condemn the empty labour and trifling of these authors, because there have neither been twenty thousand times ten thousand years from the flood to the present time, as Plato said, affirming that there had been so many years; nor yet 15 times 10,375 years, as we have already mentioned Apollonius the Egyptian gave out; nor is the world uncreated, nor is there a spontaneous production of all things, as Pythagoras and the rest dreamed; but, being indeed created, it is also governed by the providence of God, who made all things; and the whole course of time and the years are made plain to those who wish to obey the truth. Lest, then, I seem to have made things plain up to the time of Cyrus, and to neglect the subsequent periods, as if through inability to exhibit them, I will endeavour, by God's help, to give an account, according to my ability, of the course of the subsequent times.

I

Chap. XXVII.—*Roman chronology to the death of M. Aurelius.*

When Cyrus, then, had reigned twenty-nine years, and had been slain by Tomyris in the country of the Massagetæ, this being in the 62d Olympiad, then the Romans began to increase in power, God strengthening them, Rome having been founded by Romulus, the reputed child of Mars and Ilia, in the 7th Olympiad, on the 21st day of April, the year being then reckoned as consisting of ten months. Cyrus, then, having died, as we have already said, in the 62d Olympiad, this date falls 220 A.U.C., in which year also Tarquinius, surnamed Superbus, reigned over the Romans, who was the first who banished Romans and corrupted the youth, and made eunuchs of the citizens, and, moreover, first defiled virgins, and then gave them in marriage. On this account he was fitly called Superbus in the Roman language, and that is translated "the Proud." For he first decreed that those who saluted him should have their salute acknowledged by some one else. He reigned twenty-five years. After him yearly consuls were introduced, tribunes also and ediles for 453 years, whose names we consider it long and superfluous to recount. For if any one is anxious to learn them, he will ascertain them from the tables which Chryserus the nomenclator compiled: he was a freedman of Aurelius Verus, who composed a very lucid record of all things, both names and dates, from the founding of Rome to the death of his own patron, the Emperor Verus. The annual magistrates ruled the Romans, as we say, for 453 years. Afterwards those who are called emperors began in this order: first, Caius Julius, who reigned 3 years 4 months 6 days; then Augustus, 56 years 4 months 1 day; Tiberius, 22 years; then another Caius, 3 years 8 months 7 days; Claudius, 23 years 8 months 24 days; Nero, 13 years 6 months 28 days; Galba, 2 years 7 months 6 days; Otho, 3 months 5 days; Vitellius, 6 months 22 days; Vespasian, 9 years 11 months 22 days; Titus, 2 years 22 days; Domitian, 15 years 5 months 6 days; Nerva, 1 year 4 months 10 days;

Trajan, 19 years 6 months 16 days; Adrian, 20 years 10 months 28 days; Antoninus, 22 years 7 months 6 days; Verus, 19 years 10 days. The time therefore of the Cæsars to the death of the Emperor Verus is 237 years 5 days. From the death of Cyrus, therefore, and the reign of Tarquinius Superbus, to the death of the Emperor Verus, the whole time amounts to 744 years.

CHAP. XXVIII.—*Leading chronological epochs.*

And from the foundation of the world the whole time is thus traced, so far as its main epochs are concerned. From the creation of the world to the deluge were 2242 years. And from the deluge to the time when Abraham our forefather begat a son, 1036 years. And from Isaac, Abraham's son, to the time when the people dwelt with Moses in the desert, 660 years. And from the death of Moses and the rule of Joshua the son of Nun, to the death of the patriarch David, 498 years. And from the death of David and the reign of Solomon to the sojourning of the people in the land of Babylon, 518 years 6 months 10 days. And from the government of Cyrus to the death of the Emperor Aurelius Verus, 744 years. All the years from the creation of the world amount to a total of 5698 years, and the odd months and days.

CHAP. XXIX.—*Antiquity of Christianity.*

These periods, then, and all the above-mentioned facts, being viewed collectively, one can see the antiquity of the prophetical writings and the divinity of our doctrine, that the doctrine is not recent, nor our tenets mythical and false, as some think, but very ancient and true. For Thallus mentioned Belus, king of the Assyrians, and Saturn, son of Titan, alleging that Belus with the Titans made war against Jupiter and the so-called gods in his alliance; and on this occasion he says that Gyges, being defeated, fled to Tartessus. At that time Gyges ruled over that country, which then was called Acte, but now is named Attica. And whence the other countries and cities derived their names, we think it unnecessary to recount, especially to you who are acquainted with history. That Moses, and not he only, but also most of the prophets who followed him, is proved to be older than all writers, and than Saturn and Belus and the Trojan war, is manifest. For according to the history of Thallus, Belus is found to be 322 years prior to the Trojan war. But we have shown above that Moses lived somewhere about 900 or 1000 years before the sack of Troy. And as Saturn and Belus flourished at the same time, most people do not know which is Saturn and which is Belus. Some worship Saturn, and call him Bel or Bal, especially the inhabitants of the eastern countries, for they do not know who either Saturn or Belus is. And among the Romans he is called Saturn, for neither do they know which of the two is more ancient—Saturn or Bel. So far as regards the commencement of the Olympiads, they say that the observance dates from Iphitus, but according to others from Linus, who is also called Ilius. The order which the whole number of years and Olympiads holds, we have shown above. I think I have now, according to my ability, accurately discoursed both of the godlessness of your practices,[1] and of the whole number of the epochs of history. For if even a chronological error has been committed by us, of *e.g.* 50 or 100, or even 200 years, yet not of thousands and tens of thousands, as Plato and Apollonius and other mendacious authors have hitherto written. And perhaps our knowledge of the whole number of the years is not quite accurate, because the odd months and days are not set down in the sacred books. But so far as regards the periods we speak of, we are corroborated by Berosus,[2] the Chaldæan philosopher, who made the Greeks acquainted with the Chaldæan literature, and uttered some things concerning the deluge, and many other points of history, in agreement with Moses ; and with the prophets Jeremiah and Daniel also, he spoke in a measure of agreement. For he mentioned what happened to the Jews under the king of the Babylonians, whom he calls Abobassor, and who is called by the Hebrews

[1] Another reading gives, " both of the antiquity of our religion."
[2] Berosus flourished in the reign of Alexander the Great.

Nebuchadnezzar. And he also spoke of the temple of Jerusalem, how it was desolated by the king of the Chaldæans,
and that the foundations of the temple having been laid the
second year of the reign of Cyrus, the temple was completed
in the second year of the reign of Darius.

CHAP. XXX.—*Why the Greeks did not mention our histories.*

But the Greeks make no mention of the histories which
give the truth : first, because they themselves only recently
became partakers of the knowledge of letters ; and they
themselves own it, alleging that letters were invented, some
say among the Chaldæans, and others with the Egyptians, and
others again say that they are derived from the Phœnicians.
And secondly, because they sinned, and still sin, in not making
mention of God, but of vain and useless matters. For thus
they most heartily celebrate Homer and Hesiod, and the rest
of the poets, but the glory of the incorruptible and only God
they not only omit to mention, but blaspheme ; yes, and they
persecuted, and do daily persecute, those who worship Him.
And not only so, but they even bestow prizes and honours on
those who in harmonious language insult God ; but of those
who are zealous in the pursuit of virtue and practise a holy
life, some they stoned, some they put to death, and up to the
present time they subject them to savage tortures. Wherefore such men have necessarily lost the wisdom of God, and
have not found the truth.

If you please, then, study these things carefully, that you
may have a compendium[1] and pledge of the truth.

---

[1] Otto prefers σύμβουλον instead of σύμβολον, on the authority of one
MS. The sense then is, "that you may have a counsellor and pledge of
the truth,"—the counsellor and pledge of the truth being the book
written by Theophilus for Autolycus.

RECOGNITIONS OF CLEMENT.

INTRODUCTORY NOTICE.

THE *Recognitions of Clement* is a kind of philosophical and theological romance. The writer of the work seems to have had no intention of presenting his statements as facts; but, choosing the disciples of Christ and their followers as his principal characters, he has put into their mouths the most important of his beliefs, and woven the whole together by a thread of fictitious narrative.

The *Recognitions* is one of a series; the other members of which that have come down to us are the *Clementine Homilies* and two *Epitomes*.

The authorship, the date, and the doctrinal character of these books have been subjects of keen discussion in modern times. Especial prominence has been given to them by the Tübingen school. Hilgenfeld says: "There is scarcely a single writing which is of so great importance for the history of Christianity in its first stage, and which has already given such brilliant disclosures at the hands of the most renowned critics in regard to the earliest history of the Christian Church, as the writings ascribed to the Roman Clement, the *Recognitions* and *Homilies*."[1] The importance thus attached to these strange and curious documents by one school of theologians, has compelled men of all shades of belief to investigate the subject; but after all their investigations, a great variety of opinion still prevails on almost every point connected with these books.

We leave our readers to judge for themselves in regard to the doctrinal statements, and confine ourselves to a notice of

[1] *Die Clementinischen Recognitionen und Homilien nach ihrem Ursprung und Inhalt dargestellt*, von Dr Adolf Hilgenfeld, Jena, 1848, p. 1.

some of the opinions in regard to the authorship and date of the *Recognitions*.

The first question that suggests itself in regard to the *Recognitions* is, whether the *Recognitions* or the *Homilies* are the earliest form of the book, and what relation do they bear to each other ? Some maintain that they are both the productions of the same author, and that the one is a later and altered edition of the other; and they find some confirmation of this in the preface of Rufinus. Others think that both books are expansions of another work which formed the basis. And others maintain that the one book is a *rifacimento* of the other by a different hand. Of this third party, some, like Cave, Whiston, Rosenmüller, Staüdlin, Hilgenfeld, and many others, believe that the *Recognitions* was the earliest[1] of the two forms; while others, as Clericus, Möhler, Lücke, Schliemann, and Uhlhorn, give priority to the *Clementines*. Hilgenfeld supposes that the original writing was the Κήρυγμα Πέτρου, which still remains in the work; that besides this there are three parts, — one directed against Basilides, the second the *Travels of Peter* (περίοδοι), and the third the *Recognitions*. There are also, he believes, many interpolated passages of a much later date than any of these parts.

No conclusion has been reached in regard to the author. Some have believed that it is a genuine work of Clement. Whiston maintained that it was written by some of his hearers and companions. Others have attributed the work to Bardesanes. But most acknowledge that there is no possibility of discovering who was the author.

Various opinions exist as to the date of the book. It has been attributed to the first, second, third, and fourth centuries, and some have assigned even a later date. If we were to base our arguments on the work as it stands, the date assigned would be somewhere in the first half of the third century. A passage from the *Recognitions* is quoted by Origen[2] in his *Commentary on Genesis*, written in 231; and mention is made

---

[1] See Schliemann, *Die Clementinen*, Hamburg, 1844, p. 295.
[2] *Philocalia*, cap. 22.

in the work of the extension of the Roman franchise to all
nations under the dominion of Rome,—an event which took
place in the reign of Caracalla, A.D. 211. The *Recognitions*
also contains a large extract from the work *De Fato*, ascribed
to Bardesanes, but really written by a scholar of his. Some
have thought that Bardesanes or his scholar borrowed from
the *Recognitions;* but more recently the opinion has prevailed,
that the passage was not originally in the *Recognitions*, but
was inserted into the *Recognitions* towards the middle of the
third century, or even later.[1]

Those who believe the work made up of various documents
assign various dates to these documents. Hilgenfeld, for instance, believes that the Κήρυγμα Πέτρου was written before
the time of Trajan, and the *Travels of Peter* about the time
of his reign.

Nothing is known of the place in which the *Recognitions*
was written. Some, as Schliemann, have supposed Rome,
some Asia Minor, and recently Uhlhorn has tried to trace it
to Eastern Syria.[2]

The Greek of the *Recognitions* is lost. The work has come
down to us in the form of a translation by Rufinus of Aquileia
(*d.* 410 A.D.). In his letter to Gaudentius, Rufinus states
that he omitted some portions difficult of comprehension, but
that in regard to the other parts he had translated with
care, and an endeavour to be exact even in rendering the
phraseology.

The best editions of the *Recognitions* are those by Cotelerius,
often reprinted, and by Gersdorf, Lipsiæ 1838; but the text
is not in a satisfactory condition.

[1] See Merx, *Bardesanes von Edessa*, Halle, 1863, p. 113.
[2] *Die Homilien und Recognitionen des Clemens Romanus nach ihrem
Ursprung und Inhalt dargestellt*, von Gerhard Uhlhorn, Göttingen, 1854,
p. 429.

RUFINUS, PRESBYTER OF AQUILEIA;

HIS PREFACE TO CLEMENT'S BOOK OF RECOGNITIONS.

TO BISHOP GAUDENTIUS.

O thee, indeed, O Gaudentius, thou choice glory of our doctors, belongs such vigour of mind, yea, such grace of the Spirit, that whatever you say even in the course of your daily preaching, whatever you deliver in the church, ought to be preserved in books, and handed down to posterity for their instruction. But we, whom slenderness of wit renders less ready, and now old age renders slow and inactive, though after many delays, yet at length present to you the work which once the virgin Sylvia of venerable memory enjoined upon us, that we should render Clement into our language, and you afterwards by hereditary right demanded of us; and thus we contribute to the use and profit of our people, no small spoil, as I think, taken from the libraries of the Greeks, so that we may feed with foreign nourishment those whom we cannot with our own. For foreign things usually seem both more pleasant, and sometimes also more profitable. In short, almost everything is foreign that brings healing to our bodies, that opposes diseases, and neutralizes poisons. For Judæa sends us *Lacryma balsami*, Crete *Coma dictamni*, Arabia her flowers of spices, India reaps her crop of spikenard; which, although they reach us in a somewhat more broken condition than when they leave their native fields, yet retain entire the sweetness of their odour and their healing virtue. Receive therefore, my soul,[1]

---

[1] Var. readings: "magnanimous one," "my lord," "my friend."

Clement returning to you; receive him now in a Roman dress. And wonder not if haply the florid countenance of eloquence appear less in him than usual. It matters not, provided the sense tastes the same. Therefore we transport foreign merchandise into our country with much labour. And I know not with how grateful countenances my countrymen welcome me, bringing to them the rich spoils of Greece, and unlocking hidden treasures of wisdom with the key of our language. But may God grant your prayers, that no unlucky eye nor any livid aspect may meet us, lest, by an extreme kind of prodigy, while those from whom he is taken do not envy, yet those upon whom he is bestowed should repine. Truly it is right to point out the plan of our translation to you, who have read these works also in Greek, lest haply in some parts you may think the order of translation not kept. I suppose you are aware that there are two editions in Greek of this work of Clement,—the Ἀναγνώσεις, that is, *Recognitions;* and that there are two collections of books, differing in some points, but in many [containing] the same narrative. In short, the last part of this work, in which is the relation concerning the transformation of Simon, is contained in one of the collections, but is not at all in the other. There are also in both collections some dissertations concerning the unbegotten God and the Begotten, and on some other subjects, which, to say nothing more, are beyond our comprehension. These, therefore, as being beyond our powers, I have chosen to reserve for others, rather than to produce in an imperfect state. But in the rest, we have given our endeavour, so far as we could, not to vary either from the sentiments or even from the language and modes of expression; and this, although it renders the style of the narrative less ornate, yet it makes it more faithful. The epistle in which the same Clement, writing to James the Lord's brother, informs him of the death of Peter, and that he had left him his successor in his chair and teaching, and in which also the whole subject of church order is treated of, I have not prefixed to this work, both because it is of later date, and because I have already translated and published it. But I do not think it out of place to explain here what in that letter will perhaps seem to some to be inconsistent. For some ask, Since Linus and Cletus were bishops in the city of Rome before this Clement, how could Clement himself, writing to James, say that the chair of teaching was handed over to him by Peter? Now of this we have heard this explanation, that Linus and Cletus were indeed bishops in the city of Rome before Clement, but during the lifetime of Peter: that is, that they undertook the care of the episcopate, and that he fulfilled the office of the apostleship; as is found also to have been the case at Cæsarea, where, when he himself was present, he yet had Zaccheus, ordained by himself, as bishop. And in this way both statements will appear to be true, both that these bishops are reckoned before Clement, and yet that Clement received the teacher's seat on the death of Peter. But now let us see how Clement, writing to James the Lord's brother, begins his narrative.

RECOGNITIONS OF CLEMENT.

BOOK I.

CHAP. I.—*Clement's early history; doubts.*

CLEMENT, who was born in the city of Rome, was from my earliest age a lover of chastity; while the bent of my mind held me bound as with chains of anxiety and sorrow. For a thought that was in me—whence originating, I cannot tell—constantly led me to think of my condition of mortality, and to discuss such questions as these: Whether there be for me any life after death, or whether I am to be wholly annihilated: whether I did not exist before I was born, and whether there shall be no remembrance of this life after death, and so the boundlessness of time shall consign all things to oblivion and silence; so that not only we shall cease to be, but there shall be no remembrance that we have ever been. This also I revolved in my mind: when the world was made, or what was before it was made, or whether it has existed from eternity. For it seemed certain, that if it had been made, it must be doomed to dissolution; and if it be dissolved, what is to be afterwards?—unless, perhaps, all things shall be buried in oblivion and silence, or something shall be, which the mind of man cannot now conceive.

CHAP. II.—*His distress.*

While I was continually revolving in my mind these and such like questions, suggested I know not how, I was pining away wonderfully through excess of grief; and, what was worse, if at any time I thought to cast aside such cares, as being of little use, the waves of anxiety rose all the higher

upon me.   For I had in me that most excellent companion,
who would not suffer me to rest—the desire of immortality :
for, as the subsequent issue showed, and the grace of
Almighty God directed, this bent of mind led me to the
quest of truth, and the acknowledgment of the true light ;
and hence it came to pass, that ere long I pitied those whom
formerly in my ignorance I believed to be happy.

Chap. iii.—*His dissatisfaction with the schools of the philosophers.*

Having therefore such a bent of mind from my earliest
years, the desire of learning something led me to frequent the
schools of the philosophers.   There I saw that nought else
was done, save that doctrines were asserted and controverted
without end, contests were waged, and the arts of syllogisms
and the subtleties of conclusions were discussed.   If at any
time the doctrine of the immortality of the soul prevailed,
I was thankful ; if at any time it was impugned, I went
away sorrowful.   Still, neither doctrine had the power of truth
over my heart.   This only I understood, that opinions and
definitions of things were accounted true or false, not in
accordance with their nature and the truth of the arguments,
but in proportion to the talents of those who supported them.
And I was all the more tortured in the bottom of my heart,
because I was neither able to lay hold of any of those things
which were spoken as firmly established, nor was I able to
lay aside the desire of inquiry ; but the more I endeavoured
to neglect and despise them, so much the more eagerly, as I
have said, did a desire of this sort, creeping in upon me
secretly as with a kind of pleasure, take possession of my
heart and mind.

Chap. iv.—*His increasing disquiet.*

Being therefore straitened in the discovery of things, I said
to myself, Why do we labour in vain, since the end of things
is manifest ?   For if after death I shall be no more, my present torture is useless ; but if there is to be for me a life after
death, let us keep for that life the excitements that belong to

it, lest perhaps some sadder things befall me than those which I now suffer, unless I shall have lived piously and soberly; and, according to the opinions of some of the philosophers, I be consigned to the stream of dark-rolling Phlegethon, or to Tartarus, like Sisyphus and Tityus, and to eternal punishment in the infernal regions, like Ixion and Tantalus. And again I would answer to myself: But these things are fables; or if it be so, since the matter is in doubt, it is better to live piously. But again I would ponder with myself, How should I restrain myself from the lust of sin, while uncertain as to the reward of righteousness?—and all the more when I have no certainty what righteousness is, or what is pleasing to God; and when I cannot ascertain whether the soul be immortal, and be such that it has anything to hope for; nor do I know what the future is certainly to be. Yet still I cannot rest from thoughts of this sort.

Chap. v.—*His design to test the immortality of the soul.*

What, then, shall I do? This I shall do. I shall proceed to Egypt, and there I shall cultivate the friendship of the hierophants or prophets, who preside at the shrines. Then I shall win over a magician by money, and entreat him, by what they call their necromantic art, to bring me a soul from the infernal regions, as if I were desirous of consulting it about some business. But this shall be my consultation, whether the soul be immortal. Now, the proof that the soul is immortal will be put past doubt, not from what it says, or from what I hear, but from what I see: for seeing it with my eyes, I shall ever after hold the surest conviction of its immortality; and no fallacy of words or uncertainty of hearing shall ever be able to disturb the persuasion produced by sight. However, I related this project to a certain philosopher with whom I was intimate, who counselled me not to venture upon it; "for," said he, "if the soul should not obey the call of the magician, you henceforth will live more hopelessly, as thinking that there is nothing after death, and also as having tried things unlawful. If, however, you seem to see anything, what religion or what piety can arise to you from things unlawful and impious? For they say that transactions of this sort are hateful to the Divinity, and that God sets Himself in opposition to those who trouble souls after their release from the body." When I heard this, I was indeed staggered in my purpose; yet I could not in any way either lay aside my longing, or cast off the distressing thought.

Chap. vi.—*Rumars of Christ.*

Not to make a long story of it, whilst I was tossed upon these billows of my thought, a certain report, which took its rise in the regions of the East in the reign of Tiberius Cæsar, gradually reached us; and gaining strength as it passed through every place, like some good message sent from God, it was filling the whole world, and suffered not the divine will to be concealed in silence. For it was spread over all places, announcing that there was a certain person in Judæa, who, beginning in the spring-time,[1] was preaching the kingdom of God to the Jews, and saying that those should receive it who should observe the ordinances of His commandments and His doctrine. And that His speech might be believed to be worthy of credit, and full of the Divinity, He was said to perform many mighty works, and wonderful signs and prodigies by His mere word; so that, as one having power from God, He made the deaf to hear, and the blind to see, and the lame to stand erect, and expelled every infirmity and all demons from men; yea, that He even raised dead persons who were brought to Him; that He cured lepers also, looking at them from a distance; and that there was absolutely nothing which seemed impossible to Him. These and such like things were confirmed in process of time, not now by frequent rumours, but by the plain statements of persons coming from those quarters; and day by day the truth of the matter was further disclosed.

Chap. vii.—*Arrival of Barnabas at Rome.*

At length meetings began to be held in various places in the city, and this subject to be discussed in conversation, and

---

[1] V. R. in the time of Tiberius Cæsar.

to be a matter of wonder who this might be who had appeared, and what message He had brought from God to men; until, about the same year, a certain man, standing in a most crowded place in the city, made proclamation to the people, saying: "Hear me, O ye citizens of Rome. The Son of God is now in the regions of Judæa, promising eternal life to every one who will hear Him, but upon condition that he shall regulate his actions according to the will of Him by whom He hath been sent, even of God the Father. Wherefore turn ye from evil things to good, from things temporal to things eternal. Acknowledge that there is one God, ruler of heaven and earth, in whose righteous sight ye unrighteous inhabit His world. But if ye be converted, and act according to His will, then, coming to the world to come, and being made immortal, ye shall enjoy His unspeakable blessings and rewards." Now, the man who spoke these things to the people was from the regions of the East, by nation a Hebrew, by name Barnabas, who said that he himself was one of His disciples, and that he was sent for this end, that he should declare these things to those who would hear them. When I heard these things, I began, with the rest of the multitude, to follow him, and to hear what he had to say. Truly I perceived that there was nothing of dialectic artifice in the man, but that he expounded with simplicity, and without any craft of speech, such things as he had heard from the Son of God, or had seen. For he did not confirm his assertions by the force of arguments, but produced, from the people who stood round about him, many witnesses of the sayings and marvels which he related.

CHAP. VIII.—*His preaching.*

Now, inasmuch as the people began to assent willingly to the things which were sincerely spoken, and to embrace his simple discourse, those who thought themselves learned or philosophic began to laugh at the man, and to flout him, and to throw out for him the grappling-hooks of syllogisms, like strong arms. But he, unterrified, regarding their subtleties as mere ravings, did not even judge them worthy of an answer, but boldly pursued the subject which he had set before him. At length, some one having proposed this question to him as he was speaking, Why a gnat has been so formed, that though it is a small creature, and has six feet, yet it has got wings in addition; whereas an elephant, though it is an immense animal, and has no wings, yet has only four feet; he, paying no attention to the question, went on with his discourse, which had been interrupted by the unseasonable challenge, only adding this admonition at every interruption : " We have it in charge to declare to you the words and the wondrous works of Him who hath sent us, and to confirm the truth of what we speak, not by artfully devised arguments, but by witnesses produced from amongst yourselves. For I recognise many standing in the midst of you whom I remember to have heard along with us the things which we have heard, and to have seen what we have seen. But be it in your option to receive or to spurn the tidings which we bring to you. For we cannot keep back what we know to be for your advantage, because, if we be silent, woe is to us; but to you, if you receive not what we speak, destruction. I could indeed very easily answer your foolish challenges, if you asked for the sake of learning truth,—I mean as to the difference of a gnat and an elephant; but now it were absurd to speak to you of these creatures, when the very Creator and Framer of all things is unknown by you."

Chap. ix.—*Clement's interposition on behalf of Barnabas.*

When he had thus spoken, all, as with one consent, with rude voice raised a shout of derision, desiring to put him to shame, and to silence him, crying out that he was a barbarian and a madman. When I saw matters going on in this way, being filled, I know not whence, with a certain zeal, and inflamed with religious enthusiasm, I could not keep silence, but cried out with all boldness, " Most righteously does Almighty God hide His will from you, whom He foresaw to be unworthy of the knowledge of Himself, as is manifest to those who are really wise, from what you are now doing. For when you see that preachers of the will of God have come amongst you, because their speech makes no show of knowledge of the grammatical art, but in simple and unpolished language they set before you the divine commands, so that all who hear may be able to follow and to understand the things that are spoken, you deride the ministers and messengers of your salvation, not knowing that it is the condemnation of you who think yourselves skilful and eloquent, that rustic and barbarous men have the knowledge of the truth; whereas, when it has come to you, it is not even received as a guest, while, if your intemperance and lust did not oppose, it ought to have been a citizen and a native. Thus you are convicted of not being friends of truth and philosophers, but followers of boasting and vain speakers. Ye think that truth dwells not in simple, but in ingenious and subtle words, and produce countless thousands of words which are not to be rated at the worth of one word. What, then, do ye think will become of you, all ye crowd of Greeks, if there is to be, as he says, a judgment of God? But now give over laughing at this man to your own destruction, and let any one of you who pleases answer me; for, indeed, by your barking you annoy the ears even of those who desire to be saved, and by your clamour you turn aside to the fall of infidelity the minds that are prepared for faith. What pardon can there be for you who deride and do violence to the messenger of the truth when he offers to you the knowledge of God? whereas, even if he brought you nothing of truth, yet, even for the kindness of his intentions towards you, you ought to receive with gratitude and welcome."

Chap. x.—*Intercourse with Barnabas.*

While I was urging these and similar arguments, a great excitement was stirred up amongst the bystanders, some being moved with pity as towards a stranger, and approving my speech as in accordance with that feeling; others, petulant and stolid, rousing the anger of their undisciplined minds as much against me as against Barnabas. But as the day was declining to evening, I laid hold of Barnabas by the right hand, and led him away, although reluctantly, to my house; and there I made him remain, lest perchance any one of the rude rabble should lay hands upon him. While we were thus placed in contact for a few days, I gladly heard him discoursing the word of truth; yet he hastened his departure, saying that he must by all means celebrate at Judæa a festal day of his religion which was approaching, and that there he should remain in future with his countrymen and his brethren, evidently indicating that he was horrified at the wrong that had been done to him.

Chap. xi.—*Departure of Barnabas.*

At length I said to him, " Only expound to me the doctrine of that man who you say has appeared, and I will arrange your sayings in my language, and will preach the kingdom and righteousness of Almighty God; and after that, if you wish it, I shall even sail along with you, for I am extremely desirous to see Judæa, and perhaps I shall remain with you always." To this he answered, " If indeed you wish to see our country, and to learn those things which you desire, set sail with me even now; or, if there be anything that detains you now, I shall leave with you directions to my dwelling, so that when you please to come you may easily find me; for to-morrow I shall set out on my journey." When I saw him determined, I went down with him to the harbour, and carefully took from him the directions which he gave me to find his dwelling. I told him that, but for the necessity of getting some money which was due to me, I should not at all delay, but that I should speedily follow him. Having told him this, I commended him to the kindness of those who had charge of the ship, and returned sad; for I was possessed of the memory of the intercourse which I had had with an excellent guest and a choice friend.

Chap. xii.—*Clement's arrival at Cæsarea, and introduction to Peter.*

Having then stopped for a few days, and having in some measure finished the business of collecting what was owing to me (for I neglected many things through my desire of hastening, that I might not be hindered from my purpose), I set sail direct for Judæa, and after fifteen days landed at Cæsarea Stratonis, which is the largest city in Palestine. When I had landed, and was seeking for an inn, I learned from the conversation of the people, that one Peter, a most approved disciple of Him who appeared in Judæa, and showed many signs and miracles divinely performed among men, was going to hold a discussion of words and questions the next day with one Simon, a Samaritan. Having heard this, I asked to be shown his lodging; and having found it, and standing before the door, I informed the doorkeeper who I was, and whence I came; and, behold, Barnabas coming out, as soon as he saw me rushed into my arms, weeping for joy, and, seizing me by the hand, led me in to Peter. Having pointed him out to me at a distance, "This," said he, "is Peter, of whom I spoke to you as the greatest in the wisdom of God, and to whom also I have spoken constantly of you. Enter, therefore, as one well known to him. For he is well acquainted with all the good that is in thee, and has carefully made himself aware of your religious purpose, whence also he is greatly desirous to see you. Therefore I present you to him to-day as a great gift." At the same time, presenting me, he said, "This, O Peter, is Clement."

Chap. XIII.—*His cordial reception by Peter.*

But Peter most kindly, when he heard my name, immediately ran to me and kissed me. Then, having made me sit down, he said, "Thou didst well to receive as thy guest Barnabas, preacher of the truth, nothing fearing the rage of the insane people. Thou shalt be blessed. For as you have deemed an ambassador of the truth worthy of all honour, so the truth herself shall receive thee a wanderer and a stranger, and shall enroll thee a citizen of her own city; and then there shall be great joy to thee, because, imparting a small favour, thou shalt be written heir of eternal blessings. Now, therefore, do not trouble yourself to explain your mind to me; for Barnabas has with faithful speech informed me of all things about you and your dispositions, almost daily and without ceasing, recalling the memory of your good qualities. And to point out to you shortly, as to a friend already of one mind with us, what is your best course ; if there is nothing to hinder you, come along with us, and hear the word of the truth, which we are going to speak in every place until we come even to the city of Rome ; and now, if you wish anything, speak."

Chap. xiv.—*His account of himself.*

Having detailed to him what purpose I had conceived from the beginning, and how I had been distracted with vain inquiries, and all those things which at first I intimated to thee, my lord James, so that I need not repeat the same things now, I willingly agreed to travel with him ; "for that," said I, "is just what I was most eagerly desirous of. But first I should wish the scheme of truth to be expounded to me, that I may know whether the soul is mortal or immortal ; and if immortal, whether it shall be brought into judgment for those things which it does here. Further, I desire to know what that righteousness is, which is pleasing to God ; then, further, whether the world was created, and why it was created, and whether it is to be dissolved, and whether it is to be renovated and made better, or whether after this there shall be no world at all ; and, not to mention everything, I should wish to be told what is the case with respect to these and such like things." To this Peter answered, " I shall briefly impart to you the knowledge of these things, O Clement : therefore listen.

Chap. xv.—*Peter's first instruction : causes of ignorance.*

" The will and counsel of God has for many reasons been concealed from men ; first, indeed, through bad instruction, wicked associations, evil habits, unprofitable conversation, and unrighteous presumptions. On account of all these, I say, first error, then contempt, then infidelity and malice, covetousness also, and vain boasting, and other such like evils, have filled the whole house of this world, like some enormous smoke, and preventing those who dwell in it from seeing its Founder aright, and from perceiving what things are pleasing to Him. What, then, is fitting for those who are within, excepting with a cry brought forth from their inmost hearts to invoke His aid, who alone is not shut up in the smoke-filled house, that He would approach and open the door of the house, so that the smoke may be dissipated which is within, and the light of the sun which shines without may be admitted?

Chap. XVI.—*Instruction continued: the true Prophet.*

"He, therefore, whose aid is needed for the house filled with the darkness of ignorance and the smoke of vices, is He, we say, who is called the true Prophet, who alone can enlighten the souls of men, so that with their eyes they may plainly see the way of safety. For otherwise it is impossible to get knowledge of divine and eternal things, unless one learns of that true Prophet; because, as you yourself stated a little ago, the belief of things, and the opinions of causes, are estimated in proportion to the talents of their advocates: hence, also, one and the same cause is now thought just, now unjust; and what now seemed true, anon becomes false on the assertion of another. For this reason, the credit of religion and piety demanded the presence of the true Prophet, that He Himself might tell us respecting each particular, how the truth stands, and might teach us how we are to believe concerning each. And therefore, before all else, the credentials of the prophet himself must be examined with all care; and when you have once ascertained that he is a prophet, it behoves you thenceforth to believe him in everything, and not further to discuss the particulars which he teaches, but to hold the things which he speaks as certain and sacred; which things, although they seem to be received by faith, yet are believed on the ground of the probation previously instituted. For when once at the outset the truth of the prophet is established on examination, the rest is to be heard and held on the ground of the faith by which it is already established that he is a teacher of truth. And as it is certain that all things which pertain to divine knowledge ought to be held according to the rule of truth, so it is beyond doubt that from none but Himself alone can it be known what is true."

CHAP. XVII.—*Peter requests him to be his attendant.*

Having thus spoken, he set forth to me so openly and so clearly who that Prophet was, and how He might be found, that I seemed to have before my eyes, and to handle with my hand, the proofs which he produced concerning the prophetic truth; and I was struck with intense astonishment, how no one sees, though placed before his eyes, those things which all are seeking for. Whence, by his command, reducing into order what he had spoken to me, I compiled a book concerning the true Prophet, and sent it to you from Cæsarea by his command. For he said that he had received a command from you to send you every year an account of his sayings and doings. Meantime, at the beginning of his discourse which he delivered to me the first day, when he had instructed me very fully concerning the true Prophet, and very many things besides, he added also this: "See," said he, "for the future, and be present at the discussions which, whenever any necessity arises, I shall hold with those who contradict; against whom, when I dispute, even if I shall seem to be worsted, I shall not be afraid of your being led to doubt of those things which I have stated to you; because, even if I shall seem to be beaten, yet those things shall not therefore seem to be uncertain which the true Prophet has delivered to us. Yet I hope that we shall not be overcome in disputations either, if only our hearers are reasonable, and friends of truth, who can discern the force and bearing of words, and recognise what discourse comes from the sophistical art, not containing truth, but an image of truth; and what that is, which, uttered simply and without craft, depends for all its power not on show and ornament, but on truth and reason."

CHAP. XVIII.—*His profiting by Peter's instruction.*

To this I answered: "I give thanks to God Almighty, because I have been instructed as I wished and desired. At all events, you may depend upon me so far, that I can never come to doubt of those things which I have learned of you; so that even if you yourself should at any time wish to transfer my faith from the true Prophet, you should not be able, because I have drunk in with all my heart what you have spoken. And that you may not think that I am promising you a great thing when I say that I cannot be moved away from this faith, it is with me a certainty, that whoever has received this account of the true Prophet, can never afterwards so much as doubt of its truth. And therefore I am confident with respect to this heaven-taught doctrine, in which all the art of malice is overborne. For in opposition to [this] prophecy neither any art can stand, nor the subtleties of sophisms and syllogisms; but every one who hears of the true Prophet must of necessity long immediately for the truth itself, nor will he afterwards, under pretext of seeking the truth, endure diverse errors. Wherefore, O my lord Peter, be not further anxious about me, as if I were one who does not know what he has received, and how great a gift has been conferred on him. Be assured that you have conferred a favour on one who knows and understands its value: nor can I be easily deceived on that account, because I seem to have gotten quickly what I long desired; for it may be that one who desires gets quickly, while another does not even slowly attain the things which he desires."

Chap. xix.—*Peter's satisfaction.*

Then Peter, when he heard me speak thus, said: "I give thanks to my God, both for your salvation and for my own peace; for I am greatly delighted to see that you have understood what is the greatness of the prophetic virtue, and because, as you say, not even I myself, if I should wish it (which God forbid!), should be able to turn you away to another faith. Now henceforth begin to be with us, and to-morrow be present at our discussions, for I am to have a contest with Simon the magician." When he had thus spoken, he retired to take food along with his friends; but he ordered me to eat by myself; and after the meal, when he had sung praise to God and given thanks, he rendered to me an account of this proceeding, and added, " May the Lord grant to thee to be made like to us in all things, that, receiving baptism, thou mayest be able to meet with us at the same table." Having thus spoken, he ordered me to go to rest, for by this time both fatigue and the time of the day called to sleep.

CHAP. XX.—*Postponement of discussion with Simon Magus.*

Early next morning Zaccheus came in to us, and after salutation, said to Peter: " Simon puts off the discussion till the eleventh day of the present month, which is seven days hence, for he says that then he will have more leisure for the contest. But to me it seems that his putting off is also advantageous to us, so that more may come together, who may be either hearers or judges of our disputation. However, if it seem proper to you, let us occupy the interval in discussing among ourselves the things which, we suppose, may come into the controversy; so that each of us, knowing what things are to be proposed, and what answers are to be given, may consider with himself if they are all right, or if an adversary shall be able to find anything to object, or to set aside the things which we bring against him. But if the things which are to be spoken by us are manifestly impregnable on every side, we shall have confidence in entering upon the examination. And indeed, this is my opinion, that first of all it ought to be inquired what is the origin of all things, or what is the immediate[1] thing which may be called the cause of all things which are : then, with respect to all things that exist, whether they have been made, and by whom, through whom, and for whom; whether they have received their subsistence from one, or from two, or from many; and whether they have been taken and fashioned from none [previously] subsisting, or from some : then, whether there is any virtue in the highest things, or in the lower; whether there is anything which is better than all, or anything that is inferior to all; whether there are any motions, or none; whether those things which are seen were always, and shall be always; whether they have

1 Here we follow a marginal reading.

come into existence without a creator, and shall pass away
without a destroyer. If, I say, the discussion begin with
these things, I think that the things which shall be inquired
into, being discussed with diligent examination, will be easily
ascertained. And when these are ascertained, the knowledge
of those that follow will be easily found. I have stated my
opinion; be pleased to intimate what you think of the matter."

CHAP. XXI.—*Advantage of the delay.*

To this Peter answered: "Tell Simon in the meantime to
do as he pleases, and to rest assured that, Divine Providence
granting, he shall always find us ready." Then Zaccheus
went out to intimate to Simon what he had been told. But
Peter, looking at us, and perceiving that I was saddened by
the putting off of the contest, said: "He who believes that the
world is administered by the providence of the Most High
God, ought not, O Clement, my friend, to take it amiss, in
whatever way particular things happen, being assured that
the righteousness of God guides to a favourable and fitting
issue even those things which seem superfluous or contrary in
any business, and especially towards those who worship Him
more intimately; and therefore he who is assured of these
things, as I have said, if anything occur contrary to his expectation, he knows how to drive away grief from his mind on
that account, holding it unquestionable in his better judgment,
that, by the government of the good God, even what seems
contrary may be turned to good. Wherefore, O Clement,
even now let not this delay of the magician Simon sadden
you: for I believe that it has been done by the providence of
God, for your advantage; that I may be able, in this interval
of seven days, to expound to you the method of our faith
without any distraction, and the order continuously, according to the tradition of the true Prophet, who alone knows
the past as it was, the present as it is, and the future as it
shall be: which things were indeed plainly spoken [by Him],
but are not plainly written; so much so, that when they are
read, they cannot be understood without an expounder, on
account of the sin which has grown up with men, as I said

before. Therefore I shall explain all things to you, that in those things which are written you may clearly perceive what is the mind of the Lawgiver."

CHAP. XXII.—*Repetition of instructions.*

When he had said this, he began to expound to me point by point of those chapters of the law which seemed to be in question, from the beginning of the creation even to that point of time at which I came to him at Cæsarea, telling me that the delay of Simon had contributed to my learning all things in order. "At other times," said he, "we shall discourse more fully on individual points of which we have now spoken shortly, according as the occasion of our conversation shall bring them before us; so that, according to my promise, you may gain a full and perfect knowledge of all. Since, then, by this delay we have to-day on our hands, I wish to repeat to you again what has been spoken, that it may be the better recalled to your memory." Then he began in this way to refresh my recollection of what he had said: "Do you remember, O friend Clement, the account I gave you of the eternal age, that knows no end?" Then said I, "Never, O Peter, shall I retain anything, if I can lose or forget that."

CHAP. XXIII.—*Repetition continued.*

Then Peter, having heard my answer with pleasure, said: "I congratulate you because you have answered thus, not because you speak of these things easily, but because you profess that you remember them; for the most sublime truths are best honoured by means of silence. Yet, for the credit of those things which you remember concerning things not to be spoken,[1] tell me what you retain of those things which we spoke of in the second place, which can easily be spoken out, that, perceiving your tenacity of memory, I may the more readily point out to you, and freely open, the things of which I wish to speak." Then I, when I perceived that he rejoiced in the good memory of his hearers, said: "Not only am I mindful of your definition, but also of that preface which was

[1] That is, that I may be sure that you remember these things.

prefixed to the definition ; and of almost all things that you have expounded, I retain the sense complete, though not all the words ; because the things that you have spoken have been made, as it were, native to my soul, and inborn. For you have held out a most sweet cup to me in my excessive thirst. And that you may not suppose that I am occupying you with words, being unmindful of things, I shall now call to mind the things which were spoken, in which the order of your discussion greatly helps me ; for the way in which the things that you said followed by consequence upon one another, and were arranged in a balanced manner, makes them easily recalled to memory by the lines of their order. For the order of sayings is useful for remembering them : for when you begin to follow them point by point in succession, when anything is wanting, immediately the sense seeks for it ; and when it has found it, retains it, or at all events, if it cannot discover it, there will be no reluctance to ask it of the master. But not to delay in granting what you demand of me, I shall shortly rehearse what you delivered to me concerning the definition of truth.

Chap. xxiv.—*Repetition continued.*

"There always was, there is now, and there ever shall be, that by which the first Will begotten from eternity consists ; and from the first Will [proceeds] a second Will. After these came the world ; and from the world came time : from this, the multitude of men ; from the multitude the election of the beloved, from whose oneness of mind the peaceful kingdom of God is constructed. But the rest, which ought to follow these, you promised to tell me at another time. After this, when you had explained about the creation of the world, you intimated the decree of God, " which He, of His own good pleasure, announced in the presence of all the first angels," and which He ordained as an eternal law to all ; and how He established two kingdoms,—I mean that of the present time and that of the future,—and appointed times to each, and decreed that a day of judgment should be expected, which He determined, in which a severance is to be made of things and of souls: so that the wicked indeed shall be consigned to eternal fire for their sins; but those who have lived according to the will of God the Creator, having received a blessing for their good works, effulgent with brightest light, introduced into an eternal abode, and abiding in incorruption, shall receive eternal gifts of ineffable blessings."

CHAP. XXV.—*Repetition continued.*

While I was going on thus, Peter, enraptured with joy, and anxious for me as if I had been his son, lest perhaps I should fail in recollection of the rest, and be put to shame on account of those who were present, said: "It is enough, O Clement; for you have stated these things more clearly than I myself explained them." Then said I, "Liberal learning has conferred upon me the power of orderly narration, and of stating those things clearly for which there is occasion. And if we use learning in asserting the errors of antiquity, we ruin ourselves by gracefulness and smoothness of speech; but if we apply learning and grace of speech to the assertion of the truth, I think that not a little advantage is thereby gained. Be that as it may, my lord Peter, you can but imagine with what thankfulness I am transported for all the rest of your instruction indeed, but especially for the statement of that doctrine which you gave: There is one God, whose work the world is, and who, because He is in all respects righteous, shall render to every one according to his deeds. And after that you added: For the assertion of this dogma countless thousands of words will be brought forward; but in those to whom is granted knowledge of the true Prophet, all this forest of words is cut down. And on this account, since you have delivered to me a discourse concerning the true Prophet, you have strengthened me with all confidence of your assertions." And then, having perceived that the sum of all religion and piety consists in this, I immediately replied: "You have proceeded most excellently, O Peter: wherefore, in future, expound unhesitatingly, as to one who already knows what are the foundations of faith and piety, the traditions of the true Prophet, who alone, as has been clearly

proved, is to be believed.   But that exposition which requires
assertions and arguments, reserve for the unbelievers, to whom
you have not yet judged it proper to commit the indubitable
faith of prophetic grace." When I had said this, I added :
"You promised that you would give at the proper time
two things : first this exposition, at once simple and entirely
free from error; and then an exposition of each individual
point as it may be evolved in the course of the various questions which shall be raised.   And after this you expounded
the sequence of things in order from the beginning of the
world, even to the present time ; and if you please, I can
repeat the whole from memory."

Chap. XXVI.—*Friendship of God; how secured.*

To this Peter answered : " I am exceedingly delighted, O
Clement, that I commit my words to so safe a heart ; for to
be mindful of the things that are spoken is an indication of
having in readiness the faith of works.   But he from whom
the wicked demon steals away the words of salvation, and
snatches them away from his memory, cannot be saved, even
though he wish it ; for he loses the way by which life is
reached.   Wherefore let us the rather repeat what has been
spoken, and confirm it in your heart, that is, in what manner
or by whom the world was made, that we may proceed to the
friendship of the Creator.   But His friendship is secured by
living well, and by obeying His will ; which will is the law
of all that live.   We shall therefore unfold these things
briefly to you, in order that they may be the more surely
remembered.

Chap. XXVII.—*Account of the creation.*

" In the beginning, when God had made the heaven and the
earth,[1] as one house, the shadow which was cast by the mun-
dane bodies involved in darkness those things which were
enclosed in it.   But when the will of God had introduced
light, that darkness which had been caused by the shadows
of bodies was straightway dispelled : then at length light is

[1] Gen. i. 1.

L

appointed for the day, darkness for the night. And now the water which was within the world, in the middle space of that first heaven and earth, congealed as if with frost, and solid as crystal, is distended, and the middle spaces of the heaven and earth are separated as by a firmament of this sort; and that firmament the Creator called heaven, so called by the name of that previously made: and so He divided into two portions that fabric of the universe, although it was but one house. The reason of the division was this, that the upper portion might afford a dwelling-place to angels, and the lower to men. After this, the place of the sea and the chaos which had been made received that portion of the waters which remained below, by order of the eternal Will; and these flowing down to the sunk and hollow places, the dry land appeared; and the gatherings of the waters were made seas. And after this the earth, which had appeared, produced various species of herbs and shrubs. It gave forth fountains also, and rivers, not only in the plains, but on the mountains. And so all things were prepared, that men who were to dwell in it might have it in their power to use all these things according to their will, that is, either for good or evil.

Chap. XXVIII.—*Account of the creation continued.*

" After this He adorns that visible heaven with stars. He places in it also the sun and the moon, that the day might enjoy the light of the one, the night that of the other; and that at the same time they might be for an indication of things past, present, and future. For they were made for signs of seasons and of days, which, although they are seen indeed by all, are understood only by the learned and intelligent. And when, after this, He had ordered living creatures to be produced from the earth and the waters, he made Paradise, which also He named a place of delights. But after all these things He made man, on whose account He had prepared all things, whose internal species[1] is older, and for whose sake all things that are were made, given up to his service, and assigned to the uses of his habitation.

[1] That is, his soul, according to the doctrine of the pre-existence of souls.

Chap. xxix.—*The giants: the flood.*

"All things therefore being completed which are in heaven, and in earth, and in the waters, and the human race also having multiplied, in the eighth generation, righteous men, who had lived the life of angels, being allured by the beauty of women, fell into promiscuous and illicit connections with these;[1] and thenceforth acting in all things without discretion, and disorderly, they changed the state of human affairs and the divinely prescribed order of life, so that either by persuasion or force they compelled all men to sin against God their Creator. In the ninth generation are born the giants, so called from of old,[2] not dragon-footed, as the fables of the Greeks relate, but men of immense bodies, whose bones, of enormous size, are still shown in some places for confirmation. But against these the righteous providence of God brought a flood upon the world, that the earth might be purified from their pollution, and every place might be turned into a sea by the destruction of the wicked. Yet there was then found one righteous man, by name Noah, who, being delivered in an ark with his three sons and their wives, became the colonizer of the world after the subsiding of the waters, with those animals and seeds which he had shut up with him.

Chap. xxx.—*Noah's sons.*

"In the twelfth generation, when God had blessed men, and they had begun to multiply,[3] they received a commandment that they should not taste blood, for on account of this also the deluge had been sent. In the thirteenth generation, when the second of Noah's three sons had done an injury to his father, and had been cursed by him, he brought the

---

[1] Gen. vi. 2.

[2] The writer here translates the words of the Septuagint, οἱ γίγαντες οἱ ἀπ᾽ αἰῶνος οἱ ἄνθρωποι οἱ ὀνομαστοί, illi qui a seculo nominantur. We have given the translation of our authorized version. It is likely, however, that the writer believed the name to imply that they lived to a great age, as is maintained by Diodorus quoted by Suicer on the word, or he may have traced the word to γῆ.

[3] Gen. ix. 1.

condition of slavery upon his posterity. His elder brother meantime obtained the lot of a dwelling-place in the middle region of the world, in which is the country of Judæa; the younger obtained the eastern quarter, and he the western. In the fourteenth generation one of the cursed progeny first erected an altar to demons, for the purpose of magical arts, and offered there bloody sacrifices. In the fifteenth generation, for the first time, men set up an idol and worshipped it. Until that time the Hebrew language, which had been given by God to men, bore sole sway. In the sixteenth generation the sons of men migrated from the east, and, coming to the lands that had been assigned to their fathers, each one marked the place of his own allotment by his own name. In the seventeenth generation Nimrod I. reigned in Babylonia, and built a city, and thence migrated to the Persians, and taught them to worship fire.

CHAP. XXXI.—*World after the flood.*

"In the eighteenth generation walled cities were built, armies were organized and armed, judges and laws were sanctioned, temples were built, and the princes of nations were adored as gods. In the nineteenth generation the descendants of him who had been cursed after the flood, going beyond their proper bounds which they had obtained by lot in the western regions, drove into the eastern lands those who had obtained the middle portion of the world, and pursued them as far as Persia, while themselves violently took possession of the country from which they expelled them. In the twentieth generation a son for the first time died before his father,[1] on account of an incestuous crime.

CHAP. XXXII.—*Abraham.*

"In the twenty-first generation there was a certain wise man, of the race of those who were expelled, of the family of Noah's eldest son, by name Abraham, from whom our Hebrew nation is derived. When the whole world was again overspread with errors, and when for the hideousness of its

[1] Gen. xi. 28.

crimes destruction was ready for it, this time not by water, but fire, and when already the scourge was hanging over the whole earth, beginning with Sodom, this man, by reason of his friendship with God, who was well pleased with him, obtained from God that the whole world should not equally perish. From the first this same man, being an astrologer, was able, from the account and order of the stars, to recognise the Creator, while all others were in error, and understood that all things are regulated by His providence. Whence also an angel,[1] standing by him in a vision, instructed him more fully concerning those things which he was beginning to perceive. He showed him also what belonged to his race and posterity, and promised him that those districts should be restored rather than given to them.

Chap. XXXIII.—*Abraham : his posterity.*

"Therefore Abraham, when he was desirous to learn the causes of things, and was intently pondering upon what had been told him, the true Prophet appeared to him, who alone knows the hearts and purpose of men, and disclosed to him all things which he desired. He taught him the knowledge of the Divinity; intimated the origin of the world, and likewise its end; showed him the immortality of the soul, and the manner of life which was pleasing to God; declared also the resurrection of the dead, the future judgment, the reward of the good, the punishment of the evil,—all to be regulated by righteous judgment: and having given him all this information plainly and sufficiently, He departed again to the invisible abodes. But while Abraham was still in ignorance, as we said to you before, two sons were born to him, of whom the one was called Ismael, and the other Heliesdros. From the one are descended the barbarous nations, from the other the people of the Persians, some of whom have adopted the manner of living and the institutions of their neighbours, the Brachmans. Others settled in Arabia, of whose posterity some also have spread into Egypt. From them some of the Indians and of the Egyptians have learned to be circumcised,

---

[1] Gen. xv. xxii.

and to be of purer observance than others, although in process
of time most of them have turned to impiety what was the
proof and sign of purity.

Chap. xxxiv.—*The Israelites in Egypt.*

"Nevertheless, as he had got these two sons during the time
while he still lived in ignorance of things, having received the
knowledge of God, he asked of the Righteous One that he
might merit to have offspring by Sarah, who was his lawful
wife, though she was barren. She obtained a son, whom he
named Isaac, from whom came Jacob, and from him the
twelve patriarchs, and from these twelve seventy-two. These,
when famine befell, came into Egypt with all their family;
and in the course of four hundred years, being multiplied by
the blessing and promise of God, they were afflicted by the
Egyptians. And when they were afflicted the true Prophet
appeared to Moses,[1] and struck the Egyptians with ten
plagues, when they refused to let the Hebrew people depart
from them, and return to their native land; and he brought
the people of God out of Egypt. But those of the Egyptians
who survived the plagues, being infected with the animosity
of their king, pursued after the Hebrews. And when they
had overtaken them at the sea-shore, and thought to destroy
and exterminate them all, Moses, pouring out prayer to God,
divided the sea into two parts, so that the water was held
on the right hand and on the left as if it had been frozen,
and the people of God passed as over a dry road; but the
Egyptians who were pursuing them, rashly entering, were
drowned. For when the last of the Hebrews came out, the
last of the Egyptians went down into the sea; and straightway the waters of the sea, which by his command were held
bound as with frost, were loosed by his command who had
bound them, and recovering their natural freedom, inflicted
punishment on the wicked nation.

Chap. xxxv.—*The Exodus.*

" After this, Moses, by the command of God, whose provi-

[1] Exod. iii.

dence is over all, led out the people of the Hebrews into the wilderness ; and, leaving the shortest road which leads from Egypt to Judæa, he led the people through long windings of the wilderness, that, by the discipline of forty years, the novelty of a changed manner of life might root out the evils which had clung to them by a long-continued familiarity with the customs of the Egyptians. Meantime they came to Mount Sinai, and thence the law was given to them with voices and sights from heaven, written in ten precepts, of which the first and greatest was that they should worship God Himself alone, and not make to themselves any appearance or form[1] to worship. But when Moses had gone up to the mount, and was staying there forty days, the people, although they had seen Egypt struck with the ten plagues, and the sea parted and passed over by them on foot, manna also given to them from heaven for bread, and drink supplied to them out of the rock that followed[2] them, which kind of food was turned into whatever taste any one desired ; and although, being placed under the torrid region of heaven, they were shaded by a cloud in the day-time, that they might not be scorched by the heat, and by night were enlightened by a pillar of fire, lest the horror of darkness should be added to the wasteness of the wilderness;—those very people, I say, when Moses stayed in the mount, made and worshipped a golden calf's head, after the fashion of Apis, whom they had seen worshipped in Egypt; and after so many and so great marvels which they had seen, were unable to cleanse and wash out from themselves the defilements of old habit. On this account, leaving the short road which leads from Egypt to Judæa, Moses conducted them by an immense circuit of the desert, if haply he might be able, as we mentioned before, to shake off the evils of old habit by the change of a new education.

CHAP. XXXVI.—*Allowance of sacrifice for a time.*

"When meantime Moses, that faithful and wise steward, perceived that the vice of sacrificing to idols had been deeply

---

[1] That is, picture or statue.　　　　[2] Comp. 1 Cor. x. 4.

ingrained into the people from their association with the
Egyptians, and that the root of this evil could not be extracted from them, he allowed them indeed to sacrifice, but
permitted it to be done only to God, that by any means he
might cut off one half of the deeply ingrained evil, leaving
the other half to be corrected by another, and at a future
time; by Him, namely, concerning whom he said himself, ' A
prophet shall the Lord your God raise unto you, whom ye
shall hear even as myself, according to all things which He
shall say to you. Whosoever shall not hear that prophet, his
soul shall be cut off from his people.' [1]

Chap. xxxvii.—*The holy place.*

"In addition to these things, he also appointed a place in
which alone it should be lawful to them to sacrifice to God.[2]
And all this was arranged with this view, that when the fitting
time should come, and they should learn by means of the
Prophet that God desires mercy and not sacrifice,[3] they might
see Him who should teach them that the place chosen of
God, in which it was suitable that victims should be offered
to God, is his Wisdom; and that on the other hand they
might hear that this place, which seemed chosen for a time,
often harassed as it had been by hostile invasions and plunderings, was at last to be wholly destroyed.[4] And in order
to impress this upon them, even before the coming of the true
Prophet, who was to reject at once the sacrifices and the
place, it was often plundered by enemies and burnt with fire,
and the people carried into captivity among foreign nations,
and then brought back when they betook themselves to the
mercy of God; that by these things they might be taught
that a people who offer sacrifices are driven away and
delivered up into the hands of the enemy, but they who do
mercy and righteousness are without sacrifices freed from
captivity, and restored to their native land. But it fell out
that very few understood this; for the greater number,
though they could perceive and observe these things, yet

[1] Deut. xviii. 15 ; Acts iii. 22, 23.   [2] Deut. xii. 11 ; 2 Chron. vii. 12.
[3] Hos. vi. 6 ; Matt. ix. 13, xii. 7.   [4] Matt. xxiv. 2 ; Luke xix. 44.

were held by the irrational opinion of the vulgar : for right opinion with liberty is the prerogative of a few.

Chap. xxxviii.—*Sins of the Israelites.*

"Moses,[1] then, having arranged these things, and having set over the people one Ausès to bring them to the land of their fathers, himself by the command of the living God went up to a certain mountain, and there died. Yet such was the manner of his death, that till this day no one has found his burial-place. When, therefore, the people reached their fathers' land, by the providence of God, at their first onset the inhabitants of wicked races are routed, and they enter upon their paternal inheritance, which was distributed among them by lot. For some time thereafter they were ruled not by kings, but judges, and remained in a somewhat peaceful condition. But when they sought for themselves tyrants rather than kings, then also with regal ambition they erected a temple in the place which had been appointed to them for prayer ; and thus, through a succession of wicked kings, the people fell away to greater and still greater impiety.

Chap. xxxix.—*Baptism instituted in place of sacrifices.*

"But when the time began to draw near that what was wanting in the Mosaic institutions should be supplied, as we have said, and that the Prophet should appear, of whom he had foretold that He should warn them by the mercy of God to cease from sacrificing ; lest haply they might suppose that on the cessation of sacrifice there was no remission of sins for them, He instituted baptism by water amongst them, in which they might be absolved from all their sins on the invocation of His name, and for the future, following a perfect life, might abide in immortality, being purified not by the blood of beasts, but by the purification of the Wisdom of God. Subsequently also an evident proof of this great mystery is supplied [in the fact], that every one who, believing in this Prophet who had been foretold by Moses, is baptized in His name, shall be kept unhurt from the destruction of war which

[1] Deut. xxxi.–xxxiv.

impends over the unbelieving nation, and the place itself; but that those who do not believe shall be made exiles from their place and kingdom, that even against their will they may understand and obey the will of God.

Chap. xl.—*Advent of the true Prophet.*

" These things therefore having been fore-arranged, He who was expected comes, bringing signs and miracles as His credentials by which He should be made manifest. But not even so did the people believe, though they had been trained during so many ages to the belief of these things. And not only did they not believe, but they added blasphemy to un-belief, saying that He was a gluttonous man and a belly-slave, and that He was actuated by a demon,[1] even He who had come for their salvation. To such an extent does wicked-ness prevail by the agency of evil ones; so that, but for the Wisdom of God assisting those who love the truth, almost all would have been involved in impious delusion. There-fore He chose us twelve,[2] the first who believed in Him, whom He named apostles; and afterwards other seventy-two most approved disciples,[3] that, at least in this way recog-nising the pattern of Moses,[4] the multitude might believe that this is He of whom Moses foretold, the Prophet that was to come.[5]

Chap. xli.—*Rejection of the true Prophet.*

" But some one perhaps may say that it is possible for any one to imitate a number; but what shall he say of the signs and miracles which He wrought? For Moses had wrought miracles and cures in Egypt. He also of whom he foretold that He should rise up a prophet like unto himself, though He cured every sickness and infirmity among the people, wrought innumerable miracles, and preached eternal life, was hurried •by wicked men to the cross; which deed was, however, by His power turned to good. In short, while He was suffering, all the world suffered with Him; for the sun was darkened, the

[1] Matt. ix.; John. vii. [2] Matt. x. [3] Luke x.
[4] Num. xi. 16. [5] Deut. xviii. 15.

mountains were torn asunder, the graves were opened, the veil of the temple was rent,[1] as in lamentation for the destruction impending over the place. And yet, though all the world was moved, they themselves are not even now moved to the consideration of these so great things.

Chap. XLII.—*Call of the Gentiles.*

" But inasmuch as it was necessary that the Gentiles should be called into the room of those who remained unbelieving, so that the number might be filled up which had been shown to Abraham,[2] the preaching of the blessed kingdom of God is sent into all the world. On this account worldly spirits are disturbed, who always oppose those who are in quest of liberty, and who make use of the engines of error to destroy God's building; while those who press on to the glory of safety and liberty, being rendered braver by their resistance to these spirits, and by the toil of great struggles against them, attain the crown of safety not without the palm of victory. Meantime, when He had suffered, and darkness had overwhelmed the world from the sixth even to the ninth hour,[3] as soon as the sun shone out again, and things were returned to their usual course, even wicked men returned to themselves and their former practices, their fear having abated. For some of them, watching the place with all care, when they could not prevent His rising again, said that He was a magician ; others pretended that He was stolen away.[4]

Chap. XLIII.—*Success of the gospel.*

" Nevertheless, the truth everywhere prevailed; for, in proof that these things were done by divine power, we who had been very few became in the course of a few days, by the help of God, far more than they. So that the priests at one time were afraid, lest haply, by the providence of God, to their confusion, the whole of the people should come over to our faith. Therefore they often sent to us, and asked us to discourse to them concerning Jesus, whether He were the Pro-

[1] Matt. xxvii. 45, 51, 52. [2] Gen. xv. ; Acts xiii.
[3] Matt. xxvii. 45. [4] Matt. xxviii. 13.

phet whom Moses foretold, who is the eternal Christ.[1] For on this point only does there seem to be any difference between us who believe in Jesus, and the unbelieving Jews. But while they often made such requests to us, and we sought for a fitting opportunity, a week of years was completed from the passion of the Lord, the church of the Lord which was constituted in Jerusalem was most plentifully multiplied and grew, being governed with most righteous ordinances by James, who was ordained bishop in it by the Lord.

Chap. xliv.—*Challenge by Caiaphas.*

"But when we twelve apostles, on the day of the passover, had come together with an immense multitude, and entered into the church of the brethren, each one of us, at the request of James, stated briefly, in the hearing of the people, what we had done in every place. While this was going on, Caiaphas, the high priest, sent priests to us, and asked us to come to him, that either we should prove to him that Jesus is the eternal Christ, or he to us that He is not, and that so all the people should agree upon the one faith or the other; and this he frequently entreated us to do. But we often put it off, always seeking for a more convenient time."

Then I, Clement, answered to this : "I think that this very question, whether He is the Christ, is of great importance for the establishment of the faith ; otherwise the high priest would not so frequently ask that he might either learn or teach concerning the Christ."

Then Peter : "You have answered rightly, O Clement ; for as no one can see without eyes, nor hear without ears, nor smell without nostrils, nor taste without a tongue, nor handle anything without hands, so it is impossible, without the true Prophet, to know what is pleasing to God."

And I answered : "I have already learned from your instruction that this true prophet is the Christ ; but I should wish to learn what *the Christ* means, or why He is so called, that a matter of so great importance may not be vague and uncertain to me."

[1] John xii. 34.

CHAP. XLV.—*The true Prophet: why called the Christ.*

Then Peter began to instruct me in this manner : " When God had made the world, as Lord of the universe, He appointed chiefs over the several creatures, over the trees even, and the mountains, and the fountains, and the rivers, and all things which He had made, as we have told you ; for it were too long to mention them one by one.   He set, therefore, an angel as chief over the angels, a spirit over the spirits, a star over the stars, a demon over the demons, a bird over the birds, a beast over the beasts, a serpent over the serpents, a fish over the fishes, a man over men, who is Christ Jesus.   But He is called *Christ* by a certain excellent rite of religion ; for as there are certain names common to kings, as Arsaces among the Persians, Cæsar among the Romans, Pharaoh among the Egyptians, so among the Jews a king is called *Christ*.   And the reason of this appellation is this : Although indeed He was the Son of God, and the beginning of all things, He became man ; Him first God anointed with oil which was taken from the wood of the tree of life : from that anointing therefore He is called *Christ*.   Thence, moreover, He Himself also, according to the appointment of His Father, anoints with similar oil every one of the pious when they come to His kingdom, for their refreshment after their labours, as having got over the difficulties of the way; so that their light may shine, and being filled with the Holy Spirit, they may be endowed with immortality.   But it occurs to me that I have sufficiently explained to you the whole nature of that branch from which that ointment is taken.

CHAP. XLVI.—*Anointing.*

" But now also I shall, by a very short representation, recall you to the recollection of all these things.   In the present life, Aaron, the first high priest,[1] was anointed with a composition of chrism, which was made after the pattern of that spiritual ointment of which we have spoken before.   He was prince of the people, and as a king received first-fruits

[1] Exod. xxix. ; Lev. viii.

and tribute from the people, man by man ; and having under-taken the office of judging the people, he judged of things clean and things unclean. But if any one else was anointed with the same ointment, as deriving virtue from it, he became either king, or prophet, or priest. If, then, this temporal grace, compounded by men, had such efficacy, consider now how potent was that ointment extracted by God from a branch of the tree of life, when that which was made by men could confer so excellent dignities among men. For what in the present age is more glorious than a prophet, more illustrious than a priest, more exalted than a king?"

Chap. xlvii.—*Adam anointed a prophet.*

To this I replied : " I remember, Peter, that you told me of the first man that he was a prophet; but you did not say that he was anointed. If then there be no prophet without anointing, how could the first man be a prophet, since he was not anointed ?" Then Peter, smiling, said : " If the first man prophesied, it is certain that he was also anointed. For al-though he who has recorded the law in his pages is silent as to his anointing, yet he has evidently left us to understand these things. For as, if he had said that he was anointed, it would not be doubted that he was also a prophet, although it were not written in the law; so, since it is certain that he was a prophet, it is in like manner certain that he was also anointed, because without anointing he could not be a pro-phet. But you should rather have said, If the chrism was compounded by Aaron, by the perfumer's art, how could the first man be anointed before Aaron's time, the arts of com-position not yet having been discovered ?"   Then I answered, " Do not misunderstand me, Peter ; for I do not speak of that compounded ointment and temporal oil, but of that simple and eternal [ointment], which you told me was made by God, after whose likeness you say that that other was com-pounded by men."

Chap. xlviii.—*The true Prophet, a priest.*

Then Peter answered, with an appearance of indignation :

"What! do you suppose, Clement, that all of us can know all things before the time? But not to be drawn aside now from our proposed discourse, we shall at another time, when your progress is more manifest, explain these things more distinctly.

"Then, however, a priest or a prophet, being anointed with the compounded ointment, putting fire to the altar of God, was held illustrious in all the world. But after Aaron, who was a priest, another is taken out of the waters. I do not speak of Moses, but of Him who, in the waters of baptism, was called by God His Son.[1] For it is Jesus who has put out, by the grace of baptism, that fire which the priest kindled for sins; for, from the time when He appeared, the chrism has ceased, by which the priesthood or the prophetic or the kingly office was conferred.

CHAP. XLIX.—*Two comings of Christ.*

"His coming, therefore, was predicted by Moses, who delivered the law of God to men; but by another also before him, as I have already informed you. He therefore intimated that He should come, humble indeed in His first coming, but glorious in His second. And the first, indeed, has been already accomplished; since He has come and taught, and He, the Judge of all, has been judged and slain. But at His second coming He shall come to judge, and shall indeed condemn the wicked, but shall take the pious into a share and association with Himself in His kingdom. Now the faith of His second coming depends upon His first. For the prophets—especially Jacob and Moses—spoke of the first, but some also of the second. But the excellency of prophecy is chiefly shown in this, that the prophets spoke not of things to come, according to the sequence of things; otherwise they might seem merely as wise men to have conjectured what the sequence of things pointed out.

CHAP. L.—*His rejection by the Jews.*

"But what I say is this: It was to be expected that Christ

[1] Matt. iii. 17.

should be received by the Jews, to whom He came, and that they should believe on Him who was expected for the salvation of the people, according to the traditions of the fathers; but that the Gentiles should be averse to Him, since neither promise nor announcement concerning Him had been made to them, and indeed He had never been made known to them even by name. Yet the prophets, contrary to the order and sequence of things, said that He should be the expectation of the Gentiles, and not of the Jews.[1] And so it happened. For when He came, He was not at all acknowledged by those who seemed to expect Him, in consequence of the tradition of their ancestors; whereas those who had heard nothing at all of Him, both believe that He has come, and hope that He is to come. And thus in all things prophecy appears faithful, which said that He was the expectation of the Gentiles. The Jews, therefore, have erred concerning the first coming of the Lord; and on this point only there is disagreement betwixt us and them. For they themselves know and expect that Christ shall come; but that He has come already in humility—even He who is called Jesus— they do not know. And this is a great confirmation of His coming, that all do not believe on Him.

Chap. li.—*The only Saviour.*

"Him, therefore, has God appointed in the end of the world; because it was impossible that the evils of men could be removed by any other, provided that the nature of the human race were to remain entire, *i.e.* the liberty of the will being preserved. This condition, therefore, being preserved inviolate, He came to invite to His kingdom all righteous ones, and those who have been desirous to please Him. For these He has prepared unspeakable good things, and the heavenly city Jerusalem, which shall shine above the brightness of the sun, for the habitation of the saints. But the unrighteous, and the wicked, and those who have despised God, and have devoted the life given them to diverse wickednesses, and have given to the practice of evil the time which

[1] Gen. xlix. 10.

was given them for the work of righteousness, He shall hand over to fitting and condign vengeance. But the rest of the things which shall then be done, it is neither in the power of angels nor of men to tell or to describe. This only it is enough for us to know, that God shall confer upon the good an eternal possession of good things."

Chap. lii.—*The saints before Christ's coming.*

When he had thus spoken, I answered : "If those shall enjoy the kingdom of Christ, whom His coming shall find righteous, shall then those be wholly deprived of the kingdom who have died before His coming?" Then Peter says : "You compel me, O Clement, to touch upon things that are unspeakable. But so far as it is allowed to declare them, I shall not shrink from doing so. Know then that Christ, who was from the beginning, and always, was ever present with the pious, though secretly, through all their generations; especially with those who waited for Him, to whom He frequently appeared. But the time was not yet that there should be a resurrection of the bodies that were dissolved ; but this seemed rather to be their reward from God, that whoever should be found righteous, should remain longer in the body ; or, at least, as is clearly related in the writings of the law concerning a certain righteous man, that God translated him.[1] In like manner others were dealt with, who pleased His will, that, being translated to Paradise, they should be kept for the kingdom. But as to those who have not been able completely to fulfil the rule of righteousness, but have had some remnants of evil in their flesh, their bodies are indeed dissolved, but their souls are kept in good and blessed abodes, that at the resurrection of the dead, when they shall recover their own bodies, purified even by the dissolution, they may obtain an eternal inheritance in proportion to their good deeds. And therefore blessed are all those who shall attain to the kingdom of Christ; for not only shall they escape the pains of hell, but shall also remain incorruptible, and shall be the

[1] Gen. v. 24.

M

first to see God the Father, and shall obtain the rank of honour among the first in the presence of God.

CHAP. LIII.—*Animosity of the Jews.*

"Wherefore there is not the least doubt concerning Christ; and all the unbelieving Jews are stirred up with boundless rage against us, fearing lest haply He against whom they have sinned should be He. And their fear grows all the greater, because they know that, as soon as they fixed Him on the cross, the whole world showed sympathy with Him; and that His body, although they guarded it with strict care, could nowhere be found; and that innumerable multitudes are attaching themselves to His faith. Whence they, together with the high priest Caiaphas, were compelled to send to us again and again, that an inquiry might be instituted concerning the truth of His name. And when they were constantly entreating that they might either learn or teach concerning Jesus, whether He were the Christ, it seemed good to us to go up into the temple, and in the presence of all the people to bear witness concerning Him, and at the same time to charge the Jews with many foolish things which they were doing. For the people was now divided into many parties, ever since the days of John the Baptist.

CHAP. LIV.—*Jewish sects.*

"For when the rising of Christ was at hand for the abolition of sacrifices, and for the bestowal of the grace of baptism, the enemy, understanding from the predictions that the time was at hand, wrought various schisms among the people, that, if haply it might be possible to abolish the former sin,[1] the latter fault might be incorrigible. The first schism, therefore, was that of those who were called Sadducees, which took their rise almost in the time of John. These, as more righteous than others, began to separate themselves from the assembly of the people, and to deny the resurrection of the dead,[2] and to assert that by an argument of infidelity, saying that it was unworthy that God should be worshipped, as it were, under the promise

---

[1] That is, the sin of sacrifice. [2] Matt. xxii. 23.

of a reward. The first author of this opinion was Dositheus ;
the second was Simon.   Another schism is that of the
Samaritans ; for they deny the resurrection of the dead, and
assert that God is not to be worshipped in Jerusalem, but on
Mount Gerizim.   They indeed rightly, from the predictions
of Moses, expect the one true Prophet ; but by the wickedness
of Dositheus they were hindered from believing that Jesus
is He whom they were expecting.   The scribes also, and
Pharisees, are led away into another schism ; but these, being
baptized by John, and holding the word of truth received
from the tradition of Moses as the key of the kingdom of
heaven, have hid it from the hearing of the people.[1]   Yea,
some even of the disciples of John, who seemed to be great
ones, have separated themselves from the people, and proclaimed their own master as the Christ.   But all these schisms
have been prepared, that by means of them the faith of Christ
and baptism might be hindered.

Chap. lv.—*Public discussion.*

" However, as we were proceeding to say, when the high
priest had often sent priests to ask us that we might discourse
with one another concerning Jesus ; when it seemed a fit opportunity, and it pleased all the church, we went up to the
temple, and, standing on the steps together with our faithful
brethren, the people kept perfect silence ; and first the high
priest began to exhort the people that they should hear
patiently and quietly, and at the same time witness and
judge of those things that were to be spoken.   Then, in the
next place, exalting with many praises the rite of sacrifice
which had been bestowed by God upon the human race for
the remission of sins, he found fault with the baptism of our
Jesus, as having been recently brought in in opposition to the
sacrifices.   But Matthew, meeting his propositions, showed
clearly, that whosoever shall not obtain the baptism of Jesus
shall not only be deprived of the kingdom of heaven, but
shall not be without peril at the resurrection of the dead,
even though he be fortified by the prerogative of a good life

[1] Luke xi. 52.

and an upright disposition. Having made these and such like statements, Matthew stopped.

CHAP. LVI.—*Sadducees refuted.*

"But the party of the Sadducees, who deny the resurrection of the dead, were in a rage, so that one of them cried out from amongst the people, saying that those greatly err who think that the dead ever arise. In opposition to him, Andrew, my brother, answering, declared that it is not an error, but the surest matter of faith, that the dead rise, in accordance with the teaching of Him of whom Moses foretold that He should come the true Prophet. 'Or if,' says he, 'you do not think that this is He whom Moses foretold, let this first be inquired into, so that when this is clearly proved to be He, there may be no further doubt concerning the things which He taught.' These, and many such like things, Andrew proclaimed, and then stopped.

CHAP. LVII.—*Samaritan refuted.*

" But a certain Samaritan, speaking against the people and against God, and asserting that neither are the dead to rise, nor is that worship of God to be maintained which is in Jerusalem, but that Mount Gerizim is to be reverenced, added also this in opposition to us, that our Jesus was not He whom Moses foretold as a prophet to come into the world. Against him, and another who supported him in what he said, James and John, the sons of Zebedee, strove vigorously ; and although they had a command not to enter into their cities,[1] nor to bring the word of preaching to them, yet, lest their discourse, unless it were confuted, should hurt the faith of others, they replied so prudently and so powerfully, that they put them to perpetual silence. For James made an oration concerning the resurrection of the dead, with the approbation of all the people; while John showed that if they would abandon the error of Mount Gerizim, they should consequently acknowledge that Jesus was indeed He who, according to the prophecy of Moses, was expected to come; since, in-

[1] Matt. x. 3.

deed, as Moses wrought signs and miracles, so also did Jesus.
And there is no doubt but that the likeness of the signs proves
Him to be that prophet of whom he said that He should come,
'like himself.' Having declared these things, and more to
the same effect, they ceased.

CHAP. LVIII.—*Scribes refuted.*

" And, behold, one of the scribes, shouting out from the
midst of the people, says : ' The signs and miracles which
your Jesus wrought, he wrought not as a prophet, but as a
magician.' Him Philip eagerly encounters, showing that by
this argument he accused Moses also. For when Moses
wrought signs and miracles in Egypt, in like manner as Jesus
also did in Judæa, it cannot be doubted that what was said of
Jesus might as well be said of Moses. Having made these
and such like protestations, Philip was silent.

CHAP. LIX.—*Pharisees refuted.*

"Then a certain Pharisee, hearing this, chid Philip because
he put Jesus on a level with Moses. To whom Bartholomew,
answering, boldly declared that we do not only say that Jesus
was equal to Moses, but that He was greater than he, because
Moses was indeed a prophet, as Jesus was also, but that
Moses was not the Christ, as Jesus was, and therefore He is
doubtless greater who is both a prophet and the Christ, than
he who is only a prophet. After following out this train of
argument, he stopped. After him James the son of Alphæus
gave an address to the people, with the view of showing that
we are not to believe on Jesus on the ground that the prophets
foretold concerning Him, but rather that we are to believe
the prophets, that they were really prophets, because the
Christ bears testimony to them; for it is the presence and
coming of Christ that show that they are truly prophets :
for testimony must be borne by the superior to his inferiors,
not by the inferiors to their superior. After these and many
similar statements, James also was silent. After him Lebbæus
began vehemently to charge it upon the people that they did
not believe in Jesus, who had done them so much good by

teaching them the things that are of God, by comforting the afflicted, healing the sick, relieving the poor; yet for all these benefits their return had been hatred and death. When he had declared these and many more such things to the people, he ceased.

Chap. lx.—*Disciples of John refuted.*

"And, behold, one of the disciples of John asserted that John was the Christ, and not Jesus, inasmuch as Jesus Himself declared that John was greater than all men and all prophets.[1] 'If, then,' said he, 'he be greater than all, he must be held to be greater than Moses, and than Jesus himself. But if he be the greatest of all, then must he be the Christ.' To this Simon the Canaanite, answering, asserted that John was indeed greater than all the prophets, and all who are born of women, yet that he is not greater than the Son of man. Accordingly Jesus is also the Christ, whereas John is only a prophet: and there is as much difference between him and Jesus, as between the forerunner and Him whose forerunner he is; or as between Him who gives the law, and him who keeps the law. Having made these and similar statements, the Canaanite also was silent. After him Barnabas,[1] who also is called Matthias, who was substituted as an apostle in the place of Judas, began to exhort the people that they should not regard Jesus with hatred, nor speak evil of Him. For it were far more proper, even for one who might be in ignorance or in doubt concerning Jesus, to love than to hate Him. For God has affixed a reward to love, a penalty to hatred. 'For the very fact,' said he, 'that He assumed a Jewish body, and was born among the Jews, how has not this incited us all to love Him?' When he had spoken this, and more to the same effect, he stopped.

Chap. lxi.—*Caiaphas answered.*

"Then Caiaphas attempted to impugn the doctrine of Jesus, saying that He spoke vain things, for He said that the

---

[1] Matt. xi. 9, 11.

[2] We should doubtless read "Barsabas."

poor are blessed;[1] and promised earthly rewards; and placed the chief gift in an earthly inheritance; and promised that those who maintain righteousness shall be satisfied with meat and drink; and many things of this sort He is charged with teaching. Thomas, in reply, proves that his accusation is frivolous; showing that the prophets, in whom Caiaphas believes, taught these things much more, and did not show in what manner these things are to be, or how they are to be understood; whereas Jesus pointed out how they are to be taken. And when he had spoken these things, and others of like kind, Thomas also held his peace.

Chap. lxii.—*Foolishness of preaching.*

"Therefore Caiaphas, again looking at me, and sometimes in the way of warning and sometimes in that of accusation, said that I ought for the future to refrain from preaching Christ Jesus, lest I should do it to my own destruction, and lest, being deceived myself, I should also deceive others. Then, moreover, he charged me with presumption, because, though I was unlearned, a fisherman, and a rustic, I dared to assume the office of a teacher. As he spoke these things, and many more of like kind, I said in reply, that I incurred less danger, if, as he said, this Jesus were not the Christ, because I received Him as a teacher of the law; but that he was in terrible danger if this be the very Christ, as assuredly He is: for I believe in Him who has appeared; but for whom else, who has never appeared, does he reserve his faith? But if I, an unlearned and uneducated man, as you say, a fisherman and a rustic, have more understanding than wise elders, this, said I, ought the more to strike terror into you. For if I disputed with any learning, and won over you wise and learned men, it would appear that I had acquired this power by long learning, and not by the grace of divine power; but now, when, as I have said, we unskilled men convince and overcome you wise men, who that has any sense does not perceive that this is not a work of human subtlety, but of divine will and gift?

[1] Matt. v.; Luke x.

Chap. lxiii.—*Appeal to the Jews.*

" Thus we argued and bore witness; and we who were unlearned men and fishermen, taught the priests concerning the one only God of heaven; the Sadducees, concerning the resurrection of the dead; the Samaritans, concerning the sacredness of Jerusalem (not that we entered into their cities, but disputed with them in public); the scribes and Pharisees, concerning the kingdom of heaven; the disciples of John, that they should not suffer John to be a stumbling-block to them; and all the people, that Jesus is the eternal Christ. At last, however, I warned them, that before we should go forth to the Gentiles, to preach to them the knowledge of God the Father, they should themselves be reconciled to God, receiving His Son; for I showed them that in no way else could they be saved, unless through the grace of the Holy Spirit they hasted to be washed with the baptism of threefold invocation, and received the eucharist of Christ the Lord, whom alone they ought to believe concerning those things which He taught, that so they might merit to attain eternal salvation; but that otherwise it was utterly impossible for them to be reconciled to God, even if they should kindle a thousand altars and a thousand high altars to Him.

Chap. lxiv.—*Temple to be destroyed.*

" 'For we,' said I, 'have ascertained beyond doubt that God is much rather displeased with the sacrifices which you offer, the time of sacrifices having now passed away; and because ye will not acknowledge that the time for offering victims is now past, therefore the temple shall be destroyed, and the abomination of desolation[1] shall stand in the holy place; and then the gospel shall be preached to the Gentiles for a testimony against you, that your unbelief may be judged by their faith. For the whole world at different times suffers under divers maladies, either spreading generally over all, or affecting individuals specially. Therefore it needs a physician to visit it for its salvation. We therefore bear

[1] Dan. ix. 27; Matt. xxiv. 15.

witness to you, and declare to you what has been hidden from every one of you. It is for you to consider what is for your advantage.'

CHAP. LXV.—*Tumult stilled by Gamaliel.*

" When I had thus spoken, the whole multitude of the priests were in a rage, because I had foretold to them the overthrow of the temple. Which when Gamaliel, a chief of the people, saw—who was secretly our brother in the faith, but by our advice remained among them—because they were greatly enraged and moved with intense fury against us, he stood up, and said,[1] ' Be quiet for a little, O men of Israel, for ye do not perceive the trial which hangs over you. Wherefore refrain from these men ; and if what they are engaged in be of human counsel, it will soon come to an end; but if it be from God, why will you sin without cause, and prevail nothing? For who can overpower the will of God? Now therefore, since the day is declining towards evening, I shall myself dispute with these men to-morrow, in this same place, in your hearing, so that I may openly oppose and clearly confute every error.' By this speech of his their fury was to some extent checked, especially in the hope that next day we should be publicly convicted of error; and so he dismissed the people peacefully.

CHAP. LXVI.—*Discussion resumed.*

" Now when we had come to our James, while we detailed to him all that had been said and done, we supped, and re-mained with him, spending the whole night in supplication to Almighty God, that the discourse of the approaching dis-putation might show the unquestionable truth of our faith. Therefore, on the following day, James the bishop went up to the temple with us, and with the whole church. There we found a great multitude, who had been waiting for us from the middle of the night. Therefore we took our stand in the same place as before, in order that, standing on an elevation, we might be seen by all the people. Then, when

[1] Acts v. 35-39.

profound silence was obtained, Gamaliel, who, as we have said, was of our faith, but who by a dispensation remained amongst them, that if at any time they should attempt anything unjust or wicked against us, he might either check them by skilfully adopted counsel, or might warn us, that we might either be on our guard or might turn it aside;—he therefore, as if acting against us, first of all looking to James the bishop, addressed him in this manner:

Chap. LXVII.—*Speech of Gamaliel.*

" 'If I, Gamaliel, deem it no reproach either to my learning or to my old age to learn something from babes and unlearned ones, if haply there be anything which it is for profit or for safety to acquire (for he who lives reasonably knows that nothing is more precious than the soul), ought not this to be the object of love and desire to all, to learn what they do not know, and to teach what they have learned? For it is most certain that neither friendship, nor kindred, nor lofty power, ought to be more precious to men then truth. Therefore you, O brethren, if ye know anything more, shrink not from laying it before the people of God who are present, and also before your brethren; while the whole people shall willingly and in perfect quietness hear what you say. For why should not the people do this, when they see even me equally with themselves willing to learn from you, if haply God has revealed something further to you? But if you in anything are deficient, be not ye ashamed in like manner to be taught by us, that God may fill up whatever is wanting on either side. But if any fear now agitates you on account of some of our people whose minds are prejudiced against you, and if through fear of their violence you dare not openly speak your sentiments, in order that I may deliver you from this fear, I openly swear to you by Almighty God, who liveth for ever, that I will suffer no one to lay hands upon you. Since, then, you have all this people witnesses of this my oath, and you hold the covenant of our sacrament as a fitting pledge, let each one of you, without any hesitation, declare what he has learned; and let us, brethren, listen eagerly and in silence.'

Chap. lxviii.—*The rule of faith.*

"These sayings of Gamaliel did not much please Caiaphas; and holding him in suspicion, as it seemed, he began to insinuate himself cunningly into the discussions: for, smiling at what Gamaliel had said, the chief of the priests asked of James, the chief of the bishops, that the discourse concerning Christ should not be drawn but from the Scriptures; 'that we may know,' said he, 'whether Jesus be the very Christ or no.' Then said James, 'We must first inquire from what Scriptures we are especially to derive our discussion.' Then he, with difficulty, at length overcome by reason, answered, that it must be derived from the law; and afterwards he made mention also of the prophets.

Chap. lxix.—*Two comings of Christ.*

"To him our James began to show, that whatsoever things the prophets say they have taken from the law, and what they have spoken is in accordance with the law. He also made some statements respecting the books of the Kings, in what way, and when, and by whom they were written, and how they ought to be used. And when he had discussed most fully concerning the law, and had, by a most clear exposition, brought into light whatever things are in it concerning Christ, he showed by most abundant proofs that Jesus is the Christ, and that in Him are fulfilled all the prophecies which related to His humble advent. For he showed that two advents of Him are foretold: one in humiliation, which He has accomplished; the other in glory, which is hoped for to be accomplished, when He shall come to give the kingdom to those who believe in Him, and who observe all things which He has commanded. And when he had plainly taught the people concerning these things, he added this also: That unless a man be baptized in water, in the name of the threefold blessedness, as the true Prophet taught, he can neither receive remission of sins nor enter into the kingdom of heaven; and he declared that this is the prescription of the unbegotten God. To which he added this also: 'Do not think that we speak of two unbegotten Gods, or that one is divided into two, or that the same is made male and female. But we speak of the only-begotten Son of God, not sprung from another source, but ineffably self-originated; and in like manner we speak of the Paraclete.' But when he had spoken some things also concerning baptism, through seven successive days he persuaded all the people and the high priest that they should hasten straightway to receive baptism.

Chap. lxx.— *Tumult raised by Saul.*

"And when matters were at that point that they should come and be baptized, some one of our enemies,[1] entering the temple with a few men, began to cry out, and to say, 'What mean ye, O men of Israel? Why are you so easily hurried on? Why are ye led headlong by most miserable men, who are deceived by Simon, a magician?' While he was thus speaking, and adding more to the same effect, and while James the bishop was refuting him, he began to excite the people and to raise a tumult, so that the people might not be able to hear what was said. Therefore he began to drive all into confusion with shouting, and to undo what had been arranged with much labour, and at the same time to reproach the priests, and to enrage them with revilings and abuse, and, like a madman, to excite every one to murder, saying, 'What do ye? Why do ye hesitate? Oh, sluggish and inert, why do we not lay hands upon them, and pull all these fellows to pieces?' When he had said this, he first, seizing a strong brand from the altar, set the example of smiting. Then others also, seeing him, were carried away with like madness. Then ensued a tumult on either side, of the beating and the beaten. Much blood is shed; there is a confused flight, in the midst of which that enemy attacked James, and threw him headlong from the top of the steps; and supposing him to be dead, he cared not to inflict further violence upon him.

---

[1] A marginal note in one of the manuscripts states that this enemy was Saul.

Chap. lxxi.—*Flight to Jericho.*

" But our friends lifted him up, for they were both more numerous and more powerful than the others; but, from their fear of God, they rather suffered themselves to be killed by an inferior force, than they would kill others. But when the evening came the priests shut up the temple, and we returned to the house of James, and spent the night there in prayer. Then before daylight we went down to Jericho, to the number of 5000 men. Then after three days one of the brethren came to us from Gamaliel, whom we mentioned before, bringing to us secret tidings that that enemy had received a commission from Caiaphas, the chief priest, that he should arrest all who believed in Jesus, and should go to Damascus with his letters, and that there also, employing the help of the unbelievers, he should make havoc among the faithful; and that he was hastening to Damascus chiefly on this account, because he believed that Peter had fled thither.[1] And about thirty days thereafter he stopped on his way while passing through Jericho going to Damascus. At that time we were absent, having gone out to the sepulchres of two brethren which were whitened of themselves every year, by which miracle the fury of many against us was restrained, because they saw that our brethren were had in remembrance before God.

Chap. lxxii.—*Peter sent to Cæsarea.*

" While, therefore, we abode in Jericho, and gave ourselves to prayer and fasting, James the bishop sent for me, and sent me here to Cæsarea, saying that Zaccheus had written to him from Cæsarea, that one Simon, a Samaritan magician, was subverting many of our people, asserting that he was one *Stans*,—that is, in other words, the Christ, and the great power of the high God, which is superior to the Creator of the world; at the same time that he showed many miracles, and made some doubt, and others fall away to him. He informed me of all things that had been ascertained respecting this

[1] Acts xxii. 5.

man from those who had formerly been either his associates or his disciples, and had afterwards been converted to Zaccheus. ' Many therefore there are, O Peter,' said James, ' for whose safety's sake it behoves you to go and to refute the magician, and to teach the word of truth. Therefore make no delay; nor let it grieve you that you set out alone, knowing that God by Jesus will go with you, and will help you, and that soon, by His grace, you will have many associates and sympathizers. Now be sure that you send me in writing every year an account of your sayings and doings, and especially at the end of every seven years.' With these expressions he dismissed me, and in six days I arrived at Cæsarea.

CHAP. LXXIII.—*Welcomed by Zaccheus.*

" When I entered the city, our most beloved brother Zaccheus met me; and embracing me, brought me to this lodging, in which he himself stayed, inquiring of me concerning each of the brethren, especially concerning our honourable brother James. And when I told him that he was still lame on one foot, on his immediately asking the cause of this, I related to him all that I have now detailed to you, how we had been called by the priests and Caiaphas the high priest to the temple, and how James the archbishop, standing on the top of the steps, had for seven successive days shown the whole people from the Scriptures of the Lord that Jesus is the Christ; and how, when all were acquiescing that they should be baptized by him in the name of Jesus, an enemy did all those things which I have already mentioned, and which I need not repeat.

CHAP. LXXIV.—*Simon Magus challenges Peter.*

" When Zaccheus had heard these things, he told me in return of the doings of Simon; and in the meantime Simon himself—how he heard of my arrival I do not know—sent a message to me, saying, ' Let us dispute to-morrow in the hearing of the people.' To which I answered, ' Be it so, as it pleaseth you.' And this promise of mine was known over the whole city, so that even you, who arrived on that very day, learned that I was to hold a discussion with Simon on the following day, and having found out my abode, according to the directions which you had received from Barnabas, came to me. But I so rejoiced at your coming, that my mind, moved I know not how, hastened to expound all things quickly to you, yet especially that which is the main point in our faith, concerning the true Prophet, which alone, I doubt not, is a sufficient foundation for the whole of our doctrine. Then, in the next place, I unfolded to you the more secret meaning of the written law, through its several heads, which there was occasion to unfold; neither did I conceal from you the good things of the traditions. But what remains, beginning from to-morrow, you shall hear from day to day in connection with the questions which will be raised in the discussion with Simon, until by God's favour we reach that city of Rome to which we believe that our journey is to be directed."

I then declared that I owed him all thanks for what he had told me, and promised that I would most readily do all that he commanded. Then, having taken food, he ordered me to rest, and he also betook himself to rest.

RECOGNITIONS OF CLEMENT.

BOOK II.

CHAP. I.—*Power of habit.*

HEN the day dawned which had been fixed for the discussion with Simon, Peter, rising at the first cock-crowing, aroused us also : for we were sleeping in the same apartment, thirteen of us in all ; of whom, next to Peter, Zaccheus was first, then Sophonius, Joseph and Michæas, Eliesdrus, Phineas, Lazarus, and Elisæus : after these I (Clement) and Nicodemus ; then Niceta and Aquila, who had formerly been disciples of Simon, and were converted to the faith of Christ under the teaching of Zaccheus. Of the women there was no one present. As the evening light[1] was still lasting, we all sat down ; and Peter, seeing that we were awake, and that we were giving attention to him, having saluted us, immediately began to speak, as follows :

" I confess, brethren, that I wonder at the power of human nature, which I see to be fit and suited to every call upon it. This, however, it occurs to me to say of what I have found by experience, that when the middle of the night is passed, I awake of my own accord, and sleep does not come to me again. This happens to me for this reason, that I have formed the habit of recalling to memory the words of my Lord, which I heard from Himself ; and for the longing I have towards them, I constrain my mind and my thoughts to be roused, that, awaking to them, and recalling and ar-

[1] That is, the lamp which had been lighted in the evening.

ranging them one by one, I may retain them in my memory. From this, therefore, whilst I desire to cherish the sayings of the Lord with all delight in my heart, the habit of waking has come upon me, even if there be nothing that I wish to think of. Thus, in some unaccountable way, when any custom is established, the old custom is changed, provided indeed you do not force it above measure, but as far as the measure of nature admits. For it is not possible to be altogether without sleep; otherwise night would not have been made for rest."

Chap. II.—*Curtailment of sleep.*

Then I, when I heard this, said: "You have very well said, O Peter; for one custom is superseded by another. For when I was at sea, I was at first distressed, and all my system was disordered, so that I felt as if I had been beaten, and could not bear the tossing and tumult of the sea; but after a few days, when I had got accustomed to it, I began to bear it tolerably, so that I was glad to take food immediately in the morning along with the sailors, whereas before it was not my custom to eat anything before the seventh hour. Now, therefore, simply from the custom which I then acquired, hunger reminds me about that time at which I used to eat with the sailors; which, however, I hope to get rid of, when once another custom shall have been formed. I believe, therefore, that you also have acquired the habit of wakefulness, as you state; and you have wished at a fitting time to explain this to us, that we also may not grudge to throw off and dispense with some portion of our sleep, that we may be able to take in the precepts of the living doctrine. For when the food is digested, and the mind is under the influence of the silence of night, those things which are seasonably taught abide in it."

Chap. III.—*Need of caution.*

Then Peter, being pleased to hear that I understood the purport of his preface, that he had delivered it for our advantage; and commending me, doubtless for the purpose of

N

encouraging and stimulating me, began to deliver the following discourse : " It seems to me to be seasonable and necessary to have some discussion relating to those things that
are near at hand; that is, concerning Simon. For I should
wish to know of what character and of what conduct he is.
Wherefore, if any one of you has any knowledge of him, let
him not fail to inform me ; for it is of consequence to know
these things beforehand. For if we have it in charge, that
when we enter into a city we should first learn who in it is
worthy,[1] that we may eat with him, how much more is it
proper for us to ascertain who or what sort of man he is to
whom the words of immortality are to be committed ! For we
ought to be careful, yea, extremely careful, that we cast not
our pearls before swine.[2]

Chap. iv.—*Prudence in dealing with opponents.*

" But for other reasons also it is of importance that I
should have some knowledge of this man. For if I know
that in those things concerning which it cannot be doubted
that they are good, he is faultless and irreproachable,—that is
to say, if he is sober, merciful, upright, gentle, and humane,
which no one doubts to be good qualities,—then it will seem
to be fitting, that upon him who possesses these good virtues,
that which is lacking of faith and knowledge should be conferred ; and so his life, which is in other respects worthy of
approbation, should be amended in those points in which it
shall appear to be imperfect. But if he remains wrapped up
and polluted in those sins which are manifestly such, it does
not become me to speak to him at all of the more secret and
sacred things of divine knowledge, but rather to protest and
confront him, that he cease from sin, and cleanse his actions
from vice. But if he insinuate himself, and lead us on to
speak what he, while he acts improperly, ought not to hear,
it will be our part to parry him cautiously. For not to
answer him at all does not seem proper, for the sake of the
hearers, lest haply they may think that we decline the contest through want of ability to answer him, and so their

[1] Matt. x. ; Luke x.   [2] Matt. vii. 6.

faith may be injured through their misunderstanding of our purpose."

CHAP. v.—*Simon Magus, a formidable antagonist.*

When Peter had thus spoken to us, Niceta asks permission to say something to him; and Peter having granted permission, he says : " With your pardon, I beseech you, my lord Peter, to hear me, who am very anxious for thee, and who am afraid lest, in the contest which you have in hand with Simon, you should seem to be overmatched. For it very frequently happens that he who defends the truth does not gain the victory, since the hearers are either prejudiced, or have no great interest in the better cause. But over and above all this, Simon himself is a most vehement orator, trained in the dialectic art, and in the meshes of syllogisms; and what is worse than all, he is greatly skilled in the magic art. And therefore I fear, lest haply, being so strongly fortified on every side, he shall be thought to be defending the truth, whilst he is alleging falsehoods, in the presence of those who do not know him. For neither should we ourselves have been able to escape from him, and to be converted to the Lord, had it not been that, while we were his assistants, and the sharers of his errors, we had ascertained that he was a deceiver and a magician."

CHAP. vi.—*Simon Magus : his wickedness.*

When Niceta had thus spoken, Aquila also, asking that he might be permitted to speak, proceeded in manner following: "Receive, I entreat thee, most excellent Peter, the assurance of my love towards thee ; for indeed I also am extremely anxious on thy account. And do not blame us in this, for indeed to be concerned for any one cometh of affection ; whereas to be indifferent is no less than hatred. But I call God to witness that I feel for thee, not as knowing thee to be weaker in debate,—for indeed I was never present at any dispute in which thou wert engaged,—but because I well know the impieties of this man, I think of thy reputation, and at the same time the souls of the hearers, and above all, the interests of the truth itself. For this magician is vehement towards all things that he wishes, and wicked above measure. For in all things we know him well, since from boyhood we have been assistants and ministers of his wickedness; and had not the love of God rescued us from him, we should even now be engaged in the same evil deeds with him. But a certain inborn love towards God rendered his wickedness hateful to us, and the worship of God attractive to us. Whence I think also that it was the work of Divine Providence, that we, being first made his associates, should take knowledge in what manner or by what art he effects the prodigies which he seems to work. For who is there that would not be astonished at the wonderful things which he does? Who would not think that he was a god come down from heaven for the salvation of men? For myself, I confess, if I had not known him intimately, and had taken part in his doings, I would easily have been carried away with him. Whence it was no great thing for us to be separated from his society, knowing as we did that he depends upon magic arts and wicked devices. But if thou also thyself wish to know all about him—who, what, and whence he is, and how he contrives what he does—then listen.

Chap. vii.—*Simon Magus: his history.*

"This Simon's father was Antonius, and his mother Rachel. By nation he is a Samaritan, from a village of the Gettones; by profession a magician, yet exceedingly well trained in the Greek literature; desirous of glory, and boasting above all the human race, so that he wishes himself to be believed to be an exalted power, which is above God the Creator, and to be thought to be the Christ, and to be called the *Standing One*. And he uses this name as implying that he can never be dissolved, asserting that his flesh is so compacted by the power of his divinity, that it can endure to eternity. Hence, therefore, he is called the *Standing One*, as though he cannot fall by any corruption.

Chap. viii.—*Simon Magus: his history.*

" For after that John the Baptist was killed, as you yourself also know, when Dositheus had broached his heresy, with thirty other chief disciples, and one woman, who was called *Luna*—whence also these thirty appear to have been appointed with reference to the number of the days, according to the course of the moon—this Simon, ambitious of evil glory, as we have said, goes to Dositheus, and pretending friendship, entreats him, that if any one of those thirty should die, he should straightway substitute him in room of the dead: for it was contrary to their rule either to exceed the fixed number, or to admit any one who was unknown, or not yet proved; whence also the rest, desiring to become worthy of the place and number, are eager in every way to please, according to the institutions of their sect, each one of those who aspire after admittance into the number, hoping that he may be deemed worthy to be put into the place of the deceased, when, as we have said, any one dies. Therefore Dositheus, being greatly urged by this man, introduced Simon when a vacancy occurred among the number.

Chap. ix.—*Simon Magus: his profession.*

"But not long after he fell in love with that woman whom they call Luna; and he confided all things to us as his friends: how he was a magician, and how he loved Luna, and how, being desirous of glory, he was unwilling to enjoy her ingloriously, but that he was waiting patiently till he could enjoy her honourably; yet so if we also would conspire with him towards the accomplishment of his desires. And he promised that, as a reward of this service, he would cause us to be invested with the highest honours, and we should be believed by men to be gods; 'Only, however, on condition,' says he, 'that you confer the chief place upon me, Simon, who by magic art am able to show many signs and prodigies, by means of which either my glory or our sect may be established. For I am able to render myself invisible to those who wish to lay hold of me, and again to be visible when I am willing to be seen. If I wish to flee, I can dig through the mountains, and pass through rocks as if they were clay. If I should throw myself headlong from a lofty mountain, I should be borne unhurt to the earth, as if I were held up; when bound, I can loose myself, and bind those who had bound me; being shut up in prison, I can make the barriers open of their own accord; I can render statues animated, so that those who see suppose that they are men. I can make new trees suddenly spring up, and produce sprouts at once. I can throw myself into the fire, and not be burnt; I can change my countenance, so that I cannot be recognised; but I can show people that I have two faces. I shall change myself into a sheep or a goat; I shall make a beard to grow upon little boys; I shall ascend by flight into the air; I shall exhibit abundance of gold, and shall make and unmake kings. I shall be worshipped as God; I shall have divine honours publicly assigned to me, so that an image of me shall be set up, and I shall be worshipped and adored as God. And what need of more words? Whatever I wish, that I shall be able to do. For already I have achieved many things by way of experiment. In short,' says he, 'once when my mother Rachel ordered me to go to the field to reap, and I saw a sickle lying, I ordered it to go and reap; and it reaped ten times more than the others. Lately, I produced many new sprouts from the earth, and made them bear leaves and produce fruit in a moment; and the nearest mountain I successfully bored through.'

CHAP. X.—*Simon Magus: his deception.*

"But when he spoke thus of the production of sprouts and the perforation of the mountain, I was confounded on this account, because he wished to deceive even us, in whom he seemed to place confidence; for we knew that those things had been from the days of our fathers, which he represented as having been done by himself lately. We then, although we heard these atrocities from him, and worse than these, yet we followed up his crimes, and suffered others to be deceived by him, telling also many lies on his behalf; and this before he did any of the things which he had promised, so that while as yet he had done nothing, he was by some thought to be God.

CHAP. XI.—*Simon Magus, at the head of the sect of Dositheus.*

"Meantime, at the outset, as soon as he was reckoned among the thirty disciples of Dositheus, he began to depreciate Dositheus himself, saying that he did not teach purely or perfectly, and that this was the result not of ill intention, but of ignorance. But Dositheus, when he perceived that Simon was depreciating him, fearing lest his reputation among men might be obscured (for he himself was supposed to be the *Standing One*), moved with rage, when they met as usual at the school, seized a rod, and began to beat Simon; but suddenly the rod seemed to pass through his body, as if it had been smoke. On which Dositheus, being astonished, says to him, 'Tell me if thou art the *Standing One*, that I may adore thee.' And when Simon answered that he was, then Dositheus, perceiving that he himself was not the Standing One, fell down and worshipped him, and gave up his own place as chief to Simon, ordering all the rank of thirty men to obey him; himself taking the inferior place which Simon formerly occupied. Not long after this he died.

CHAP. XII.—*Simon Magus and Luna.*

"Therefore, after the death of Dositheus, Simon took Luna to himself; and with her he still goes about, as you see, deceiving multitudes, and asserting that he himself is a certain power which is above God the Creator, while Luna, who is with him, has been brought down from the higher heavens, and that she is Wisdom, the mother of all things, for whom, says he, the Greeks and barbarians contending, were able in some measure to see an image of her; but of herself, as she is, as the dweller with the first and only God, they were wholly ignorant. Propounding these and other things of the same sort, he has deceived many. But I ought also to state this, which I remember that I myself saw. Once, when this

Luna of his was in a certain tower, a great multitude had assembled to see her, and were standing around the tower on all sides; but she was seen by all the people to lean forward, and to look out through all the windows of that tower.[1] Many other wonderful things he did and does; so that men, being astonished at them, think that he himself is the great God.

Chap. XIII.—*Simon Magus: secret of his magic.*

"Now when Niceta and I once asked him to explain to us how these things could be effected by magic art, and what was the nature of that thing, Simon began thus to explain it to us as his associates. 'I have,' said he, 'made the soul of a boy, unsullied and violently slain, and invoked by unutterable adjurations, to assist me; and by it all is done that I command.' 'But,' said I, 'is it possible for a soul to do these things?' He answered: 'I would have you know this, that the soul of man holds the next place after God, when once it is set free from the darkness of his body. And immediately it acquires prescience: wherefore it is invoked for necromancy.' Then I answered: 'Why, then, do not the souls of persons who are slain take vengeance on their slayers?' 'Do you not remember,' said he, 'that I told you, that when it goes out of the body it acquires knowledge of the future?' 'I remember,' said I. 'Well, then,' said he, 'as soon as it goes out of the body, it immediately knows that there is a judgment to come, and that every one shall suffer punishment for those evils that he hath done; and therefore they are unwilling to take vengeance on their slayers, because they themselves are enduring torments for their own evil deeds which they had done here, and they know that severer punishments await them in the judgment. Moreover, they are not permitted by the angels who preside over them to go out, or to do anything.' 'Then,' I replied, 'if the angels do not permit them to come hither, or to do what they please, how can the souls obey the magician who invokes

[1] The meaning seems to be, that she was seen at all the windows at once.—Tr.

them ?'   'It is not,' said he, 'that they grant indulgence to
the souls that are willing to come; but when the presiding
angels are adjured by one greater than themselves, they have
the excuse of our violence who adjure them, to permit the
souls which we invoke to go out: for they do not sin who
suffer violence, but we who impose necessity upon them.'
Thereupon Niceta, not able longer to refrain, hastily answered, as indeed I also was about to do, only I wished first
to get information from him on several points; but, as I
said, Niceta, anticipating me, said : ' And do you not fear
the day of judgment, who do violence to angels, and invoke
souls, and deceive men, and bargain for divine honour to
yourself from men ?   And how do you persuade us that
there shall be no judgment, as some of the Jews confess,
and that souls are not immortal, as many suppose, though
you see them with your very eyes, and receive from them
assurance of the divine judgment ?'

Chap. xiv.—*Simon Magus, professes to be God.*

"At those sayings of his Simon grew pale ; but after a little,
recollecting himself, he thus answered : ' Do not think that
I am a man of your race.   I am neither magician, nor lover
of Luna, nor son of Antonius.   For before my mother Rachel
and he came together, she, still a virgin, conceived me, while
it was in my power to be either small or great, and to appear
as a man among men.   Therefore I have chosen you first as
my friends, for the purpose of trying you, that I may place
you first in my heavenly and unspeakable places when I shall
have proved you.   Therefore I have pretended to be a man,
that I might more clearly ascertain if you cherish entire
affection towards me.'   But when I heard that, judging him
indeed to be a wretch, yet wondering at his impudence ; and
blushing for him, and at the same time fearing lest he should
attempt some evil against us, I beckoned to Niceta to feign
for a little along with me, and said to him : ' Be not angry
with us, corruptible men, O thou incorruptible God, but
rather accept our affection, and our mind willing to know

who God is ; for we did not till now know who thou art, nor did we perceive that thou art he whom we were seeking.'

CHAP. XV.—*Simon Magus, professed to have made a boy of air.*

"As we spoke these and such like words with looks suited to the occasion, this most vain fellow believed that we were deceived ; and being thereby the more elated, he added also this : 'I shall now be propitious to you, for the affection which you bear towards me as God; for you loved me while you did not know me, and were seeking me in ignorance. But I would not have you doubt that this is truly to be God, when one is able to become small or great as he pleases ; for I am able to appear to man in whatever manner I please. Now, then, I shall begin to unfold to you what is true. Once on a time, I, by my power, turning air into water, and water again into blood, and solidifying it into flesh, formed a new human creature—a boy—and produced a much nobler work than God the Creator. For He created a man from the earth, but I from air—a far more difficult matter ; and again I unmade him and restored him to air, but not until I had placed his picture and image in my bed-chamber, as a proof and memorial of my work.' Then we understood that he spake concerning that boy, whose soul, after he had been slain by violence, he made use of for those services which he required."

CHAP. XVI.—*Simon Magus : hopelessness of his case.*

But Peter, hearing these things, said with tears : "Greatly do I wonder at the infinite patience of God, and, on the other hand, at the audacity of human rashness in some. For what further reason can be found to persuade Simon that God judges the unrighteous, since he persuades himself that he employs the obedience of souls for the service of his crimes ? But, in truth, he is deluded by demons. Yet, although he is sure by these very things that souls are immortal, and are judged for the deeds which they have done, and although he thinks that he really sees those things which we believe by faith; though, as I said, he is deluded by demons, yet he thinks that he sees the very substance of the soul. How shall such a man, I say, be brought to confess either that he acts wickedly while he occupies such an evil position, or that he is to be judged for those things which he hath done, who, knowing the judgment of God, despises it, and shows himself an enemy to God, and dares commit such horrid things? Wherefore it is certain, my brethren, that some oppose the truth and religion of God, not because it appears to them that reason can by no means stand with faith, but because they are either involved in excess of wickedness, or prevented by their own evils, or elated by the swelling of their heart, so that they do not even believe those things which they think that they see with their own eyes.

Chap. XVII.—*Men enemies to God.*

"But, inasmuch as inborn affection towards God the Creator seemed to suffice for salvation to those who loved Him, the enemy studies to pervert this affection in men, and to render them hostile and ungrateful to their Creator. For I call heaven and earth to witness, that if God permitted the enemy to rage as much as he desires, all men should have perished long ere now; but for His mercy's sake God doth not suffer him. But if men would turn their affection towards God, all would doubtless be saved, even if for some faults they might seem to be corrected for righteousness. But now the most of men have been made enemies of God, whose hearts the wicked one has entered, and has turned aside towards himself the affection which God the Creator had implanted in them, that they might have it towards Him. But of the rest, who seemed for a time to be watchful, the enemy, appearing in a phantasy of glory and splendour, and promising them certain great and mighty things, has caused their mind and heart to wander away from God; yet it is for some just reason that he is permitted to accomplish these things."

CHAP. XVIII.—*Responsibility of men.*

To this Aquila answered: " How, then, are men in fault, if the wicked one, transforming himself into the brightness of light,[1] promises to men greater things than the Creator Himself does?" Then Peter answered: "I think," says he, " that nothing is more unjust than this; and now listen while I tell you how unjust it is. If your son, whom you have trained and nourished with all care, and brought to man's estate, should be ungrateful to you, and should leave you and go to another, whom perhaps he may have seen to be richer, and should show to him the honour which he owed to you, and, through hope of greater profit, should deny his birth, and refuse you your paternal rights, would this seem to you right or wicked?" Then Aquila answered: " It is manifest to all that it would be wicked." Then Peter said: " If you say that this would be wicked among men, how much more so is it in the case of God, who, above all men, is worthy of honour from men; whose benefits we not only enjoy, but by whose means and power it is that we began to be when we were not, and whom, if we please, we shall obtain from Him to be for ever in blessedness! In order, therefore, that the unfaithful may be distinguished from the faithful, and the pious from the impious, it has been permitted to the wicked one to use those arts by which the affections of every one towards the true Father may be proved. But if there were in truth some strange God, were it right to leave our own God, who created us, and who is our Father and our Maker, and to pass over to another?" " God forbid!" said Aquila. Then said Peter: " How, then, shall we say that the wicked one is the cause of our sin, when this is done by permission of God, that those may be proved and condemned in the day of judgment, who, allured by greater promises, have abandoned their duty towards their true Father and Creator; while those who have kept the faith and the love of their own Father, even with poverty, if so it has befallen, and with tribulation, may enjoy heavenly gifts and immortal dignities

[1] 2 Cor. xi. 14.

in His kingdom?   But we shall expound these things more carefully at another time.   Meantime I desire to know what Simon did after this."

Chap. xix.—*Disputation begun.*

And Niceta answered : " When he perceived that we had found him out, having spoken to one another concerning his crimes, we left him, and came to Zaccheus, telling him those same things which we have now told to you.   But he, receiving us most kindly, and instructing us concerning the faith of our Lord Jesus Christ, enrolled us in the number of the faithful."   When Niceta had done speaking, Zaccheus, who had gone out a little before, entered, saying, " It is time, O Peter, that you proceed to the disputation ; for a great crowd, collected in the court of the house, is awaiting you, in the midst of whom stands Simon, supported by many attendants."   Then Peter, when he heard this, ordering me to withdraw for the sake of prayer (for I had not yet been washed from the sins which I had committed in ignorance), said to the rest, " Brethren, let us pray that God, for His unspeakable mercy through His Christ, would help me going out on behalf of the salvation of men who have been created by Him."   Having said this, and having prayed, he went forth to the court of the house, in which a great multitude of people were assembled ; and when he saw them all looking intently on him in profound silence, and Simon the magician standing in the midst of them like a standard-bearer, he began in manner following.

Chap. xx.—*The kingdom of God and His righteousness.*

" Peace be to all of you who are prepared to give your right hands to truth : for whosoever are obedient to it seem indeed themselves to confer some favour upon God ; whereas they do themselves obtain from Him the gift of His greatest bounty, walking in His paths of righteousness.   Wherefore the first duty of all is to inquire into the righteousness of God and His kingdom ;[1] His righteousness, that we may be

[1] Matt. vi. 33.

taught to act rightly ; His kingdom, that we may know what
is the reward appointed for labour and patience ; in which
kingdom there is indeed a bestowal of eternal good things
upon the good, but upon those who have acted contrary to
the will of God, a worthy infliction of penalties in proportion
to the doings of every one. It becomes you, therefore, whilst
you are here,—that is, whilst you are in the present life,—
to ascertain the will of God, while there is opportunity also
of doing it. For if any one, before he amends his doings,
wishes to investigate concerning things which he cannot discover, such investigation will be foolish and ineffectual. For
the time is short, and the judgment of God shall be occupied
with deeds, not questions. Therefore before all things let us
inquire into this, what or in what manner we must act that
we may merit to obtain eternal life.

Chap. xxi.—*Righteousness the way to the kingdom.*

" For if we occupy the short time of this life with vain and
useless questions, we shall without doubt go into the presence
of God empty and void of good works, when, as I have said,
our works shall be brought into judgment. For everything
has its own time and place. This is the place, this the time
of works; the world to come, that of recompenses. That we
may not therefore be entangled, by changing the order of
places and times, let us inquire, in the first place, what is
the righteousness of God ; so that, like persons going to set
out on a journey, we may be filled with good works as with
abundant provision, so that we may be able to come to the
kingdom of God, as to a very great city. For to those who
think aright, God is manifest even by the operations of the
world which He hath made, using the evidence of His creation ;[1] and therefore, since there ought to be no doubt about
God, we have now to inquire only about His righteousness
and His kingdom. But if our mind suggest to us to make
any inquiry concerning secret and hidden things before we
inquire into the works of righteousness, we ought to render
to ourselves a reason, because if acting well we shall merit

[1] Rom. i. 20.

to obtain salvation : then, going to God chaste and clean, we shall be filled with the Holy Spirit, and shall know all things that are secret and hidden, without any cavilling of questions ; whereas now, even if any one should spend the whole of his life in inquiring into these things, he not only shall not be able to find them, but shall involve himself in greater errors, because he did not first enter through the way of righteousness, and strive to reach the haven of life.

CHAP. XXII.—*Righteousness ; what it is.*

" And therefore I advise that His righteousness be first inquired into, that, pursuing our journey through it, and placed in the way of truth, we may be able to find the true Prophet, running not with swiftness of foot, but with goodness of works, and that, enjoying His guidance, we may be under no danger of mistaking the way. For if under His guidance we shall merit to enter that city to which we desire to come, all things concerning which we now inquire we shall see with our eyes, being made, as it were, heirs of all things. Understand, therefore, that the way is this course of our life ; the travellers are those who do good works ; the gate is the true Prophet, of whom we speak ; the city is the kingdom in which dwells the Almighty Father, whom only those can see who are of pure heart.[1] Let us not then think the labour of this journey hard, because at the end of it there shall be rest. For the true Prophet Himself also from the beginning of the world, through the course of time, hastens to rest. For He is present with us at all times ; and if at any time it is necessary, He appears and corrects us, that He may bring to eternal life those who obey Him. Therefore this is my judgment, as also it is the pleasure of the true Prophet, that inquiry should first be made concerning righteousness, by those especially who profess that they know God. If therefore any one has anything to propose which he thinks better, let him speak ; and when he has spoken, let him hear, but with patience and quietness : for in order to this at the first, by way of salutation, I prayed for peace to you all."

[1] Matt. v. 8.

CHAP. XXIII.—*Simon refuses peace.*

To this Simon answered : " We have no need of your peace; for if there be peace and concord, we shall not be able to make any advance towards the discovery of truth. For robbers and debauchees have peace among themselves, and every wickedness agrees with itself ; and if we have met with this view, that for the sake of peace we should give assent to all that is said, we shall confer no benefit upon the hearers ; but, on the contrary, we shall impose upon them, and shall depart friends. Wherefore, do not invoke peace, but rather battle, which is the mother of peace ; and if you can, exterminate errors. And do not seek for friendship obtained by unfair admissions ; for this I would have you know, above all, that when two fight with each other, then there will be peace when one has been defeated and has fallen. And therefore fight as best you can, and do not expect peace without war, which is impossible ; or if it can be attained, show us how."

CHAP. XXIV.—*Peter's explanation.*

To this Peter answered : " Hear with all attention, O men, what we say. Let us suppose that this world is a great plain, and that from two states, whose kings are at variance with each other, two generals were sent to fight : and suppose the general of the good king gave this counsel, that both armies should without bloodshed submit to the authority of the better king, whereby all should be safe without danger ; but that the opposite general should say, No, but we must fight ; that not he who is worthy, but he who is stronger, may reign, with those who shall escape ;—which, I ask you, would you rather choose ? I doubt not but that you would give your hands to the better king, with the safety of all. And I do not now wish, as Simon says that I do, that assent should be given, for the sake of peace, to those things that are spoken amiss ; but that truth be sought for with quietness and order.

Chap. xxv.—*Principles on which the discussion should be conducted.*

"For some, in the contest of disputations, when they perceive that their error is confuted, immediately begin, for the sake of making good their retreat, to create a disturbance, and to stir up strifes, that it may not be manifest to all that they are defeated ; and therefore I frequently entreat that the investigation of the matter in dispute may be conducted with all patience and quietness, so that if perchance anything seem to be not rightly spoken, it may be allowed to go back over it, and explain it more distinctly. For sometimes a thing may be spoken in one way and heard in another, while it is either advanced too obscurely, or not attended to with sufficient care ; and on this account I desire that our conversation should be conducted patiently, so that neither should the one snatch it away from the other, nor should the unseasonable speech of one contradicting interrupt the speech of the other ; and that we should not cherish the desire of finding fault, but that we should be allowed, as I have said, to go over again what has not been clearly enough spoken, that by fairest examination the knowledge of the truth may become clearer. For we ought to know, that if any one is conquered by the truth, it is not he that is conquered, but the ignorance which is in him, which is the worst of all demons ; so that he who can drive it out receives the palm of salvation. For it is our purpose to benefit the hearers, not that we may conquer badly, but that we may be well conquered for the acknowledgment of the truth. For if our speech be actuated by the desire of seeking the truth, even although we shall speak anything imperfectly through human frailty, God in His unspeakable goodness will fill up secretly in the understandings of the hearers those things that are lacking. For He is righteous ; and according to the purpose of every one, He enables some to find easily what they seek, while to others He renders even that obscure which is before their eyes. Since, then, the way of God is the way of peace, let us with peace seek the things which are God's. If any one has anything to

o

advance in answer to this, let him do so; but if there is no one who wishes to answer, I shall begin to speak, and I myself shall bring forward what another may object to me, and shall refute it."

CHAP. XXVI.—*Simon's interruption.*

When therefore Peter had begun to continue his discourse, Simon, interrupting his speech, said: "Why do you hasten to speak whatever you please? I understand your tricks. You wish to bring forward those matters whose explanation you have well studied, that you may appear to the ignorant crowd to be speaking well; but I shall not allow you this subterfuge. Now therefore, since you promise, as a brave man, to answer to all that any one chooses to bring forward, be pleased to answer me in the first place." Then Peter said: "I am ready, only provided that our discussion may be with peace." Then Simon said: "Do not you see, O simpleton, that in pleading for peace you act in opposition to your Master, and that what you propose is not suitable to him who promises that he will overthrow ignorance? Or, if you are right in asking peace from the audience, then your Master was wrong in saying, 'I have not come to send peace on earth, but a sword.'[1] For either you say well, and he not well; or else, if your Master said well, then you not at all well: for you do not understand that your statement is contrary to his, whose disciple you profess yourself to be."

CHAP. XXVII.—*Questions and answers.*

Then Peter: "Neither He who sent me did amiss in sending a sword upon the earth, nor do I act contrary to Him in asking peace of the hearers. But you both unskilfully and rashly find fault with what you do not understand: for you have heard that the Master came not to send peace on earth; but that He also said, 'Blessed are the peacemakers, for they shall be called the very sons of God,'[2] you have not heard. Wherefore my sentiments are not different from those of the Master when I recommend peace, to the

[1] Matt. x. 34.   [2] Matt. v. 9.

keepers of which He assigned blessedness." Then Simon said: "In your desire to answer for your Master, O Peter, you have brought a much more serious charge against him, if he himself came not to make peace, yet enjoined upon others to keep it. Where, then, is the consistency of that other saying of his, 'It is enough for the disciple that he be as his master?'"[1]

Chap. XXVIII.—*Consistency of Christ's teaching.*

To this Peter answered: "Our Master, who was the true Prophet, and ever mindful of Himself, neither contradicted Himself, nor enjoined upon us anything different from what Himself practised. For whereas He said, 'I am not come to send peace on earth, but a sword; and henceforth you shall see father separated from son, son from father, husband from wife and wife from husband, mother from daughter and daughter from mother, brother from brother, father-in-law from daughter-in-law, friend from friend,' all these contain the doctrine of peace; and I will tell you how. At the beginning of His preaching, as wishing to invite and lead all to salvation, and induce them to bear patiently labours and trials, He blessed the poor, and promised that they should obtain the kingdom of heaven for their endurance of poverty, in order that under the influence of such a hope they might bear with equanimity the weight of poverty, despising covetousness; for covetousness is one, and the greatest, of most pernicious sins. But He promised also that the hungry and the thirsty should be satisfied with the eternal blessings of righteousness, in order that they might bear poverty patiently, and not be led by it to undertake any unrighteous work. In like manner, also, He said that the pure in heart are blessed, and that thereby they should see God, in order that every one desiring so great a good might keep himself from evil and polluted thoughts.

Chap. XXIX.—*Peace and strife.*

"Thus, therefore, our Master, inviting His disciples to

[1] Matt. x. 25.

patience, impressed upon them that the blessing of peace was
also to be preserved with the labour of patience. But, on the
other hand, He mourned over those who lived in riches and
luxury, who bestowed nothing upon the poor; proving that
they must render an account, because they did not pity their
neighbours, even when they were in poverty, whom they ought
to love as themselves. And by such sayings as these He
brought some indeed to obey Him, but others He rendered
hostile. The believers therefore, and the obedient, He charges
to have peace among themselves, and says to them, ' Blessed
are the peacemakers, for they shall be called the very sons of
God.'[1] But to those who not only did not believe, but set themselves in opposition to His doctrine, He proclaims the war of
the word and of confutation, and says that ' henceforth ye
shall see son separated from father, and husband from wife,
and daughter from mother, and brother from brother, and
daughter-in-law from mother-in-law, and a man's foes shall
be they of his own house.'[2] For in every house, when there
begins to be a difference betwixt believer and unbeliever, there
is necessarily a contest: the unbelievers, on the one hand,
fighting against the faith; and the believers, on the other,
confuting the old error and the vices of sins in them.

CHAP. XXX.—*Peace to the sons of peace.*

" In like manner, also, during the last period of His teaching, He wages war against the scribes and Pharisees, charging them with evil deeds and unsound doctrine, and with
hiding the key of knowledge which they had handed down to
them from Moses, by which the gate of the heavenly kingdom might be opened.[3] But when our Master sent us forth
to preach, He commanded us, that into whatsoever city or
house we should enter, we should say, ' Peace be to this house.'
' And if,' said He, ' a son of peace be there, your peace shall
come upon him; but if there be not, your peace shall return
to you.' Also that, going out from that house or city, we
should shake off upon them the very dust which adhered to

---

[1] Matt. v. 9.   [2] Matt. x. 34, 35; Luke xii. 53.
[3] Matt. xxiii.; Luke xi.

our feet. 'But it shall be more tolerable for the land of Sodom and Gomorrha in the day of judgment than for that city or house.'[1] This indeed He commanded to be done at length, if first the word of truth be preached in the city or house, whereby they who receive the faith of the truth may become sons of peace and sons of God ; and those who will not receive it may be convicted as enemies of peace and of God.

Chap. xxxi.—*Peace and war.*

"Thus, therefore, we, observing the commands of our Master, first offer peace to our hearers, that the way of salvation may be known without any tumult. But if any one do not receive the words of peace, nor acquiesce in the truth, we know how to direct against him the war of the word, and to rebuke him sharply by confuting his ignorance and charging home upon him his sins. Therefore of necessity we offer peace, that if any one is a son of peace, our peace may come upon him ; but from him who makes himself an enemy of peace, our peace shall return to ourselves. We do not therefore, as you say, propose peace by agreement with the wicked, for indeed we should straightway have given you the right hand ; but only in order that, through our discussing quietly and patiently, it might be more easily ascertained by the hearers which is the true speech. But if you differ and disagree with yourself, how shall you stand ? He must of necessity fall who is divided in himself ; ' for every kingdom divided against itself shall not stand.'[2] If you have aught to say to this, say on."

Chap. xxxii.—*Simon's challenge.*

Then said Simon: "I am astonished at your folly. For you so propound the words of your Master, as if it were held to be certain concerning him that he is a prophet; while I can very easily prove that he often contradicted himself. In short, I shall refute you from those words which you have yourself brought forward. For you say, that he said that every kingdom or every city divided in itself shall not stand ; and elsewhere you say, that he said that he would send a

[1] Matt. x. 12-15 ; Luke x. 5, 6.   [2] Matt. xii. 25.

sword, that he might separate those who are in one house, so that son shall be divided from father, daughter from mother, brother from brother; so that if there be five in one house, three shall be divided against two, and two against three.[1] If, then, everything that is divided falls, he who makes divisions furnishes causes of falling; and if he is such, assuredly he is wicked. Answer this if you can."

Chap. xxxiii.—*Authority.*

Then Peter: "Do not rashly take exception, O Simon, against the things which you do not understand. In the first place, I shall answer your assertion, that I set forth the words of my Master, and from them resolve matters about which there is still doubt. Our Lord, when He sent us apostles to preach, enjoined us to teach all nations[2] the things which were committed to us. We cannot therefore speak those things as they were spoken by Himself. For our commission is not to *speak*, but to *teach* those things, and from them to show how every one of them rests upon truth. Nor, again, are we permitted to speak anything of our own. For we are sent; and of necessity he who is sent delivers the message as he has been ordered, and sets forth the will of the sender. For if I should speak anything different from what He who sent me enjoined me, I should be a false apostle, not saying what I am commanded to say, but what seems good to myself. Whoever does this, evidently wishes to show himself to be better than he is by whom he is sent, and without doubt is a traitor. If, on the contrary, he keeps by the things that he is commanded, and brings forward most clear assertions of them, it will appear that he is accomplishing the work of an apostle; and it is by striving to fulfil this that I displease you. Blame me not, therefore, because I bring forward the words of Him who sent me. But if there is aught in them that is not fairly spoken, you have liberty to confute me; but this can in no wise be done, for He is a prophet, and cannot be contrary to Himself. But if you do not think that He is a prophet, let this be first inquired into."

[1] Luke xii. 52.　　　　　[2] Matt. xxviii. 19, 20.

CHAP. XXXIV.—*Order of proof.*

Then said Simon: "I have no need to learn this from you, but how these things agree with one another. For if he shall be shown to be inconsistent, he shall be proved at the same time not to be a prophet." Then says Peter: "But if I first show Him to be a prophet, it will follow that what seems to be inconsistency is not such. For no one can be proved to be a prophet merely by consistency, because it is possible for many to attain this; but if consistency does not make a prophet, much more inconsistency does not. Because, therefore, there are many things which to some seem inconsistent, which yet have consistency in them on a more profound investigation; as also other things which seem to have consistency, but which, being more carefully discussed, are found to be inconsistent; for this reason I do not think that there is any better way to judge of these things than to ascertain in the first instance whether He be a prophet who has spoken those things which appear to be inconsistent. For it is evident that, if He be found to be a prophet, those things which seem to be contradictory must have consistency, but are misunderstood. Concerning these things, therefore, proofs will be properly demanded. For we apostles are sent to expound the sayings and affirm the judgments of Him who has sent us; but we are not commissioned to say anything of our own, but to unfold the truth, as I have said, of His words."

CHAP. XXXV.—*How error cannot stand with truth.*

Then Simon said: "Instruct us, therefore, how it can be consistent that he who causes divisions, which divisions cause those who are divided to fall, can either seem to be good, or to have come for the salvation of men." Then Peter said: "I will tell you how our Master said that every kingdom and every house divided against itself cannot stand; and whereas He Himself did this, see how it makes for salvation. By the word of truth He certainly divides the kingdom of the world, which is founded in error, and every house in it, that error may fall, and truth may reign. But if it happen to any house, that error, being introduced by any one, divides the truth, then, where error has gained a footing, it is certain that truth cannot stand." Then Simon said: "But it is uncertain whether your master divides error or truth." Then Peter: "That belongs to another question; but if you are agreed that everything which is divided falls, it remains that I show, if only you will hear in peace, that our Jesus has divided and dispelled error by teaching truth."

Chap. xxxvi.—*Altercation.*

Then said Simon: "Do not repeat again and again your talk of peace, but expound briefly what it is that you think or believe." Peter answered: "Why are you afraid of hearing frequently of peace? or do you not know that peace is the perfection of law? For wars and disputes spring from sins; and where there is no sin, there is peace of soul; but where there is peace, truth is found in disputations, righteousness in works." Then Simon: "You seem to me not to be able to profess what you think." Then Peter: "I shall speak, but according to my own judgment, not under constraint of your tricks. For I desire that what is salutary and profitable be brought to the knowledge of all; and therefore I shall not delay to state it as briefly as possible. There is one God; and He is the creator of the world, a righteous judge, rendering to every one at some time or other according to his deeds. But now for the assertion of these things I know that countless thousands of words can be called forth."

Chap. xxxvii.—*Simon's subtlety.*

Then Simon said: "I admire, indeed, the quickness of your wit, yet I do not embrace the error of your faith. For you have wisely foreseen that you may be contradicted; and you have even politely confessed, that for the assertion of these things countless thousands of words will be called forth, for no one agrees with the profession of your faith. In short, as to there being one God, and the world being His work, who can receive this doctrine? Neither, I think, any one of the pagans, even if he be an unlearned man, and certainly

no one of the philosophers; but not even the rudest and most
wretched of the Jews, nor I myself, who am well acquainted
with their law." Then Peter said: "Put aside the opinions of
those who are not here, and tell us face to face what is your
own." Then Simon said: "I can state what I really think;
but this consideration makes me reluctant to do so, that if I say
what is neither acceptable to you, nor seems right to this unskilled rabble, you indeed, as confounded, will straightway shut
your ears, that they may not be polluted with blasphemy, forsooth, and will take to flight because you cannot find an answer;
while the unreasoning populace will assent to you, and embrace you as one teaching those things which are commonly
received among them; and will curse me, as professing things
new and unheard of, and instilling my error into the minds
of others."

Chap. xxxviii.—*Simon's creed.*

Then Peter: "Are not you making use of long preambles,
as you accused us of doing, because you have no truth to
bring forward? or if you have, begin without circumlocution,
if you have so much confidence. And if, indeed, what you say
be displeasing to any one of the hearers, he will withdraw;
and those who remain shall be compelled by your assertion
to approve what is true. Begin, therefore, to expound what
seemeth to you to be right." Then Simon said: "I say that
there are many gods; but that there is one incomprehensible
and unknown to all, and that He is the God of all these
gods." Then Peter answered: "This God whom you assert to
be incomprehensible and unknown to all, can you prove His
existence from the Scriptures of the Jews, which are held
to be of authority, or from some others of which we are all
ignorant, or from the Greek authors, or from your own
writings? Certainly you are at liberty to speak from whatever writings you please, yet so that you first show that they
are prophetic; for so their authority will be held without
question."

Chap. xxxix.—*Argument for polytheism.*

Then Simon said: "I shall make use of assertions from the law of the Jews only. For it is manifest to all who take interest in religion, that this law is of universal authority, yet that every one receives the understanding of this law according to his own judgment. For it has so been written by Him who created the world, that the faith of things is made to depend upon it. Whence, whether any one wishes to bring forward truth, or any one to bring forward falsehood, no assertion will be received without this law. Inasmuch, therefore, as my knowledge is most fully in accordance with the law, I rightly declared that there are many gods, of whom one is more eminent than the rest, and incomprehensible, even He who is God of gods. But that there are many gods, the law itself informs me. For, in the first place, [it says this in the passage] where one in the figure of a serpent speaks to Eve, the first woman, 'On the day ye eat of the tree of the knowledge of good and evil, ye shall be as gods,'[1] that is, as those who made man; and after they have tasted of the tree, God Himself testifies, saying to the rest of the gods, 'Behold, Adam is become as one of us;'[2] thus, therefore, it is manifest that there were many gods engaged in the making of man. Also, whereas at the first God said to the other gods, 'Let us make man after our image and likeness;'[3] also His saying, 'Let us drive him out;'[4] and again, 'Come, let us go down, and confound their language;'[5] all these things indicate that there are many gods. But this also is written, 'Thou shalt not curse the gods, nor curse the chief of thy people;'[6] and again this writing, 'God alone led them, and there was no strange god with them,'[7] shows that there are many gods. There are also many other testimonies which might be adduced from the law, not only obscure, but plain, by which it is taught that there are many gods. One of these was chosen by lot, that he might be the god of the Jews. But it is not of him that I speak, but of

---

[1] Gen. iii. 5.   [2] Gen. iii. 22.   [3] Gen. i. 26.   [4] Gen. iii. 22.
[5] Gen. xi. 17.   [6] Exod. xxii. 28.   [7] Deut. xxxii. 12.

that God who is also his God, whom even the Jews themselves did not know. For he is not their God, but the God
of those who know him."

Chap. xl.—*Peter's answer.*

When Peter had heard this, he answered : "Fear nothing,
Simon : for, behold, we have neither shut our ears, nor fled ;
but we answer with words of truth to those things which
you have spoken falsely, asserting this first, that there is one
God, even the God of the Jews, who is the only God, the
Creator of heaven and earth, who is also the God of all those
whom you call gods. If, then, I shall show you that none
is superior to Him, but that He Himself is above all, you
will confess that your error is above all." Then Simon said :
"Why, indeed, though I should be unwilling to confess it,
would not the hearers who stand by charge me with un-
willingness to profess the things that are true ?"

Chap. xli.—*The answer, continued.*

"Listen, then," says Peter, "that you may know, first of all,
that even if there are many gods, as you say, they are subject
to the God of the Jews, to whom no one is equal, than whom
no one can be greater ; for it is written that the prophet
Moses thus spoke to the Jews : 'The Lord your God is the
God of gods, and the Lord of lords, the great God.'[1] Thus,
although there are many that are called gods, yet He who
is the God of the Jews is alone called the God of gods. For
not every one that is called God is necessarily God. Indeed,
even Moses is called a god to Pharaoh,[2] and it is certain that
he was a man ; and judges were called gods, and it is evident that they were mortal. The idols also of the Gentiles
are called gods, and we all know that they are not ; but
this has been inflicted as a punishment on the wicked, that
because they would not acknowledge the true God, they
should regard as God whatever form or image should occur
to them. Because they refused to receive the knowledge of
the One who, as I said, is God of all, therefore it is permitted

[1] Deut. x. 17.   [2] Exod. vii. 1.

to them to have as gods those who can do nothing for their worshippers. For what can either dead images or living creatures confer upon men, since the power of all things is with One?

Chap. XLII.—*Guardian angels.*

"Therefore the name *God* is applied in three ways: either because he to whom it is given is truly God, or because he is the servant of him who is truly; and for the honour of the sender, that his authority may be full, he that is sent is called by the name of him who sends, as is often done in respect of angels: for when they appear to a man, if he is a wise and intelligent man, he asks the name of him who appears to him, that he may acknowledge at once the honour of the sent, and the authority of the sender. For every nation has an angel, to whom God has committed the government of that nation; and when one of these appears, although he be thought and called God by those over whom he presides, yet, being asked, he does not give such testimony to himself. For the Most High God, who alone holds the power of all things, has divided all the nations of the earth into seventy-two parts, and over these He hath appointed angels as princes. But to the one among the archangels who is greatest, was committed the government of those who, before all others, received the worship and knowledge of the Most High God. But holy men also, as we have said, are made gods to the wicked, as having received the power of life and death over them, as we mentioned above with respect to Moses and the judges. Wherefore it is also written concerning them, 'Thou shalt not curse the gods, and thou shalt not curse the prince of thy people.'[1] Thus the princes of the several nations are called gods. But Christ is God of princes, who is Judge of all. Therefore neither angels, nor men, nor any creature, can be truly gods, forasmuch as they are placed under authority, being created and changeable: angels, for they were not, and are; men, for they are mortal; and every creature, for it is capable of dissolution, if only He dissolve

[1] Exod. xxii. 28.

it who made it. And therefore He alone is the true God, who not only Himself lives, but also bestows life upon others, which He can also take away when it pleaseth Him.

Chap. xliii.—*No God but Jehovah.*

"Wherefore the Scripture exclaims, in name of the God of the Jews, saying, 'Behold, behold, seeing that I am God, and there is none else besides me, I will kill, and I will make alive; I will smite, and I will heal; and there is none who can deliver out of my hands.'[1] See therefore how, by some ineffable virtue, the Scripture, opposing the future errors of those who should affirm that either in heaven or on earth there is any other god besides Him who is the God of the Jews, decides thus: 'The Lord your God is one God, in heaven above, and in the earth beneath; and besides Him there is none else.'[2] How, then, hast thou dared to say that there is any other god besides Him who is the God of the Jews? And again the Scripture says, 'Behold, to the Lord thy God belong the heaven, and the heaven of heavens, the earth, and all things that are in them: nevertheless I have chosen your fathers, that I might love them, and you after them.'[3] Thus that judgment is supported by the Scripture on every side, that He who created the world is the true and only God.

Chap. xliv.—*The serpent, the author of polytheism.*

"But even if there be others, as we have said, who are called gods, they are under the power of the God of the Jews; for thus saith the Scripture to the Jews, 'The Lord our God, He is God of gods, and Lord of lords.'[4] Him alone the Scripture also commands to be worshipped, saying, 'Thou shalt worship the Lord thy God, and Him only shalt thou serve;'[5] and, 'Hear, O Israel: the Lord thy God is one God.'[6] Yea, also the saints, filled with the Spirit of God, and bedewed with the drops of His mercy, cried out, saying, 'Who is like unto Thee among the gods? O Lord, who is

[1] Deut. xxxii. 39.   [2] Deut. iv. 39.   [3] Deut. x. 14, 15.
[4] Deut. x. 17.   [5] Deut. vi. 13, x. 20.   [6] Deut. vi. 4.

like unto Thee?'[1]   And again, 'Who is God, but the Lord;
and who is God, but our Lord?'[2]   Therefore Moses, when
he saw that the people were advancing, by degrees initiated
them in the understanding of the monarchy and the faith of
one God, as he says in the following words: 'Thou shalt not
make mention of the names of other gods;'[3] doubtless remembering with what penalty the serpent was visited, which
had first named *gods*.[4]   For it is condemned to feed upon
dust, and is judged worthy of such food, for this cause, that
it first of all introduced the name of *gods* into the world.
But if you also wish to introduce many gods, see that you
partake not the serpent's doom.

Chap. xlv.—*Polytheism inexcusable.*

"For be sure of this, that you shall not have us partici-
pators in this attempt ; nor will we suffer ourselves to be
deceived by you.   For it will not serve us for an excuse
in the judgment, if we say that you deceived us; because
neither could it excuse the first woman, that she had unhappily believed the serpent; but she was condemned to death,
because she believed badly.   For this cause therefore, Moses,
also commending the faith of one God to the people, says,
'Take heed to thyself, that thou be not seduced from the
Lord thy God.'[5]   Observe that he makes use of the same
word which the first woman also made use of in excusing
herself, saying that she was seduced ; but it profited her
nothing.   But over and above all this, even if some true
prophet should arise, who should perform signs and miracles,
but should wish to persuade us to worship other gods besides the God of the Jews, we should never be able to believe
him.   For so the divine law has taught us, handing down a
secret injunction more purely by means of tradition, for thus
it saith : 'If there arise among you a prophet, or one dreaming
a dream, and give you signs or wonders, and these signs or
wonders come to pass, and he say to you, Let us go and
worship strange gods, whom ye know not; ye shall not hear

[1] Ps. lxxxv. 8, lxx. 19.   [2] Ps. xvii. 32.   [3] Josh. xxiii. 7, in Sept.
[4] Gen. iii.   [5] Deut. viii. 11.

the words of that prophet, nor the dream of that dreamer, because proving he hath proved you, that he may see if ye love the Lord your God.'[1]

CHAP. XLVI.—*Christ acknowledged the God of the Jews.*

" Wherefore also our Lord, who wrought signs and wonders, preached the God of the Jews; and therefore we are right in believing what He preached. But as for you, even if you were really a prophet, and performed signs and wonders, as you promise to do, if you were to announce other gods besides Him who is the true God, it would be manifest that you were raised up as a trial to the people of God; and therefore you can by no means be believed. For He alone is the true God, who is the God of the Jews; and for this reason our Lord Jesus Christ did not teach them that they must inquire after God, for Him they knew well already, but that they must seek His kingdom and righteousness,[2] which the scribes and Pharisees, having received the key of knowledge, had not shut in, but shut out.[3] For if they had been ignorant of the true God, surely He would never have left the knowledge of this thing, which was the chief of all, and blamed them for small and little things, as for enlarging their fringes, and claiming the uppermost rooms in feasts, and praying standing in the highways, and such like things; which assuredly, in comparison of this great charge, ignorance of God, seem to be small and insignificant matters."

CHAP. XLVII.—*Simon's cavil.*

To this Simon replied: " From the words of your master I shall refute you, because even he introduces to all men a certain God who was unknown. For although both Adam knew the God who was his creator, and the maker of the world; and Enoch knew him, inasmuch as he was translated by him; and Noah, since he was ordered by him to construct the ark; and although Abraham, and Isaac, and Jacob, and Moses, and all, even every people and all nations, know the maker of the world, and confess him to be a God, yet

[1] Deut. xiii. 1-3.   [2] Matt. vi. 33.   [3] Luke xi. 52.

your Jesus, who appeared long after the patriarchs, says:
' No one knows the Son, but the Father; neither knoweth
any one the Father, but the Son, and he to whom the Son
has been pleased to reveal Him.'[1] Thus, therefore, even your
Jesus confesses that there is another God, incomprehensible
and unknown to all."

Chap. xlviii.—*Peter's answer.*

Then Peter says: " You do not perceive that you are
making statements in opposition to yourself. For if our
Jesus also knows Him whom ye call the unknown God, then
He is not known by you alone. Yea, if our Jesus knows
Him, then Moses also, who prophesied that Jesus should
come, assuredly could not himself be ignorant of Him. For
he was a prophet; and he who prophesied of the Son doubtless knew the Father. For if it is in the option of the Son
to reveal the Father to whom He will, then the Son, who has
been with the Father from the beginning, and through all
generations, as He revealed the Father to Moses, so also to
the other prophets; but if this be so, it is evident that the
Father has not been unknown to any of them. But how
could the Father be revealed to you, who do not believe in
the Son, since the Father is known to none except him to
whom the Son is pleased to reveal Him ? But the Son
reveals the Father to those who honour the Son as they
honour the Father."[2]

Chap. xlix.—*The supreme light.*

Then Simon said: " Remember that you said that God
has a son, which is doing Him wrong; for how can He have
a son, unless He is subject to passions, like men or animals ?
But on these points there is not time now to show your profound folly, for I hasten to make a statement concerning the
immensity of the supreme light; and so now listen. My
opinion is, that there is a certain power of immense and
ineffable light, whose greatness may be held to be incomprehensible, of which power even the maker of the world is
ignorant, and Moses the lawgiver, and Jesus your master."

[1] Matt. xi. 27.   [2] John v. 23.

Chap. l.—*Simon's presumption.*

Then Peter: "Does it not seem to you to be madness, that any one should take upon himself to assert that there is another God than the God of all; and should say that he supposes there is a certain power, and should presume to affirm this to others, before he himself is sure of what he says? Is any one so rash as to believe your words, of which he sees that you are yourself doubtful, and to admit that there is a certain power unknown to God the Creator, and to Moses, and the prophets, and the law, and even to Jesus our Master, which power is so good, that it will not make itself known to any but to one only, and that one such an one as thou! Then, further, if that is a new power, why does it not confer upon us some new sense, in addition to those five which we possess, that by that new sense, bestowed upon us by it, we may be able to receive and understand itself, which is new? Or if it cannot bestow such a sense upon us, how has it bestowed it upon you? Or if it has revealed itself to you, why not also to us? But if you of yourself understand things which not even the prophets were able to perceive or understand, come, tell us what each one of us is thinking now; for if there is such a spirit in you that you know those things which are above the heavens, which are unknown to all, and incomprehensible by all, much more easily do you know the thoughts of men upon the earth. But if you cannot know the thoughts of us who are standing here, how can you say that you know those things which, you assert, are known to none?

Chap. li.—*The sixth sense.*

"But believe me, that you could never know what light is unless you had received both vision and understanding from light itself; so also in other things. Hence, having received understanding, you are framing in imagination something greater and more sublime, as if dreaming, but deriving all your hints from those five senses, to whose Giver you are unthankful. But be sure of this, that until you find some new

P

sense which is beyond those five which we all enjoy, you cannot assert the existence of a new God." Then Simon answered : " Since all things that exist are in accordance with those five senses, that power which is more excellent than all cannot add anything new." Then Peter said : " It is false ; for there is also a sixth sense, namely that of foreknowledge : for those five senses are capable of knowledge, but the sixth is that of fore-knowledge ; and this the prophets possessed. How, then, can you know a God who is unknown to all, who do not know the prophetic sense, which is that of prescience ? " Then Simon began to say : " This power of which I speak, incom-prehensible and more excellent than all, ay, even than that God who made the world, neither any of the angels has known, nor of the demons, nor of the Jews, nay, nor any creature which subsists by means of God the creator. How, then, could that creator's law teach me that which the creator himself did not know, since neither did the law itself know it, that it might teach it ? "

CHAP. LII.—*Reductio ad absurdum.*

Then Peter said : " I wonder how you have been able to learn more from the law than the law was able to know or to teach ; and how you say that you adduce proofs from the law of those things which you are pleased to assert, when you declare that neither the law, nor He who gave the law—that is, the Creator of the world—knows those things of which you speak ! But this also I wonder at, how you, who alone know these things, should be standing here now with us all, circum-scribed by the limits of this small court." Then Simon, seeing Peter and all the people laughing, said : " Do you laugh, Peter, while so great and lofty matters are under dis-cussion ? " Then said Peter : " Be not enraged, Simon, for we are doing no more than keeping our promise : for we are neither shutting our ears, as you said, nor did we take to flight as soon as we heard you propound your unutterable things ; but we have not even stirred from the place. For indeed you do not even propound things that have any resem-blance to truth, which might to a certain extent frighten us.

Yet, at all events, disclose to us the meaning of this saying, how from the law you have learned of a God whom the law itself does not know, and of whom He who gave the law is ignorant." Then Simon said: "If you have done laughing, I shall prove it by clear assertions." Then Peter said: "Assuredly I shall give over, that I may learn from you how you have learned from the law what neither the law nor the God of the law Himself knows."

CHAP. LIII.—*Simon's blasphemy.*

Then says Simon: "Listen: it is manifest to all, and ascertained in a manner of which no account can be given,[1] that there is one God, who is better than all, from whom all that is took its beginning; whence also of necessity all things that are after him are subject to him, as the chief and most excellent of all. When, therefore, I had ascertained that the God who created the world, according to what the law teaches, is in many respects weak, whereas weakness is utterly incompatible with a perfect God, and I saw that he is not perfect, I necessarily concluded that there is another God who is perfect. For this God, as I have said, according to what the writing of the law teaches, is shown to be weak in many things. In the first place, because the man whom he formed was not able to remain such as he had intended him to be; and because he cannot be good who gave a law to the first man, that he should eat of all the trees of paradise, but that he should not touch the tree of knowledge; and if he should eat of it, he should die. For why should he forbid him to eat, and to know what is good and what evil, that, knowing, he might shun the evil and choose the good? But this he did not permit; and because he did eat in violation of the commandment, and discovered what is good, and learned for the sake of honour to cover his nakedness (for he perceived it to be unseemly to stand naked before his Creator), he con-

---

[1] We render by a periphrasis the expression *ineffabili quadam ratione compertum.* The meaning seems to be, that the belief of the existence and unity of God is not the result of reasoning, but of intuition or instinct.

demns to death him who had learned to do honour to God, and curses the serpent who had shown him these things. But truly, if man was to be injured by this means, why did he place the cause of injury in paradise at all? But if that which he placed in paradise was good, it is not the part of one that is good to restrain another from good.

CHAP. LIV.—*How Simon learned from the law what the law does not teach.*

"Thus, then, since he who made man and the world is, according to what the law relates, imperfect, we are given to understand, without doubt, that there is another who is perfect. For it is of necessity that there be one most excellent of all, on whose account also every creature keeps its rank. Whence also I, knowing that it is every way necessary that there be some one more benignant and more powerful than that imperfect God who gave the law, understanding what is perfect from comparison of the imperfect, understood even from the Scripture that God who is not mentioned there. And in this way I was able, O Peter, to learn from the law what the law did not know. But even if the law had not given indications from which it might be gathered that the God who made the world is imperfect, it was still possible for me to infer from those evils which are done in this world, and are not corrected, either that its creator is powerless, if he cannot correct what is done amiss; or else, if he does not wish to remove the evils, that he is himself evil; but if he neither can nor will, that he is neither powerful nor good. And from this it cannot but be concluded that there is another God more excellent and more powerful than all. If you have aught to say to this, say on."

CHAP. LV.—*Simon's objections turned against himself.*

Peter answered: "O Simon, they are wont to conceive such absurdities against God who do not read the law with the instruction of masters, but account themselves teachers, and think that they can understand the law, though he has not explained it to them who has learned of the Master. Nevertheless now, that we also may seem to follow the book of the law according to your apprehension of it; inasmuch as you say that the creator of the world is shown to be both impotent and evil, how is it that you do not see that that power of yours, which you say is superior to all, falls and lies under the very same charges? For the very same thing may be said of it, that it is either powerless, since it does not correct those things which here are done amiss; or if it can and will not, it is evil; or if it neither can nor will, then it is both impotent and imperfect. Whence that new power of yours is not only found liable to a similar charge, but even to a worse one, if, in addition to all these things, it is believed to be, when it is not. For He who created the world, His existence is manifest by His very operation in creating the world, as you yourself also confess. But this power which you say that you alone know, affords no indication of itself, by which we might perceive, at least, that it is, and subsists.

Chap. LVI.—*No God above the Creator.*

"What kind of conduct, then, would it be that we should forsake God, in whose world we live and enjoy all things necessary for life, and follow I know not whom, from whom we not only obtain no good, but cannot even know that he exists? Nor truly does he exist. For whether you call him light, and brighter than that light which we see, you borrow that very name from the Creator of the world; or whether you say that he is a substance above all, you derive from Him the idea with enlargement of speech.[1] Whether you make mention of mind, or goodness, or life, or whatever else, you borrow the words from Him. Since, then, you have nothing new concerning that power you speak of, not only as regards understanding, but even in respect of naming him, how do you introduce a new God, for whom you cannot even find a new name? For not only is the Creator of the world called a Power, but even the ministers of His glory, and all the heavenly host. Do you not then think it better that we should

---

[1] That is, you take the idea of substance from the God of the Jews, and only enlarge it by the addition of the words *above all.*

follow our Creator God, as a Father who trains us and endows us as He knows how? But if, as you say, there be some God more benignant than all, it is certain that he will not be angry with us; or if he be angry, he is evil. For if our God is angry and punishes, He is not evil, but righteous, for He corrects and amends His own sons. But he who has no concern with us, if he shall punish us, how should he be good? Inflicting punishments upon us because we have not been drawn by vain imaginations to forsake our own Father and follow him, how can you assert that he is so good, when he cannot be regarded as even just?"

CHAP. LVII.—*Simon's inconsistency.*

Then Simon: "Do you so far err, Peter, as not to know that our souls were made by that good God, the most excellent of all, but they have been brought down as captives into this world?" To this Peter answered: "Then he is not unknown by all, as you said a little while ago; and yet how did the good God permit his souls to be taken captive, if he be a power over all?" Then Simon said: "He sent God the creator to make the world; and he, when he had made it, gave out that himself was God." Then Peter said: "Then he is not, as you said, unknown to Him who made the world; nor are souls ignorant of him, if indeed they were stolen away from him. To whom, then, can he be unknown, if both the Creator of the world know him, as having been sent by him; and all souls know him, as having been violently withdrawn from him? Then, further, I wish you would tell us whether he who sent the creator of the world did not know that he would not keep faith? For if he did not know it, then he was not prescient; while if he foreknew it, and suffered it, he is himself guilty of this deed, since he did not prevent it; but if he could not, then he is not omnipotent. But if, knowing it as good, he did not prohibit it, he is found to be better, who presumed to do that which he who sent him did not know to be good."

CHAP. LVIII.—*Simon's God unjust.*

Then Simon said: "He receives those who will come to

him, and does them good." Peter answered : " But there is
nothing new in this ; for He whom you acknowledge to be
the Creator of the world also does so." Then Simon : " But
the good God bestows salvation if he is only acknowledged ;
but the creator of the world demands also that the law be
fulfilled." Then said Peter : " He saves adulterers and
men-slayers, if they know him ; but good, and sober, and
merciful persons, if they do not know him, in consequence
of their having no information concerning him, he does not
save ! Great and good truly is he whom you proclaim, who
is not so much the saviour of the evil, as he is one who shows
no mercy to the good." Then Simon : " It is truly very
difficult for man to know him, as long as he is in the flesh ;
for blacker than all darkness, and heavier than all clay, is
this body with which the soul is surrounded." Then says
Peter : " That good God of yours demands things which are
difficult ; but He who is truly God seeks easier things. Let
him then, since he is so good, leave us with our Father and
Creator ; and when once we depart from the body, and leave
that darkness that you speak of, we shall more easily know
Him ; and then the soul shall better understand that God is
its Creator, and shall remain with Him, and shall no more be
harassed with diverse imaginations ; nor shall wish to betake
itself to another power, which is known to none but Simon
only, and which is of such goodness that no one can come to
it, unless he be first guilty of impiety towards his own father !
I know not how this power can be called either good or just,
which no one can please except by acting impiously towards
him by whom he was made ! "

Chap. lix.—*The Creator our Father.*

Then Simon : " It is not impious for the sake of greater
profit and advantage to flee to him who is of richer glory."
Then Peter : " If, as you say, it is not impious to flee to a
stranger, it is at all events much more pious to remain with
our own father, even if he be poor. But if you do not think
it impious to leave our father, and flee to another, as being
better than he ; and you do not believe that our Creator will

take this amiss; much more the good God will not be angry, because, when we were strangers to him, we have not fled to him, but have remained with our own Creator. Yea, I think he will rather commend us the more for this, that we have kept faith with God our Creator; for he will consider that, if we had been his creatures, we should never have been seduced by the allurements of any other to forsake him. For if any one, allured by richer promises, shall leave his own father and betake himself to a stranger, it may be that he will leave him in his turn, and go to another who shall promise him greater things, and this the rather because he is not his son, since he could leave even him who by nature was his father." Then Simon said: "But what if souls are from him, and do not know him, and he is truly their father?"

Chap. LX.—*The Creator the Supreme God.*

Then Peter said: "You represent him as weak enough. For if, as you say, he is more powerful than all, it can never be believed the weaker wrenched the spoils from the stronger.[1] Or if God the Creator was able by violence to bring down souls into this world, how can it be that, when they are separated from the body and freed from the bonds of captivity, the good God shall call them to the sufferance of punishment, on the ground that they, either through his remissness or weakness, were dragged away to this place, and were involved in the body, as in the darkness of ignorance? You seem to me not to know what a father and a God is: but I could tell you both whence souls are, and when and how they were made; but it is not permitted to me now to disclose these things to you, who are in such error in respect of the knowledge of God." Then said Simon: "A time will come when you shall be sorry that you did not understand me speaking of the ineffable power." Then said Peter: "Give us then, as I have often said, as being yourself a new God, or as having yourself come down from him, some new sense, by means of which we may know that new God of whom you speak; for those five senses, which God our Creator

[1] Luke xi. 22.

has given us, keep faith to their own Creator, and do not perceive that there is any other God, for so their nature necessitates them."

CHAP. LXI.—*Imagination.*

To this Simon answered : "Apply your mind to those things which I am going to say, and cause it, walking in peaceable paths, to attain to those things which I shall demonstrate. Listen now, therefore. Did you never in thought reach forth your mind into regions or islands situated far away, and remain so fixed in them, that you could not even see the people that were before you, or know where yourself were sitting, by reason of the delightfulness of those things on which you were gazing?" And Peter said : "It is true, Simon, this has often occurred to me." Then Simon said : "In this way now reach forth your sense into heaven, yea above the heaven, and behold that there must be some place beyond the world, or outside the world, in which there is neither heaven nor earth, and where no shadow of these things produces darkness; and consequently, since there are neither bodies in it, nor darkness occasioned by bodies, there must of necessity be immense light; and consider of what sort that light must be, which is never succeeded by darkness. For if the light of this sun fills this whole world, how great do you suppose that bodiless and infinite light to be? So great, doubtless, that this light of the sun would seem to be darkness and not light, in comparison."

CHAP. LXII.—*Peter's experience of imagination.*

When Simon thus spoke, Peter answered : "Now listen patiently concerning both these matters, that is, concerning the example of stretching out the senses, and concerning the immensity of light. I know that I myself, O Simon, have sometimes in thought extended my sense, as you say, into regions and islands situated afar off, and have seen them with my mind not less than if it had been with my eyes. When I was at Capernaum, occupied in the taking of fishes, and sat upon a rock, holding in my hand a hook attached to a line, and fitted for deceiving the fishes, [I was so absorbed]

that I did not feel a fish adhering to it while my mind eagerly
ran through my beloved Jerusalem, to which I had frequently
gone up, waking, for the sake of offerings and prayers.   But
I was accustomed also to admire this Cæsarea, hearing of it
from others, and to long to see it; and I seemed to myself to
see it, although I had never been in it; and I thought of it
what was suitable to be thought of a great city, its gates, walls,
baths, streets, lanes, markets, and the like, in accordance with
what I had seen in other cities; and to such an extent was I
delighted with the intentness of such inspection, that, as you
said, I neither saw one who was present and standing by me,
nor knew where myself was sitting."   Then said Simon:
"Now you say well."

Chap. lxiii.—*Peter's reverie.*

Then Peter: "In short, when I did not perceive, through
the occupation of my mind, that I had caught a very large
fish which was attached to the hook, and that although it
was dragging the hook-line from my hand, my brother
Andrew, who was sitting by me, seeing me in a reverie and
almost ready to fall, thrusting his elbow into my side as
if he would awaken me from sleep, said: 'Do you not see,
Peter, what a large fish you have caught?   Are you out of
your senses, that you are thus in a stupor of astonishment?
Tell me, What is the matter with you?'   But I was angry
with him for a little, because he had withdrawn me from the
delight of those things which I was contemplating; then I
answered that I was not suffering from any malady, but that
I was mentally gazing on the beloved Jerusalem, and at the
same time on Cæsarea; and that, while I was indeed with
him in the body, in my mind I was wholly carried away
thither.   But he, I know not whence inspired, uttered a
hidden and secret word of truth.

Chap. lxiv.—*Andrew's rebuke.*

"'Give over,' says he, 'O Peter.   What is it that you are
doing?   For those who are beginning to be possessed with a
demon, or to be disturbed in their minds, begin in this way.
They are first carried away by fancies to some pleasant and

delightful things, then they are poured out in vain and fond motions towards things which have no existence. Now this happens from a certain disease of mind, by reason of which they see not the things which are, but long to bring to their sight those which are not. But thus it happens also to those who are suffering phrenzy, and seem to themselves to see many images, because their soul, being torn and withdrawn from its place by excess of cold or of heat, suffers a failure of its natural service. But those also who are in distress through thirst, when they fall asleep, seem to themselves to see rivers and fountains, and to drink; but this befalls them through being distressed by the dryness of the unmoistened body. Wherefore it is certain that this occurs through some ailment either of the soul or body.'

Chap. lxv.—*Fallacy of imagination.*

"In short, that you may receive the faith of the matter; concerning Jerusalem, which I had often seen, I told my brother what places and what gatherings of people I had seemed to myself to see. But also concerning Cæsarea, which I had never seen, I nevertheless contended that it was such as I had conceived it in my mind and thought. But when I came hither, and saw nothing at all like to those things which I had seen in phantasy, I blamed myself, and observed distinctly, that I had assigned to it gates, and walls, and buildings from others which I had seen, taking the likeness in reality from others. Nor indeed can any one imagine anything new, and of which no form has ever existed. For even if any one should fashion from his imagination bulls with five heads, he only forms them with five heads out of those which he has seen with one head. And you therefore, now, if truly you seem to yourself to perceive anything with your thought, and to look above the heavens, there is no doubt but that you imagine them from those things which you see, placed as you are upon the earth. But if you think that there is easy access for your mind above the heavens, and that you are able to conceive the things that are there, and to apprehend knowledge of that immense light, I think

that for him who can comprehend these things, it were easier
to throw his sense, which knows how to ascend thither, into
the heart and breast of some one of us who stand by, and to
tell what thoughts he is cherishing in his breast. If therefore
you can declare the thoughts of the heart of any one of us,
who is not pre-engaged in your favour, we shall perhaps be
able to believe you, that you are able to know those things
that are above the heavens, although these are much loftier."

CHAP. LXVI.—*Existence and conception.*

To this Simon replied: "O thou who hast woven a web of
many frivolities, listen now. It is impossible that anything
which comes into a man's thoughts should not also subsist in
truth and reality. For things that do not subsist, have no
appearances;[1] but things that have no appearances, cannot
present themselves to our thoughts." Then said Peter: "If
everything that can come into our thoughts has a subsistence,
then, with respect to that place of immensity which you say
is outside the world, if one thinks in his heart that it is light,
and another that it is darkness, how can one and the same
place be both light and darkness, according to their different
thoughts concerning it?" Then said Simon: "Let pass for
the present what I have said; and tell us what you suppose
to be above the heavens."

CHAP. LXVII.—*The law teaches of immensity.*

Then said Peter: "If you believed concerning the true
fountain of light, I could instruct you what and of what
sort is that which is immense, and should render, not a vain
fancy, but a consistent and necessary account of the truth,
and should make use, not of sophistical assertions, but testimonies of the law and nature, that you might know that the
law especially contains what we ought to believe in regard to
immensity. But if the doctrine of immensity is not unknown
to the law, then assuredly nought else can be unknown to it;
and therefore it is a false supposition of yours, that there is

---

[1] That is, have no visible or sensible *species*, according to the Platonic
theory of perception.

anything of which the law is not cognisant. Much more shall nothing be unknown to Him who gave the law. Yet I cannot speak anything to you of immensity and of those things which are without limit, unless first you either accept our account of those heavens which are bounded by a certain limit, or else propound your own account of them. But if you cannot understand concerning those which are comprehended within fixed boundaries, much more can you neither know nor learn anything concerning those which are without limit."

Chap. lxviii.—*The visible and the invisible heaven.*

To this Simon answered : " It seems to me to be better to believe simply that God is, and that that heaven which we see is the only heaven in the whole universe." But Peter said : " Not so ; but it is proper to confess one God who truly is ; but that there are heavens, which were made by Him, as also the law says, of which one is the higher, in which also is contained the visible firmament ; and that that higher heaven is perpetual and eternal, with those who dwell in it ; but that this visible heaven is to be dissolved and to pass away at the end of the world, in order that that heaven which is older and higher may appear after the judgment to the holy and the worthy." To this Simon answered : " That these things are so, as you say, may appear to those who believe them ; but to him who seeks for reasons of these things, it is impossible that they can be produced from the law, and especially concerning the immensity of light."

Chap. lxix.—*Faith and reason.*

Then Peter : " Do not think that we say that these things are only to be received by faith, but also that they are to be asserted by reason. For indeed it is not safe to commit these things to bare faith without reason, since assuredly truth cannot be without reason. And therefore he who has received these things fortified by reason, can never lose them ; whereas he who receives them without proofs, by an assent to a simple statement of them, can neither keep them safely, nor is certain if they are true ; because he who easily believes, also easily yields. But he who has sought reason for those things which he has believed and received, as though bound by chains of reason itself, can never be torn away or separated from those things which he hath believed. And therefore, according as any one is more anxious in demanding a reason, by so much will he be the firmer in preserving his faith."

Chap. lxx.—*Adjournment.*

To this Simon replied: "It is a great thing which you promise, that the eternity of boundless light can be shown from the law." And when Peter said, "I shall show it whenever you please," Simon answered: "Since now it is a late hour, I shall stand by you and oppose you to-morrow; and if you can prove that this world was created, and that souls are immortal, you shall have me to assist you in your preaching." When he had said thus, he departed, and was followed by a third part of all the people who had come with him, who were about one thousand men. But the rest with bended knees prostrated themselves before Peter; and he, invoking upon them the name of God, cured some who had demons, healed others who were sick, and so dismissed the people rejoicing, commanding them to come early the next day. But Peter, when the crowds had withdrawn, commanded the table to be spread on the ground, in the open air, in the court where the disputation had been held, and sat down together with those eleven; but I dined reclining with some others who also had made a beginning of hearing the word of God, and were greatly beloved.

Chap. lxxi.—*Separation from the unclean.*

But Peter, most benignantly regarding me, lest haply that separation might cause me sorrow, says to me: "It is not from pride, O Clement, that I do not eat with those who have not yet been purified; but I fear lest perhaps I should injure myself, and do no good to them. For this I would have you know for certain, that every one who has at any time worshipped idols, and has adored those whom the pagans call gods, or has eaten of the things sacrificed to them, is not without an unclean spirit; for he has become a guest of demons, and has been partaker with that demon of which he has formed the image in his mind, either through fear or love.[1] And by these means he is not free from an unclean spirit, and therefore needs the purification of baptism, that the unclean spirit may go out of him, which has made its abode in the inmost affections of his soul, and what is worse, gives no indication that it lurks within, for fear it should be exposed and expelled.

CHAP. LXXII.—*The remedy.*

" For these unclean spirits love to dwell in the bodies of men, that they may fulfil their own desires by their service, and, inclining the motions of their souls to those things which they themselves desire, may compel them to obey their own lusts, that they may become wholly vessels of demons. One of whom is this Simon, who is seized with such disease, and cannot now be healed, because he is sick in his will and purpose. Nor does the demon dwell in him against his will; and therefore, if any one would drive it out of him, since it is inseparable from himself, and, so to speak, has now become his very soul, he should seem rather to kill him, and to incur the guilt of manslaughter. Let no one of you therefore be saddened at being separated from eating with us, for every one ought to observe that it is for just so long a time as he pleases. For he who wishes soon to be baptized is separated but for a little time, but he for a longer who wishes to be baptized later. Every one therefore has it in his own power to demand a shorter or a longer time for his repentance; and therefore it lies with you, when you wish it, to come to our table ; and not with us, who are not permitted to take food with any one who has not been baptized. It is rather you, therefore, who hinder us from eating with you, if you interpose delays in the way of your purification, and defer your baptism." Having said thus, and having blessed, he took food. And afterwards, when he had given thanks to God, he went into the house and went to bed ; and we all did the like, for it was now night.

[1] 1 Cor. x. 20.

RECOGNITIONS OF CLEMENT.

BOOK III.

CHAP. I.—*Pearls before swine.*

EANTIME Peter, rising at the crowing of the cock, and wishing to rouse us, found us awake, the evening light still burning; and when, according to custom, he had saluted us, and we had all sat down, he thus began. "Nothing is more difficult, my brethren, than to reason concerning the truth in the presence of a mixed multitude of people. For that which is may not be spoken to all as it is, on account of those who hear wickedly and treacherously; yet it is not proper to deceive, on account of those who desire to hear the truth sincerely. What, then, shall he do who has to address a mixed multitude? Shall he conceal what is true? How, then, shall he instruct those who are worthy? But if he set forth pure truth to those who do not desire to obtain salvation, he does injury to Him by whom he has been sent, and from whom he has received commandment not to throw the pearls of His words before swine and dogs,[1] who, striving against them with arguments and sophisms, roll them in the mud of carnal understanding, and by their barkings and base answers break and weary the preachers of God's word. Wherefore I also, for the most part, by using a certain circumlocution, endeavour to avoid publishing the chief knowledge concerning the Supreme Divinity to unworthy ears." Then, beginning from the Father, and the Son, and the Holy Spirit, he briefly and

[1] Matt. vii. 6.

plainly expounded to us, so that all of us hearing him wondered that men have forsaken the truth, and have turned themselves to vanity.

Chap. XII.[1]—*Second day's discussion.*

But when the day had dawned, some one came in and said : " There is a very great multitude waiting in the court, and in the midst of them stands Simon, endeavouring to preoccupy the ears of the people with most wicked persuasions." Then Peter, immediately going out, stood in the place where he had disputed the day before, and all the people turning to him with joy, gave heed to him. But when Simon perceived that the people rejoiced at the sight of Peter, and were moved to love him, he said in confusion : " I wonder at the folly of men, who call me a magician, and love Peter; whereas, having knowledge of me of old, they ought to love me rather. And therefore from this sign those who have sense may understand that Peter may rather seem to be the magician, since affection is not borne to me, to whom it is almost due from acquaintance, but is abundantly expended upon him, to whom it is not due by any familiarity."

Chap. XIII.—*Simon a seducer.*

While Simon was talking on in this style, Peter, having saluted the people in his usual way, thus answered : " O Simon, his own conscience is sufficient for every one to confute him; but if you wonder at this, that those who are acquainted with you not only do not love you but even hate you, learn the reason from me. Since you are a seducer, you profess to proclaim the truth ; and on this account you had many friends who had a desire to learn the truth. But when they saw in you things contrary to what you professed, they being, as I said, lovers of truth, began not only not to love you, but even to hate you. But yet they did not immediately

[1] Chaps. ii.-xii. are wanting in the mss. of best authority; and it seems to us indisputable that they form no part of the original work. For this reason, and because we have found them utterly untranslatable, we have omitted them.

forsake you, because you still promised that you could show them what is true. As long, therefore, as no one was present who could show them, they bore with you ; but since the hope of better instruction has dawned upon them, they despise you, and seek to know what they understand to be better. And you indeed, acting by nefarious arts, thought at first that you should escape detection. But you are detected. For you are driven into a corner, and, contrary to your expectation, you are made notorious, not only as being ignorant of the truth, but as being unwilling to hear it from those who know it. For if you had been willing to hear, that saying would have been exemplified in you, of Him who said that 'there is nothing hidden which shall not be known, nor covered which shall not be disclosed.'"[1]

CHAP. XIV.—*Simon claims the fulfilment of Peter's promise.*

While Peter spoke these words, and others to the same effect, Simon answered : " I will not have you detain me with long speeches, Peter ; I claim from you what you promised yesterday. You then said that you could show that the law teaches concerning the immensity of the eternal light, and that there are only two heavens, and these created, and that the higher is the abode of that light, in which the ineffable Father dwells alone for ever ; but that after the pattern of that heaven is made this visible heaven, which you asserted is to pass away. You said, therefore, that the Father of all is one, because there cannot be two infinites ; else neither of them would be infinite, because in that in which the one subsists, he makes a limit of the subsistence of the other. Since then you not only promised this, but are able to show it from the law, leave off other matters and set about this." Then Peter said : " If I were asked to speak of these things only on your account, who come only for the purpose of contradicting, you should never hear a single discourse from me ; but seeing it is necessary that the husbandman, wishing to sow good ground, should sow some seeds, either in stony places, or places that are to be trodden of men, or in places filled with brambles

[1] Matt. x. 26.

and briers (as our Master also set forth, indicating by these the diversities of the purposes of several souls),[1] I shall not delay."

CHAP. XV.—*Simon's arrogance.*

Then said Simon : " You seem to me to be angry; but if it be so, it is not necessary to enter into the conflict." Then Peter : " I see that you perceive that you are to be convicted, and you wish politely to escape from the contest ; for what have you seen to have made me angry against you, a man desiring to deceive so great a multitude, and when you have nothing to say, pretending moderation, who also command, forsooth, by your authority that the controversy shall be conducted as you please, and not as order demands ?" Then Simon : " I shall enforce myself to bear patiently your unskilfulness, that I may show that you indeed wish to seduce the people, but that I teach the truth. But now I refrain from a discussion concerning that boundless light. Answer me, therefore, what I ask of you. Since God, as you say, made all things, whence comes evil?" Then said Peter : " To put questions in this way is not the part of an opponent, but of a learner. If therefore you wish to learn, confess it ; and I shall first teach you how you ought to learn, and when you have learned to listen, then straightway I shall begin to teach you. But if you do not wish to learn, as though you knew all things, I shall first set forth the faith which I preach, and do you also set forth what you think to be true ; and when the profession of each of us has been disclosed, let our hearers judge whose discourse is supported by truth." To this Simon answered : " This is a good joke : behold a fellow who offers to teach me ! Nevertheless I shall suffer you, and bear with your ignorance and your arrogance. I confess, then, I do wish to learn ; let us see how you can teach me."

CHAP. XVI.—*Existence of evil.*

Then Peter said : " If you truly wish to learn, then first learn this, how unskilfully you have framed your question ;

[1] Luke viii. 5.

for you say, Since God has created all things, whence is evil? But before you asked this, three sorts of questions should have had the precedence: *First,* Whether there be evil? *Secondly,* What evil is? *Thirdly,* To whom it is, and whence?" To this Simon answered: "Oh thou most unskilful and unlearned, is there any man who does not confess that there is evil in this life? Whence I also, thinking that you had even the common sense of all men, asked, whence evil is; not as wishing to learn, since I know all things, least of all from you, who know nothing, but that I might show you to be ignorant of all things. And that you may not suppose that it is because I am angry that I speak somewhat sternly, know that I am moved with compassion for those who are present, whom you are attempting to deceive." Then Peter said: "The more wicked are you, if you can do such wrong, not being angry; but smoke must rise where there is fire. Nevertheless I shall tell you, lest I should seem to take you up with words, so as not to answer to those things which you have spoken disorderly. You say that all confess the existence of evil, which is verily false; for, first of all, the whole Hebrew nation deny its existence."

Chap. XVII.—*Not admitted by all.*

Then Simon, interrupting his discourse, said: "They do rightly who say that there is no evil." Then Peter answered: "We do not propose to speak of this now, but only to state the fact that the existence of evil is not universally admitted. But the second question that you should have asked is, What is evil?—a substance, an accident, or an act? And many other things of the same sort. And after that, towards what, or how it is, or to whom it is evil,—whether to God, or to angels, or to men, to the righteous or the wicked, to all or to some, to one's self or to no one? And then you should inquire, Whence it is?—whether from God, or from nothing; whether it has always been, or has had its beginning in time; whether it is useful or useless? and many other things which a proposition of this sort demands." To this Simon answered: "Pardon me; I was in error concerning the first question; but suppose that I now ask first, whether evil is or not?"

CHAP. XVIII.—*Manner of conducting the discussion.*

Then Peter said: "In what way do you put the question; as wishing to learn, or to teach, or for the sake of raising the question? If indeed as wishing to learn, I have something to teach you first, that coming by consequence and the right order of doctrine, you may understand from yourself what evil is. But if you put the question as an instructor, I have no need to be taught by you, for I have a Master from whom I have learned all things. But if you ask merely for the sake of raising a question and disputing, let each of us first set forth his opinion, and so let the matter be debated. For it is not reasonable that you should ask as one wishing to learn, and contradict as one teaching, so that after my answer it should be in your discretion to say whether I have spoken well or ill. Wherefore you cannot stand in the place of a gainsayer and be judge of what we say. And therefore, as I said, if a discussion is to be held, let each of us state his sentiments; and while we are placed in conflict, these religious hearers will be just judges."

CHAP. XIX.—*Desire of instruction.*

Then Simon said: "Does it not seem to you to be absurd that an unskilled people should sit in judgment upon our sayings?" Then Peter: "It is not so; for what perhaps is less clear to one, can be investigated by many, for oftentimes even a popular rumour has the aspect of a prophecy. But in addition to all this, all these people stand here constrained by the love of God, and by a desire to know the truth, and therefore all these are to be regarded as one, by reason of their affection being one and the same towards the truth; as, on the other hand, two are many and diverse, if they disagree with each other. But if you wish to receive an indication how all these people who stand before us are as one man, consider from their very silence and quietness how with all patience, as you see, they do honour to the truth of God, even before they learn it, for they have not yet learned the greater observance which they owe to it. Wherefore I hope, through the mercy of God, that He will accept the religious purpose of their mind towards Him, and will give the palm of victory to him who preaches the truth, that He may make manifest to them the herald of truth."

Chap. xx.—*Common principles.*

Then Simon: "On what subject do you wish the discussion to be held? Tell me, that I also may define what I think, and so the inquiry may begin." And Peter answered: "If, indeed, you will do as I think right, I would have it done according to the precept of my Master, who first of all commanded the Hebrew nation, whom He knew to have knowledge of God, and that it is He who made the world, not that they should inquire about Him whom they knew, but that, knowing Him, they should investigate His will and His righteousness; because it is placed in men's power that, searching into these things, they may find, and do, and observe those things concerning which they are to be judged. Therefore He commanded us to inquire, not whence evil cometh, as you asked just now, but to seek the righteousness of the good God, and His kingdom; and all these things, says He, shall be added to you."[1] Then Simon said: "Since these things are commanded to Hebrews, as having a right knowledge of God, and being of opinion that every one has it in his power to do those things concerning which he is to be judged,—but my opinion differs from theirs,—where do you wish me to begin?"

Chap. xxi.—*Freedom of the will.*

Then said Peter: "I advise that the first inquiry be, whether it be in our power to know whence we are to be judged." But Simon said: "Not so; but concerning God, about whom all who are present are desirous to hear." Then Peter: "You admit, then, that something is in the power of the will: only confess this, if it is so, and let us inquire, as

[1] Matt. vi. 33.

you say, concerning God." To this Simon answered : "By no means." Then Peter said : "If, then, nothing is in our power, it is useless for us to inquire anything concerning God, since it is not in the power of those who seek to find; hence I said well, that this should be the first inquiry, whether anything is in the power of the will." Then said Simon : "We cannot even understand this that you say, if there is anything in the power of the will." But Peter, seeing that he was turning to contention, and, through fear of being overcome, was confounding all things as being in general uncertain, answered : "How then do you know that it is not in the power of man to know anything, since this very thing at least you know ?"

Chap. XXII.—*Responsibility.*

Then Simon said : "I know not whether I know even this; for every one, according as it is decreed to him by fate, either does, or understands, or suffers." Then Peter said : "See, my brethren, into what absurdities Simon has fallen, who before my coming was teaching that men have it in their power to be wise and to do what they will, but now, driven into a corner by the force of my arguments, he denies that man has any power either of perceiving or of acting ; and yet he presumes to profess himself to be a teacher ! But tell me how then God judges according to truth every one for his doings, if men have it not in their own power to do anything ? If this opinion be held, all things are torn up by the roots ; vain will be the desire of following after goodness ; yea, even in vain do the judges of the world administer laws and punish those who do amiss, for they had it not in their power not to sin ; vain also will be the laws of nations which assign penalties to evil deeds. Miserable also will those be who laboriously keep righteousness ; but blessed those who, living in pleasure, exercise tyranny, living in luxury and wickedness. According to this, therefore, there can be neither righteousness, nor goodness, nor any virtue, nor, as you would have it, any God. But, O Simon, I know why you have spoken thus : truly because you wish to avoid inquiry, lest you should be openly confuted; and therefore you say that it is not in the power of man to perceive or to discern anything. But if this had really been your opinion, you would not surely, before my coming, have professed yourself before the people to be a teacher. I say, therefore, that man is under his own control." Then said Simon: "What is the meaning of being under his own control? Tell us." To this Peter: "If nothing can be learned, why do you wish to hear?" And Simon said: "You have nothing to answer to this."

Chap. xxiii.—*Origin of evil.*

Then said Peter: "I shall speak, not as under compulsion from you, but at the request of the hearers. The power of choice is the sense of the soul, possessing a quality by which it can be inclined towards what acts it wills." Then Simon, applauding Peter for what he had spoken, said: "Truly you have expounded it magnificently and incomparably, for it is my duty to bear testimony to your speaking well. Now if you will explain to me this which I now ask you, in all things else I shall submit to you. What I wish to learn, then, is this: if what God wishes to be, is; and what He does not wish to be, is not. Answer me this." Then Peter: "If you do not know that you are asking an absurd and incompetent question, I shall pardon you and explain; but if you are aware that you are asking inconsequently, you do not well." Then Simon said: "I swear by the Supreme Divinity, whatsoever that may be, which judges and punishes those who sin, that I know not what I have said inconsequently, or what absurdity there is in my words, that is, in those that I have just uttered."

Chap. xxiv.—*God the author of good, not of evil.*

To this Peter answered: "Since, then, you confess that you are ignorant, now learn. Your question demanded our deliverance on two matters that are contrary to one another. For every motion is divided into two parts, so that a certain part is moved by necessity, and another by will; and those things which are moved by necessity are always in motion, those which are moved by will, not always. For example, the sun's motion is performed by necessity to complete its appointed circuit, and every state and service of heaven depends upon necessary motions. But man directs the voluntary motions of his own actions. And thus there are some things which have been created for this end, that in their services they should be subject to necessity, and should be unable to do aught else than what has been assigned to them; and when they have accomplished this service, the Creator of all things, who thus arranged them according to His will, preserves them. But there are other things, in which there is a power of will, and which have a free choice of doing what they will. These, as I have said, do not remain always in that order in which they were created; but according as their will leads them, and the judgment of their mind inclines them, they effect either good or evil; and therefore He hath proposed rewards to those who do well, and penalties to those who do evil.

CHAP. XXV.—" *Who hath resisted His will?*"

" You say, therefore, if God wishes anything to be, it is; and if He do not wish it, it is not. But if I were to answer that what He wishes is, and what He wishes not is not, you would say that then He wishes the evil things to be which are done in the world, since everything that He wishes is, and everything that He wishes not is not. But if I had answered that it is not so that what God wishes is, and what He wishes not is not, then you would retort upon me that God must then be powerless, if He cannot do what He wills; and you would be all the more petulant, as thinking that you had got a victory, though you had said nothing to the point. Therefore you are ignorant, O Simon, yea very ignorant, how the will of God acts in each individual case. For some things, as we have said, He has so willed to be, that they cannot be otherwise than as they are ordained by Him; and to these He has assigned neither rewards nor punishments; but those which He has willed to be so that they have it in their power to do what they will, He has assigned to them according to their actions and their wills, to earn either rewards or punishments. Since, therefore, as I have informed you, all things that are moved are divided into two parts, according to the distinction that I formerly stated, everything that God wills is, and everything that He wills not is not."

Chap. xxvi.—*No goodness without liberty.*

To this Simon answered: "Was not He able to make us all such that we should be good, and that we should not have it in our power to be otherwise?" Peter answered: "This also is an absurd question. For if He had made us of an unchangeable nature and incapable of being moved away from good, we should not be really good, because we could not be aught else; and it would not be of our purpose that we were good; and what we did would not be ours, but of the necessity of our nature. But how can that be called good which is not done of purpose? And on this account the world required long periods, until the number of souls which were predestined to fill it should be completed, and then that visible heaven should be folded up like a scroll, and that which is higher should appear, and the souls of the blessed, being restored to their bodies, should be ushered into light; but the souls of the wicked, for their impure actions being surrounded with fiery spirit, should be plunged into the abyss of unquenchable fire, to endure punishments through eternity. Now that these things are so, the true Prophet has testified to us; concerning whom, if you wish to know that He is a prophet, I shall instruct you by innumerable declarations. For of those things which were spoken by Him, even now everything that He said is being fulfilled; and those things which He spoke with respect to the future are believed to be about to be fulfilled, for faith is given to the future from those things which have already come to pass."

Chap. xxvii.—*The visible heaven; why made.*

But Simon, perceiving that Peter was clearly assigning a reason from the head of prophecy, from which the whole question is settled, declined that the discourse should take this turn; and thus answered: "Give me an answer to the questions that I put, and tell me, if that visible heaven is, as you say, to be dissolved, why was it made at first?" Peter answered: "It was made for the sake of this present life of men, that there might be some sort of interposition and separation, lest any unworthy one might see the habitation of the celestials and the abode of God Himself, which are prepared in order to be seen by those only who are of pure heart.[1] But now, that is in the time of the conflict, it has pleased Him that those things be invisible, which are destined as a reward to the conquerors." Then Simon said: "If the Creator is good, and the world is good, how shall He who is good ever destroy that which is good? But if He shall destroy that which is good, how shall He Himself be thought to be good? But if He shall dissolve and destroy it as evil, how shall He not appear to be evil, who has made that which is evil?"

Chap. XXVIII.—*Why to be dissolved.*

To this Peter replied: "Since we have promised not to run away from your blasphemies, we endure them patiently, for you shall yourself render an account for the things that you speak. Listen now, therefore. If indeed that heaven which is visible and transient had been made for its own sake, there would have been some reason in what you say, that it ought not to be dissolved. But if it was made not for its own sake, but for the sake of something else, it must of necessity be dissolved, that that for which it seems to have been made may appear. As I might say, by way of illustration, however fairly and carefully the shell of the egg may seem to have been formed, it is yet necessary that it be broken and opened, that the chick may issue from it, and that may appear for which the form of the whole egg seems to have been moulded. So also, therefore, it is necessary that the condition of this world pass away, that that sublimer condition of the heavenly kingdom may shine forth."

[1] Matt. v. 8.

CHAP. XXIX.—*Corruptible and temporary things made by the Incorruptible and Eternal.*

Then Simon : " It does not seem to me that the heaven, which has been made by God, can be dissolved. For things made by the Eternal One are eternal, while things made by a corruptible one are temporary and decaying." Then Peter : " It is not so. Indeed corruptible and temporary things of all sorts are made by mortal creatures ; but the Eternal does not always make things corruptible, nor always incorruptible ; but according to the will of God the Creator, so will be the things which He creates. For the power of God is not subject to law, but His will is law to His creatures." Then Simon answered : " I call you back to the first question. You said now that God is visible to no one ; but when that heaven shall be dissolved, and that superior condition of the heavenly kingdom shall shine forth, then those who are pure in heart[1] shall see God ; which statement is contrary to the law, for there it is written that God said, ' None shall see my face and live.' "[2]

CHAP. XXX.—*How the pure in heart see God.*

Then Peter answered : " To those who do not read the law according to the tradition of Moses, my speech appears to be contrary to it ; but I will show you how it is not contradictory. God is seen by the mind, not by the body ; by the spirit, not by the flesh. Whence also angels, who are spirits, see God ; and therefore men, as long as they are men, cannot see Him. But after the resurrection of the dead, when they shall have been made like the angels,[3] they shall be able to see God. And thus my statement is not contrary to the law ; neither is that which our Master said, ' Blessed are they of a pure heart, for they shall see God.'[4] For He showed that a time shall come in which of men shall be made angels, who in the spirit of their mind shall see God." After these and many similar sayings, Simon began to assert with many oaths, saying : " Concerning one thing only render me a reason,

[1] Matt. v. 8.   [2] Ex. xxxiii. 20.   [3] Matt. xxii. 30.   [4] Matt. v. 8.

whether the soul is immortal, and I shall submit to your will
in all things.   But let it be to-morrow, for to-day it is late."
When therefore Peter began to speak, Simon went out, and
with him a very few of his associates; and that for shame.
But all the rest, turning to Peter, on bended knees prostrated
themselves before him; and some of those who were afflicted
with diverse sicknesses, or invaded by demons, were healed by
the prayer of Peter, and departed rejoicing, as having obtained
at once the doctrine of the true God, and also His mercy.
When therefore the crowds had withdrawn, and only we his
attendants remained with him, we sat down on couches placed
on the ground, each one recognising his accustomed place, and
having taken food, and given thanks to God, we went to sleep.

Chap. xxxi.—*Diligence in study.*

But on the following day, Peter, as usual, rising before
dawn, found us already awake and ready to listen; and thus
began: "I entreat you, my brethren and fellow-servants,
that if any of you is not able to wake, he should not torment
himself through respect to my presence, because sudden
change is difficult; but if for a long time one gradually
accustoms himself, that will not be distressing which comes
of use.   For we had not all the same training; although in
course of time we shall be able to be moulded into one habit,
for they say that custom holds the place of a second nature.
But I call God to witness that I am not offended, if any one
is not able to wake; but rather by this, if, when any one
sleeps all through the night, he does not in the course of the
day fulfil that which he omitted in the night.   For it is
necessary to give heed intently and unceasingly to the study
of doctrine, that our mind may be filled with the thought
of God only; because in the mind which is filled with the
thought of God, no place will be given to the wicked one."

Chap. xxxii.—*Peter's private instruction.*

When Peter spoke thus to us, every one of us eagerly
assured him, that ere now we were awake, being satisfied
with short sleep, but that we were afraid to arouse him,

because it did not become the disciples to command the master; "and yet even this, O Peter, we had almost ventured to take upon ourselves, because our hearts, agitated with longing for your words, drove sleep wholly from our eyes. But again our affection towards you opposed it, and did not suffer us violently to rouse you." Then Peter said: "Since therefore you assert that you are willingly awake through desire of hearing, I wish to repeat to you more carefully, and to explain in their order, the things that were spoken yesterday without arrangement. And this I propose to do throughout these daily disputations, that by night, when privacy of time and place is afforded, I shall unfold in correct order, and by a straight line of explanation, anything that in the controversy has not been stated with sufficient fulness." And then he began to point out to us how the yesterday's discussion ought to have been conducted, and how it could not be so conducted on account of the contentiousness or the unskilfulness of his opponent; and how therefore he only made use of assertion, and only overthrew what was said by his adversary, but did not expound his own doctrines either completely or distinctly. Then repeating the several matters to us, he discussed them in regular order and with full reason.

Chap. XXXIII.—*Learners and cavillers.*

But when the day began to be light, after prayer he went out to the crowds and stood in his accustomed place, for the discussion; and seeing Simon standing in the middle of the crowd, he saluted the people in his usual way, and said to them: "I confess that I am grieved with respect to some men, who come to us in this way that they may learn something, but when we begin to teach them, they profess that they themselves are masters, and while indeed they ask questions as ignorant persons, they contradict as knowing ones. But perhaps some one will say, that he who puts a question, puts it indeed in order that he may learn, but when that which he hears does not seem to him to be right, it is necessary that he should answer, and that seems to be contradiction which is not contradiction, but further inquiry.

Chap. xxxiv.—*Against order is against reason.*

"Let such a one then hear this : The teaching of all doctrine has a certain order, and there are some things which must be delivered first, others in the second place, and others in the third, and so all in their order; and if these things be delivered in their order, they become plain; but if they be brought forward out of order, they will seem to be spoken against reason. And therefore order is to be observed above all things, if we seek for the purpose of finding what we seek. For he who enters rightly upon the road, will observe the second place in due order, and from the second will more easily find the third; and the further he proceeds, so much the more will the way of knowledge become open to him, even until he arrive at the city of truth, whither he is bound, and which he desires to reach. But he who is unskilful, and knows not the way of inquiry,—as a traveller in a foreign country, ignorant and wandering, if he will not employ a native of the country as a guide,—undoubtedly when he has strayed from the way of truth, shall remain outside the gates of life, and so, involved in the darkness of black night, shall walk through the paths of perdition. Inasmuch therefore, as, if those things which are to be sought, be sought in an orderly manner, they can most easily be found, but the unskilful man is ignorant of the order of inquiry, it is right that the ignorant man should yield to the knowing one, and first learn the order of inquiry, that so at length he may find the method of asking and answering."

Chap. xxxv.—*Learning before teaching.*

To this Simon replied : "Then truth is not the property of all, but of those only who know the art of disputation, which is absurd; for it cannot be, since He is equally the God of all, that all should not be equally able to know His will." Then Peter : "All were made equal by Him, and to all He has given equally to be receptive of truth. But that none of those who are born, are born with education, but education is subsequent to birth, no one can doubt. Since, therefore, the birth of men holds equity in this respect, that all are equally capable of receiving discipline, the difference is not in nature, but in education. Who does not know that the things which any one learns, he was ignorant of before he learned them?" Then Simon said : " You say truly." Then Peter said : "If then in those arts which are in common use, one first learns and then teaches, how much more ought those who profess to be the educators of souls, first to learn, and so to teach, that they may not expose themselves to ridicule, if they promise to afford knowledge to others, when they themselves are unskilful?" Then Simon : " This is true in respect of those arts which are in common use; but in the word of knowledge, as soon as any one has heard, he has learned."

Chap. XXXVI.—*Self-evidence of the truth.*

Then said Peter : "If indeed one hear in an orderly and regular manner, he is able to know what is true ; but he who refuses to submit to the rule of a reformed life and a pure conversation, which truly is the proper result of knowledge of the truth, will not confess that he knows what he does know. For this is exactly what we see in the case of some who, abandoning the trades which they learned in their youth, betake themselves to other performances, and by way of excusing their own sloth, begin to find fault with the trade as unprofitable." Then Simon : " Ought all who hear to believe that whatever they hear is true ?" Then Peter : " Whoever hears an orderly statement of the truth, cannot by any means gainsay it, but knows that what is spoken is true, provided he also willingly submit to the rules of life. But those who, when they hear, are unwilling to betake themselves to good works, are prevented by the desire of doing evil from acquiescing in those things which they judge to be right. Hence it is manifest that it is in the power of the hearers to choose which of the two they prefer. But if all who hear were to obey, it would be rather a necessity of nature, leading all in one way. For as no one can be persuaded to become shorter or taller, because the force of nature does not permit it ; so also, if either all were converted to the truth by a word, or all were not converted, it would be the force of nature which compelled all in the one case, and none at all in the other, to be converted."

CHAP. XXXVII.—*God righteous as well as good.*

Then said Simon: "Inform us, therefore, what he who desires to know the truth must first learn." Then Peter: "Before all things it must be inquired what it is possible for man to find out. For of necessity the judgment of God turns upon this, if a man was able to do good and did it not. And therefore men must inquire whether they have it in their power by seeking to find what is good, and to do it when they have found it; for this is that for which they are to be judged. But more than this there is no occasion for any one but a prophet to know; for what is the need for men to know how the world was made? This, indeed, would be necessary to be learned if we had to enter upon a similar construction. But now it is sufficient for us, in order to the worship of God, to know that He made the world; but how He made it is no subject of inquiry for us, because, as I have said, it is not incumbent upon us to acquire the knowledge of that art, as though we were about to make something similar. But neither are we to be judged for this, why we have not learned how the world was made, but only for that, if we be without knowledge of its Creator. For we shall know that the Creator of the world is the righteous and good God, if we seek Him in the paths of righteousness. For if we only know regarding Him that He is good, such knowledge is not sufficient for salvation. For in the present life not only the worthy, but also the unworthy, enjoy His goodness and His benefits. But if we believe Him to be not only good, but also righteous, and if, according to what we believe concerning God, we observe righteousness in the whole course of our life, we shall enjoy His goodness for ever. In a word, to the Hebrews, whose opinion concerning God was that He is only good, our Master said that they should seek also His righteousness;[1] that is, that they should know that He is good indeed in this pre-

[1] Matt. vi. 33.

R

sent time, that all may live in His goodness, but that He shall be righteous at the day of judgment, to bestow eternal rewards upon the worthy, from which the unworthy shall be excluded.

Chap. XXXVIII.—*God's justice shown at the day of judgment.*

Then Simon : " How can one and the same being be both good and righteous ?"   Peter answered : " Because without righteousness, goodness would be unrighteousness ; for it is the part of a good God to bestow His sunshine and rain equally on the just and the unjust ;[1] but this would seem to be unjust, if He treated the good and the bad always with equal fortune, and were it not that He does it for the sake of the fruits, which all may equally enjoy who are born in this world.   But as the rain given by God equally nourishes the corn and the tares, but at the time of harvest the crops are gathered into the barn, but the chaff or the tares are burnt in the fire,[2] so in the day of judgment, when the righteous shall be introduced into the kingdom of heaven, and the unrighteous shall be cast out, then also the justice of God shall be shown.   For if He remained for ever alike to the evil and the good, this would not only not be good, but even unrighteous and unjust ; that the righteous and the un-righteous should be held by Him in one order of desert."

Chap. XXXIX.—*Immortality of the soul.*

Then said Simon : " The one point on which I should wish to be satisfied is, whether the soul is immortal ; for I cannot take up the burden of righteousness unless I know first con-cerning the immortality of the soul ; for indeed if it is not immortal, the profession of your preaching cannot stand." Then said Peter : " Let us first inquire whether God is just ; for if this were ascertained, the perfect order of religion would straightway be established."   Then Simon : " With all your boasting of your knowledge of the order of dis-cussion, you seem to me now to have answered contrary to order ; for when I ask you to show whether the soul is immortal, you say that we must first inquire whether God

[1] Matt. v. 45.   [2] Matt. iii. 12.

is just." Then said Peter: "That is perfectly right and regular." Simon: "I should wish to learn how."

CHAP. XL.—*Proved by the success of the wicked in this life.*

"Listen, then," said Peter: "Some men who are blasphemers against God, and who spend their whole life in injustice and pleasure, die in their own bed and obtain honourable burial; while others who worship God, and maintain their life frugally with all honesty and sobriety, die in deserted places for their observance of righteousness, so that they are not even thought worthy of burial. Where, then, is the justice of God, if there be no immortal soul to suffer punishment in the future for impious deeds, or enjoy rewards for piety and rectitude?" Then Simon said: "It is this indeed that makes me incredulous, because many well-doers perish miserably, and again many evil-doers finish long lives in happiness."

CHAP. XLI.—*Cavils of Simon.*

Then said Peter: "This very thing which draws you into incredulity, affords to us a certain conviction that there shall be a judgment. For since it is certain that God is just, it is a necessary consequence that there is another world, in which every one receiving according to his deserts, shall prove the justice of God. But if all men were now receiving according to their deserts, we should truly seem to be deceivers when we say that there is a judgment to come; and therefore this very fact, that in the present life a return is not made to every one according to his deeds, affords, to those who know that God is just, an indubitable proof that there shall be a judgment." Then said Simon: "Why, then, am I not persuaded of it?" Peter: "Because you have not heard the true Prophet saying, 'Seek first His righteousness, and all these things shall be added to you.'[1] Then said Simon: "Pardon me if I am unwilling to seek righteousness, before I know if the soul is immortal." Then Peter: "You also pardon me this one thing, because I cannot do otherwise than the Prophet of truth has instructed me." Then said Simon:

[1] Matt. vi. 33.

"It is certain that you cannot assert that the soul is immortal, and therefore you cavil, knowing that if it be proved to be mortal, the whole profession of that religion which you are attempting to propagate will be plucked up by the roots. And therefore, indeed, I commend your prudence, while I do not approve your persuasiveness; for you persuade many to embrace your religion, and to submit to the restraint of pleasure, in hope of future good things; to whom it happens that they lose the enjoyment of things present, and are deceived with hopes of things future. For as soon as they die, their soul shall at the same time be extinguished."

CHAP. XLII.—"*Full of all subtlety and all mischief.*"

But Peter, when he heard him speak thus, grinding his teeth, and rubbing his forehead with his hand, and sighing with profound grief, said : "Armed with the cunning of the old serpent, you stand forth to deceive souls; and therefore, as the serpent is more subtile than any other beast, you profess that you are a teacher from the beginning. And again, like the serpent you wished to introduce many gods; but now, being confuted in that, you assert that there is no God at all. For by occasion of I know not what unknown God, you denied that the Creator of the world is God, but asserted that He is either an evil being, or that He has many equals, or, as we have said, that He is not God at all. And when you had been overcome in this position, you now assert that the soul is mortal, so that men may not live righteously and uprightly in hope of things to come. For if there be no hope for the future, why should not mercy be given up, and men indulge in luxury and pleasures, from which it is manifest that all unrighteousness springs? And while you introduce so impious a doctrine into the miserable life of men, you call yourself pious, and me impious, because, under the hope of future good things, I will not suffer men to take up arms and fight against one another, plunder and subvert everything, and attempt whatsoever lust may dictate. And what will be the condition of that life which you would introduce, that men will attack and be attacked, be enraged and disturbed, and live always in fear? For those who do evil to others must expect like evil to themselves. Do you see that you are a leader of disturbance and not of peace, of iniquity and not of equity? But I feigned anger, not because I could not prove that the soul is immortal, but because I pity the souls which you are endeavouring to deceive. I shall speak, therefore, but not as compelled by you; for I know how I should speak; and you will be the only one who wants not so much persuasion as admonition on this subject. But those who are really ignorant of this, I shall instruct as is suitable."

Chap. XLIII.—*Simon's subterfuges.*

Then says Simon: "If you are angry, I shall neither ask you any questions, nor do I wish to hear you." Then Peter: "If you are now seeking a pretext for escaping, you have full liberty, and need not use any special pretext. For all have heard you speaking all amiss, and have perceived that you can prove nothing, but that you only asked questions for the sake of contradiction; which any one can do. For what difficulty is there in replying, after the clearest proofs have been adduced, 'You have said nothing to the purpose?' But that you may know that I am able to prove to you in a single sentence that the soul is immortal, I shall ask you with respect to a point which all know; answer me, and I shall prove to you in one sentence that it is immortal." Then Simon, who had thought that he had got, from the anger of Peter, a pretext for departing, stopped on account of the remarkable promise that was made to him, and said: "Ask me then, and I shall answer you what all know, that I may hear in a single sentence, as you have promised, how the soul is immortal."

Chap. XLIV.—*Sight or hearing?*

Then Peter: "I shall speak so that it may be proved to you before all the rest. Answer me, therefore, which of the two can better persuade an incredulous man, seeing or hearing?" Then Simon said: "Seeing." Then Peter: "Why then do you wish to learn from me by words, what is proved to you by the thing itself and by sight?" Then Simon: "I know not what you mean." Then Peter: "If you do not know, go now to your house, and entering the inner bed-chamber you will see an image placed, containing the figure of a murdered boy clothed in purple; ask him, and he will inform you either by hearing or seeing. For what need is there to hear from him if the soul is immortal, when you see it standing before you? For if it were not in being, it assuredly could not be seen. But if you know not what image I speak of, let us straightway go to your house, with ten other men, of those who are here present."

CHAP. XLV.—*A home-thrust.*

But Simon hearing this, and being smitten by his conscience, changed colour and became bloodless; for he was afraid, if he denied it, that his house would be searched, or that Peter in his indignation would betray him more openly, and so all would learn what he was. Thus he answered: "I beseech thee, Peter, by that good God who is in thee, to overcome the wickedness that is in me. Receive me to repentance, and you shall have me as an assistant in your preaching. For now I have learned in very deed that you are a prophet of the true God, and therefore you alone know the secret and hidden things of men." Then said Peter: "You see, brethren, Simon seeking repentance; in a little while you shall see him returning again to his infidelity. For, thinking that I am a prophet, forasmuch as I have disclosed his wickedness, which he supposed to be secret and hidden, he has promised that he will repent. But it is not lawful for me to lie, nor must I deceive, whether this infidel be saved or not saved. For I call heaven and earth to witness, that I spoke not by a prophetic spirit what I said, and what I intimated, as far as was possible, to the listening crowds; but I learned from some who once were his associates in his works, but have now been converted to our faith, what things he did in secret. Therefore I spoke what I knew, not what I foreknew."

Chap. XLVI.—*Simon's rage.*

But when Simon heard this, he assailed Peter with curses and reproaches, saying : " Oh most wicked and most deceitful of men, to whom fortune, not truth, hath given the victory. But I sought repentance not for defect of knowledge, but in order that you, thinking that by repentance I should become your disciple, might entrust to me all the secrets of your profession, and so at length, knowing them all, I might confute you. But as you cunningly understood for what reason I had pretended penitence, and acquiesced as if you did not understand my stratagem, that you might first expose me in presence of the people as unskilful, then foreseeing that being thus exposed to the people, I must of necessity be indignant, and confess that I was not truly penitent, you anticipated me, that you might say that I should, after my penitence, again return to my infidelity, that you might seem to have conquered on all sides, both if I continued in the penitence which I had professed, and if I did not continue ; and so you should be believed to be wise, because you had foreseen these things, while I should seem to be deceived, because I did not foresee your trick. But you foreseeing mine, have used subtlety and circumvented me. But, as I said, your victory is the result of fortune, not of truth : yet I know why I did not foresee this ; because I stood by you and spoke with you in my goodness, and bore patiently with you. But now I shall show you the power of my divinity, so that you shall quickly fall down and worship me.

Chap. XLVII.—*Simon's vaunt.*

" I am the first power, who am always, and without beginning. But having entered the womb of Rachel, I was born of her as a man, that I might be visible to men. I have flown through the air ; I have been mixed with fire, and been made one body with it ; I have made statues to move ; I have animated lifeless things ; I have made stones bread ; I have flown from mountain to mountain ; I have moved from place to place, upheld by angels' hands, and have lighted on the earth. Not only have I done these things; but even now I am able to do them, that by facts I may prove to all, that I am the Son of God, enduring to eternity, and that I can make those who believe on me endure in like manner for ever. But your words are all vain; nor can you perform any real works [such as I have now mentioned], as he also who sent you is a magician, who yet could not deliver himself from the suffering of the cross."

Chap. XLVIII.—*Attempts to create a disturbance.*

To this speech of Simon, Peter answered: "Do not meddle with the things that belong to others; for that you are a magician, you have confessed and made manifest by the very deeds that you have done; but our Master, who is the Son of God and of man, is manifestly good; and that He is truly the Son of God has been told, and shall be told to those to whom it is fitting. But if you will not confess that you are a magician, let us go, with all this multitude, to your house, and then it will be evident who is a magician." While Peter was speaking thus, Simon began to assail him with blasphemies and curses, that he might make a riot, and excite all so that he could not be refuted, and that Peter, withdrawing on account of his blasphemy, might seem to be overcome. But he stood fast, and began to charge him more vehemently.

Chap. XLIX.—*Simon's retreat.*

Then the people in indignation cast Simon from the court, and drove him forth from the gate of the house; and only one person followed him when he was driven out. Then silence being obtained, Peter began to address the people in this manner: "You ought, brethren, to bear with wicked men patiently; knowing that although God could cut them off, yet He suffers them to remain even till the day appointed, in which judgment shall pass upon all. Why then should not we bear with those whom God suffers? Why should not we bear with fortitude the wrongs that they do to us, when He who is almighty does not take vengeance on them, that both His own goodness and the impiety of the wicked may be known? But if the wicked one had not found Simon to be his minister, he would doubtless have found another: for it is of necessity that in this life offences come, 'but woe to that man by whom they come;'[1] and therefore Simon is rather to be mourned over, because he has become a choice vessel for the wicked one, which undoubtedly would not have happened had he not received power over him for his former sins. For why should I further say that he once believed in our Jesus, and was persuaded that souls are immortal?[2] Although in this he is deluded by demons, yet he has persuaded himself that he has the soul of a murdered boy ministering to him in whatever he pleases to employ it in; in which truly, as I have said, he is deluded by demons, and therefore I spoke to him according to his own ideas: for he has learned from the Jews, that judgment and vengeance are to be brought forth against those who set themselves against the true faith, and do not repent. But there are men to whom, as being perfect in crimes, the wicked one appears, that he may deceive them, so that they may never be turned to repentance.

Chap. l.—*Peter's benediction.*

"You therefore who are turned to the Lord by repentance, bend to Him your knees." When he had said this, all the multitude bent their knees to God; and Peter, looking towards heaven, prayed for them with tears, that God, for His goodness, would deign to receive those betaking themselves to Him. And after he had prayed, and had instructed them to meet early the next day, he dismissed the multitude. Then, according to custom, having taken food, we went to sleep.

Chap. li.—*Peter's accessibility.*

Peter, therefore, rising at the usual hour of the night, found us waking; and when, saluting us in his usual manner, he had taken his seat, first of all Niceta said: "If you will permit me, my lord Peter, I have something to ask of you." Then Peter said: "I permit not only you, but all, and not only now, but always, that every one confess what moves him,

[1] Matt. xviii. 7. [2] Acts viii. 13.

and the part in his mind that is pained, in order that he may obtain healing. For things which are covered with silence, and are not made known to us, are cured with difficulty, like maladies of long standing; and therefore, since the medicine of seasonable and necessary discourse cannot easily be applied to those who keep silence, every one ought to declare in what respect his mind is feeble through ignorance. But to him who keeps silence, it belongs to God alone to give a remedy. We indeed also can do it, but by the lapse of a long time. For it is necessary that the discourse of doctrine, proceeding in order from the beginning, and meeting each single question, should disclose all things, and resolve and reach to all things, even to that which every one requires in his mind; but that, as I have said, can only be done in the course of a long time. Now, then, ask what you please."

Chap. LII.—*False signs and miracles.*

Then Niceta said: "I give you abundant thanks, O most clement Peter; but this is what I desire to learn, how Simon, who is the enemy of God, is able to do such and so great things? For indeed he told no lie in his declaration of what he has done." To this the blessed Peter thus answered: "God, who is one and true, has resolved to prepare good and faithful friends for His first begotten; but knowing that none can be good, unless they have in their power that perception by which they may become good, that they may be of their own intent what they choose to be,—and otherwise they could not be truly good, if they were kept in goodness not by purpose, but by necessity,—has given to every one the power of his own will, that he may be what he wishes to be. And again, foreseeing that that power of will would make some choose good things and others evil, and so that the human race would necessarily be divided into two classes, He has permitted each class to choose both a place and a king, whom they would. For the good King rejoices in the good, and the wicked one in the evil. And although I have expounded those things more fully to you, O Clement, in that treatise in which I discoursed on predestination and the end, yet it is fitting that I should now make clear to Niceta also, as he asks me, what is the reason that Simon, whose thoughts are against God, is able to do so great marvels.

Chap. LIII.—*Self-love the foundation of goodness.*

"First of all, then, he is evil, in the judgment of God, who will not inquire what is advantageous to himself. For how can any one love another, if he does not love himself? Or to whom will that man not be an enemy, who cannot be a friend to himself? In order, therefore, that there might be a distinction between those who choose good and those who choose evil, God has concealed that which is profitable to men, *i.e.* the possession of the kingdom of heaven, and has laid it up and hidden it as a secret treasure, so that no one can easily attain it by his own power or knowledge. Yet He has brought the report of it, under various names and opinions, through successive generations, to the hearing of all: so that whosoever should be lovers of good, hearing it, might inquire and discover what is profitable and salutary to them; but that they should ask it, not from themselves, but from Him who has hidden it, and should pray that access and the way of knowledge might be given to them: which way is opened to those only who love it above all the good things of this world; and on no other condition can any one even understand it, however wise he may seem; but that those who neglect to inquire what is profitable and salutary to themselves, as self-haters and self-enemies, should be deprived of its good things, as lovers of evil things.

Chap. LIV.—*God to be supremely loved.*

"It behoves, therefore, the good to love that [way] above all things, that is, above riches, glory, rest, parents, relatives, friends, and everything in the world. But he who perfectly loves this possession of the kingdom of heaven, will undoubtedly cast away all practice of evil habit, negligence, sloth, malice, anger, and such like. For if you prefer any of these to it, as loving the vices of your own lust more than God, you shall not attain to the possession of the heavenly kingdom; for truly it is foolish to love anything more than God. For whether they be parents, they die; or relatives, they do not continue; or friends, they change. But God alone is eternal, and abideth unchangeable. He, therefore, who will not seek after that which is profitable to himself, is evil, to such an extent that his wickedness exceeds the very prince of impiety. For he abuses the goodness of God to the purpose of his own wickedness, and pleases himself; but the other neglects the good things of his own salvation, that by his own destruction he may please the evil one.

CHAP. LV.—*Ten commandments corresponding to the plagues of Egypt.*

"On account of those, therefore, who by neglect of their own salvation please the evil one, and those who by study of their own profit seek to please the good One, ten things have been prescribed as a test to this present age, according to the number of the ten plagues which were brought upon Egypt. For when Moses, according to the commandment of God, demanded of Pharaoh that he should let the people go, and in token of his heavenly commission showed signs, his rod being thrown upon the ground was turned into a serpent.[1] And when Pharaoh could not by these means be brought to consent, as having freedom of will, again the magicians seemed to do similar signs, by permission of God, that the purpose of the king might be proved from the freedom of his will, whether he would rather believe the signs wrought by Moses, who was sent by God, or those which the magicians rather seemed to work than actually wrought. For truly he ought to have understood from their very name that they were not workers of truth, because they were not called messengers of God, but magicians, as the tradition also intimates. Moreover, they seemed to maintain the contest up to a certain point, and afterwards they confessed of themselves, and yielded to their superior.[2] Therefore the last plague is inflicted,[3] the destruction of the first-born, and then Moses is commanded to consecrate the people by the sprinkling of

[1] Ex. vii. viii.   [2] Ex. viii. 19.   [3] Ex. xii.

blood ; and so, gifts being presented, with much entreaty he is asked to depart with the people.

Chap. lvi.—*Simon resisted Peter, as the magicians Moses.*

"In a similar transaction I see that I am even now engaged. For as then, when Moses exhorted the king to believe God, the magicians opposed him by a pretended exhibition of similar signs, and so kept back the unbelievers from salvation ; so also now, when I have come forth to teach all nations to believe in the true God, Simon the magician resists me, acting in opposition to me, as they also did in opposition to Moses ; in order that whosoever they be from among the nations that do not use sound judgment, they may be made manifest ; but that those may be saved who rightly distinguish signs from signs." While Peter thus spoke, Niceta answered : "I beseech you that you would permit me to state whatever occurs to my mind." Then Peter, being delighted with the eagerness of his disciples, said : "Speak what you will."

Chap. lvii.—*Miracles of the magicians.*

Then said Niceta : "In what respect did the Egyptians sin in not believing Moses, since the magicians wrought like signs, even although they were done rather in appearance than in truth ? For if I had been there then, should I not have thought, from the fact that the magicians did like things to those which Moses did, either that Moses was a magician, or that the magicians wrought their signs by divine commission ? For I should not have thought it likely that the same things could be effected by magicians, even in appearance, which he who was sent by God performed. And now, in what respect do they sin who believe Simon, since they see him do so great marvels ? Or is it not marvellous to fly through the air, to be so mixed with fire as to become one body with it, to make statues walk, brazen dogs bark, and other such like things, which assuredly are sufficiently wonderful to those who know not how to distinguish ? Yea, he has also been seen to make bread of stones. But if he sins who believes those who do signs, how shall it appear that

he also does not sin who has believed our Lord for His signs
and works of power?"

CHAP. LVIII.—*Truth veiled with love.*

Then said Peter: "I take it well that you bring the truth
to the rule, and do not suffer hindrances of faith to lurk in
your soul. For thus you can easily obtain the remedy. Do
you remember that I said, that the worst of all things is
when any one neglects to learn what is for his good?" Niceta
answered: "I remember." Then Peter: "And again, that
God has veiled His truth, that He may disclose it to those
who faithfully follow Him?" "Neither," said Niceta, "have
I forgotten this." Then said Peter: "What think you then?
That God has buried His truth deep in the earth, and has
heaped mountains upon it, that it may be found by those only
who are able to dig down into the depths? It is not so; but
as He has surrounded the mountains and the earth with the
expanse of heaven, so hath He veiled the truth with the cur-
tain of His own love, that he alone may be able to reach it,
who has first knocked at the gate of divine love.

CHAP. LIX.—*Good and evil in pairs.*

"For, as I was beginning to say, God has appointed for
this world certain pairs; and he who comes first of the pairs
is of evil, he who comes second, of good. And in this is
given to every man an occasion of right judgment, whether
he is simple or prudent. For if he is simple, and believes him
who comes first, though moved thereto by signs and prodigies,
he must of necessity, for the same reason, believe him who
comes second; for he will be persuaded by signs and prodigies, as he was before. When he believes this second one,
he will learn from him that he ought not to believe the
first, who comes of evil; and so the error of the former is
corrected by the emendation of the latter. But if he will not
receive the second, because he has believed the first, he will
deservedly be condemned as unjust; for unjust it is, that
when he believed the first on account of his signs, he will not
believe the second, though he bring the same, or even greater

signs. But if he has not believed the first, it follows that he may be moved to believe the second. For his mind has not become so completely inactive but that it may be roused by the redoubling of marvels. But if he is prudent, he can make distinction of the signs. And if indeed he has believed in the first, he will be moved to the second by the increase in the miracles, and by comparison he will apprehend which are better ; although clear tests [of miracles] are recognised by all learned men, as we have shown in the regular order of our discussion. But if any one, as being whole and not needing a physician, is not moved to the first, he will be drawn to the second by the very continuance of the thing, and will make a distinction of signs and marvels after this fashion ;—he who is of the evil one, the signs that he works do good to no one ; but those which the good man worketh are profitable to men.

CHAP. LX.—*Uselessness of pretended miracles.*

"For tell me, I pray you, what is the use of showing statues walking, dogs of brass or stone barking, mountains dancing, of flying through the air, and such like things, which you say that Simon did ? But those [signs] which are of the good One, are directed to the advantage of men, as are those which were done by our Lord, who gave sight to the blind and hearing to the deaf, raised up the feeble and the lame, drove away sicknesses and demons, raised the dead, and did other like things, as you see also that I do. Those signs, therefore, which make for the benefit of men, and confer some good upon them, the wicked one cannot do, excepting only at the end of the world. For then it shall be permitted him to mix up with his signs some good ones, as the expelling of demons or the healing of diseases ; by this means going beyond his bounds, and being divided against himself, and fighting against himself, he shall be destroyed. And therefore the Lord has foretold, that in the last times there shall be such temptation, that, if it be possible, the very elect shall be deceived ; that is to say, that by the marks of signs being confused, even those must be disturbed who seem to be expert in discovering spirits and distinguishing miracles.

Chap. LXI.—*Ten pairs.*

" The ten pairs of which we have spoken have therefore been assigned to this world from the beginning of time. Cain and Abel were one pair. The second was the giants and Noah ; the third, Pharaoh and Abraham ; the fourth, the Philistines and Isaac ; the fifth, Esau and Jacob ; the sixth, the magicians and Moses the lawgiver ; the seventh, the tempter and the Son of man ; the eighth, Simon and I, Peter ; the ninth, all nations, and he who shall be sent to sow the word among the nations ; the tenth, Antichrist and Christ. Concerning these pairs we shall give you fuller information at another time." When Peter spoke thus, Aquila said : " Truly there is need of constant teaching, that one may learn what is true about everything."

Chap. LXII.—*The Christian life.*

But Peter said : " Who is he that is earnest toward instruction, and that studiously inquires into every particular, except him who loves his own soul to salvation, and renounces all the affairs of this world, that he may have leisure to attend to the word of God only ? Such is he whom alone the true Prophet deems wise, even he who sells all that he has and buys the one true pearl,[1] who understands what is the difference between temporal things and eternal, small and great, men and God. For he understands what is the eternal hope in presence of the true and good God. But who is he that loves God, save him who knows His wisdom ? And how can any one obtain knowledge of God's wisdom, unless he be constant in hearing His word ? Whence it comes, that he conceives a love for Him, and venerates Him with worthy honour, pouring out hymns and prayers to Him, and most pleasantly resting in these, accounteth it his greatest damage if at any time he speak or do aught else even for a moment of time ; because, in reality, the soul which is filled with the love of God can neither look upon anything except what pertains to God, nor, by reason of love of Him, can be satisfied with

[1] Matt. xiii. 46.

meditating upon those things which it knows to be pleasing
to Him. But those who have not conceived affection for Him,
nor bear His love lighted up in their mind, are as it were
placed in darkness and cannot see light ; and therefore, even
before they begin to learn anything of God, they immediately
faint as though worn out by labour; and filled with weariness,
they are straightway hurried by their own peculiar habits to
those words with which they are pleased. For it is wearisome
and annoying to such persons to hear anything about God ;
and that for the reason I have stated, because their mind
has received no sweetness of divine love."

Chap. lxiii.—*A deserter from Simon's camp.*

While Peter was thus speaking, the day dawned ; and,
behold, one of the disciples of Simon came, crying out : " I
beseech thee, O Peter, receive me, a wretch, who have been
deceived by Simon the magician, to whom I gave heed as
to a heavenly God, by reason of those miracles which I saw
him perform. But when I heard your discourses, I began
to think him a man, and indeed a wicked man ; nevertheless,
when he went out from this I alone followed him, for I had
not yet clearly perceived his impieties. But when he saw
me following him, he called me blessed, and led me to his
house ; and about the middle of the night he said to me, ' I
shall make you better than all men, if you will remain with
me even till the end.' When I had promised him this, he
demanded of me an oath of perseverance ; and having got
this, he placed upon my shoulders some of his polluted and
accursed secret things, that I might carry them, and ordered
me to follow him. But when we came to the sea, he went
aboard a boat which happened to be there, and took from
my neck what he had ordered me to carry. And as he came
out a little after, bringing nothing with him, he must have
thrown it into the sea. Then he asked me to go with him,
saying that he was going to Rome, and that there he would
please the people so much, that he should be reckoned a god,
and publicly gifted with divine honours. ' Then,' said he, ' if
you wish to return hither, I shall send you back, loaded with

s

all riches, and upheld by various services.' When I heard this, and saw nothing in him in accordance with this profession, but perceived that he was a magician and a deceiver, I answered: 'Pardon me, I pray you; for I have a pain in my feet, and therefore I am not able to leave Cæsarea. Besides, I have a wife and little children, whom I cannot leave by any means.' When he heard this, he charged me with sloth, and set out towards Dora, saying, 'You will be sorry, when you hear what glory I shall get in the city of Rome.' And after this he set out for Rome, as he said; but I hastily returned hither, entreating you to receive me to penitence, because I have been deceived by him."

Chap. lxiv.—*Declaration of Simon's wickedness.*

When he who had returned from Simon had thus spoken, Peter ordered him to sit down in the court. And he himself going forth, and seeing immense crowds, far more than on the previous days, stood in his usual place; and pointing out him who had come, began to discourse as follows: "This man whom I point out to you, brethren, has just come to me, telling me of the wicked practices of Simon, and how he has thrown the implements of his wickedness into the sea, not induced to do so by repentance, but being afraid lest, being detected, he should be subjected to the public laws. And he asked this man, as he tells me, to remain with him, promising him immense gifts; and when he could not persuade him to do so, he left him, reproaching him for sluggishness, and set out for Rome." When Peter had intimated this to the crowd, the man himself who had returned from Simon stood up, and began to state to the people everything relating to Simon's crimes. And when they were shocked by the things which they heard that Simon had done by his magical acts, Peter said:

Chap. lxv.—*Peter resolves to follow Simon.*

" Be not, my brethren, distressed by those things that have been done, but give heed to the future: for what is passed is ended; but the things which threaten are dangerous to those who shall fall in with them. For offences shall never be wanting in this world,[1] so long as the enemy is permitted to act according to his will; in order that the prudent and those who understood his wiles may be conquerors in the contests which he raises against them; but that those who neglect to learn the things that pertain to the salvation of their souls, may be taken by him with merited deceptions. Since, therefore, as you have heard, Simon has gone forth to preoccupy the ears of the Gentiles who are called to salvation, it is necessary that I also follow upon his track, so that whatever disputations he raises may be corrected by us. But inasmuch as it is right that greater anxiety should be felt concerning you who are already received within the walls of life,—for if that which has been actually acquired perish, a positive loss is sustained; while with respect to that which has not yet been acquired, if it can be got, there is so much gain; but if not, the only loss is that there is no gain; —in order, therefore, that you may be more and more confirmed in the truth, and the nations who are called to salvation may in no way be prevented by the wickedness of Simon, I have thought good to ordain Zaccheus as pastor over you, and to remain with you myself for three months; and so to go to the Gentiles, lest through our delaying longer, and the crimes of Simon stalking in every direction, they should become incurable."

Chap. lxvi.—*Zaccheus made bishop of Cæsarea; presbyters and deacons ordained.*

At this announcement all the people wept, hearing that he was going to leave them; and Peter, sympathizing with them, himself also shed tears; and looking up to heaven, he said: "To Thee, O God, who hast made heaven and earth, and all things that are in them, we pour out the prayer of supplication, that Thou wouldest comfort those who have recourse to Thee in their tribulation. For by reason of the affection that they have towards Thee, they do love me who

[1] Matt. xviii. 7 ; Luke xvii. 1.

have declared to them Thy truth. Wherefore guard them with the right hand of Thy compassion; for neither Zaccheus nor any other man can be a sufficient guardian to them." When he had said this, and more to the same effect, he laid his hands upon Zaccheus, and prayed that he might blamelessly discharge the duty of his bishopric. Then he ordained twelve presbyters and four deacons, and said: "I have ordained you this Zaccheus as a bishop, knowing that he has the fear of God, and is expert in the Scriptures. You ought therefore to honour him as holding the place of Christ, obeying him for your salvation, and knowing that whatever honour and whatever injury is done to him, redounds to Christ, and from Christ to God. Hear him therefore with all attention, and receive from him the doctrine of the faith; and from the presbyters the monitions of life; and from the deacons the order of discipline. Have a religious care of widows; vigorously assist orphans; take pity on the poor; teach the young modesty;—and in a word, sustain one another as circumstances shall demand; worship God, who created heaven and earth; believe in Christ; love one another; be compassionate to all; and fulfil charity not only in word, but in act and deed."

CHAP. LXVII.—*Invitation to baptism.*

When he had given them these and such like precepts, he made proclamation to the people, saying: "Since I have resolved to stay three months with you, if any one desires it, let him be baptized; that, stripped of his former evils, he may for the future, in consequence of his own conduct, become heir of heavenly blessings, as a reward for his good actions. Whosoever will, then, let him come to Zaccheus and give his name to him, and let him hear from him the mysteries of the kingdom of heaven. Let him attend to frequent fastings, and approve himself in all things, that at the end of these three months he may be baptized on the day of the festival. But every one of you shall be baptized in ever flowing waters, the name of the Trine Beatitude being invoked over him; he being first anointed with oil sanctified by prayer, that so at length, being consecrated by these things, he may attain a perception of holy things."[1]

CHAP. LXVIII.—*Twelve sent before him.*

And when he had spoken at length on the subject of baptism, he dismissed the crowd, and betook himself to his usual place of abode; and there, while the twelve stood around him (viz. Zaccheus and Sophonias, Joseph and Michæus, Eleazar and Phineas, Lazarus and Eliseus, I Clement and Nicodemus, Niceta and Aquila), he addressed us to the following effect: "Let us, my brethren, consider what is right; for it is our duty to bring some help to the nations, which are called to salvation. You have yourselves heard that Simon has set out, wishing to anticipate our journey. Him we should have followed step by step, that wheresoever he tries to subvert any, we might immediately confute him. But since it appears to me to be unjust to forsake those who have been already converted to God, and to bestow our care upon those who are still afar off, I think it right that I should remain three months with those in this city who have been turned to the faith, and should strengthen them; and yet that we should not neglect those who are still far off, lest haply, if they be long infected with the power of pernicious doctrine, it be more difficult to recover them. Therefore I wish (only, however, if you also think it right), that for Zaccheus, whom we have now ordained bishop, Benjamin the son of Saba be substituted; and for Clement (whom I have resolved to have always by me, because, coming from the Gentiles, he has a great desire to hear the word of God) there be substituted Ananias the son of Safra; and for Niceta and Aquila, who have been but lately converted to the faith of Christ, Rubelus the brother of Zaccheus, and Zacharias the builder. I wish, therefore, to complete the number of twelve by substituting these four for the other four, that Simon may feel that I in them am always with him."

[1] This may be translated, "that he may partake of holy things." Cotelerius supposes the words "holy things" to mean the body and blood of Christ.

Chap. lxix.—*Arrangements approved by all the brethren.*

Having therefore separated me, Clement, and Niceta and Aquila, he said to those twelve : "I wish you the day after to-morrow to proceed to the Gentiles, and to follow in the footsteps of Simon, that you may inform me of all his proceedings. You will also inquire diligently the sentiments of every one, and announce to them that I shall come to them without delay ; and, in short, in all places instruct the Gentiles to expect my coming." When he had spoken these things, and others to the same effect, he said : "You also, my brethren, if you have anything to say to these things, say on, lest haply it be not right which seems good to me alone." Then all, with one voice applauding him, said : "We ask you rather to arrange everything according to your own judgment, and to order what seems good to yourself ; for this we think to be the perfect work of piety, if we fulfil what you command."

Chap. lxx.—*Departure of the twelve.*

Therefore, on the day appointed, when they had ranged themselves before Peter, they said : "Do not think, O Peter, that it is a small grief to us that we are to be deprived of the privilege of hearing you for three months ; but since it is good for us to do what you order, we shall most readily obey. We shall always retain in our hearts the remembrance of your face ; and so we set out actively, as you have commanded us." Then he, having poured out a prayer to the Lord for them, dismissed them. And when those twelve who had been sent forward had gone, Peter entered, according to custom, and stood in the place of disputation. And a multitude of people had come together, even a larger number than usual ; and all with tears gazed upon him, by reason of what they had heard from him the day before, that he was about to go forth on account of Simon. Then, seeing them weeping, he himself also was similarly affected, although he endeavoured to conceal and to restrain his tears. But the trembling of his voice, and the interruption of his discourse, betrayed that he was distressed by similar emotion.

CHAP. LXXI.—*Peter prepares the Cæsareans for his departure.*

However, rubbing his forehead with his hand, he said: "Be of good courage, my brethren, and comfort your sorrowful hearts by means of counsel, referring all things to God, whose will alone is to be fulfilled and to be preferred in all things. For let us suppose for a moment, that by reason of the affection that we have towards you, we should act against His will, and remain with you, is He not able, by sending death upon me, to appoint to me a longer separation from you? And therefore it is better for us to carry out this shorter separation with His will, as those to whom it is prescribed to obey God in all things. Hence you also ought to obey Him with like submission, inasmuch as you love me from no other reason than on account of your love of Him. As friends of God, therefore, acquiesce in His will; but also judge yourselves what is right. Would it not have seemed wicked, if, when Simon was deceiving you, I had been detained by the brethren in Jerusalem, and had not come to you, and that although you had Zaccheus among you, a good and eloquent man? So now also consider that it would be wicked, if, when Simon has gone forth to assail the Gentiles, who are wholly without a defender, I should be detained by you, and should not follow him. Wherefore let us see to it, that we do not, by an unreasonable affection, accomplish the will of the wicked one.

CHAP. LXXII.—*More than ten thousand baptized.*

"Meantime I shall remain with you three months, as I promised. Be ye constant in hearing the word; and at the end of that time, if any are able and willing to follow us, they may do so, if duty will admit of it. And when I say *if duty will admit*, I mean that no one by his departure must sadden any one who ought not to be saddened, as by leaving parents who ought not to be left, or a faithful wife, or any other person to whom he is bound to afford comfort for God's sake." Meantime, disputing and teaching day by day, he filled up the time appointed with the labour of teaching;

and when the festival day arrived, upwards of ten thousand were baptized.

Chap. LXXIII.—*Tidings of Simon.*

But in those days a letter was received from the brethren who had gone before, in which were detailed the crimes of Simon, how going from city to city he was deceiving multitudes, and everywhere maligning Peter, so that, when he should come, no one might afford him a hearing. For he asserted that Peter was a magician, a godless man, injurious, cunning, ignorant, and professing impossible things. " For," says he, " he asserts that the dead shall rise again, which is impossible. But if any one attempts to confute him, he is cut off by secret snares by him, through means of his attendants. Wherefore, I also," says he, " when I had vanquished him and triumphed over him, fled for fear of his snares, lest he should destroy me by incantations, or compass my death by plots." They intimated also that he mainly stayed at Tripolis.

Chap. LXXIV.—*Farewell to Cæsarea.*

Peter therefore ordered the letter to be read to the people; and after the reading of it, he addressed them and gave them full instructions about everything, but especially that they should obey Zaccheus, whom he had ordained bishop over them. Also he commended the presbyters and the deacons to the people, and not less the people to them. And then, announcing that he should spend the winter at Tripolis, he said : " I commend you to the grace of God, being about to depart to-morrow, with God's will." But during the whole three months which he spent at Cæsarea, for the sake of instruction, whatever he discoursed of in the presence of the people in the day-time, he explained more fully and perfectly in the night, in private to us, as more faithful and completely approved by him. And at the same time he commanded me, because he understood that I carefully stored in my memory what I heard, to commit to writing whatever seemed worthy of record, and to send it to you, my lord James, as also I did, in obedience to his command.

CHAP. LXXV.—*Contents of Clement's despatches to James.*

The first book,[1] therefore, of those that I formerly sent to you, contains an account of the true Prophet, and of the peculiarity of the understanding of the law, according to what the tradition of Moses teacheth.   The second contains an account of the beginning, and whether there be one beginning or many, and that the law of the Hebrews knows what immensity is. The third, concerning God, and those things that have been ordained by Him.   The fourth, that though there are many that are called gods, there is but one true God, according to the testimonies of the Scriptures.   The fifth, that there are two heavens, one of which is that visible firmament which shall pass away, but the other is eternal and invisible.   The sixth, concerning good and evil ; and that all things are subjected to good by the Father ; and why, and how, and whence evil is, and that it co-operates with good, but not with a good purpose ; and what are the signs of good, and what those of evil ; and what is the difference between duality and conjunction.   The seventh, what are the things which the twelve apostles treated of in the presence of the people in the temple. The eighth, concerning the words of the Lord which seem to be contradictory, but are not ; and what is the explanation of them.   The ninth, that the law which has been given by God is righteous and perfect, and that it alone can make pure.   The tenth, concerning the carnal birth of men, and concerning the generation which is by baptism ; and what is the succession of carnal seed in man ; and what is the account of his soul, and how the freedom of the will is in it, which, seeing it is not unbegotten, but made, could not be immoveable from good. Concerning these several subjects, therefore, whatever Peter discoursed at Cæsarea, according to his command, as I have said, I have sent you written in ten volumes.   But on the next day, as had been determined, we set out from Cæsarea with some faithful men, who had resolved to accompany Peter.

---

[1] Cotelerius remarks that these ten books previously sent to James (if they ever existed) ought to be distinguished from the ten books of the *Recognitions,* which were addressed to the same James, but written after those now mentioned.

RECOGNITIONS OF CLEMENT.

BOOK IV.

Chap. i.—*Halt at Dora.*

AVING set out from Cæsarea on the way to
Tripolis, we made our first stoppage at a small
town called Dora, because it was not far distant;
and almost all those who had believed through
the preaching of Peter could scarcely bear to be separated
from him, but walked along with us, again and again gazing
upon him, again and again embracing him, again and again
conversing with him, until we came to the inn. On the
following day we came to Ptolemais, where we stayed ten
days; and when a considerable number had received the word
of God, we signified to some of them who seemed particularly
attentive, and wished to detain us longer for the sake of instruction, that they might, if so disposed, follow us to Tripolis.
We acted in the same way at Tyre, and Sidon, and Berytus,
and announced to those who desired to hear further discourses,
that we were to spend the winter at Tripolis. Therefore, as
all those who were anxious followed Peter from each city, we
were a great multitude of elect ones when we entered into
Tripolis. On our arrival, the brethren who had been sent
before met us before the gates of the city; and taking us
under their charge, conducted us to the various lodgings
which they had prepared. Then there arose a commotion in
the city, and a great assemblage of persons desirous to see
Peter.

Chap. ii.—*Reception in the house of Maro.*

And when we had come to the house of Maro, in which

preparation had been made for Peter, he turned to the crowd, and told them that he would address them the day after to-morrow.   Therefore the brethren who had been sent before assigned lodgings to all who had come with us.   Then, when Peter had entered into the house of Maro, and was asked to partake of food, he answered that he would by no means do so, until he had ascertained whether all those that had accompanied him were provided with lodgings.   Then he learned from the brethren who had been sent before, that the citizens had received them not only hospitably, but with all kindness, by reason of their love towards Peter; so much so, that several were disappointed because there were no guests for them; for that all had made such preparations, that even if many more had come, there would still have been a deficiency of guests for the hosts, not of hosts for the guests.

Chap. iii.—*Simon's flight.*

Thereupon Peter was greatly delighted, and praised the brethren, and blessed them, and requested them to remain with him.   Then, when he had bathed in the sea, and had taken food, he went to sleep in the evening; and rising, as usual, at cock-crow, while the evening light was still burning, he found us all awake.   Now there were in all sixteen of us, viz. Peter and I, Clement, Niceta and Aquila, and those twelve who had preceded us.   Saluting us, then, as was his wont, Peter said: " Since we are not taken up with others to-day, let us be taken up with ourselves.   I shall tell you what took place at Cæsarea after your departure, and you shall tell us of the doings of Simon here."   And while the conversation was going on on these subjects, at daybreak some of the members of the family came in and told Peter that Simon, when he heard of Peter's arrival, departed in the night, on the way to Syria.   They also stated that the crowds thought that the day which he had said was to intervene was a very long time for their affection, and that they were standing in impatience before the gate, conversing among themselves about those things which they wished to hear, and that they

hoped that they should by all means see him before the time
appointed; and that as the day became lighter the multitudes
were increasing, and that they were trusting confidently,
whatever they might be presuming upon, that they should
hear a discourse from him.   "Now then," said they, "instruct
us to tell them what seems good to you; for it is absurd that
so great a multitude should have come together, and should
depart with sadness, through no answer being returned to
them.   For they will not consider that it is they that have
not waited for the appointed day, but rather they will think
that you are slighting them."

Chap. iv.—*The harvest plenteous.*

Then Peter, filled with admiration, said: "You see,
brethren, how every word of the Lord spoken prophetically
is fulfilled.   For I remember that He said, 'The harvest indeed
is plenteous, but the labourers are few; ask therefore the
Lord of the harvest, that He would send out labourers into
His harvest.'[1] Behold, therefore, the things which are foretold
in a mystery are fulfilled.   But whereas He said also, 'Many
shall come from the east and the west, from the north and
the south, and shall recline in the bosom of Abraham, and
Isaac, and Jacob;'[2] this also is, as you see, in like manner
fulfilled.   Wherefore I entreat you, my fellow-servants and
helpers, that you would learn diligently the order of preaching,
and the ways of absolutions, that ye may be able to save the
souls of men, which by the secret power of God acknowledge
whom they ought to love, even before they are taught.   For
you see that these men, like good servants, long for him
whom they expect to announce to them the coming of their
Lord, that they may be able to fulfil His will when they have
learned it.   The desire, therefore, of hearing the word of
God, and inquiring into His will, they have from God; and
this is the beginning of the gift of God, which is given to
the Gentiles, that by this they may be able to receive the
doctrine of truth.

[1] Matt. ix. 37, 38.   [2] Luke xiii. 29; Matt. viii. 11.

Chap. v.—*Moses and Christ.*

" For so also it was given to the people of the Hebrews from
the beginning, that they should love Moses, and believe his
word; whence also it is written: 'The people believed God,
and Moses His servant.'[1]   What, therefore, was of peculiar
gift from God toward the nation of the Hebrews, we see now
to be given also to those who are called from among the
Gentiles to the faith.   But the method of works is put into
the power and will of every one, and this is their own; but
to have an affection towards a teacher of truth, this is a gift
of the heavenly Father.   But salvation is in this, that you do
His will of whom you have conceived a love and affection
through the gift of God; lest that saying of His be addressed
to you which He spoke, 'Why call ye me Lord, Lord, and do
not what I say?'[2]   It is therefore the peculiar gift bestowed
by God upon the Hebrews, that they believe Moses; and the
peculiar gift bestowed upon the Gentiles is that they love
Jesus.   For this also the Master intimated, when He said, 'I
will confess to Thee, O Father, Lord of heaven and earth,
because Thou hast concealed these things from the wise and
prudent, and hast revealed them to babes.'[3]   By which it is
certainly declared, that the people of the Hebrews, who were
instructed out of the law, did not know Him; but the people
of the Gentiles have acknowledged Jesus, and venerate Him;
on which account also they shall be saved, not only acknowledging Him, but also doing His will.   But he who is of the
Gentiles, and who has it of God to believe Moses, ought also
to have it of his own purpose to love Jesus also.   And again,
the Hebrew, who has it of God to believe Moses, ought to
have it also of his own purpose to believe in Jesus; so that
each of them, having in himself something of the divine gift,
and something of his own exertion, may be perfect by both.
For concerning such an one our Lord spoke, as of a rich man,
'Who brings forth from his treasures things new and old.'[4]

[1] Ex. xiv. 31.   [2] Luke vi. 46.
[3] Matt. xi. 25.   [4] Matt. xiii. 52.

Chap. vi.—*A congregation.*

"But enough has been said of these things; for time presses, and the religious devotion of the people invites us to address them." And when he had thus spoken, he asked where there was a suitable place for discussion. And Maro said: "I have a very spacious hall[1] which can hold more than five hundred men, and there is also a garden within the house; or if it please you to be in some public place, all would prefer it, for there is nobody who does not desire at least to see your face." Then Peter said: "Show me the hall, or the garden." And when he had seen the hall, he went in to see the garden also; and suddenly the whole multitude, as if some one had called them, rushed into the house, and thence broke through into the garden, where Peter was already standing, selecting a fit place for discussion.

Chap. vii.—*The sick healed.*

But when he saw that the crowds had, like the waters of a great river, poured over the narrow passage, he mounted upon a pillar which happened to stand near the wall of the garden, and first saluted the people in a religious manner. But some of those who were present, and who had been for a long time distressed by demons, threw themselves on the ground, while the unclean spirits entreated that they might be allowed but for one day to remain in the bodies that they had taken possession of. But Peter rebuked them, and commanded them to depart; and they went out without delay. After these, others who had been afflicted with long-standing sicknesses asked Peter that they might receive healing; and he promised that he would entreat the Lord for them as soon as his discourse of instruction was completed. But as soon as he promised, they were freed from their sicknesses; and he ordered them to sit down apart, with those who had been freed from the demons, as after the fatigue of labour. Meantime, while this was going on, a vast multitude assembled, attracted not only by the desire of hearing Peter, but also by the report of the cures

[1] *Ædes,* in the singular, probably a temple.

which had been accomplished. But Peter, beckoning with his hand to the people to be still, and settling the crowds in tranquillity, began to address them as follows :

Chap. viii.—*Providence vindicated.*

" It seems to me necessary, at the outset of a discourse concerning the true worship of God, first of all to instruct those who have not as yet acquired any knowledge of the subject, that throughout the divine providence must be maintained to be without blame, by which the world is ruled and governed. Moreover, the reason of the present undertaking, and the occasion offered by those whom the power of God has healed, suggest this subject for a beginning, viz. to show that for good reason very many persons are possessed of demons, that so the justice of God may appear. For ignorance will be found to be the mother of almost all evils. But now let us come to the reason.

Chap. ix.—*State of innocence a state of enjoyment.*

" When God had made man after His own image and likeness, He grafted into His work a certain breathing and odour of His divinity, that so men, being made partakers of His Only-begotten, might through Him be also friends of God and sons of adoption. Whence also He Himself, as the true Prophet, knowing with what actions the Father is pleased, instructed them in what way they might obtain that privilege. At that time, therefore, there was among men only one worship of God—a pure mind and an uncorrupted spirit. And for this reason every creature kept an inviolable covenant with the human race. For by reason of their reverence of the Creator, no sickness, or bodily disorder, or corruption of food, had power over them ; whence it came to pass, that a life of a thousand years did not fall into the frailty of old age.

Chap. x.—*Sin the cause of suffering.*

" But when men, leading a life void of distress, began to think that the continuance of good things was granted them

not by the divine bounty, but by the chance of things, and to
accept as a debt of nature, not as a gift of God's goodness,
their enjoyment without any exertion of the delights of the
divine complaisance,—men, being led by these things into
contrary and impious thoughts, came at last, at the instigation of idleness, to think that the life of gods was theirs by
nature, without any labours or merits on their part. Hence
they go from bad to worse, to believe that neither is the world
governed by the providence of God, nor is there any place
for virtues, since they knew that they themselves possessed
the fulness of ease and delights, without the assignment of
any works previously, and without any labours were treated
as the friends of God.

Chap. XI.—*Suffering salutary.*

" By the most righteous judgment of God, therefore, labours
and afflictions are assigned as a remedy to men languishing
in the vanity of such thoughts. And when labour and tribulations came upon them, they were excluded from the place
of delights and amenity. Also the earth began to produce
nothing to them without labour; and then men's thoughts
being turned in them, they were warned to seek the aid of
their Creator, and by prayers and vows to ask for the divine
protection. And thus it came to pass, that the worship of
God, which they had neglected by reason of their prosperity,
they recovered through their adversity; and their thoughts
towards God, which indulgence had perverted, affliction corrected. So therefore the divine providence, seeing that this
was more profitable to man, removed from them the ways of
benignity and abundance, as being hurtful, and introduced
the way of vexation and tribulation.

Chap. XII.—*Translation of Enoch.*

" But that He might show that these things were done on
account of the ungrateful, He translated to immortality a
certain one of the first race of men, because He saw that he
was not unmindful of His grace, and because he hoped to

call on the name of God;[1] while the rest, who were so ungrateful that they could not be amended and corrected even
by labours and tribulations, were condemned to a terrible
death.   Yet amongst them also He found a certain one, who
was righteous with his house,[2] whom He preserved, having
enjoined him to build an ark, in which he and those who were
commanded to go with him might escape, when all things
should be destroyed by a deluge: in order that, the wicked
being cut off by the overflow of waters, the world might
receive a purification; and he who had been preserved for
the continuance of the race, being purified by water, might
anew repair the world.

Chap. XIII.—*Origin of idolatry.*

" But when all these things were done, men turned again
to impiety; and on this account a law was given by God to
instruct them in the manner of living.   But in process of
time, the worship of God and righteousness were corrupted
by the unbelieving and the wicked, as we shall show more
fully by and by.   Moreover, perverse and erratic religions
were introduced, to which the greater part of men gave themselves up, by occasion of holidays and solemnities, instituting
drinkings and banquets, following pipes, and flutes, and harps,
and diverse kinds of musical instruments, and indulging
themselves in all kinds of drunkenness and luxury.   Hence
every kind of error took rise; hence they invented groves
and altars, fillets and victims, and after drunkenness they
were agitated as if with mad emotions.   By this means power
was given to the demons to enter into minds of this sort,
so that they seemed to lead insane dances and to rave like
Bacchanalians; hence were invented the gnashing of teeth,
and bellowing from the depth of their bowels; hence a
terrible countenance and a fierce aspect in men, so that he
whom drunkenness had subverted and a demon had instigated,

---

[1] There seems to be here a mixing up of the translation of *Enoch* with
the statement that in the days of *Enos* men began to call on the name
of the Lord; Gen. iv. 26.

[2] Gen. vi. 9.

T

was believed by the deceived and the erring to be filled with
the Deity.

Chap. xiv.—*God both good and righteous.*

" Hence, since so many false and erratic religions have
been introduced into the world, we have been sent, as good
merchants, bringing unto you the worship of the true God,
handed down from the fathers, and preserved ; as the seeds of
which we scatter these words amongst you, and place it in
your choice to choose what seems to you to be right. For
if you receive those things which we bring you, you shall not
only be able yourselves to escape the incursions of the demon,
but also to drive them away from others ; and at the same
time you shall obtain the rewards of eternal good things.
But those who shall refuse to receive those things which are
spoken by us, shall be subject in the present life to diverse
demons and disorders of sicknesses, and their souls after their
departure from the body shall be tormented for ever. For
God is not only good, but also just ; for if He were always
good, and never just to render to every one according to
his deeds, goodness would be found to be injustice. For it
were injustice if the impious and the pious were treated by
Him alike.

Chap. xv.—*How demons get power over men.*

" Therefore demons, as we have just said, when once they
have been able, by means of opportunities afforded them, to
convey themselves through base and evil actions into the bodies
of men, if they remain in them a long time through their own
negligence, because they do not seek after what is profitable
to their souls, they necessarily compel them for the future
to fulfil the desires of the demons who dwell in them. But
what is worst of all, at the end of the world, when that demon
shall be consigned to eternal fire, of necessity the soul also
which obeyed him, shall with him be tortured in eternal fires,
together with its body which it hath polluted.

Chap. xvi.—*Why they wish to possess men.*

"Now that the demons are desirous of occupying the bodies of men, this is the reason. They are spirits having their purpose turned to wickedness. Therefore by immoderate eating and drinking, and lust, they urge men on to sin; but only those who entertain the purpose of sinning, who, while they seem simply desirous of satisfying the necessary cravings of nature, give opportunity to the demons to enter into them, because through excess they do not maintain moderation. For as long as the measure of nature is kept, and legitimate moderation is preserved, the mercy of God does not give them liberty to enter into men. But when either the mind falls into impiety, or the body is filled with immoderate meat or drink, then, as if invited by the will and purpose of those who thus neglect themselves, they receive power as against those who have broken the law imposed by God.

Chap. xvii.—*The gospel gives power over demons.*

"You see, then, how important is the acknowledgment of God, and the observance of the divine religion, which not only protects those who believe from the assaults of the demon, but also gives them command over those who rule over others. And therefore it is necessary for you, who are of the Gentiles, to betake yourselves to God, and to keep yourselves from all uncleanness, that the demons may be expelled, and God may dwell in you. And at the same time, by prayers, commit yourselves to God, and call for His aid against the impudence of the demons; for 'whatever things ye ask, believing, ye shall receive.'[1] But even the demons themselves, in proportion as they see faith grow in a man, in that proportion they depart from him, residing only in that part in which something of infidelity still remains; but from those who believe with full faith, they depart without any delay. For when a soul has come to the faith of God, it obtains the virtue of heavenly water, by which it extinguishes the demon like a spark of fire.

[1] Matt. xxi. 22.

CHAP. XVIII.—*This power in proportion to faith.*

"There is therefore a measure of faith, which, if it be perfect, drives the demon perfectly from the soul; but if it has
any defect, something on the part of the demon still remains
in the portion of infidelity; and it is the greatest difficulty
for the soul to understand when or how, whether fully or
less fully, the demon has been expelled from it. For if he
remains in any quarter, when he gets an opportunity, he
suggests thoughts to men's hearts; and they, not knowing
whence they come, believe the suggestions of the demons,
as if they were the perceptions of their own souls. Thus
they suggest to some to follow pleasure by occasion of bodily
necessity; they excuse the passionateness of others by excess
of gall; they colour over the madness of others by the vehe-
mence of melancholy; and even extenuate the folly of some
as the result of abundance of phlegm. But even if this were
so, still none of these could be hurtful to the body, except
from the excess of meats and drinks; because, when these
are taken in excessive quantities, their abundance, which the
natural warmth is not sufficient to digest, curdles into a sort
of poison, and it, flowing through the bowels and all the veins
like a common sewer, renders the motions of the body un-
healthy and base. Wherefore moderation is to be attained in
all things, that neither may place be given to demons, nor the
soul, being possessed by them, be delivered along with them
to be tormented in eternal fires.

CHAP. XIX.—*Demons incite to idolatry.*

"There is also another error of the demons, which they suggest to the senses of men, that they should think that those
things which they suffer, they suffer from such as are called
gods, in order that thereby, offering sacrifices and gifts, as if
to propitiate them, they may strengthen the worship of false
religion, and avoid us who are interested in their salvation,
that they may be freed from error; but this they do, as I have
said, not knowing that these things are suggested to them by
demons, for fear they should be saved. It is therefore in the

power of every one, since man has been made possessed of free-will, whether he shall hear us to life, or the demons to destruction. Also to some, the demons, appearing visibly under various figures, sometimes throw out threats, sometimes promise relief from sufferings, that they may instil into those whom they deceive the opinion of their being gods, and that it may not be known that they are demons. But they are not concealed from us, who know the mysteries of the creation, and for what reason it is permitted to the demons to do those things in the present world ; how it is allowed them to transform themselves into what figures they please, and to suggest evil thoughts, and to convey themselves, by means of meats and of drink consecrated to them, into the minds or bodies of those who partake of it, and to concoct vain dreams to further the worship of some idol.

Chap. xx.—*Folly of idolatry.*

" And yet who can be found so senseless as to be persuaded to worship an idol, whether it be made of gold or of any other metal ? To whom is it not manifest that the metal is just that which the artificer pleased? How then can the divinity be thought to be in that which would not be at all unless the artificer had pleased? Or how can they hope that future things should be declared to them by that in which there is no perception of present things ? For although they should divine something, they should not straightway be held to be gods ; for divination is one thing, divinity is another. For the Pythons also seem to divine, yet they are not gods ; and, in short, they are driven out of men by Christians. And how can that be God which is put to flight by a man ? But perhaps you will say, What as to their effecting cures, and their showing how one can be cured? On this principle, physicians ought also to be worshipped as gods, for they cure many ; and in proportion as any one is more skilful, the more he will cure.

Chap. xxi.—*Heathen oracles.*

" Whence it is evident that they, since they are demoniac

spirits, know some things both more quickly and more perfectly [than men] ; for they are not retarded in their learning by the heaviness of a body. And therefore they, as being spirits, know without delay and without difficulty what physicians attain after a long time and by much labour. It is not wonderful, therefore, if they know somewhat more than men do ; but this is to be observed, that what they know they do not employ for the salvation of souls, but for the deception of them, that by means of it they may indoctrinate them in the worship of false religion. But God, that the error of so great deception might not be concealed, and that He Himself might not seem to be a cause of error in permitting them so great licence to deceive men by divinations, and cures, and dreams, has of His mercy furnished men with a remedy, and has made the distinction of falsehood and truth patent to those who desire to know. This, therefore, is that distinction : what is spoken by the true God, whether by prophets or by diverse visions, is always true ; but what is foretold by demons is not always true. It is therefore an evident sign that those things are not spoken by the true God, in which at any time there is falsehood ; for in truth there is never falsehood. But in the case of those who speak falsehoods, there may occasionally be a slight mixture of truth, to give as it were seasoning to the falsehoods.

Chap. XXII.—*Why they sometimes come true.*

"But if any one say, What is the use of this, that they should be permitted even sometimes to speak truth, and thereby so much error be introduced amongst men ? let him take this for answer : If they had never been allowed to speak any truth, then they would not foretell anything at all ; while if they did not foretell, they would not be known to be demons. But if demons were not known to be in this world, the cause of our struggle and contest would be concealed from us, and we should suffer openly what was done in secret, that is, if the power were granted to them of only acting against us, and not of speaking. But now, since they sometimes speak truth, and sometimes falsehood, we ought to acknowledge, as I have said, that their responses are of demons, and not of God, with whom there is never falsehood.

Chap. xxiii.—*Evil not in substance.*

" But if any one, proceeding more curiously, inquire: What then was the use of God's making these evil things, which should have so great a tendency to subvert the minds of men ? To one proposing such a question, we answer that we must first of all inquire whether there is any evil in substance. And although it would be sufficient to say to him that it is not suitable that the creature judge the Creator, but that to judge the work of another belongs to him who is either of equal skill or equal power ; yet, to come directly to the point, we say absolutely that there is no evil in substance. But if this be so, then the Creator of substance is vainly blamed.

Chap. xxiv.—*Why God permits evil.*

" But you will meet me by saying, Even if it has come to this through freedom of will, was the Creator ignorant that those whom He created would fall away into evil ? He ought therefore not to have created those who, He foresaw, would deviate from the path of righteousness. Now we tell those who ask such questions, that the purpose of assertions of the sort made by us is to show why the wickedness of those who as yet were not, did not prevail over the goodness of the Creator.[1] For if, wishing to fill up the number and measure of His creation, He had been afraid of the wickedness of those who were to be, and like one who could find no other way of remedy and cure, except only this, that He should refrain from His purpose of creating, lest the wickedness of those who were to be should be ascribed to Him ; what else would this show but unworthy suffering and unseemly feebleness on the part of

---

[1] There is considerable variety of reading in this sentence, and the precise meaning is somewhat obscure. The general sense, however, is sufficiently evident, that if God had refrained from creating those who, He foresaw, would fall into evil, this would have been to subject His goodness to their evil.

the Creator, who should so fear the actings of those who as yet were not, that He refrained from His purposed creation?

Chap. XXV.—*Evil beings turned to good account.*

"But, setting aside these things, let us consider this earnestly, that God the Creator of the universe, foreseeing the future differences of His creation, foresaw and provided diverse ranks and different offices to each of His creatures, according to the peculiar movements which were produced from freedom of will; so that while all men are of one substance in respect of the method of creation, there should yet be diversity in ranks and offices, according to the peculiar movements of minds, to be produced from liberty of will. Therefore He foresaw that there would be faults in His creatures; and the method of His justice demanded that punishment should follow faults, for the sake of amendment. It behoved, therefore, that there should be ministers of punishment, and yet that freedom of will should draw them into that order. Moreover, those also must have enemies to conquer, who had undertaken the contests for the heavenly rewards. Thus, therefore, neither are those things destitute of utility which are thought to be evil, since the conquered unwillingly acquire eternal rewards for those by whom they are conquered. But let this suffice on these points, for in process of time even more secret things shall be disclosed.

Chap. XXVI.—*Evil angels seducers.*

"Now therefore, since you do not yet understand how great darkness of ignorance surrounds you, meantime I wish to explain to you whence the worship of idols began in this world. And by idols, I mean those lifeless images which you worship, whether made of wood, or earthenware, or stone, or brass, or any other metals: of these the beginning was in this wise. Certain angels, having left the course of their proper order, began to favour the vices of men, and in some measure to lend unworthy aid to their lust, in order that by these means they might indulge their own pleasures the more; and then, that they might not seem to be inclined of their own accord to unworthy services, taught men that demons could, by certain arts—that is, by magical invocations—be made to obey men; and so, as from a furnace and workshop of wickedness, they filled the whole world with the smoke of impiety, the light of piety being withdrawn.

Chap. XXVII.—*Ham the first magician.*

" For these and some other causes, a flood was brought upon the world, as we have said already, and shall say again; and all who were upon the earth were destroyed, except the family of Noah, who survived, with his three sons and their wives. One of these, by name Ham, unhappily discovered the magical act, and handed down the instruction of it to one of his sons, who was called Mesraim, from whom the race of the Egyptians and Babylonians and Persians are descended. Him the nations who then existed called Zoroaster, admiring him as the first author of the magic art; under whose name also many books on this subject exist. He therefore, being much and frequently intent upon the stars, and wishing to be esteemed a god among them, began to draw forth, as it were, certain sparks from the stars, and to show them to men, in order that the rude and ignorant might be astonished, as with a miracle; and desiring to increase this estimation of him, he attempted these things again and again, until he was set on fire, and consumed by the demon himself, whom he accosted with too great importunity.

Chap. XXVIII.—*Tower of Babel.*

" But the foolish men who were then, whereas they ought to have abandoned the opinion which they had conceived of him, inasmuch as they had seen it confuted by his mortal punishment, extolled him all the more. For raising a sepulchre to his honour, they went so far as to adore him as a friend of God, and one who had been removed to heaven in a chariot of lightning, and to worship him as if he were a living star. Hence also his name was called Zoroaster after his death—that is, *living star*—by those who, after one generation, had been taught to speak the Greek language. In fine, by this example,

even now many worship those who have been struck with lightning, honouring them with sepulchres, and worshipping them
as friends of God. But this man was born in the fourteenth
generation, and died in the fifteenth, in which the tower was
built, and the languages of men were divided into many.

CHAP. XXIX.—*Fire-worship of the Persians.*

"First among whom is named a certain king Nimrod, the
magic art having been handed down to him as by a flash,
whom the Greeks also called Ninus, and from whom the city
of Nineveh took its name. Thus, therefore, diverse and
erratic superstitions took their beginning from the magic
art. For, because it was difficult to draw away the human
race from the love of God, and attach them to deaf and
lifeless images, the magicians made use of higher efforts, that
men might be turned to erratic worship, by signs among the
stars, and motions brought down as it were from heaven, and
by the will of God. And those who had been first deceived,
collecting the ashes of Zoroaster,—who, as we have said, was
burnt up by the indignation of the demon, to whom he had
been too troublesome,—brought them to the Persians, that
they might be preserved by them with perpetual watching, as
divine fire fallen from heaven, and might be worshipped as a
heavenly God.

CHAP. XXX.—*Hero-worship.*

"By a like example, other men in other places built temples,
set up statues, instituted mysteries and ceremonies and sacrifices, to those whom they had admired, either for some arts or
for virtue, or at least had held in very great affection; and
rejoiced, by means of all things belonging to gods, to hand
down their fame to posterity; and that especially, because,
as we have already said, they seemed to be supported by some
phantasies of magic art, so that by invocation of demons
something seemed to be done and moved by them towards the
deception of men. To these they add also certain solemnities,
and drunken banquets, in which men might with all freedom
indulge; and demons, conveyed into them in the chariot of

repletion, might be mixed with their very bowels, and holding a place there, might bind the acts and thoughts of men to their own will. Such errors, then, having been introduced from the beginning, and having been aided by lust and drunkenness, in which carnal men chiefly delight, the religion of God, which consisted in continence and sobriety, began to become rare amongst men, and to be well-nigh abolished.

Chap. xxxi.—*Idolatry led to all immorality.*

"For whereas at first, men worshipping a righteous and all-seeing God, neither dared sin nor do injury to their neighbours, being persuaded that God sees the actions and movements of every one; when religious worship was directed to lifeless images, concerning which they were certain that they were incapable of hearing, or sight, or motion, they began to sin licentiously, and to go forward to every crime, because they had no fear of suffering anything at the hands of those whom they worshipped as gods. Hence the madness of wars burst out; hence plunderings, rapines, captivities, and liberty reduced to slavery; each one, as he could, satisfied his lust and his covetousness, although no power can satisfy covetousness. For as fire, the more fuel it gets, is the more extensively kindled and strengthened, so also the madness of covetousness is made greater and more vehement by means of those things which it acquires.

Chap. xxxii.—*Invitation.*

"Wherefore begin now with better understanding to resist yourselves in those things which you do not rightly desire; if so be that you can in any way repair and restore in yourselves that purity of religion and innocence of life which at first were bestowed upon man by God, that thereby also the hope of immortal blessings may be restored to you. And give thanks to the bountiful Father of all, by Him whom He has constituted King of peace, and the treasury of unspeakable honours, that even at the present time your sins may be washed away with the water of the fountain, or river, or even sea; the threefold name of blessedness being called over you, that by it not only evil spirits may be driven out, if any dwell in you, but also that, when you have forsaken your sins, and have with entire faith and entire purity of mind believed in God, you may drive out wicked spirits and demons from others also, and may be able to set others free from sufferings and sicknesses. For the demons themselves know and acknowledge those who have given themselves up to God, and sometimes they are driven out by the mere presence of such, as you saw a little while ago, how, when we had only addressed to you the word of salutation, straightway the demons, on account of their respect for our religion, began to cry out, and could not bear our presence even for a little.

Chap. XXXIII.—*The weakest Christian more powerful than the strongest demon.*

"Is it, then, that we are of another and a superior nature, and that therefore the demons are afraid of us? Nay, we are of one and the same nature with you, but we differ in religion. But if you will also be [like us], we do not grudge it, but rather we exhort you, and wish you to be assured, that when the same faith and religion and innocence of life shall be in you that is in us, you will have equal and the same power and virtue against demons, through God rewarding your faith. For as he who has soldiers under him, although he may be inferior, and they superior to him in strength, yet ' says to this one, Go, and he goeth; and to another, Come, and he cometh; and to another, Do this, and he doeth it;'[1] and this he is able to do, not by his own power, but by the fear of Cæsar; so every faithful one commands the demons, although they seem to be much stronger then men, and that not by means of his own power, but by means of the power of God, who has put them in subjection. For even that which we have just spoken of, that Cæsar is held in awe by all soldiers, and in every camp, and in his whole kingdom, though he is but one man, and perhaps feeble in respect of bodily strength, this is

[1] Matt. viii. 9.

not effected but by the power of God, who inspires all with fear, that they may be subject to one.

Chap. xxxiv.—*Temptation of Christ.*

"This we would have you know assuredly, that a demon has no power against a man, unless one voluntarily submit himself to his desires. Whence even that one who is the prince of wickedness, approached Him who, as we have said, is appointed of God King of peace, tempting Him, and began to promise Him all the glory of the world; because he knew that when he had offered this to others, for the sake of deceiving them, they had worshipped him. Therefore, impious as he was, and unmindful of himself, which indeed is the special peculiarity of wickedness, he presumed that he should be worshipped by Him by whom he knew that he was to be destroyed. Therefore our Lord, confirming the worship of one God, answered him : 'It is written, Thou shalt worship the Lord thy God, and Him only shalt thou serve.'[1] And he, terrified by this answer, and fearing lest the true religion of the one and true God should be restored, hastened straightway to send forth into this world false prophets, and false apostles, and false teachers, who should speak indeed in the name of Christ, but should accomplish the will of the demon.

Chap. xxxv.—*False apostles.*

"Wherefore observe the greatest caution, that you believe no teacher, unless he bring from Jerusalem the testimonial of James the Lord's brother, or of whosoever may come after him. For no one, unless he has gone up thither, and there has been approved as a fit and faithful teacher for preaching the word of Christ,—unless, I say, he brings a testimonial thence, is by any means to be received. But let neither prophet nor apostle be looked for by you at this time, besides us. For there is one true Prophet, whose words we twelve apostles preach; for He is the accepted year of God, having us apostles as His twelve months. But for what reason the world itself was made, or what diversities have occurred in it,

[1] Matt. iv. 10.

and why our Lord, coming for its restoration, has chosen and sent us twelve apostles, shall be explained more at length at another time. Meantime He has commanded us to go forth to preach, and to invite you to the supper of the heavenly King, which the Father hath prepared for the marriage of His Son, and that we should give you wedding garments, that is, the grace of baptism;[1] which whosoever obtains, as a spotless robe with which he is to enter to the supper of the King, ought to beware that it be not in any part of it stained with sin, and so he be rejected as unworthy and reprobate.

Chap. XXXVI.—*The garments unspotted.*

" But the ways in which this garment may be spotted are these: If any one withdraw from God the Father and Creator of all, receiving another teacher besides Christ, who alone is the faithful and true Prophet, and who has sent us twelve apostles to preach the word; if any one think otherwise than worthily of the substance of the Godhead, which excels all things;— these are the things which even fatally pollute the garment of baptism. But the things which pollute it in actions are these: murders, adulteries, hatreds, avarice, evil ambition. And the things which pollute at once the soul and the body are these: to partake of the table of demons, that is, to taste things sacrificed, or blood, or a carcase which is strangled, and if there be aught else which has been offered to demons. Be this therefore the first step to you of three; which step brings forth thirty commands, and the second sixty, and the third a hundred,[2] as we shall expound more fully to you at another time."

Chap. XXXVII.—*The congregation dismissed.*

When he had thus spoken, and had charged them to come to the same place in good time on the following day, he dismissed the crowds; and when they were unwilling to depart, Peter said to them: "Do me this favour on account of the fatigue of yesterday's journey; and now go away, and meet in good time to-morrow." And so they departed with joy.

[1] Matt. xxii. 2-14.   [2] Matt. xiii. 23.

But Peter, commanding me to withdraw a little for the purpose of prayer,[1] afterwards ordered the couches to be spread in that part of the garden which was covered with shade; and every one, according to custom, recognising the place of his own rank, we took food. Then, as there was still some portion of the day left, he conversed with us concerning the Lord's miracles; and when evening was come, he entered his bed-chamber and went to sleep.

[1] Clement being not yet baptized, is represented as not permitted to join with the disciples even in prayer.

RECOGNITIONS OF CLEMENT.

BOOK V.

CHAP. I.—*Peter's salutation.*

UT on the following day, Peter rising a little earlier than usual, found us asleep; and when he saw it, he gave orders that silence should be kept for him, as though he himself wished to sleep longer, that we might not be disturbed in our rest. But when we rose refreshed with sleep, we found him, having finished his prayer, waiting for us in his bed-chamber. And as it was already dawn, he addressed us shortly, saluting us according to his custom, and forthwith proceeded to the usual place for the purpose of teaching; and when he saw that many had assembled there, having invoked peace upon them according to the first religious form, he began to speak as follows:

CHAP. II.—*Suffering the effect of sin.*

"God, the Creator of all, at the beginning made man after His own image, and gave him dominion over the earth and sea, and over the air; as the true Prophet has told us, and as the very reason of things instructs us: for man alone is rational, and it is fitting that reason should rule over the irrational. At first, therefore, while he was still righteous, he was superior to all disorders and all frailty; but when he sinned, as we taught you yesterday, and became the servant of sin, he became at the same time liable to frailty. This therefore is written, that men may know that, as by impiety they have been made liable to suffer, so by piety they may be made free from suffering; and not only free from suffering, but by even a little faith in God be able to cure the sufferings of others. For thus the true Prophet promised us, saying, 'Verily I say to you, that if ye have faith as a grain of mustard seed, ye shall say to this mountain, Remove hence, and it shall remove.' [1] Of this saying you have yourselves also had proofs; for you saw yesterday how at our presence the demons removed and were put to flight, with those sufferings which they had brought upon men.

Chap. iii.—*Faith and unbelief.*

" Whereas therefore some men suffer, and others cure those who suffer, it is necessary to know the cause at once of the suffering and the cure; and this is proved to be nought else than unbelief on the part of the sufferers, and faith on the part of those who cure them. For unbelief, while it does not believe that there is to be a judgment by God, affords licence to sin, and sin makes men liable to sufferings; but faith, believing that there is to be a judgment of God, restrains men from sin; and those who do not sin are not only free from demons and sufferings, but can also put to flight the demons and sufferings of others.

Chap. iv.—*Ignorance the mother of evils.*

"From all these things, therefore, it is concluded that all evil springs from ignorance; and ignorance herself, the mother of all evils, is sprung from carelessness and sloth, and is nourished, and increased, and rooted in the senses of men by negligence; and if any one teach that she is to be put to flight, she is with difficulty and indignantly torn away, as from an ancient and hereditary abode. And therefore we must labour for a little, that we may search out the presumptions of ignorance, and cut them off by means of knowledge, especially in those who are preoccupied with some erroneous opinions, by means of which ignorance is the more firmly rooted in them, as under the appearance of a certain kind of knowledge; for nothing is worse than for one to believe that he knows what he is ignorant of, and to maintain that to be true which is false. This is as if a drunk man should think

[1] Matt. xvii. 19.

U

himself to be sober, and should act indeed in all respects as a drunk man, and yet think himself to be sober, and should wish to be called so by others. Thus, therefore, are those also who do not know what is true, yet hold some appearance of knowledge, and do many evil things as if they were good, and hasten to destruction as if it were to salvation.

CHAP. V.—*Advantages of knowledge.*

" Wherefore we must, above all things, hasten to the knowledge of the truth, that, as with a light kindled thereat, we may be able to dispel the darkness of errors : for ignorance, as we have said, is a great evil; but because it has no substance, it is easily dispelled by those who are in earnest. For ignorance is nothing else than not knowing what is good for us ; once know this, and ignorance perishes. Therefore the knowledge of truth ought to be eagerly sought after ; and no one can confer it except the true Prophet. For this is the gate of life to those who will enter, and the road of good works to those going to the city of salvation.

CHAP. VI.—*Free-will.*

" Whether any one, truly hearing the word of the true Prophet, is willing or unwilling to receive it, and to embrace His burden, that is, the precepts of life, he has either in his power, for we are free in will. For if it were so, that those who hear had it not in their power to do otherwise than they had heard, there were some power of nature in virtue of which it were not free to him to pass over to another opinion. Or if, again, no one of the hearers could at all receive it, this also were a power of nature which should compel the doing of some one thing, and should leave no place for the other course. But now, since it is free for the mind to turn its judgment to which side it pleases, and to choose the way which it approves, it is clearly manifest that there is in men a liberty of choice.

CHAP. VII.—*Responsibility of knowledge.*

" Therefore, before any one hears what is good for him, it is certain that he is ignorant ; and being ignorant, he wishes and desires to do what is not good for him ; wherefore he is not judged for that. But when once he has heard the causes of his error, and has received the method of truth, then, if he remain in those errors with which he had been long ago pre-occupied, he shall rightly be called into judgment, to suffer punishment, because he has spent in the sport of errors that portion of life which was given him to be spent in living well. But he who, hearing those things, willingly receives them, and is thankful that the teaching of good things has been brought to him, inquires more eagerly, and does not cease to learn, until he ascertains whether there be truly another world, in which rewards are prepared for the good. And when he is assured of this, he gives thanks to God because He has shown him the light of truth ; and for the future directs his actions in all good works, for which he is assured that there is a reward prepared in the world to come ; while he constantly wonders and is astonished at the errors of other men, and that no one sees the truth which is placed before his eyes. Yet he himself, rejoicing in the riches of wisdom which he hath found, desires insatiably to enjoy them, and is delighted with the practice of good works ; hastening to attain, with a clean heart and a pure conscience, the world to come, when he shall be able even to see God, the King of all.

CHAP. VIII.—*Desires of the flesh to be subdued.*

" But the sole cause of our wanting and being deprived of all these things is ignorance. For while men do not know how much good there is in knowledge, they do not suffer the evil of ignorance to be removed from them ; for they know not how great a difference is involved in the change of one of these things for the other. Wherefore I counsel every learner willingly to lend his ear to the word of God, and to hear with love of the truth what we say, that his mind, receiving the best seed, may bring forth joyful fruits by good deeds. For if, while I teach the things which pertain to salvation, any one refuses to receive them, and strives to resist them with a mind occupied by evil opinions, he shall have the cause of his perishing, not from us, but from himself. For it is his duty to examine with just judgment the things which we say, and to understand that we speak the words of truth, that, knowing how things are, and directing his life in good actions, he may be found a partaker of the kingdom of heaven, subjecting to himself the desires of the flesh, and becoming lord of them, that so at length he himself also may become the pleasant possession of the Ruler of all.

Chap. ix.—*The two kingdoms.*

"For he who persists in evil, and is the servant of evil, cannot be made a portion of good so long as he persists in evil, because from the beginning, as we have said, God instituted two kingdoms, and has given to each man the power of becoming a portion of that kingdom to which he shall yield himself to obey. And since it is decreed by God that no one man can be a servant of both kingdoms, therefore endeavour with all earnestness to betake yourselves to the covenant and laws of the good King. Wherefore also the true Prophet, when He was present with us, and saw some rich men negligent with respect to the worship of God, thus unfolded the truth of this matter : ' No one,' said He, ' can serve two masters ; ye cannot serve God and mammon ;'[1] calling riches, in the language of His country, *mammon.*

Chap. x.—*Jesus the true Prophet.*

"He therefore is the true Prophet, who appeared to us, as you have heard, in Judæa, who, standing in public places, by a simple command made the blind see, the deaf hear, cast out demons, restored health to the sick, and life to the dead ; and since nothing was impossible to Him, He even perceived the thoughts of men, which is possible for none but God only. He proclaimed the kingdom of God ; and we believed Him as a true Prophet in all that He spoke, deriving the confirmation of our faith not only from His words, but also from His works ; and also because the sayings of the law, which many generations before had set forth His coming, were fulfilled in Him ; and the figures of the doings of

[1] Matt. vi. 24.

Moses, and of the patriarch Jacob before him, bore in all respects a type of Him. It is evident also that the time of His advent, that is, the very time at which He came, was foretold by them; and, above all, it was contained in the sacred writings, that He was to be waited for by the Gentiles. And all these things were equally fulfilled in Him.

Chap. XI.—*The expectation of the Gentiles.*

"But that which a prophet of the Jews foretold, that He was to be waited for by the Gentiles,[1] confirms above measure the faith of truth in Him. For if he had said that He was to be waited for by the Jews, he would not have seemed to prophesy anything extraordinary, that He whose coming had been promised for the salvation of the world should be the object of hope to the people of the same tribe with Himself, and to His own nation : for that this would take place, would seem rather to be a matter of natural inference than one requiring the grandeur of a prophetic utterance. But now, whereas the prophets say that all that hope which is set forth concerning the salvation of the world, and the newness of the kingdom which is to be established by Christ, and all things which are declared concerning Him are to be transferred to the Gentiles; the grandeur of the prophetic office is confirmed, not according to the sequence of things, but by an incredible fulfilment of the prophecy. For the Jews from the beginning had understood by a most certain tradition that this man should at some time come, by whom all things should be restored; and daily meditating and looking out for His coming, when they saw Him amongst them, and accomplishing the signs and miracles, as had been written of Him, being blinded with envy, they could not recognise Him when present, in the hope of whom they rejoiced while He was absent; yet the few of us who were chosen by Him understood it.

Chap. XII.—*Call of the Gentiles.*

"But this happened by the providence of God, that the knowledge of this good One should be handed over to the

[1] Gen. xlix. 10.

Gentiles, and those who had never heard of Him, nor had learned from the prophets, should acknowledge Him, while those who had acknowledged Him in their daily meditations should not know Him. For, behold, by you who are now present, and desire to hear the doctrine of His faith, and to know what, and how, and of what sort is His coming, the prophetic truth is fulfilled. For this is what the prophets foretold, that He is to be sought for by you, who never heard of Him.[1] And, therefore, seeing that the prophetic sayings are fulfilled even in yourselves, you rightly believe in Him alone, you rightly wait for Him, you rightly inquire concerning Him, that you not only may wait for Him, but also believing, you may obtain the inheritance of His kingdom; according to what Himself said, that every one is made the servant of him to whom he yields subjection.[2]

Chap. XIII.—*Invitation of the Gentiles.*

" Wherefore awake, and take to yourselves our Lord and God, even that Lord who is Lord both of heaven and earth, and conform yourselves to His image and likeness, as the true Prophet Himself teaches, saying, 'Be ye merciful, as also your heavenly Father is merciful, who makes His sun to rise upon the good and the evil, and rains upon the just and the unjust.'[3] Imitate Him, therefore, and fear Him, as the commandment is given to men, 'Thou shalt worship the Lord thy God, and Him only shalt thou serve.'[4] For it is profitable to you to serve this Lord alone, that through Him knowing the one God, ye may be freed from the many whom ye vainly feared. For he who fears not God the Creator of all, but fears those whom he himself with his own hands hath made, what does he do but make himself subject to a vain and senseless fear, and render himself more vile and abject than those very things, the fear of which he has conceived in his mind? But rather, by the goodness of Him who inviteth you, return to your former nobleness, and by good deeds show that you bear the image of your Creator, that by

[1] Isa. lxv. 1.   [2] John viii. 34.   [3] Luke vi. 36 ; Matt. v. 45.
[4] Deut. vi. 13 ; Matt. iv. 10.

contemplation of His likeness ye may be believed to be even His sons.

CHAP. XIV.—*Idols unprofitable.*

" Begin, therefore, to cast out of your minds the vain ideas of idols, and your useless and empty fears, that at the same time you may also escape the condition of unrighteous bondage. For those have become your lords, who could not even have been profitable servants to you. For how should lifeless images seem fit even to serve you, when they can neither hear, nor see, nor feel anything ? Yea, even the material of which they are made, whether it be gold or silver, or even brass or wood, though it might have profited you for necessary uses, you have rendered wholly inefficient and useless by fashioning gods out of it. We therefore declare to you the true worship of God, and at the same time warn and exhort the worshippers, that by good deeds they imitate Him whom they worship, and hasten to return to His image and likeness, as we said before.

CHAP. XV.—*Folly of idolatry.*

" But I should like if those who worship idols would tell me if they wish to become like to those whom they worship ? Does any one of you wish to see in such sort as they see ? or to hear after the manner of their hearing ? or to have such understanding as they have ? Far be this from any of my hearers ! For this were rather to be thought a curse and a reproach to a man, who bears in himself the image of God, although he has lost the likeness. What sort of gods, then, are they to be reckoned, the imitation of whom would be execrable to their worshippers, and to have whose likeness would be a reproach ? What then ? Melt your useless images, and make useful vessels. Melt the unserviceable and inactive metal, and make implements fit for the use of men. But, says one, human laws do not allow us. He says well ; for it is human laws, and not their own power, that prevents it. What kind of gods, then, are those which are defended by human laws, and not by their own energies ? And so also they are preserved from thieves by watch-dogs and the protection of bolts, at least if they be of silver, or gold, or even of brass; for those that are of stone and earthenware are protected by their own worthlessness, for no one will steal a stone or a crockery god. Hence those seem to be the more miserable whose more precious metal exposes them to the greater danger. Since, then, they can be stolen, since they must be guarded by men, since they can be melted, and weighed out, and forged with hammers, ought men possessed of understanding to hold them as gods?

CHAP. XVI.—*God alone a fit object of worship.*

"Oh! into what wretched plight the understanding of men has fallen! For if it is reckoned the greatest folly to fear the dead, what shall we judge of those who fear something that is worse than the dead are? For those images are not even to be reckoned among the number of the dead, because they never were alive. Even the sepulchres of the dead are preferable to them, since, although they are now dead, yet they once had life; but those whom you worship never possessed even such base life as is in all, the life of frogs and owls. But why say more about them, since it is enough to say to him who adores them: Do you not see that he whom you adore sees not, hear that he whom you adore hears not, and understand that he understands not?—for he is the work of man's hand, and necessarily is void of understanding. You therefore worship a god without sense, whereas every one who has sense believes that not even those things are to be worshipped which have been made by God and have sense,[1] such as the sun, moon, and stars, and all things that are in heaven and upon earth. For they think it reasonable, that not those things which have been made for the service of the world, but the Creator of those things themselves, and of the whole world, should be worshipped. For even these things rejoice when He is adored and worshipped, and do not take it well that the honour of the Creator should be bestowed

---

[1] It was a very prevalent opinion among the ancient philosophers, that the heavenly bodies have some kind of life and intelligence.

on the creature.   For the worship of God alone is acceptable
[to them], who alone is uncreated, and all things also are His
creatures.   For as it belongs to him who alone is uncreated to
be God, so everything that has been created is not truly God.

Chap. xvii.—*Suggestions of the old serpent.*

" Above all, therefore, you ought to understand the deception of the old serpent and his cunning suggestions, who de-
ceives you as it were by prudence, and as by a sort of reason
creeps through your senses; and beginning at the head, he
glides through your inner marrow, accounting the deceiving
of you a great gain.   Therefore he insinuates into your
minds opinions of gods of whatsoever kinds, only that he may
withdraw you from the faith of one God, knowing that your
sin is his comfort.   For he, for his wickedness, was condemned from the beginning to eat dust, for that he caused to
be again resolved into dust him who had been taken from the
dust, even till the time when your souls shall be restored,
being brought through the fire; as we shall instruct you
more fully at another time.   From him, therefore, proceed
all the errors and doubts, by which you are driven from the
faith and belief of one God.

Chap. xviii.—*His first suggestion.*

" And first of all he suggests to men's thoughts not to hear
the words of truth, by which they might put to flight the
ignorance of those things which are evils.   And this he does,
as by the presentation of another knowledge, making a show
of that opinion which very many hold, to think that they shall
not be held guilty if they have been in ignorance, and that
they shall not be called to account for what they have not
heard; and thereby he persuades them to turn aside from
hearing the word.   But I tell you, in opposition to this, that
ignorance is in itself a most deadly poison, which is sufficient
to ruin the soul without any aid from without.   And therefore
there is no one who is ignorant who shall escape through his
ignorance, but it is certain that he shall perish.   For the power
of sin naturally destroys the sinner.   But since the judgment

shall be according to reason, the cause and origin of ignorance shall be inquired into, as well as of every sin. For he who is unwilling to know how he may attain to life, and prefers to be in ignorance lest he thereby be made guilty, from this very fact is judged as if he knew and had knowledge. For he knew what it was that he was unwilling to hear; and the cunning obtained by the artifice of the serpent will avail him nothing for an excuse, for he will have to do with Him to whom the heart is open. But that you may know that ignorance of itself brings destruction, [I assure you that] when the soul departs from the body, if it leave it in ignorance of Him by whom it was created, and from whom in this world it obtained all things that were necessary for its uses, it is driven forth from the light of His kingdom as ungrateful and unfaithful.

Chap. xix.—*His second suggestion.*

" Again, the wicked serpent suggests another opinion to men, which many of you are in the habit of bringing forward, —that there is, as we say, one God, who is Lord of all; but these also, they say, are gods. For as there is one Cæsar, and he has under him many judges,—for example, prefects, consuls, tribunes, and other officers,—in like manner we think, that while there is one God greater than all, yet still that these gods are ordained in this world, after the likeness of those officers of whom we have spoken, subject indeed to that greater God, yet ruling us and the things that are in this world. In answer to this, I shall show you how, in those very things which you propose for deception, you are confuted by the reasons of truth. You say that God occupies the place of Cæsar, and those who are called gods represent his judges and officers. Hold then, as you have adduced it, by the example of Cæsar; and know that, as no one of Cæsar's judges or administrators, as prefects, proconsuls, generals, or tribunes, may lawfully take the name of Cæsar,—or else both he who should take it and those who should confer it should be destroyed together,—so also in this case you ought to observe, that if any one give the name of God to any but Himself, and he accept it, they shall partake one and the same destruction, by a much more terrible fate than the servants of Cæsar. For he who offends against Cæsar shall undergo temporal destruction; but he who offends against Him who is the sole and true God, shall suffer eternal punishment, and that deservedly, as having injured by a wrongful condition the name which is unique.[1]

Chap. xx.—*Egyptian idolatry.*

" Although this word God is not the *name* of God, but meantime that word is employed by men as His name ; and therefore, as I have said, when it is used reproachfully, the re-proach is referred to the injury of the true name.   In short, the ancient Egyptians, who thought that they had discovered the theory of the heavenly revolutions and the nature of the stars, nevertheless, through the demon's blocking up their senses, subjected the incommunicable name to all kinds of indignity.   For some taught that their ox, which is called Apis, ought to be worshipped; others taught that the he-goat, others that cats, the ibis, a fish also, a serpent, onions, drains, crepitus ventris, ought to be regarded as deities, and innumer-able other things, which I am ashamed even to mention."

Chap. xxi.—*Egyptian idolatry more reasonable than others.*

When Peter was speaking thus, all we who heard him laughed.   Then said Peter : " You laugh at the absurdities of others, because through long custom you do not see your own.   For indeed it is not without reason that you laugh at the folly of the Egyptians, who worship dumb animals, while they themselves are rational.   But I will tell you how they also laugh at you ; for they say, We worship living animals, though mortal ; but you worship and adore things which never were alive at all.   They add this also, that they are figures and allegories of certain powers by whose help the race of men is governed.   Taking refuge in this for shame, they fabricate these and similar excuses, and so endeavour to screen their error.   But this is not the time to answer the Egyptians, and

---

[1] The writer means, that insult is offered to that name which belongs to God alone by giving it to others, and thus placing it in a position which is unjust to it.

leaving the care of those who are present to heal the diseases of the absent. For it is a certain indication that you are held to be free from sickness of this sort, since you do not grieve over it as your own, but laugh at it as that of others.

CHAP. XXII.—*Second suggestion continued.*

"But let us come back to you, whose opinion it is that God should be regarded as Cæsar, and the gods as the ministers and deputies of Cæsar. Follow me attentively, and I shall presently show you the lurking-places of the serpent, which lie in the crooked windings of this argument. It ought to be regarded by all as certain and beyond doubt, that no creature can be on a level with God, because He was made by none, but Himself made all things; nor indeed can any one be found so irrational, as to suppose that the thing made can be compared with the maker. If therefore the human mind, not only by reason, but even by a sort of natural instinct, rightly holds this opinion, that that is called *God* to which nothing can be compared or equalled, but which exceeds all and excels all; how can it be supposed that that name which is believed to be above all, is rightly given to those whom you think to be employed for the service and comfort of human life? But we shall add this also. This world was undoubtedly made, and is corruptible, as we shall show more fully by and by; meantime it is admitted both that it has been made and that it is corruptible. If therefore the world cannot be called God, and rightly so, because it is corruptible, how shall parts of the world take the name of God? For inasmuch as the whole world cannot be God, much more its parts cannot. Therefore, if we come back to the example of Cæsar, you will see how far you are in error. It is not lawful for any one, though a man of the same nature with him, to be compared with Cæsar: do you think, then, that any one ought to be compared with God, who excels all in this respect, that He was made by none, but Himself made all things? But, indeed, you dare not give the name of Cæsar to any other, because he immediately punishes one who offends against him; you dare give that of

God to others, because He delays the punishment of offenders against Him, in order to their repentance.

Chap. xxiii.—*Third suggestion.*

" Through the mouths of others also that serpent is wont to speak in this wise : We adore visible images in honour of the invisible God. Now this is most certainly false. For if you really wished to worship the image of God, you would do good to man, and so worship the true image of God in him. For the image of God is in every man, though His likeness is not in all, but where the soul is benign and the mind pure. If, therefore, you wish truly to honour the image of God, we declare to you what is true, that you should do good to and pay honour and reverence to man, who is made in the image of God ; that you minister food to the hungry, drink to the thirsty, clothing to the naked, hospitality to the stranger, and necessary things to the prisoner ; and that is what will be regarded as truly bestowed upon God. And so far do these things go to the honour of God's image, that he who does not these things is regarded as casting reproach upon the divine image. What, then, is that honour of God which consists in running from one stone or wooden figure to another, in venerating empty and lifeless figures as deities, and despising men in whom the image of God is of a truth? Yea, rather be assured, that whoever commits murder or adultery, or anything that causes suffering or injury to men, in all these the image of God is violated. For to injure men is a great impiety towards God. Whenever, therefore, you do to another what you would not have another do to you, you defile the image of God with undeserved distresses. Understand, therefore, that that is the suggestion of the serpent lurking within you, which persuades you that you may seem to be pious when you worship insensible things, and may not seem impious when you injure sensible and rational beings.

Chap. xxiv.—*Fourth suggestion.*

" But to these things the serpent answers us with another

mouth, and says: If God did not wish these things to be, then they should not be. I am not telling you how it is that many contrary things are permitted to be in this world for the probation of every one's mind. But this is what is suitable to be said in the meantime: If, according to you, everything that was to be worshipped ought not to have been, there would have been almost nothing in this world. For what is there that you have left without worshipping it? The sun, the moon, the stars, the water, the earth, mountains, trees, stones, men; there is no one of these that ye have not worshipped. According to your saying, therefore, none of these ought to have been made by God, that you might not have anything that you could worship! Yea, He ought not even to have made men themselves to be the worshippers! But this is the very thing which that serpent which lurks within you desires: for he spares none of you; he would have no one of you escape from destruction. But it shall not be so. For I tell you, that not that which is worshipped is in fault, but he who worships. For with God is righteous judgment; and He judges in one way the sufferer, and in another way the doer, of wrong.

Chap. xxv.—*Fifth suggestion.*

"But you say: Then those who adore what ought not to be adored, should be immediately destroyed by God, to prevent others doing the like. But are you wiser than God, that you should offer Him counsel?[1] He knows what to do. For with all who are placed in ignorance He exercises patience, because He is merciful and gracious; and He foresees that many of the ungodly become godly, and that even some of those who worship impure statues and polluted images have been converted to God, and forsaking their sins and doing good works, attain to salvation. But it is said: We ought never to have come even to the thought of doing these things. You do not know what freedom of will is, and you forget that he is good who is so by his own intention; but he who is retained in goodness by necessity cannot be called good,

[1] Rom. xi. 34.

because it is not of himself that he is so. Because, therefore, there is in every one liberty to choose good or evil, he either acquires rewards, or brings destruction on himself. Nay, it is said, God brings to our minds whatsoever we think. What mean ye, O men? Ye blaspheme. For if He brings all our thoughts into our minds, then it is He that suggests to us thoughts of adultery, and covetousness, and blasphemy, and every kind of effeminacy. Cease, I entreat of you, these blasphemies, and understand what is the honour worthy of God. And say not, as some of you are wont to say, that God needs not honour from men. Indeed, He truly is in need of none; but you ought to know that the honour which you bestow upon God is profitable to yourselves. For what is so execrable, as for a man not to render thanks to his Creator?

CHAP. XXVI.—*Sixth suggestion.*

"But it is said: We do better, who give thanks both to Himself, and to all with Him. In this you do not understand that there is the ruin of your salvation. For it is as if a sick man should call in for his cure at once a physician and poisoners; since these could indeed injure him, but not cure him; and the true physician would refuse to mix his remedies with their poisons, lest either the man's destruction should be ascribed to the good, or his recovery to the injurious. But you say: Is God then indignant or envious, if, when He benefits us, our thanks be rendered to others? Even if He be not indignant, at all events He does not wish to be the author of error, that by means of His work credit should be given to a vain idol. And what is so impious, so ungrateful, as to obtain a benefit from God, and to render thanks to blocks of wood and stone? Wherefore arise, and understand your salvation. For God is in need of no one, nor does He require anything, nor is He hurt by anything; but we are either helped or hurt, in that we are grateful or ungrateful. For what does God gain from our praises, or what does He lose by our blasphemies? Only [this we must remember], that God brings into proximity and friendship with Himself the soul that renders thanks to Him.   But the wicked demon possesses the ungrateful soul.

CHAP. XXVII.—*Creatures take vengeance on sinners.*

" But this also I would have you know, that upon such souls God does not take vengeance directly, but His whole creation rises up and inflicts punishments upon the impious; and although in the present world the goodness of God bestows the light of the world and the services of the earth alike upon the pious and the impious, yet not without grief does the sun afford his light, and the other elements perform their service, to the impious.   And, in short, sometimes even in opposition to the goodness of the Creator, the elements are wearied out by the crimes of the wicked; and thence it is that either the fruit of the earth is blighted, or the composition of the air is vitiated, or the heat of the sun is increased beyond measure, or there is an excessive amount of rain or of cold.   Thence pestilence, and famine, and death in various forms stalk forth, for the creature hastens to take vengeance on the wicked; yet the goodness of God restrains it, and bridles its indignation against the wicked, and compels it to be obedient to His mercy, rather than to be inflamed by the sins and the crimes of men. For the patience of God waiteth for the conversion of men, as long as they are in this body.

CHAP. XXVIII.—*Eternity of punishments.*

" But if any persist in impiety till the end of life, then as soon as the soul, which is immortal, departs, it shall pay the penalty of its persistence in impiety.   For even the souls of the impious are immortal, though perhaps they themselves would wish them to end with their bodies.   But it is not so; for they endure without end the torments of eternal fire, and to their destruction they have not the quality of mortality. But perhaps you will say to me, You terrify us, O Peter. And how shall we speak to you the things which are in reality? Can we declare to you the truth by keeping silence?   We cannot state the things which are, otherwise than as they are. But if we were silent, we should make ourselves the cause of the ignorance that is ruinous to you, and should satisfy the serpent that lurks within you, and blocks up your senses, who cunningly suggests these things to you, that he may make you always the enemies of God.   But we are sent for this end, that we may betray his disguises to you; and melting your enmities, may reconcile you to God, that you may be converted to Him, and may please Him by good works.   For man is at enmity with God, and is in an unreasonable and impious state of mind and wicked disposition towards Him, especially when he thinks that he knows something, and is in ignorance.   But when you lay aside these, and begin to be pleased and displeased with the same things which please and displease God, and to will what God willeth, then ye shall truly be called His friends.

Chap. xxix.—*God's care of human things.*

"But perhaps some of you will say, God has no care of human things; and if we cannot even attain to the knowledge of Him, how shall we attain to His friendship?   That God does concern Himself with the affairs of men, His government of the world bears witness: for the sun daily waits upon it, the showers minister to it; the fountains, rivers, winds, and all elements, attend upon it; and the more these things become known to men, the more do they indicate God's care over men.   For unless by the power of the Most High, the more powerful would never minister to the inferior; and by this God is shown to have not only a care over men, but some great affection, since He has deputed such noble elements to their service.   But that men may also attain to the friendship of God, is proved to us by the example of those to whose prayers He has been so favourable, that He has withheld the heaven from rain when they wished, and has again opened it when they prayed.[1]   And many other things He has bestowed upon those who do His will, which could not be bestowed but upon His friends.   But you will say, What harm is done to God if these things also are worshipped by us?   If any one of you should pay to another the honour that is due to his father,

---

[1] 1 Kings xvii. xviii.; Jas. v. 17, 18.

from whom he has received innumerable benefits, and should reverence a stranger and foreigner as his father, should you not think that he was undutiful towards his father, and most deserving to be disinherited?

CHAP. XXX.—*Religion of fathers to be abandoned.*

" Others say, It is wicked if we do not worship those [idols] which have come down to us from our fathers, and prove false to the religion bequeathed to us by our ancestors. On this principle, if any one's father was a robber or a base fellow, he ought not to change the manner of life handed down to him by his fathers, nor to be recalled from his father's errors to a better way; and it is reckoned impious if one do not sin with his parents, or does not persist in impiety with them. Others say, We ought not to be troublesome to God, and to be always burdening Him with complaints of our miseries, or with the exigencies of our petitions. How foolish and witless an answer! Do you think it is troublesome to God if you thank Him for His benefits, while you do not think it troublesome to Him if, for His gifts, you render thanks to stocks and stones? And how comes it, that when rain is withheld in a long drought, we all turn our eyes to heaven, and entreat the gift of rain from God Almighty, and all of us with our little ones pour out prayers to God, and entreat His compassion? But truly ungrateful souls, when they obtain the blessing, quickly forget: for as soon as they have gathered in their harvest or their vintage, straightway they offer the first-fruits to deaf and dumb images, and pay vows in temples or groves for those things which God has bestowed upon them, and then offer sacrifices to demons; and having received a favour, deny the bestower of the favour.[1]

CHAP. XXXI.—*Paganism—its enormities.*

" But some say, These things are instituted for the sake of joy, and for refreshing our minds; and they have been devised for this end, that the human mind may be relaxed for a little from cares and sorrows. See now what a charge

[1] Literally, " change the bestower of it for another."

you yourselves bring upon the things which you practise. If these things have been invented for the purpose of lightening sorrow and affording enjoyment, how is it that the invocations of demons are performed in groves and woods? What is the meaning of the insane whirlings, and the slashing of limbs, and the cutting off of members? How is it that mad rage is produced in them? How is insanity produced? How is it that women are driven violently, raging with dishevelled hair? Whence the shrieking and gnashing of teeth? Whence the bellowing of the heart and the bowels, and all those things which, whether they are pretended or are contrived by the ministration of demons, are exhibited to the terror of the foolish and ignorant? Are these things done for the sake of lightening the mind, or rather for the sake of oppressing it? Do ye not yet perceive nor understand, that these are the counsels of the serpent lurking within you, which draws you away from the apprehension of truth by irrational suggestions of errors, that he may hold you as slaves and servants of lust and concupiscence and every disgraceful thing?

Chap. xxxii.—*True religion calls to sobriety and modesty.*

" But I protest to you with the clear voice of preaching, that, on the contrary, the religion of God calls you to sobriety and modesty; orders you to refrain from effeminacy and madness, and by patience and gentleness to prevent the inroads of anger; to be content with your own possessions, and with the virtue of frugality ; not even when driven by poverty to plunder the goods of others, but in all things to observe justice ; to withdraw yourselves wholly from the idol sacrifices: for by these things you invite demons to you, and of your own accord give them the power of entering into you ; and so you admit that which is the cause either of madness or of unlawful love.

Chap. xxxiii.—*Origin of impiety.*

" Hence is the origin of all impiety ; hence murders, adulteries, thefts ; and a nursery is formed of all evils and wickednesses, while you indulge in profane libations and odours, and give to wicked spirits an opportunity of ruling and obtaining some sort of authority over you. For when they invade your senses, what do they else than work the things which belong to lust and injustice and cruelty, and compel you to be obedient to all things that are pleasing to them? God, indeed, permits you to suffer this at their hands by a certain righteous judgment, that from the very disgrace of your doings and your feelings you may understand how unworthy it is to be subject to demons and not to God. Hence also, by the friendship of demons, men are brought to disgraceful and base deeds; hence, men proceed even to the destruction of life, either through the fire of lust, or through the madness of anger through excess of grief, so that, as is well[1] known, some have even laid violent hands upon themselves. And this, as we have said, by a just sentence of God they are not prevented from doing, that they may both understand to whom they have yielded themselves in subjection, and know whom they have forsaken.

Chap. xxxiv.—*Who are worshippers of God?*

" But some one will say, These passions sometimes befall even those who worship God. It is not true. For we say that he is a worshipper of God, who does the will of God, and observes the precepts of His law. For in God's estimation he is not a Jew who is called a Jew among men (nor is he a Gentile that is called a Gentile), but he who, believing in God, fulfils His law and does His will, though he be not circumcised.[2] He is the true worshipper of God, who not only is himself free from passions, but also sets others free from them; though they be so heavy that they are like mountains, he removes them by means of the faith with which he believes in God.[3] Yea, by faith he truly removes mountains with their trees, if it be necessary. But he who seems to worship God, but is neither fortified by a full faith,

---

[1] The original has here, " as is often known;" that is, as people know from many instances having occurred within their own knowledge.

[2] Rom. ii. 28 ; Rev. ii. 9.   [3] Matt. xvii. 9 ; Luke xvii. 6.

nor by obedience to the commandments, but is a sinner, has given a place in himself, by reason of his sins, to passions, which are appointed of God for the punishment of those who sin, that they may exact from them the deserts of their sins by means of punishments inflicted, and may bring them purified to the general judgment of all, provided always that their faith do not fail them in their chastisement. For the chastisement of unbelievers in the present life is a judgment, by which they begin to be separated from future blessings; but the chastisement of those who worship God, while it is inflicted upon them for sins into which they have fallen, exacts from them the due of what they have done, that, preventing the judgment, they may pay the debt of their sin in the present life, and be freed, at least in half, from the eternal punishments which are there prepared.

CHAP. xxxv.—*Judgment to come.*

" But he does not receive these things as true who does not believe that there is to be a judgment of God, and therefore, being bound by the pleasures of the present life, is shut out from eternal good things; and therefore we do not neglect to proclaim to you what we know to be necessary for your salvation, and to show you what is the true worship of God, that, believing in God, you may be able, by means of good works, to be heirs with us of the world to come. But if you are not yet convinced that what we say is true, meantime, in the first instance, you ought not to take it amiss and to be hostile to us because we announce to you the things which we consider to be good, and because we do not grudge to bestow also upon you that which we believe brings salvation to ourselves, labouring, as I have said, with all eagerness, that we may have you as fellow-heirs of the blessings which we believe are to befall ourselves. But whether those things which we declare to you are certainly true, you shall not be able to know otherwise than by rendering obedience to the things which are commanded, that you may be taught by the issue of things, and the most certain end of blessedness.

Chap. xxxvi.—*Conclusion of discourse.*

" And, therefore, although the serpent lurking within you occupies your senses with a thousand arts of corruption, and throws in your way a thousand obstacles, by which he may turn you away from the hearing of saving instruction, all the more ought you to resist him, and despising his suggestions, to come together the more frequently to hear the word and receive instruction from us, because nobody can learn anything who is not taught."

And when he had done speaking, he ordered those to be brought to him who were oppressed by sicknesses or demons, and laid his hands upon them with prayer; and so he dismissed the crowds, charging them to resort to the hearing of the word during the days that he was to remain there. Therefore, when the crowds had departed, Peter washed his body in the waters which ran through the garden, with as many of the others as chose to do so; and then ordered the couches to be spread on the ground under a very shady tree, and directed us to recline according to the order established at Cæsarea. And thus, having taken food and given thanks to God after the manner of the Hebrews, as there was yet some portion of the day remaining, he ordered us to question him on any matters that we pleased. And although we were with him twenty in all, he explained to every one whatever he pleased to ask of him; the particulars of which I set down in books and sent to you some time ago. And when evening came we entered with him into the lodging, and went to sleep, each one in his own place.

RECOGNITIONS OF CLEMENT.

———◆———

BOOK VI.

Chap. i.—*Diligence in study.*

BUT as soon as day began to advance the dawn upon the retiring darkness, Peter having gone into the garden to pray, and returning thence and coming to us, by way of excuse for awaking and coming to us a little later than usual, said this: "Now that the spring-time has lengthened the day, of course the night is shorter; if, therefore, one desires to occupy some portion of the night in study, he must not keep the same hours[1] for waking at all seasons, but should spend the same length of time in sleeping, whether the night be longer or shorter, and be exceedingly careful that he do not cut off from the period which he is wont to have for study, and so add to his sleep and lessen his time of keeping awake. And this also is to be observed, lest haply if sleep be interrupted while the food is still undigested, the undigested mass load the mind, and by the exhalation of crude spirits render the inner sense confused and disturbed. It is right, therefore, that that part also be cherished with sufficient rest, so that, those things being sufficiently accomplished which are due to it, the body may be able in other things to render due service to the mind."

Chap. ii.—*Much to be done in a little time.*

When he had said this, as very many had already assembled

[1] It will be remembered that the *hours* were variable periods, and began to be reckoned from sunrise.

in the accustomed place of the garden to hear him, Peter went forth; and having saluted the crowds in his usual manner, began to speak as follows: " Since, indeed, as land neglected by the cultivator necessarily produces thorns and thistles, so your sense, by long neglect, has produced a plentiful crop of noxious opinions of things and dogmas of false science; there is need now of much care in cultivating the field of your mind, that the word of truth, which is the true and diligent husbandman of the heart, may cultivate it with continual instructions. It is therefore your part to render obedience to it, and to lop off superfluous occupations and anxieties, lest a noxious growth choke the good seed of the word. For it may be that a short and earnest diligence may repair a long time's neglect; for the time of every one's life is uncertain, and therefore we must hasten to salvation, lest haply sudden death seize upon him who delays.

Chap. iii.—*Righteous anger.*

" And all the more eagerly must we strive on this account, that while there is time, the collected vices of evil custom may be cut off. And this you shall not be able to do otherwise, than by being angry with yourselves on account of your profitless and base doings. For this is righteous and necessary anger, by which every one is indignant with himself, and accuses himself for those things in which he has erred and done amiss; and by this indignation a certain fire is kindled in us, which, applied as it were to a barren field, consumes and burns up the roots of vile pleasure, and renders the soil of the heart more fertile for the good seed of the word of God. And I think that you have sufficiently worthy causes of anger, from which that most righteous fire may be kindled, if you consider into what errors the evil of ignorance has drawn you, and how it has caused you to fall and rush head-long into sin, from what good things it has withdrawn you, and into what evils it has driven you, and, what is of more importance than all the rest, how it has made you liable to eternal punishments in the world to come. Is not the fire of most righteous indignation kindled within you for all these things, now that the light of truth has shone upon you; and does not the flame of that anger which is pleasing to God rise within you, that every sprout may be burnt up and destroyed from the root, if haply any shoot of evil concupiscence has budded within you?

Chap. iv.—*Not peace, but a sword.*

"Hence, also, He who hath sent us, when He had come, and had seen that all the world had fallen into wickedness, did not forthwith give peace to him who is in error, lest He should confirm him in evil; but set the knowledge of truth in opposition to the ruins of ignorance of it, that, if haply men would repent and look upon the light of truth, they might rightly grieve that they had been deceived and drawn away into the precipices of error, and might kindle the fire of salutary anger against the ignorance that had deceived them. On this account, therefore, He said, 'I have come to send fire on the earth; and how I wish that it were kindled!'[1] There is therefore a certain fight, which is to be fought by us in this life; for the word of truth and knowledge necessarily separates men from error and ignorance, as we have often seen putrified and dead flesh in the body separated by the cutting knife from its connection with the living members. Such is the effect produced by knowledge of the truth. For it is necessary that, for the sake of salvation, the son, for example, who has received the word of truth, be separated from his unbelieving parents; or again, that the father be separated from his son, or the daughter from her mother. And in this manner the battle of knowledge and ignorance, of truth and error, arises between believing and unbelieving kinsmen and relations. And therefore He who has sent us said again, 'I am not come to send peace on earth, but a sword.'[2]

Chap. v.—*How the fight begins.*

"But if any one say, How does it seem right for men to be separated from their parents? I will tell you how. Because, if they remained with them in error, they would do no

[1] Luke xii. 49.　　　　　　[2] Matt. x. 34.

good to them, and they would themselves perish with them. It is therefore right, and very right, that he who will be saved be separated from him who will not. But observe this also, that this separation does not come from those who understand aright; for they wish to be with their relatives, and to do them good, and to teach them better things. But it is the vice peculiar to ignorance, that it will not bear to have near it the light of truth, which confutes it; and therefore that separation originates with them. For those who receive the knowledge of the truth, because it is full of goodness, desire, if it be possible, to share it with all, as given by the good God; yea, even with those who hate and persecute them: for they know that ignorance is the cause of their sin. Wherefore, in short, the Master Himself, when He was being led to the cross by those who knew Him not, prayed the Father for His murderers, and said, 'Father, forgive their sin, for they know not what they do!'[1] The disciples also, in imitation of the Master, even when themselves were suffering, in like manner prayed for their murderers.[2] But if we are taught to pray even for our murderers and persecutors, how ought we not to bear the persecutions of parents and relations, and to pray for their conversion?

Chap. vi.—*God to be loved more than parents.*

" Then let us consider carefully, in the next place, what reason we have for loving our parents. For this cause, it is said, we love them, because they seem to be the authors of our life. But our parents are not authors of our life, but means of it. For they do not bestow life, but afford the means of our entering into this life; while the one and sole author of life is God. If therefore we would love the Author of our life, let us know that it is He that is to be loved. But then it is said, We cannot know Him; but them we know, and hold in affection. Be it so: you cannot know *what* God is, but you can very easily know what God is *not*. For how can any man fail to know that wood, or stone, or brass, or other such matter, is not God? But if you will not

---

[1] Luke xxiii. 54.   [2] Acts vii. 59.

give your mind to consider the things which you might easily apprehend, it is certain that you are hindered in the knowledge of God, not by impossibility, but by indolence; for if you had wished it, even from these useless images you might have been set on the way of understanding.

Chap. vii.—*The earth made for men.*

" For it is certain that these images are made with iron tools; but iron is wrought by fire, which fire is extinguished by water. But water is moved by spirit; and spirit has its beginning from God. For thus saith the prophet Moses: ' In the beginning God made the heaven and the earth. But the earth was invisible, and unarranged; and darkness was over the deep: and the Spirit of God was upon the waters.'[1] Which Spirit, like the Creator's hand, by command of God separated light from darkness; and after that invisible heaven produced this visible one, that He might make the higher places a habitation for angels, and the lower for men. For your sake, therefore, by command of God, the water which was upon the face of the earth withdrew, that the earth might produce fruits for you; and into the earth also He inserted veins of moisture, that fountains and rivers might flow forth from it for you. For your sake it was commanded to bring forth living creatures, and all things which could serve for your use and pleasure. Is it not for you that the winds blow, that the earth, conceiving by them, may bring forth fruits? Is it not for you that the showers fall, and the seasons change? Is it not for you that the sun rises and sets, and the moon undergoes her changes? For you the sea offers its service, that all things may be subject to you, ungrateful as you are. For all these things shall there not be a righteous punishment of vengeance, because beyond all else you are ignorant of the bestower of all these things, whom you ought to acknowledge and reverence above all?

Chap. viii.—*Necessity of baptism.*

" But now I lead you to understanding by the same paths.

[1] Gen. i. 1, 2.

For you see that all things are produced from waters. But water was made at first by the Only-begotten; and the Almighty God is the head of the Only-begotten, by whom we come to the Father in such order as we have stated above. But when you have come to the Father, you will learn that this is His will, that you be born anew by means of waters, which were first created. For he who is regenerated by water, having filled up the measure of good works, is made heir of Him by whom he has been regenerated in incorruption. Wherefore, with prepared minds, approach as sons to a father, that your sins may be washed away, and it may be proved before God that ignorance was their sole cause. For if, after the learning of these things, you remain in unbelief, the cause of your destruction will be imputed to yourselves, and not to ignorance. And do not suppose that you can have hope towards God, even if you cultivate all piety and all righteousness, but do not receive baptism. Yea rather, he will be worthy of greater punishment, who does good works not well; for merit accrues to men from good works, but only if they be done as God commands. Now God has ordered every one who worships Him to be sealed by baptism; but if you refuse, and obey your own will rather than God's, you are doubtless contrary and hostile to His will.

CHAP. IX.—*Use of baptism.*

"But you will perhaps.say, What does the baptism of water contribute towards the worship of God? In the first place, because that which hath pleased God is fulfilled. In the second place, because, when you are regenerated and born again of water and of God, the frailty of your former birth, which you have through men, is cut off, and so at length you shall be able to attain salvation; but otherwise it is impossible. For thus hath the true prophet testified to us with an oath: 'Verily I say to you, That unless a man is born again of water, he shall not enter into the kingdom of heaven.'[1] Therefore make haste; for there is in these waters a certain power of mercy which was borne upon them at the beginning,

[1] John iii. 5.

and acknowledges those who are baptized under the name of the threefold sacrament, and rescues them from future punishments, presenting as a gift to God the souls that are consecrated by baptism. Betake yourselves therefore to these waters, for they alone can quench the violence of the future fire; and he who delays to approach to them, it is evident that the idol of unbelief remains in him, and by it he is prevented from hastening to the waters which confer salvation. For whether you be righteous or unrighteous, baptism is necessary for you in every respect: for the righteous, that perfection may be accomplished in him, and he, may be born again to God; for the unrighteous, that pardon may be vouchsafed him of the sins which he has committed in ignorance. Therefore all should hasten to be born again to God without delay, because the end of every one's life is uncertain.

CHAP. X.—*Necessity of good works.*

" But when you have been regenerated by water, show by good works the likeness in you of that Father who hath begotten you. Now you know God, honour Him as a father; and His honour is, that you live according to His will. And His will is, that you so live as to know nothing of murder or adultery, to flee from hatred and covetousness, to put away anger, pride, and boasting, to abhor envy, and to count all such things entirely unsuitable to you. There is truly a certain peculiar observance of our religion, which is not so much imposed upon men, as it is sought out by every worshipper of God by reason of its purity. By reason of chastity, I say, of which there are many kinds, but first, that every one be careful that he ' come not near a menstruous woman;' for this the law of God regards as detestable. But though the law had given no admonition concerning these things, should we willingly, like beetles, roll ourselves in filth? For we ought to have something more than the animals, as reasonable men, and capable of heavenly senses, whose chief study it ought to be to guard the conscience from every defilement of the heart.

Chap. xi.—*Inward and outward cleansing.*

"Moreover, it is good, and tends to purity, also to wash the body with water. I call it good, not as if it were that prime good of the purifying of the mind, but because this of the washing of the body is the sequel of that good. For so also our Master rebuked some of the Pharisees and scribes, who seemed to be better than others, and separated from the people, calling them hypocrites, because they purified only those things which were seen of men, but left defiled and sordid their hearts, which God alone sees. To some therefore of them—not to all—He said, 'Woe to you, scribes and Pharisees, hypocrites! because ye cleanse the outside of the cup and platter, but the inside is full of pollution. O blind Pharisees, first make clean what is within, and what is without shall be clean also.'[1] For truly, if the mind be purified by the light of knowledge, when once it is clean and clear, then it necessarily takes care of that which is without a man, that is, his flesh, that it also may be purified. But when that which is without, the cleansing of the flesh, is neglected, it is certain that there is no care taken of the purity of the mind and the cleanness of the heart. Thus therefore it comes to pass, that he who is clean inwardly is without doubt cleansed outwardly also, but not always that he who is clean outwardly is also cleansed inwardly—to wit, when he does these things that he may please men.

Chap. xii.—*Importance of chastity.*

"But this kind of chastity is also to be observed, that sexual intercourse must not take place heedlessly and for the sake of mere pleasure, but for the sake of begetting children. And since this observance is found even amongst some of the lower animals, it were a shame if it be not observed by men, reasonable, and worshipping God. But there is this further reason why chastity should be observed by those who hold the true worship of God, in those forms of it of which we have spoken, and others of like sort, that it is observed strictly even amongst

[1] Matt. xxiii. 25, 26.

those who are still held by the devil in error, for even amongst
them there is in some degree the observance of chastity.
What then ?   Will you not observe, now that you are reformed, what you observed when you were in error ?

Chap. XIII.—*Superiority of Christian morality.*

" But perhaps some one of you will say, Must we then observe all things which we did while we worshipped idols ?   Not
all.   But whatever things were done well, these you ought
to observe even now ; because, if anything is rightly done by
those who are in error, it is certain that that is derived from
the truth ; whereas, if anything is not rightly done in the
true religion, that is, without doubt, borrowed from error.   For
good is good, though it be done by those who are in error ;
and evil is evil, though it be done by those who follow the
truth.   Or shall we be so foolish, that if we see a worshipper
of idols to be sober, we shall refuse to be sober, lest we should
seem to do the same things which he does who worships idols?
It is not so.   But let this be our study, that if those who err
do not commit murder, we should not even be angry ; if they
do not commit adultery, we should not even covet another's
wife ; if they love their neighbours, we should love even our
enemies ; if they lend to those who have the means of paying,
we should give to those from whom we do not hope to receive
anything.   And in all things, we who hope for the inheritance
of the eternal world ought to excel those who know only the
present world ; knowing that if their works, when compared
with our works, be found like and equal in the day of judgment, there will be confusion to us, because we are found
equal in our works to those who are condemned on account
of ignorance, and had no hope of the world to come.

Chap. XIV.—*Knowledge enhances responsibility.*

" And truly confusion is our worthy portion, if we have
done no more than those who are inferior to us in knowledge.   But if it be confusion to us to be found equal to
them in works, what shall become of us if the examination
that is to take place find us inferior and worse than them ?

Hear, therefore, how our true Prophet has taught us concerning these things; for, with respect to those who neglect to hear the words of wisdom, He speaks thus: 'The queen of the south shall rise in judgment with this generation, and shall condemn it, because she came from the ends of the earth to hear the wisdom of Solomon; and, behold, a greater than Solomon is here, and they hear Him not.'[1] But with respect to those who refused to repent of their evil deeds, He spoke thus: 'The men of Nineve shall rise in the judgment with this generation, and shall condemn it: for they repented at the preaching of Jonas; and, behold, a greater than Jonas is here.'[2] You see, therefore, how He condemned those who were instructed out of the law, by adducing the example of those who came from Gentile ignorance, and showing that the former were not even equal to those who seemed to live in error. From all these things, then, the statement that He propounded is proved, that chastity, which is observed to a certain extent even by those who live in error, should be held much more purely and strictly, in all its forms, as we showed above, by us who follow the truth; and the rather because with us eternal rewards are assigned to its observance."

CHAP. XV.—*Bishops, presbyters, deacons, and widows ordained at Tripolis.*

When he had said these things, and others to the same effect, he dismissed the crowds; and having, according to his custom, supped with his friends, he went to sleep. And while in this manner he was teaching the word of God for three whole months, and converting multitudes to the faith, at the last he ordered me to fast; and after the fast he conferred on me the baptism of ever-flowing water, in the fountains which adjoin the sea. And when, for the grace of regeneration divinely conferred upon me, we had joyfully kept holiday with our brethren, Peter ordered those who had been appointed to go before him, to proceed to Antioch, and there to wait three months more. And they having gone, he him-

---

[1] Matt. xii. 42; Luke xi. 31.　　　[2] Matt. xii. 41; Luke xi. 32.

self led down to the fountains, which, I have said, are near
the sea, those who had fully received the faith of the Lord,
and baptized them; and celebrating[1] the Eucharist with them,
he appointed, as bishop over them, Maro, who had entertained
him in his house, and who was now perfect in all things;
and with him he ordained twelve presbyters and deacons at
the same time. He also instituted the order of widows, and
arranged all the services of the church; and charged them
all to obey Maro their bishop in all things that he should
command them. And thus all things being suitably arranged,
when the three months were fulfilled, we bade farewell to
those who were at Tripolis, and set out for Antioch.

[1] Literally, " breaking the Eucharist."

RECOGNITIONS OF CLEMENT.

BOOK VII.

CHAP. I.—*Journey from Tripolis.*

T length leaving Tripolis, a city of Phœnicia, we made our first halt at Ortosias, not far from Tripolis; and there we remained the next day also, because almost all those that had believed in the Lord, unable to part from Peter, followed him thus far. Thence we came to Antharadus. But because there were many in our company, Peter said to Niceta and Aquila: "As there are immense crowds of brethren with us, and we bring upon ourselves no little envy as we enter into every city, it seems to me that we must take means, without doing so unpleasing a thing as to prevent their following us, to secure that the wicked one shall not stir up envy against us on account of any display! I wish, therefore, that you, Niceta and Aquila, would go before us with them, so that you may lead the multitude divided into two sections, that we may enter every city of the Gentiles travelling apart, rather than in one assemblage.

CHAP. II.—*Disciples divided into two bands.*

"But I know that you think it sad to be separated from me for the space of at least two days. Believe me, that in whatever degree you love me, my affection towards you is tenfold greater. But if, by reason of our mutual affection, we will not do the things that are right and honourable, such love will appear to be unreasonable. And therefore, without bating a tittle of our love, let us attend to those things which seem useful and necessary; especially since not a day can pass in which you may not be present at my discussions. For I purpose to pass through the most noted cities of the provinces one by one, as you also know, and to reside three months in each for the sake of teaching. Now, therefore, go before me to Laodicea, which is the nearest city, and I shall follow you after two or three days, so far as I purpose. But you shall wait for me at the inn nearest to the gate of the city ; and thence again, when we have spent a few days there, you shall go before me to more distant cities. And this I wish you to do at every city, for the sake of avoiding envy as much as in us lies, and also that the brethren who are with us, finding lodgings prepared in the several cities by your foresight, may not seem to be vagabonds."

CHAP. III.—*Order of march.*

When Peter thus spoke, they of course acquiesced, saying : " It does not greatly sadden us to do this, because we are ordered by you, who have been chosen by the foresight of Christ to do and to counsel well in all things ; but also because, while it is a heavy loss not to see our lord Peter for one, or it may be two days, yet it is not intolerable. And we think of our twelve brethren who go before us, and who are deprived of the advantage of hearing and seeing you for a whole month out of the three that you stay in every city. Therefore we shall not delay doing as you order, because you order all things aright." And thus saying, they went forward, having received instructions that they should speak to the brethren who journeyed with them outside the city, and request them not to enter the cities in a crowd and with tumult, but apart, and divided into two bands.

CHAP. IV.—*Clement's joy at remaining with Peter.*

But when they were gone, I Clement rejoiced greatly because he had kept me with himself, and I said to him : " I give thanks to God that you have not sent me forward with the others, for I should have died through sadness." Then said Peter : " And what will happen if necessity shall demand that you be sent anywhere for the purpose of teaching ?

Would you die if you were separated from me for a good purpose? Would you not put a restraint upon yourself, to bear patiently what necessity has laid upon you? Or do you not know that friends are always together, and are joined in memory, though they be separated bodily; as, on the other hand, some persons are near to one another in body, but are separate in mind?"

Chap. v.—*Clement's affection for Peter.*

Then I answered: "Think not, my lord, that I suffer these things unreasonably; but there is a certain cause and reason of this affection of mine towards you. For I have you alone as the object of all my affections, instead of father and mother, and brethren; but above all this, is the fact that you alone are the cause of my salvation and knowledge of the truth. And also this I do not count of least moment, that my youthful age is subject to the snares of lusts; and I am afraid to be without you, by whose sole presence all effeminacy, however irrational it be, is put to shame; although I trust, by the mercy of God, that even my mind, from what it has conceived through your instruction, shall be unable to receive aught else into its thoughts. Besides, I remember your saying at Cæsarea, 'If any one wishes to accompany me, without violating dutifulness, let him accompany me.' And by this you meant that he should not make any one sad, to whom he ought according to God's appointment to cleave; for example, that he should not leave a faithful wife, or parents, or the like. Now from these I am entirely free, and so I am fit for following you; and I wish you would grant me that I might perform to you the service of a servant."

Chap. vi.—*Peter's simplicity of life.*

Then Peter, laughing, said: "And do you not think, Clement, that very necessity must make you my servant? For who else can spread my sheets, and arrange my beautiful coverlets? Who will be at hand to keep my rings, and prepare my robes, which I must be constantly changing? Who shall superintend my cooks, and provide various and choice meats to be prepared by most recondite and various art ; and all those things which are procured at enormous expense, and are brought together for men of delicate up-bringing, yea rather, for their appetite, as for some enormous beast ? But perhaps, although you live with me, you do not know my manner of life. I live on bread alone, with olives, and seldom even with pot-herbs ; and my dress is what you see, a tunic with a pallium : and having these, I require nothing more. This is sufficient for me, because my mind does not regard things present, but things eternal, and therefore no present and visible thing delights me. Whence I embrace and admire indeed your good mind towards me ; and I commend you the more, because, though you have been accustomed to so great abundance, you have been able so soon to abandon it, and to accommodate yourself to this life of ours, which makes use of necessary things alone. For we—that is, I and my brother Andrew—have grown up from our childhood, not only orphans, but also extremely poor, and through necessity have become used to labour, whence now also we easily bear the fatigues of our journeyings. But rather, if you would consent and allow it, I, who am a working man, could more easily discharge the duty of a servant to you."

CHAP. VII.—*Peter's humility.*

But I trembled when I heard this, and my tears immediately gushed forth, because so great a man, who is worth more than the whole world, had addressed such a proposal to me. Then he, when he saw me weeping, inquired the reason ; and I answered him : "How have I so sinned against you, that you should distress me with such a proposal ? " Then Peter : " If it is evil that I said I should serve you, you were first in fault in saying the same thing to me." Then said I : " The cases are not alike : for it becomes me to do this to you ; but it is grievous that you, who are sent as the herald of the Most High God to save the souls of men, should say it to me." Then said Peter : " I should agree with you, were it not that our Lord, who came for the salvation of the whole world, and who was nobler than any creature, submitted to be a servant, that He might persuade us not to be ashamed to perform the ministry of servants to our brethren." Then said I : "It were foolishness in me to suppose that I can prevail with you ; nevertheless I give thanks to the providence of God, because I have merited to have you instead of parents."

Chap. VIII.—*Clement's family history.*

Then said Peter : "Is there then no one of your family surviving ?" I answered : "There are indeed many powerful men, coming of the stock of Cæsar; for Cæsar himself gave a wife to my father, as being his relative, and educated along with him, and of a suitably noble family. By her my father had twin sons, born before me, not very like one another, as my father told me ; for I never knew them. But indeed I have not a distinct recollection even of my mother ; but I cherish the remembrance of her face, as if I had seen it in a dream. My mother's name was Matthidia, my father's Faustinianus ; my brothers', Faustinus and Faustus. Now, when I was barely five years old, my mother saw a vision— so I learned from my father—by which she was warned that, unless she speedily left the city with her twin sons, and was absent for ten years, she and her children should perish by a miserable fate.

Chap. IX.—*Disappearance of his mother and brothers.*

"Then my father, who tenderly loved his sons, put them on board a ship with their mother, and sent them to Athens to be educated, with slaves and maid-servants, and a sufficient supply of money; retaining me only to be a comfort to him, and thankful for this, that the vision had not commanded me also to go with my mother. And at the end of a year my father sent men to Athens with money for them, desiring also to know how they did ; but those who were sent never returned. Again, in the third year, my sorrowful father sent other men with money, who returned in the fourth year, and related that they had seen neither my mother nor my brothers, that they had never reached Athens, and that no trace had been found of any one of those who had been with them.

Chap. x.—*Disappearance of his father.*

"My father hearing this, and confounded with excessive sorrow, not knowing whither to go or where to seek, went down with me to the harbour, and began to ask of the sailors whether any of them had seen or heard of the bodies of a mother and two little children being cast ashore anywhere, four years ago; when one told one story and another another, but nothing definite was disclosed to us searching in this boundless sea. Yet my father, by reason of the great affection which he bore to his wife and children, was fed with vain hopes, until he thought of placing me under guardians and leaving me at Rome, as I was now twelve years old, and himself going in quest of them. Therefore he went down to the harbour weeping, and going on board a ship, took his departure; and from that time till now I have never received any letters from him, nor do I know whether he is alive or dead. But I rather suspect that he also has perished, either through a broken heart or by shipwreck; for twenty years have now elapsed since then, and no tidings of him have ever reached me."

Chap. xi.—*Different effects of suffering on heathens and Christians.*

Peter, hearing this, shed tears of sympathy, and said to his friends who were present: "If any one who is a worshipper of God had endured what this man's father has endured, immediately men would assign his religion as the cause of his calamities; but when these things happen to miserable Gentiles, they charge their misfortunes upon fate. I call them miserable, because they are both vexed with errors here, and are deprived of future hope; whereas, when the worshippers of God suffer these things, their patient endurance of them contributes to their cleansing from sin."

Chap. XII.—*Excursion to Aradus.*

After this, one of those present began to ask Peter, that early next day we should go to a neighbouring island called Aradus, which was not more than six furlongs off, to see a certain wonderful work that was in it, viz. vine-wood[1] columns of immense size. To this Peter assented, as he was very complaisant; but he charged us that, when we left the ship, we should not rush all together to see it : " for," said he, " I do not wish you to be noticed by the crowd." When therefore, next day, we reached the island by ship in the course of an hour, forthwith we hastened to the place where the wonderful columns were. They were placed in a certain temple, in which there were very magnificent works of Phidias, on which every one of us gazed earnestly.

Chap. XIII.—*The beggar woman.*

But when Peter had admired only the columns, being no wise ravished with the grace of the painting, he went out, and saw before the gates a poor woman asking alms of those who went in ; and looking earnestly at her, he said : " Tell me, O woman, what member of your body is wanting, that you subject yourself to the indignity of asking alms, and do not rather gain your bread by labouring with your hands which God has given you." But she, sighing, said : " Would that I had hands which could be moved ; but now only the appearance of hands has been preserved, for they are lifeless, and have been rendered feeble and without feeling by my gnawing of them." Then Peter said : " What has been the cause of your inflicting so great an injury upon yourself ?" " Want of courage," said she, " and naught else ; for if I had had any bravery in me, I could either have thrown myself from a precipice, or cast myself into the depths of the sea, and so ended my griefs."

Chap. XIV.—*The woman's grief.*

Then Peter said : " Do you think, O woman, that those

---

[1] Various reading, " glass."

who destroy themselves are set free from torments, and not rather that the souls of those who lay violent hands upon themselves are subjected to greater punishments?" Then said she: "I wish I were sure that souls live in the infernal regions, for I would gladly embrace the suffering of the penalty of suicide, only that I might see my darling children, if it were but for an hour." Then Peter: "What thing is it so great, that affects you with so heavy sadness? I should like to know. For if you informed me of the cause, I might be able both to show you clearly, O woman, that souls do live in the infernal regions; and instead of the precipice or the deep sea, I might give you some remedy, that you may be able to end your life without torment."

Chap. xv.—*The woman's story.*

Then the woman, hearing this welcome promise, began to say: "It is neither easy of belief, nor do I think it necessary to tell, what is my extraction, or what is my country. It is enough only to explain the cause of my grief, why I have rendered my hands powerless by gnawing them. Being born of noble parents, and having become the wife of a suitably powerful man, I had two twin sons, and after them one other. But my husband's brother was vehemently enflamed with unlawful love towards me; and as I valued chastity above all things, and would neither consent to so great wickedness, nor wished to disclose to my husband the baseness of his brother, I considered whether in any way I could escape unpolluted, and yet not set brother against brother, and so bring the whole race of a noble family into disgrace. I made up my mind, therefore, to leave my country with my two twins, until the incestuous love should subside, which the sight of me was fostering and enflaming; and I thought that our other son should remain to comfort his father to some extent.

Chap. xvi.—*The woman's story continued.*

"Now in order to carry out this plan, I pretended that I had had a dream, in which some deity stood by me in a vision, and told me that I should immediately depart from the city with my twins, and should be absent until he should command me to return ; and that, if I did not do so, I should perish with all my children. And so it was done. For as soon as I told the dream to my husband, he was terrified ; and sending with me my twin sons, and also slaves and maid-servants, and giving me plenty of money, he ordered me to sail to Athens, where I might educate my sons, and that I should stay there, until he who had commanded me to depart should give me leave to return. While I was sailing along with my sons, I was shipwrecked in the night by the violence of the winds, and, wretch that I am, was driven to this place ; and when all had perished, a powerful wave caught me, and cast me upon a rock. And while I sat there with this only hope, that haply I might be able to find my sons, I did not throw myself into the deep, although then my soul, disturbed and drunk with grief, had both the courage and the power to do it.

Chap. XVII.—*The woman's story continued.*

" But when the day dawned, and I with shouting and howl-ing was looking around, if I could even see the corpses of my unhappy sons anywhere washed ashore, some of those who saw me were moved with compassion, and searched, first over the sea, and then also along the shores, if they could find either of my children. But when neither of them was anywhere found, the women of the place, taking pity on me, began to comfort me, every one telling her own griefs, that I might take consolation from the likeness of their calamities to my own. But this saddened me all the more ; for my disposition was not such that I could regard the misfortunes of others as comforts to me. And when many desired to receive me hospitably, a certain poor woman who dwells here constrained me to enter into her hut, saying that she had had a husband who was a sailor, and that he had died at sea while a young man, and that, although many afterwards asked her in mar-riage, she preferred widowhood through love of her husband. ' Therefore,' said she, ' we shall share whatever we can gain by the labour of our hands.'

Chap. XVIII.—*The woman's story continued.*

" And, not to detain you with a long and profitless story, I willingly dwelt with her on account of the faithful affection which she retained for her husband. But not long after, my hands (unhappy woman that I was!), long torn with gnawing, became powerless, and she who had taken me in fell into palsy, and now lies at home in her bed; also the affection of those women who had formerly pitied me grew cold. We are both helpless. I, as you see, sit begging; and when I get anything, one meal serves two wretches. Behold, now you have heard enough of my affairs; why do you delay the fulfilment of your promise, to give me a remedy, by which both of us may end our miserable life without torment?"

Chap. XIX.—*Peter's reflections on the story.*

While she was speaking, Peter, being distracted with much thought, stood like one thunder-struck; and I Clement coming up, said: " I have been seeking you everywhere, and now what are we to do?" But he commanded me to go before him to the ship, and there to wait for him ; and because he must not be gainsayed, I did as he commanded me. But he, as he afterwards told me the whole, being struck with a sort of suspicion, asked of the woman her family, and her country, and the names of her sons; "and straightway," he said, "if you tell me these things, I shall give you the remedy." But she, like one suffering violence, because she would not confess these things, and yet was desirous of the remedy, feigned one thing after another, saying that she was an Ephesian, and her husband a Sicilian, and giving false names to her sons. Then Peter, supposing that she had answered truly, said: "Alas! O woman, I thought that some great joy should spring up to us to-day; for I suspected that you were a certain woman, concerning whom I lately learned certain like things." But she adjured him, saying: " I entreat you to tell me what they are, that I may know if amongst women there be one more unfortunate than myself."

CHAP. XX.—*Peter's statement to the woman.*

Then Peter, incapable of deception, and moved with compassion, began to say: "There is a certain young man among those who follow me for the sake of religion and sect, a Roman citizen, who told me that he had a father and two twin brothers, of whom not one is left to him. ' My mother,' he said, ' as I learned from my father, saw a vision, that she should depart from the Roman city for a time with her twin sons, else they should perish by a dreadful death; and when she had departed, she was never more seen.' And afterwards his father set out to search for his wife and sons, and was also lost."

CHAP. XXI.—*A discovery.*

When Peter had thus spoken, the woman, struck with astonishment, fainted. Then Peter began to hold her up, and to comfort her, and to ask what was the matter, or what she suffered. But she at length, with difficulty recovering her breath, and nerving herself up to the greatness of the joy which she hoped for, and at the same time wiping her face, said: "Is he here, the youth of whom you speak?" But Peter, when he understood the matter, said: "Tell me first, or else you shall not see him." Then she said: "I am the mother of the youth." Then says Peter: "What is his name?" And she answered: "Clement." Then said Peter: "It is himself; and he it was that spoke with me a little while ago, and whom I ordered to go before me to the ship." Then she fell down at Peter's feet, and began to entreat him that he would hasten to the ship. Then Peter said: "Yes, if you will promise me that you will do as I say." Then she said: "I will do anything; only show me my only son, for I think that in him I shall see my twins also." Then Peter said: "When you have seen him, dissemble for a little time, until we leave the island." "I will do so," she said.

CHAP. XXII.—*A happy meeting.*

Then Peter, holding her hand, led her to the ship. And

when I saw him giving his hand to the woman, I began to laugh; yet, approaching to do him honour, I tried to substitute my hand for his, and to support the woman. But as soon as I touched her hand, she uttered a loud scream, and rushed into my embrace, and began to devour me with a mother's kisses. But I, being ignorant of the whole matter, pushed her off as a mad woman; and at the same time, though with reverence, I was somewhat angry with Peter.

Chap. XXIII.—*A miracle.*

But he said: "Cease: what mean you, O Clement, my son? Do not push away your mother." But I, as soon as I heard these words, immediately bathed in tears, fell upon my mother, who had fallen down, and began to kiss her. For as soon as I heard, by degrees I recalled her countenance to my memory; and the longer I gazed, the more familiar it grew to me. Meantime a great multitude assembled, hearing that the woman who used to sit and beg was recognised by her son, who was a good man.[1] And when we wished to sail hastily away from the island, my mother said to me: "My darling son, it is right that I should bid farewell to the woman who took me in; for she is poor, and paralytic, and bedridden." When Peter and all who were present heard this, they admired the goodness and prudence of the woman; and immediately Peter ordered some to go and to bring the woman in her bed as she lay. And when she had been brought, and placed in the midst of the crowd, Peter said, in the presence of all: "If I am a preacher of truth, for confirming the faith of all those who stand by, that they may know and believe that there is one God, who made heaven and earth, in the name of Jesus Christ, His Son, let this woman rise." And as soon as he had said this, she arose whole, and fell down at Peter's feet; and greeting her friend and acquaintance with kisses, asked of her what was the meaning of it all. But she shortly related to her the whole proceeding of the *Recognition,* so that the crowds standing around wondered.

[1] Perhaps, "a man in good position."

CHAP. XXIV.—*Departure from Aradus.*

Then Peter, so far as he could, and as time permitted, addressed the crowds on the faith of God, and the ordinances of religion ; and then added, that if any one wished to know more accurately about these things, he should come to Antioch, " where," said he, " we have resolved to stay three months, and to teach fully the things which pertain to salvation. For if," said he, " men leave their country and their parents for commercial or military purposes, and do not fear to undertake long voyages, why should it be thought burdensome or difficult to leave home for three months for the sake of eternal life ?" When he had said these things, and more to the same purpose, I presented a thousand drachmas to the woman who had entertained my mother, and who had recovered her health by means of Peter, and in the presence of all committed her to the charge of a certain good man, the chief person in that town, who promised that he would gladly do what we demanded of him. I also distributed a little money among some others, and among those women who were said formerly to have comforted my mother in her miseries, to whom I also expressed my thanks. And after this we sailed, along with my mother, to Antaradus.

CHAP. XXV.—*Journeyings.*

And when we had come to our lodging, my mother began to ask of me what had become of my father ; and I told her that he had gone to seek her, and never returned. But she, hearing this, only sighed ; for her great joy on my account lightened her other sorrows. And the next day she journeyed with us, sitting with Peter's wife ; and we came to Balaneæ, where we stayed three days, and then went on to Pathos, and afterwards to Gabala ; and so we arrived at Laodicea, where Niceta and Aquila met us before the gates, and kissing us, conducted us to a lodging. But Peter, seeing that it was a large and splendid city, said that it was worthy that we should stay in it ten days, or even longer. Then Niceta and Aquila asked of me who was this unknown woman ; and I answered :

" It is my mother, whom God has given back to me by means of my lord Peter."

CHAP. XXVI.—*Recapitulation.*

And when I had said this, Peter began to relate the whole matter to them in order, and said : " When we had come to Aradus,[1] and I had ordered you to go on before us, the same day after you had gone, Clement was led in the course of conversation to tell me of his extraction and his family, and how he had been deprived of his parents, and had had twin brothers older than himself, and that, as his father told him, his mother once saw a vision, by which she was ordered to depart from the city of Rome with her twin sons, else she and they should suddenly perish. And when she had told his father the dream, he, loving his sons with tender affection, and afraid of any evil befalling them, put his wife and sons on board a ship with all necessaries, and sent them to Athens to be educated. Afterwards he sent once and again persons to inquire after them, but nowhere found even a trace of them. At last the father himself went on the search, and until now he is nowhere [to be found]. When Clement had given me this narrative, there came one to us, asking us to go to the neighbouring island of Aradus, to see vine-wood columns of wonderful size. I consented; and when we came to the place, all the rest went into the interior of the temple ; but I—for what reason I know not — had no mind to go farther.

CHAP. XXVII.— *Recapitulation continued.*

"But while I was waiting outside for them, I began to notice this woman, and to wonder in what part of her body she was disabled, that she did not seek her living by the labour of her hands, but submitted to the shame of beggary. I therefore asked of her the reason of it. She confessed that she was sprung of a noble race, and was married to a no less noble husband, 'whose brother,' said she, 'being inflamed by unlawful love towards me, desired to defile his brother's

[1] There is a confusion in the text between Aradus and Antaradus.

bed. This I abhorring, and yet not daring to tell my husband of so great wickedness, lest I should stir up war between the brothers, and bring disgrace upon the family, judged it better to depart from my country with my two twin sons, leaving the younger boy to be a comfort to his father. And that this might be done with an honourable appearance, I thought good to feign a dream, and to tell my husband that there stood by me in a vision a certain deity, who told me to set out from the city immediately with my two twins, and remain until he should instruct me to return.' She told me that her husband, when he heard this, believed her, and sent her to Athens, with the twin children to be educated there; but that they were driven by a terrible tempest upon that island, where, when the ship had gone to pieces, she was lifted by a wave upon a rock, and delayed killing herself only for this, 'until,' said she, 'I could embrace at least the dead limbs of my unfortunate sons, and commit them to burial. But when the day dawned, and crowds had assembled, they took pity upon me, and threw a garment over me. But I, miserable, entreated them with many tears, to search if they could find anywhere the bodies of my unfortunate sons. And I, tearing all my body with my teeth, with wailing and howlings cried out constantly, Unhappy woman that I am, where is my Faustus? where my Faustinus?'"

Chap. XXVIII.—*More recognitions.*

And when Peter said this, Niceta and Aquila suddenly started up, and being astonished, began to be greatly agitated, saying: "O Lord, Thou Ruler and God of all, are these things true, or are we in a dream?" Then Peter said: "Unless we be mad, these things are true." But they, after a short pause, and wiping their faces, said: "We are Faustinus and Faustus: and even at the first, when you began this narrative, we immediately fell into a suspicion that the matters that you spoke of might perhaps relate to us; yet again considering that many like things happen in men's lives, we kept silence, although our hearts were struck by some hope. Therefore we waited for the end of your story, that, if it were entirely manifest that it related to us, we might then confess it." And when they had thus spoken, they went in weeping to our mother. And when they found her asleep, and wished to embrace her, Peter prevented them, saying: "Permit me first to prepare your mother's mind, lest haply by the great and sudden joy she lose her reason, and her understanding be disturbed, especially as she is now stupified with sleep."

Chap. xxix.—"*Nothing common or unclean.*"

Therefore, when our mother had risen from her sleep, Peter began to address her, saying: "I wish you to know, O woman, an observance of our religion. We worship one God, who made the world, and we keep His law, in which He commands us first of all to worship Him, and to reverence His name, to honour our parents, and to preserve chastity and uprightness. But this also we observe, not to have a common table with Gentiles, unless when they believe, and on the reception of the truth are baptized, and consecrated by a certain threefold invocation of the blessed name; and then we eat with them. Otherwise, even if it were a father or a mother, or wife, or sons, or brothers, we cannot have a common table with them. Since, therefore, we do this for the special cause of religion, let it not seem hard to you that your son cannot eat with you, until you have the same judgment of the faith that he has."

Chap. xxx.—" *Who can forbid water?*"

Then she, when she heard this, said: "And what hinders me to be baptized to-day? For even before I saw you I was wholly alienated from those whom they call gods, because they were not able to do anything for me, although I frequently, and almost daily, sacrificed to them. And as to chastity, what shall I say, when neither in former times did pleasures deceive me, nor afterwards did poverty compel me to sin? But I think you know well enough how great was my love of chastity, when I pretended that dream that I might escape the snares of unhallowed love, and that I might

z

go abroad with my two twins, and when I left this my son Clement alone to be a comfort to his father. For if two were scarcely enough for me, how much more would it have saddened their father, if he had had none at all? For he was wretched through his great affection towards our sons, so that even the authority of the dream could scarce prevail upon him to give up to me Faustinus and Faustus, the brothers of this Clement, and that himself should be content with Clement alone."

CHAP. XXXI.—*Too much joy.*

While she was yet speaking, my brothers could contain themselves no longer, but rushed into their mother's embrace with many tears, and kissed her. But she said: "What is the meaning of this?" Then said Peter: "Be not disturbed, O woman; be firm. These are your sons Faustinus and Faustus, whom you supposed to have perished in the deep; but how they are alive, and how they escaped in that horrible night, and how the one of them is called Niceta and the other Aquila, they will be able to explain to you themselves, and we also shall hear it along with you." When Peter had said this, our mother fainted, being overcome with excess of joy; and after some time, being restored and come to herself, she said: "I beseech you, darling sons, tell me what has befallen you since that dismal and cruel night."

CHAP. XXXII.—*"He bringeth them unto their desired haven."*

Then Niceta began to say: "On that night, O mother, when the ship was broken up, and we were being tossed upon the sea, supported on a fragment of the wreck, certain men, whose business it was to rob by sea, found us, and placed us in their boat, and overcoming the power of the waves by rowing, by various stretches brought us to Cæsarea Stratonis. There they starved us, and beat us, and terrified us, that we might not disclose the truth; and having changed our names, they sold us to a certain widow, a very honourable woman, named Justa. She, having bought us, treated us as sons, so that she carefully educated us in Greek literature and liberal arts. And when we grew up, we also attended to philosophic studies, that we might be able to confute the Gentiles, by supporting the doctrines of the divine religion by philosophic disputations.

CHAP. XXXIII.—*Another wreck prevented.*

"But we adhered, for friendship's sake, and boyish companionship, to one Simon, a magician, who was educated along with us, so that we were almost deceived by him. For there is mention made in our religion of a certain Prophet, whose coming was hoped for by all who observe that religion, through whom immortal and happy life is promised to be given to those who believe in Him. Now we thought that this Simon was he. But these things shall be explained to you, O mother, at a more convenient season. Meanwhile, when we were almost deceived by Simon, a certain colleague of my lord Peter, Zaccheus by name, warned us that we should not be duped by the magician, but presented us to Peter on his arrival, that by him we might be taught the things which were sound and perfect. And this we hope will happen to you also, even as God has vouchsafed it to us, that we may be able to eat and have a common table with you. Thus therefore it was, O mother, that you believed that we were drowned in the sea, while we were stolen by pirates."

CHAP. XXXIV.—*Baptism must be preceded by fasting.*

When Niceta had spoken thus, our mother fell down at Peter's feet, entreating and beseeching him that both herself and her hostess might be baptized without delay; "that," said she, "I may not even for a single day suffer the loss of the company and society of my sons." In like manner, we her sons also entreated Peter. But he said: "What! Do you think that I alone am unpitiful, and that I do not wish you to enjoy your mother's society at meals? But she must fast at least one day first, and so be baptized; and this because I have heard from her a certain declaration, by which her faith has been made manifest to me, and which has given evidence of her belief; otherwise she must have been instructed and taught many days before she could have been baptized."

Chap. xxxv.—*Desiring the salvation of others.*

Then said I: "I pray you, my lord Peter, tell us what is that declaration which you say afforded you evidence of her faith?" Then Peter: "It is her asking that her hostess, whose kindnesses she wishes to requite, may be baptized along with her. Now she would not ask that this grace be bestowed upon her whom she loves, unless she believed that there is some great boon in baptism. Whence, also, I find fault with very many, who, when they are themselves baptized and believe, yet do nothing worthy of faith with those whom they love, such as wives, or children, or friends, whom they do not exhort to that which they themselves have attained, [as they would do] if indeed they believed that eternal life is thereby bestowed. In short, if they see them to be sick, or to be subject to any danger bodily, they grieve and mourn, because they are sure that in this destruction threatens them. So, then, if they were sure of this, that the punishment of eternal fire awaits those who do not worship God, when would they cease warning and exhorting? Or, if they refused, how would they not mourn and bewail them, being sure that eternal torments awaited them? Now, therefore, we shall send for that woman at once, and see if she loves the faith of our religion; and as we find, so shall we act. But since your mother has judged so faithfully concerning baptism, let her fast only one day before baptism."

Chap. xxxvi.—*The sons' pleading.*

But she declared with an oath, in presence of my lord Peter's wife, that from the time she recognised her son, she had been unable to take any food from excess of joy, excepting only that yesterday she drank a cup of water. Peter's wife also bore witness, saying that it was even so. Then Aquila said: "What, then, hinders her being baptized?" Then Peter, smiling, said: "But this is not the fast of baptism, for it was not done in order to baptism." Then Niceta said: "But perhaps God, wishing that our mother, on our recognition, should not be separated even for one day from participation of our table, pre-ordained this fasting. For as in her ignorance she preserved her chastity, that it might profit her in order to the grace of baptism; so she fasted before she knew the reason of fasting, that it might profit her in order to baptism, and that immediately, from the beginning of our acquaintance, she might enjoy communion of the table with us."

Chap. xxxvii.—*Peter inexorable.*

Then said Peter: "Let not the wicked one prevail against us, taking occasion from a mother's love; but let you, and me with you, fast this day along with her, and to-morrow she shall be baptized: for it is not right that the precepts of truth be relaxed and weakened in favour of any person or friendship. Let us not shrink, then, from suffering along with her, for it is a sin to transgress any commandment. But let us teach our bodily senses, which are without us, to be in subjection to our inner senses; and not compel our inner senses, which savour the things that be of God, to follow the outer senses, which savour the things that be of the flesh. For to this end also the Lord commanded, saying: 'Whosoever shall look upon a woman to lust after her, hath committed adultery with her already in his heart.' And to this He added: 'If thy right eye offend thee, pluck it out, and cast it from thee: for it is profitable for thee that one of thy members perish, rather than thy whole body be cast into hell-fire.'[1] He does not say, *has offended thee*, that you should then cast away the cause of sin after you have sinned; but, *if it offend you*, that is, that before you sin you should cut off the cause of the sin that provokes and irritates you. But let none of you think, brethren, that the Lord commended the cutting off of the members. His meaning is, that the purpose should be cut off, not the members, and the causes which allure to sin, in order that our thought, borne up on the chariot of sight, may push towards the love of God, supported by the bodily senses;[2] and not give loose reins to the

---

[1] Matt. v. 28, 29.

[2] Here a marginal reading is followed. The reading of the text is: "In order that our thought, borne on the chariot of contemplation, may hasten on, invisible to the bodily senses, towards the love of God." But the translation of *aspectus* by "contemplation" is doubtful.

eyes of the flesh as to wanton horses, eager to turn their running outside the way of the commandments, but may subject the bodily sight to the judgment of the mind, and not suffer those eyes of ours, which God intended to be viewers and witnesses of His work, to become panders of evil desire. And therefore let the bodily senses as well as the internal thought be subject to the law of God, and let them serve His will, whose work they acknowledge themselves to be."

Chap. XXXVIII.—*Reward of chastity.*

Therefore, as the order and reason of the mystery demanded, on the following day she was baptized in the sea, and returning to the lodging, was initiated in all the mysteries of religion in their order. And we her sons, Niceta and Aquila, and I Clement, were present. And after this we dined with her, and glorified God with her, thankfully acknowledging the zeal and teaching of Peter, who showed us, by the example of our mother, that the good of chastity is not lost with God; "as, on the other hand," said he, "unchastity does not escape punishment, though it may not be punished immediately, but slowly. But so well pleasing," said he, "is chastity to God, that it confers some grace in the present life even upon those who are in error; for future blessedness is laid up for those only who preserve chastity and righteousness by the grace of baptism. In short, that which has befallen your mother is an example of this, for all this welfare has been restored to her in reward of her chastity, for the guarding and preserving of which continence alone is not sufficient; but when any one perceives that snares and deceptions are being prepared, he must straightway flee as from the violence of fire or the attack of a mad dog, and not trust that he can easily frustrate snares of this kind by philosophizing or by humouring them; but, as I have said, he must flee and withdraw to a distance, as your mother also did through her true and entire love of chastity. And on this account she has been preserved to you, and you to her; and in addition, she has been endowed with the knowledge of eternal life." When he had said this, and much more to the same effect, the evening having come, we went to sleep.

RECOGNITIONS OF CLEMENT.

BOOK VIII.

CHAP. I—*The old workman.*

OW the next morning Peter took my brothers and me with him, and we went down to the harbour to bathe in the sea, and thereafter we retired to a certain secret place for prayer. But a certain poor old man, a workman, as he appeared by his dress, began to observe us eagerly, without our seeing him, that he might see what we were doing in secret. And when he saw us praying, he waited till we came out, and then saluted us, and said : " If you do not take it amiss, and regard me as an inquisitive and importunate person, I should wish to converse with you ; for I take pity on you, and would not have you err under the appearance of truth, and be afraid of things that have no existence ; or if you think that there is any truth in them, then declare it to me. If, therefore, you take it patiently, I can in a few words instruct you in what is right ; but if it be unpleasant to you, I shall go on, and do my business." To him Peter answered : " Speak what you think good, and we will gladly hear, whether it be true or false ; for you are to be welcomed, because, like a father anxious on behalf of his children, you wish to put us in possession of what you regard as good."

CHAP. II.—*Genesis.*

Then the old man proceeded to say : " I saw you bathe in the sea, and afterwards retire into a secret place ; wherefore observing, without your noticing me, what you were doing, I saw you praying. Therefore, pitying your error, I waited till you came out, that I might speak to you, and instruct you not to err in an observance of this sort; because there is neither any God, nor any worship, neither is there any providence in the world, but all things are done by fortuitous chance and *genesis*, as I have discovered most clearly for myself, being accomplished beyond others in the discipline of learning. Do not err, therefore: for whether you pray, or whether you do not pray, whatever your *genesis* contains, that shall befall you." Then I Clement was affected, I know not how, in my heart, recollecting many things in him that seemed familiar to me; for some one says well, that that which is sprung from any one, although it may be long absent, yet a spark of relationship is never extinguished. Therefore I began to ask of him who and whence he was, and how descended. But he, not wishing to answer these questions, said: "What has that to do with what I have told you? But first, if you please, let us converse of those matters which we have propounded; and afterwards, if circumstances require, we can disclose to one another, as friends to friends, our names, and families, and country, and other things connected with these." Yet we all admired the eloquence of the man, and the gravity of his manners, and the calmness of his speech.

Chap. III.—*A friendly conference.*

But Peter, walking along leisurely while conversing, was looking out for a suitable place for a conference. And when he saw a quiet recess near the harbour, he made us sit down; and so he himself first began. Nor did he hold the old man in any contempt, nor did he look down upon him because his dress was poor and mean. He said, therefore: "Since you seem to me to be a learned man, and a compassionate, inasmuch as you have come to us, and wish that to be known to us which you consider to be good, we also wish to expound to you what things we believe to be good and right; and if you do not think them true, you will take in good part our good intentions towards you, as we do yours towards us." While

Peter was thus speaking, a great multitude assembled. Then said the old man : " Perhaps the presence of a multitude disconcerts you." Peter replied : " Not at all, except only on this account, that I am afraid lest haply, when the truth is made manifest in the course of our discussion, you be ashamed in presence of the multitude to yield and assent to the things which you may have understood to be spoken truly." To this the old man answered : " I am not such a fool in my old age, that, understanding what is true, I should deny it for the favour of the rabble."

Chap. iv.— *The question stated.*

Then Peter began to say : " Those who speak the word of truth, and who enlighten the souls of men, seem to me to be like the rays of the sun, which, when once they have come forth and appeared to the world, can no longer be concealed or hidden, while they are not so much seen by men, as they afford sight to all. Therefore it was well said by One to the heralds of the truth, ' Ye are the light of the world, and a city set upon a hill cannot be hid ; neither do men light a candle and put it under a bushel, but upon a candlestick, that it may enlighten all who are in the house.'"[1] Then said the old man : " He said well, whoever he is. But let one of you state what, according to his opinion, ought to be followed, that we may direct our speech to a definite aim. For, in order to find the truth, it is not sufficient to overthrow the things that are spoken on the other side, but also that one should himself bring forward what he who is on the other side may oppose. Therefore, in order that both parties may be on an equal footing, it seems to me to be right that each of us should first enunciate what opinion he holds. And, if you please, I shall begin first. I say, then, that the world is not governed according to the providence of God, because we see that many things in it are done unjustly and disorderly ; but I say that it is *genesis* that does and regulates all things."

[1] Matt. v. 14, 15.

Chap. v.—*Freedom of discussion allowed.*

When Peter was about to reply to this, Niceta, anticipating him, said: "Would my lord Peter allow me to answer to this; and let it not be thought forward that I, a young man, should have an encounter with an old man, but rather let me converse as a son with a father." Then said the old man: "Not only do I wish, my son, that you should set forth your opinions; but also if any one of your associates, if any one even of the bystanders, thinks that he knows anything, let him unhesitatingly state it: we shall gladly hear it; for it is by the contribution of many that the things that are unknown are more easily found out." Then Niceta therefore answered: "Do not deem me to have done rashly, my father, because I have interrupted the speech of my lord Peter; but rather I meant to honour him by doing this. For he is a man of God, full of all knowledge, who is not ignorant even of Greek learning, because he is filled with the Spirit of God, to whom nothing is unknown. But because it is suitable to him to speak of heavenly things, I shall answer concerning those things which pertain to the babbling of the Greeks. But after we have disputed in the Grecian manner, and we have come to that point where no issue appears, then he himself, as filled with the knowledge of God, shall openly and clearly disclose to us the truth on all matters, so that not we only, but also all who are around us as hearers, shall learn the way of truth. And therefore now let him sit as umpire; and when either of us shall yield, then let him, taking up the matter, give an unquestionable judgment."

Chap. vi.—*The other side of the question stated.*

When Niceta had thus spoken, those who had assembled conversed among themselves: "Is this that Peter of whom we heard, the most approved disciple of Him who appeared in Judæa, and wrought many signs and miracles?" And they stood gazing upon him with great fear and veneration, as conferring upon the Lord the honour of His good servant. Which when Peter observed, he said to them: "Let us hear with all attention, holding an impartial judgment of what shall be said by each; and after their encounter we also shall add what may seem necessary." And when Peter had said this, the crowds rejoiced. Then Niceta began to speak as follows: "You have laid down, my father, that the world is not governed by the providence of God, but that all things are subject to *genesis*, whether the things which relate to the dispositions, or those which relate to the doings of every one. This I could answer immediately; but because it is right to observe order, we also lay down what we hold, as you yourself requested should be done. I say that the world is governed by the providence of God, at least in those things which need His government. For He it is alone who holds all things in His hand, who also made the world; the just God, who shall at some time render to every one according to his deeds. Now, then, you have our position; go on as you please, either overthrowing mine or establishing your own, that I may meet your statements. Or if you wish me to speak first, I shall not hesitate."

CHAP. VI.—*The way cleared.*

Then the old man answered: "Whether it pleases you, my son, to speak first, or whether you prefer that I should speak, makes no difference, especially with those who discuss in a friendly spirit. However, speak you first, and I will gladly hear; and I wish you may be able even to follow out those things that are to be spoken by me, and to put in opposition to them those things that are contrary to them, and from the comparison of both to show the truth." Niceta answered: "If you wish it, I can even state your side of the argument, and then answer it." Then the old man: "Show me first how you can know what I have not yet spoken, and so I shall believe that you can follow out my side of the argument." Then Niceta: "Your sect is manifest, even by the proposition which you have laid down, to those who are skilled in doctrines of this sort; and its consequence is certain. And because I am not ignorant what are the propositions of the philosophers, I know what follows from those things which you have propounded; especially because I have frequented the schools of Epicurus in preference to the other philosophers. But my brother Aquila has attended more to the Pyrrhonists, and our other brother to the Platonists and Aristotelians; therefore you have to do with learned hearers." Then said the old man: "You have well and logically informed us how you perceived the things that follow from the statements which have been enunciated. But I professed something more than the tenet of Epicurus; for I introduced the *genesis*, and asserted that it is the cause of all the doings of men."

Chap. viii.—*Instincts.*

When the old man had said this, I Clement said to him: "Hear, my father: if my brother Niceta bring you to acknowledge that the world is not governed without the providence of God, I shall be able to answer you in that part which remains concerning the *genesis;* for I am well acquainted with this doctrine." And when I had thus spoken, my brother Aquila said: "What is the use of our calling him *father,* when we are commanded to call no man father upon earth?"[1] Then, looking to the old man, he said, "Do not take it amiss, my father, that I have found fault with my brother for calling you *father,* for we have a precept not to call any one by that name." When Aquila said that, all the assembly of the bystanders, as well as the old man and Peter, laughed. And when Aquila asked the reason of their all laughing, I said to him: "Because you yourself do the very thing which you find fault with in another; for you called the old man *father.*" But he denied it, saying: "I am not aware that I called him *father.*" Meantime Peter was moved with certain suspicions, as he told us afterwards; and looking to Niceta, he said, "Go on with what you have proposed."

Chap. ix.—*Simple and compound.*

Then Niceta began as follows: "Everything that is, is either simple or compound. That which is simple is without

[1] Matt. xxiii. 9.

number, division, colour, difference, roughness, smoothness, weight, lightness, quality, quantity, and therefore without end. But that which is compound is either compounded of two, or of three, or even of four [elements], or at all events of several; and things which are compounded can also of necessity be divided." The old man, hearing this, said: "You speak most excellently and learnedly, my son." Then Niceta went on: "Therefore that which is simple, and which is without any of those things by which that which subsists can be dissolved, is without doubt incomprehensible and infinite, knowing neither beginning nor end, and therefore is one and alone, and subsisting without an author. But that which is compound is subject to number, and diversity, and division,—is necessarily compounded by some author, and is a diversity collected into one species. That which is infinite is therefore, in respect of goodness, a Father; in respect of power, a Creator. Nor can the power of creating cease in the Infinite, nor the goodness be quiescent; but He is impelled by goodness to change existing things, and by power to arrange and strengthen them. Therefore some things, as we have said, are changed, and composed of two or three, some of four, others of more elements. But since our inquiry at present is concerning the method of the world and its substance, which, it is agreed, is compounded of four elements, to which all those ten differences belong which we have mentioned above, let us begin at these lower steps, and come to the higher. For a way is afforded us to intellectual and invisible things from those which we see and handle; as is contained in arithmetical instructions, where, when inquiry is made concerning divine things, we rise from the lower to the higher numbers; but when the method respecting present and visible things is expounded, the order is directed from the higher to the lower numbers. Is it not so?"

CHAP. X.—*Creation implies providence.*

Then the old man said: "You are following it out exceedingly well." Then Niceta: "Now, then, we must inquire concerning the method of the world; of which the first in-

quiry is divided into two parts. For it is asked whether
it has been made or not? And if it has not been made,
itself must be that Unbegotten from which all things are.
But if it has been made, concerning this again the question
is divided into two parts, whether it was made by itself,
or by another. And if indeed it was made by itself, then
without doubt providence is excluded. If providence is
not admitted, in vain is the mind incited to virtue, in vain
justice is maintained, if there be no one to render to the just
man according to his merits. But even the soul itself will
not appear to be immortal, if there be no dispensation of providence to receive it after its escape from the body.

Chap. XI.—*General or special providence.*

"Now, if it be taught that there is a providence, and
that the world was made by it, other questions meet us which
must be discussed. For it will be asked, In what way providence acts, whether generally towards the whole, or specially
towards the parts, or generally also towards the parts, or both
generally towards the whole, and specially towards the parts?
But by general providence we mean this: as if God, at first
making the world, has given an order and appointed a course
to things, and has ceased to take any further care of what is
done. But special providence towards the parts is of this
sort, that He exercises providence over some men or places,
but not over others. But general over all, and at the same
time special over the parts, is in this wise: if God made all
things at first, and exercises providence over each individual
even to the end, and renders to every one according to his
deeds.

Chap. XII.—*Prayer inconsistent with* genesis.

"Therefore that first proposition, which declares that God
made all things in the beginning, and having imposed a
course and order upon things, takes no further account of
them, affirms that all things are done according to *genesis.*
To this, therefore, we shall first reply; and especially to
those who worship the gods and defend *genesis.* Assuredly,

these men, when they sacrifice to the gods and pray to them, hope that they shall obtain something in opposition to *genesis*, and so they annul *genesis*. But when they laugh at those who incite to virtue and exhort to continence, and say that nobody can do or suffer anything unless what is decreed to him by fate, they assuredly cut up by the roots all worship of the Divinity. For why should you worship those from whom you can obtain nothing which the method of what is decreed does not allow? Let this suffice in the meantime, in opposition to these men. But I say that the world is made by God, and that it is at some time to be destroyed by Him, that that world may appear which is eternal, and which is made for this end, that it may be always, and that it may receive those who, in the judgment of God, are worthy of it. But that there is another and invisible world, which contains this visible world within itself,—after we have finished our discussion concerning the visible world, we shall come to it also.

Chap. XIII.—*A Creator necessary.*

"Now, in the meantime, that this visible world has been made, very many wise men among the philosophers do testify. But that we may not seem to make use of assertions as witnesses, as though we needed them, let us inquire, if you please, concerning its principles. That this visible world is material, is sufficiently evident from the fact that it is visible. But every body receives [one of] two *differentiæ;* for it is either compact and solid, or divided and separate. And if the body of which the world was made was compact and solid, and that body was parted and divided through diverse species and parts according to its differences, there must necessarily be understood to have been some one to separate the body which was compact and solid, and to draw it into many parts and diverse forms; or if all this mass of the world was compounded and compacted from diverse and dispersed parts of bodies, still there must be understood to have been some one to collect into one the dispersed parts, and to invest these things with their different species.

Chap. xiv.—*Mode of creation.*

" And, indeed, I know that several of the philosophers were rather of this opinion, that God the Creator made divisions and distinctions from one body, which they call *matter*, which yet consisted of four elements, mingled into one by a certain tempering of divine providence. For I think that what some have said is vain, that the body of the world is simple, that is, without any conjunction; since it is evident that what is simple can neither be a body, nor can be mixed, or propagated, or dissolved; all which, we see, happen to the bodies of the world. For how could it be dissolved if it were simple, and had not within it that from which it might be resolved and divided? But if bodies seem to be composed of two, or three, or even of four elements,—who that has even a small portion of sense does not perceive that there must have been some one who collected several into one, and preserving the measure of tempering, made a solid body out of diverse parts? This *some one*, therefore, we call God, the Creator of the world, and acknowledge Him as the author of the universe.

Chap. xv.—*Theories of creation.*

" For the Greek philosophers, inquiring into the beginnings of the world, have gone, some in one way and some in another. In short, Pythagoras says that numbers are the elements of its beginnings; Callistratus, that qualities; Alcmæon, that contrarieties; Anaximander, that immensity; Anaxagoras, that equalities of parts; Epicurus, that atoms; Diodorus, that ἀμερῆ, that is, things in which there are no parts; Asclepius, that ὄγκοι, which we may call tumours or swellings; the geometricians, that ends; Democritus, that ideas; Thales, that water; Heraclitus, that fire; Diogenes, that air; Parmenides, that earth; Zeno, Empedocles, Plato, that fire, water, air, and earth. Aristotle also introduces a fifth element, which he called ἀκατονόμαστον; that is, that which cannot be named; without doubt indicating Him who made the world, by joining the four elements into one. Whether, therefore, there be two, or three, or four, or more, or innumerable elements, of which the world consists, in every supposition there is shown to be a God, who collected many into one; and again drew them, when collected, into diverse species; and by this it is proved that the machine of the world could not have subsisted without a maker and a disposer.

Chap. XVI.—*The world made of nothing by a Creator.*

"But from this fact also, that in the conjunction of the elements, if one be deficient or in excess, the others are loosened and fall, is shown that they took their beginning from nothing. For if, for example, moisture be wanting in any body, neither will the dry stand; for dry is fed by moisture, as also cold by heat; in which, as we have said, if one be defective, the whole are dissolved. And in this they give indications of their origin, that they were made out of nothing. Now if matter itself is proved to have been made, how shall its parts and its species, of which the world consists, be thought to be unmade? But about matter and its qualities this is not the time to speak: only let it suffice to have taught this, that God is the Creator of all things, because neither, if the body of which the world consists was solid and united, could it be separated and distinguished without a Creator; nor, if it was collected into one from diverse and separate parts, could it be collected and mixed without a Maker. Therefore, if God is so clearly shown to be the Creator of the world, what room is there for Epicurus to introduce atoms, and to assert that not only sensible bodies, but even intellectual and rational minds, are made of insensible corpuscles?

Chap. XVII.—*Doctrine of atoms untenable.*

"But you will say, according to the opinion of Epicurus, that successions of atoms coming in a ceaseless course, and mixing with one another, and conglomerating through unlimited and endless periods of time, are made solid bodies. I do not treat this opinion as a pure fiction, and that, too, a badly contrived one; but let us examine it, whatever be its character, and see if what is said can stand. For they say that those corpuscles, which they call atoms, are of different qualities: that some are moist, and therefore

2 A

heavy, and tending downwards; others dry and earthy, and therefore still heavy; but others fiery, and therefore always pushing upwards; others cold and inert, and always remaining in the middle. Since then some, as being fiery, always tend upward, and others, as being moist and dry, always downwards, and others keep a middle and unequal course, how could they meet together and form one body? For if any one throw down from a height small pieces of straw, for example, and pieces of lead of the same size, will the light straws be able to keep up with the pieces of lead, though they be equal in size? Nay; the heavier reach the bottom far more quickly. So also atoms, though they be equal in size, yet, being unequal in weight, the lighter will never be able to keep pace with the heavier; but if they cannot keep pace, certainly neither can they be mixed or form one body.

CHAP. XVIII.—*The concourse of atoms could not make the world.*

"Then, in the next place, if they are ceaselessly borne about, and always coming, and being added to things whose measure is already complete, how can the universe stand, when new weights are always being heaped upon so vast weights? And this also I ask: If this expanse of heaven which we see was constructed by the gradual concurrence of atoms, how did it not collapse while it was in construction, if indeed the yawning top of the structure was not propped and bound by any stays? For as those who build circular domes, unless they bind the fastening of the central top, the whole falls at once; so also the circle of the world, which we see to be brought together in so graceful a form, if it was not made at once, and under the influence of a single forth-putting of divine energy by the power of a Creator, but by atoms gradually concurring and constructing it, not as reason demanded, but as a fortuitous issue befell, how did it not fall down and crumble to pieces before it could be brought together and fastened? And further, I ask this: What is the pavement on which the foundations of such an immense mass are laid? And again, what you call the pavement, on what does it rest? And again that other, what supports it? And so I go on asking, until the answer comes to nothing and vacuity!

Chap. xix.—*More difficulties of the atomic theory.*

"But if any one say that atoms of a fiery quality, being joined together, formed a body, and because the quality of fire does not tend downwards, but upwards, that the nature of fire, always pushing upwards, supports the mass of the world placed upon it; to this we answer: How could atoms of a fiery quality, which always make for the highest place, descend to the lower, and be found in the lowest place of all, so as to form a foundation for all; whereas rather the heavier qualities, that is, the earthy or watery, always come before the lighter, as we have said; hence, also, they assert that the heaven, as the higher structure, is composed of fiery atoms, which are lighter, and always fly upwards? Therefore the world cannot have foundations of fire, or any other; nor can there be any association or compacting of the heavier atoms with the lighter, that is, of those which are always borne downwards, with those that always fly upwards. Thus it is sufficiently shown that the bodies of the world are consolidated by the union of atoms; and that insensible bodies, even if they could by any means concur and be united, could not give forms and measures to bodies, form limbs, or effect qualities, or express quantities; all which, therefore, by their exactness, attest the hand of a Maker, and show the operation of reason, which reason I call the Word, and God.

Chap. xx.—*Plato's testimony.*

"But some one will say that these things are done by nature. Now, in this, the controversy is about a name. For while it is evident that it is a work of mind and reason, what you call nature, I call God the Creator. It is evident that neither the species of bodies, arranged with so necessary distinctions, nor the faculties of minds, could or can be made by irrational and senseless work. But if you regard the philosophers as fit witnesses, Plato testifies concerning these things in the

Timæus, where, in a discussion on the making of the world, he asks, whether it has existed always, or had a beginning, and decides that it was made. 'For,' says he, 'it is visible and palpable, and corporeal; but it is evident that all things which are of this sort have been made; but what has been made has doubtless an author, by whom it was made. This Maker and Father of all, however, it is difficult to discover; and when discovered, it is impossible to declare Him to the vulgar.' Such is the declaration of Plato; but though he and the other Greek philosophers had chosen to be silent about the making of the world, would it not be manifest to all who have any understanding? For what man is there, having even a particle of sense, who, when he sees a house having all things necessary for useful purposes, its roof fashioned into the form of a globe, painted with various splendour and diverse figures, adorned with large and splendid lights; who is there, I say, that, seeing such a structure, would not immediately pronounce that it was constructed by a most wise and powerful artificer? And so, who can be found so foolish, as, when he gazes upon the fabric of the heaven, perceives the splendour of the sun and moon, sees the courses and beauty of the stars, and their paths assigned to them by fixed laws and periods, will not cry out that these things are made, not so much by a wise and rational artificer, as by wisdom and reason itself?

Chap. xxi.—*Mechanical theory.*

"But if you would rather have the opinions of others of the Greek philosophers,—and you are acquainted with mechanical science,—you are of course familiar with what is their deliverance concerning the heavens. For they suppose a sphere, equally rounded in every direction, and looking indifferently to all points, and at equal distances in all directions from the centre of the earth, and so stable by its own symmetry, that its perfect equality does not permit it to fall off to any side; and so the sphere is sustained, although supported by no prop. Now if the fabric of the world really has this form, the divine work is evident in it. But if, as others think, the sphere is placed upon the waters, and is supported by them, or floating in them, even so the work of a great contriver is shown in it.

Chap. XXII.—*Motions of the stars.*

"But lest the assertion may seem doubtful respecting things which are not manifest to all, let us come to those things of which nobody is ignorant. Who disposed the courses of the stars with so great reason, ordained their risings and settings, and appointed to each one to accomplish the circuit of the heavens in certain and regular times? Who assigned to some to be always approaching to the setting, and others to be returning to the rising? Who put a measure upon the courses of the sun, that he might mark out, by his diverse motions, hours, and days, and months, and changes of seasons? —that he might distinguish, by the sure measurement of his course, now winter, then spring, summer, and afterwards autumn, and always, by the same changes of the year, complete the circle with variety, without confusion? Who, I say, will not pronounce that the director of such order is the very wisdom of God? And these things we have spoken according to the relations given us by the Greeks respecting the science of the heavenly bodies.

Chap. XXIII.—*Providence in earthly things.*

"But what of those things also which we see on the earth, or in the sea? Are we not plainly taught, that not only the work, but also the providence, of God is in them? For whereas there are on the earth lofty mountains in certain places, [the object of this is] that the air, being compressed and confined by them through the appointment of God, may be forced and pressed out into winds, by which fruits may germinate, and the summer heat may be moderated when the Pleiades glow, fired with the blaze of the sun. But you still say, Why that blaze of the sun, that moderating should be required? How, then, should fruits be ripened which are necessary for the uses of men? But observe this also, that at the meridian axis,[1] where the

[1] That is, the equator.

heat is greatest, there is no great collection of clouds, nor an abundant fall of rain, lest disease should be produced among the inhabitants; for watery clouds, if they are acted on by rapid heat, render the air impure and pestilential. And the earth also, receiving the warm rain, does not afford nourishment to the crops, but destruction. In this who can doubt that there is the working of divine providence? In short, Egypt, which is scorched with the heat of Æthiopia, in its neighbourhood, lest its air should be incurably vitiated by the effects of showers, its plains do not receive rain furnished to them from the clouds, but, as it were, an earthly shower from the overflow of the Nile.

CHAP. XXIV.—*Rivers and seas.*

" What shall we say of fountains and rivers, which flow with perpetual motion into the sea? And, by the divine providence, neither does their abundant supply fail, nor does the sea, though it receives so great quantities of water, experience any increase, but both those elements which contribute to it and those which are thus contributed remain in the same proportion. But you will say to me : The salt water naturally consumes the fresh water which is poured into it. Well, in this is manifest the work of providence, that it made that element salt into which it turned the courses of all the waters which it had provided for the use of men. So that through so great spaces of time the channel of the sea has not been filled, and produced a deluge destructive to the earth and to men. Nor will any one be so foolish as to think that this so great reason and so great providence has been arranged by irrational nature.

CHAP. XXV.—*Plants and animals.*

" But what shall I say of plants, and what of animals? Is it not providence that has ordained that plants, when they decay by old age, should be reproduced by the suckers or the seeds which they have themselves produced, and animals by propagation? And by a certain wonderful dispensation of providence, milk is prepared in the udders of the dams for the animals before they are born; and as soon as they are born, with no one to guide them, they seek out the store of nourish-ment provided for them. And not only males are produced, but females also, that by means of both the race may be per-petuated. But lest this should seem, as some think, to be done by a certain order of nature, and not by the appointment of the Creator, He has, as a proof and indication of His providence, ordained a few animals to preserve their stock on the earth in an exceptional way : for example, the crow con-ceives through the mouth, and the weasel brings forth through the ear; and some birds, such as hens, sometimes produce eggs conceived of wind or dust; other animals convert the male into the female, and change their sex every year, as hares and hyænas, which they call monsters; others spring from the earth, and get their bodies from it, as moles; others from ashes, as vipers; others from putrifying flesh, as wasps from horse-flesh, bees from ox-flesh; others from cow-dung, as beetles; others from herbs, as the scorpion from the basil; and again, herbs from animals, as parsley and asparagus from the horn of the stag or the she-goat.

Chap. XXVI.—*Germination of seeds.*

" And what occasion is there to mention more instances in which divine providence has ordained the production of animals to be effected in various ways, that order being super-seded which is thought to be assigned by nature, from which not an irrational course of things, but one arranged by his own reason, might be evinced ? And in this also is there not a full work of providence shown, when seeds sown are pre-pared by means of earth and water for the sustenance of men ? For when these seeds are committed to the earth, the soil milks upon the seeds, as from its teats, the moisture which it has received into itself by the will of God. For there is in water a certain power of the spirit given by God from the beginning, by whose operation the structure of the body that is to be begins to be formed in the seed itself, and to be de-veloped by means of the blade and the ear; for the grain of seed being swelled by the moisture, that power of the spirit which has been made to reside in water, running as an incorporeal substance through certain strait passages of veins, excites the seeds to growth, and forms the species of the growing plants. By means, therefore, of the moist element in which that vital spirit is contained and inborn, it is caused that not only is it revived, but also that an appearance and form in all respects like to the seeds that had been sown is reproduced. Now, who that has even a particle of sense will think that this method depends upon irrational nature, and not upon divine wisdom? Lastly, also these things are done in a resemblance of the birth of men; for the earth seems to take the place of the womb, into which the seed being cast, is both formed and nourished by the power of water and spirit, as we have said above.

Chap. XXVII.—*Power of water.*

"But in this also the divine providence is to be admired, that it permits us to see and know the things that are made, but has placed in secrecy and concealment the way and manner in which they are done, that they may not be competent to the knowledge of the unworthy, but may be laid open to the worthy and faithful, when they shall have deserved it. But to prove by facts and examples that nothing is imparted to seeds of the substance of the earth, but that all depends upon the element of water, and the power of the spirit which is in it,—suppose, for example, that a hundred talents' weight of earth are placed in a very large trough, and that there are sown in it several kinds of seeds, either of herbs or of shrubs, and that water enough is supplied for watering them, and that that care is taken for several years, and that the seeds which are gathered are stored up, for example of corn or barley and other sorts separately from year to year, until the seeds of each sort amount to a hundred talents' weight, then also let the stalks be pulled up by the roots and weighed; and after all these have been taken from the trough, let the earth be weighed, it will still give back its hundred talents' weight undiminished. Whence, then, shall we say that all that weight, and all the quantity of different seeds and stalks, has come? Does it not appear manifestly that it has come from the water? For the earth retains entire what is its own, but the water which has been poured in all through is nowhere, on account of the powerful virtue of the divine condition, which by the one species of water both prepares the substances of so many seeds and shrubs, and forms their species, and preserves the kind while multiplying the increase.

Chap. xxviii.—*The human body.*

"From all these things I think it is sufficiently and abundantly evident that all things are produced; and the universe consists by a designing sense, and not by the irrational operation of nature. But let us come now, if you please, to our own substance, that is, the substance of man, who is a small world [a microcosm] in the great world; and let us consider with what reason it is compounded: and from this especially you will understand the wisdom of the Creator. For although man consists of different substances, one mortal and the other immortal, yet, by the skilful contrivance of the Creator, their diversity does not prevent their union, and that although the substances be diverse and alien the one from the other. For the one is taken from the earth and formed by the Creator, but the other is given from immortal substances; and yet the honour of its immortality is not violated by this union. Nor does it, as some think, consist of reason, and concupiscence, and passion, but rather such affections seem to be in it, by which it may be moved in each of these directions. For the body, which consists of bones and flesh, takes its beginning from the seed of a man, which is extracted from the marrow by warmth, and conveyed into the womb as into a soil, to which it adheres, and is gradually moistened from the fountain of the blood, and so is changed into flesh and bones, and is formed into the likeness of him who injected the seed.

Chap. xxix.—*Symmetry of the body.*

"And mark in this the work of the Designer, how He has inserted the bones like pillars, on which the flesh might be sustained and carried. Then, again, how an equal measure is preserved on either side, that is, the right and the left, so that foot answers to foot, hand to hand, and even finger to finger, so that each agrees in perfect equality with each; and also eye to eye, and ear to ear, which not only are suitable to and matched with each other, but also are formed fit for necessary uses. The hands, for instance, are so made as to be fit for work; the feet for walking; the eyes, protected with sentinel eyebrows, to serve the purpose of sight; the ears so formed for hearing, that, like a cymbal, they vibrate the sound of the word that falls upon them, and send it inward, and transmit it even to the understanding of the heart; whereas the tongue, striking against the teeth in speaking, performs the part of a fiddle-bow. The teeth also are formed, some for cutting and dividing the food, and handing it over to the inner ones; and these, in their turn, bruise and grind it like a mill, that it may be more conveniently digested when it is conveyed into the stomach; whence also they are called grinders.

Chap. xxx.—*Breath and blood.*

" The nostrils also are made for the purpose of collecting, inspiring, and expiring air, that by the renewal of the breath, the natural heat which is in the heart may, by means of the lungs, be either warmed or cooled, as the occasion may require; while the lungs are made to abide in the breast, that by their softness they may soothe and cherish the vigour of the heart, in which the life seems to abide;—the life, I say, not the soul. And what shall I say of the substance of the blood, which, proceeding as a river from a fountain, and first borne along in one channel, and then spreading through innumerable veins, as through canals, irrigates the whole territory of the human body with vital streams, being supplied by the agency of the liver, which is placed in the right side, for effecting the digestion of food and turning it into blood? But in the left side is placed the spleen, which draws to itself, and in some way cleanses, the impurities of the blood.

Chap. xxxi.—*The intestines.*

" What reason also is employed in the intestines, which are

arranged in long circular windings, that they may gradually carry off the refuse of the food, so as neither to render places suddenly empty, and so as not to be hindered by the food that is taken afterwards! But they are made like a membrane, that the parts that are outside of them may gradually receive moisture, which if it were poured out suddenly would empty the internal parts; and not hindered by a thick skin, which would render the outside dry, and disturb the whole fabric of man with distressing thirst.

Chap. XXXII.—*Generation.*

" Moreover, the female form, and the cavity of the womb, most suitable for receiving, and cherishing, and vivifying the germ, who does not believe that it has been made as it is by reason and foresight?—because in that part alone of her body the female differs from the male, in which the fœtus being placed, is kept and cherished. And again the male differs from the female only in that part of his body in which is the power of injecting seed and propagating mankind. And in this there is a great proof of providence, from the necessary difference of members; but more in this, where, under a likeness of form, there is found to be diversity of use and variety of office. For males and females equally have teats, but only those of the female are filled with milk; that, as soon as they have brought forth, the infant may find nourishment suited to him. But if we see the members in man arranged with such method, that in all the rest there is seen to be similarity of form, and a difference only in those in which their use requires a difference, and we neither see anything superfluous nor anything wanting in man, nor in woman anything deficient or in excess, who will not, from all these things, acknowledge the operation of reason, and the wisdom of the Creator?

Chap. XXXIII.—*Correspondences in creation.*

" With this agrees also the reasonable difference of other animals, and each one being suited to its own use and service. This also is testified by the variety of trees and the diversity of herbs, varying both in form and in juices. This also is asserted by the change of seasons, distinguished into four periods, and the circle closing the year with certain hours, days, months, and not deviating from the appointed reckoning by a single hour. Hence, in short, the age of the world itself is reckoned by a certain and fixed account, and a definite number of years.

Chap. xxxiv.—*Time of making the world.*

" But you will say, When was the world made? And why so late? This you might have objected, though it had been made sooner. For you might say, Why not also before this? And so, going back through unmeasured ages, you might still ask, And why not sooner? But we are not now discussing this, why it was not made sooner; but whether it was made at all. For if it is manifest that it was made, it is necessarily the work of a powerful and supreme Artificer; and if this is evident, it must be left to the choice and judgment of the wise Artificer, when He should please to make it; unless indeed you think that all this wisdom, which has constructed the immense fabric of the world, and has given to the several objects their forms and kinds, assigning to them a habit not only in accordance with beauty, but also most convenient and necessary for their future uses,—unless, I say, you think that this alone has escaped it, that it should choose a convenient season for so magnificent a work of creation. He has doubtless a certain reason and evident causes why, and when, and how He made the world; but it were not proper that these should be disclosed to those who are reluctant to inquire into and understand the things which are placed before their eyes, and which testify of His providence. For those things which are kept in secret, and are hidden within the senses of Wisdom, as in a royal treasury, are laid open to none but those who have learned of Him, with whom these things are sealed and laid up. It is God, therefore, who made all things, and Himself was made by none. But those who speak of nature instead of God, and declare that all things were made by nature, do not perceive the mistake of the name which they use. For if they think that nature is irrational, it is most foolish to suppose that a rational creature can proceed from an irrational creator. But if it is Reason—that is, Logos—by which it appears that all things were made, they change the name without purpose, when they make statements concerning the reason of the Creator. If you have anything to say to these things, my father, say on."

CHAP. XXXV.—*A contest of hospitality.*

When Niceta had thus spoken, the old man answered: "You indeed, my son, have conducted your argument wisely and vigorously; so much so, that I do not think the subject of providence could be better treated. But as it is now late, I wish to say some things to-morrow in answer to what you have argued; and if on these you can satisfy me, I shall confess myself a debtor to your favour." And when the old man said this, Peter rose up. Then one of those present, a chief man of the Laodiceans, requested of Peter and us that he might give the old man other clothes instead of the mean and torn ones that he wore. This man Peter and we embraced; and praising him for his honourable and excellent intention, said: "We are not so foolish and impious as not to bestow the things which are necessary for bodily uses upon him to whom we have committed so precious words; and we hope that he will willingly receive them, as a father from his sons, and also we trust that he will share with us our house and our living." While we said this, and that chief man of the city strove to take the old man away from us with the greatest urgency and with many blandishments, while we the more eagerly strove to keep him with us, all the people cried out that it should rather be done as the old man himself pleased; and when silence was obtained, the old man, with an oath, said: "To-day I shall stay with no one, nor take anything from any one, lest the choice of the one should prove the sorrow of the other; afterwards these things may be, if so it seem right."

CHAP. XXXVI.—*Arrangements for to-morrow.*

And when the old man had said this, Peter said to the chief man of the city : "Since you have shown your good-will in our presence, it is not right that you should go away sorrowful ; but we will accept from you favour for favour. Show us your house, and make it ready, so that the discussion which is to be to-morrow may be held there, and that any who wish to be present to hear it may be admitted." When the chief man of the city heard this, he rejoiced greatly ; and all the people also heard it gladly. And when the crowds had dispersed, he pointed out his house ; and the old man also was preparing to depart. But I commanded one of my attendants to follow the old man secretly, and find out where he stayed. And when we returned to our lodging, we told our brethren all our dealings with the old man ; and so, as usual, we supped and went to sleep.

CHAP. XXXVII.—" *The form of sound words, which ye have heard of me.*"

But on the following day Peter arose early and called us, and we went together to the secret place in which we had been on the previous day, for the purpose of prayer. And when, after prayer, we were coming thence to the appointed place, he exhorted us by the way, saying : "Hear me, most beloved fellow-servants : It is good that every one of you, according to his ability, contribute to the advantage of those who are approaching to the faith of our religion ; and there-fore do not shrink from instructing the ignorant, and teach-ing according to the wisdom which has been bestowed upon you by the providence of God, yet so that you only join the eloquence of your discourse with those things which you have heard from me, and which have been committed to you. But do not speak anything which is your own, and which has not been committed to you, though it may seem to yourselves to be true ; but hold forth those things, as I have said, which I myself have received from the true Prophet, and have delivered to you, although they may seem to be less full of authority. For thus it often happens that men turn away from the truth, while they believe that they have found out, by their own thoughts, a form of truth more true and powerful."

CHAP. XXXVIII.—*The chief man's house.*

To these counsels of Peter we willingly assented, saying to him that we should do nothing but what was pleasing to him. Then said he: "That you may therefore be exercised without danger, each of you conduct the discussion in my presence, one succeeding another, and each one elucidating his own questions. Now, then, as Niceta discoursed sufficiently yesterday, let Aquila conduct the discussion to-day; and after Aquila, Clement; and then I, if the case shall require it, will add something." Meantime, while we were talking in this way, we came to the house; and the master of the house welcomed us, and led us to a certain apartment, arranged after the manner of a theatre, and beautifully built. There we found great crowds waiting for us, who had come during the night, and amongst them the old man who had argued with us yesterday. Therefore we entered, having Peter in the midst of us, looking about if we could see the old man anywhere; and when Peter saw him hiding in the midst of the crowd, he called him to him, saying: "Since you possess a soul more enlightened than most, why do you hide yourself, and conceal yourself in modesty? Rather come hither, and propound your sentiments."

CHAP. XXXIX.—*Recapitulation of yesterday's argument.*

When Peter had thus spoken, immediately the crowd began to make room for the old man. And when he had come forward, he thus began : "Although I do not remember the words of the discourse which the young man delivered yesterday, yet I recollect the purport and the order of it; and therefore I think it necessary, for the sake of those who were not present yesterday, to call up what was said, and to repeat everything shortly, that, although something may have escaped me, I may be reminded of it by him who delivered the discourse, who is now present. This, then, was the purport of yesterday's discussion : that all things that we see, inasmuch as they consist in a certain proportion, and art, and form, and species, must be believed to have been made by intelligent power ; but if it be mind and reason that has formed them, it follows that the world is governed by the providence of the same reason, although the things which are done in the world may seem to us to be not quite rightly done. But it follows, that if God and mind is the creator of all things, He must also be just ; but if He is just, He necessarily judges. If He judges, it is of necessity that men be judged with respect to their doings ; and if every one is judged in respect of his doings, there shall at some time be a righteous separation between righteous men and sinners. This, I think, was the substance of the whole discourse.

Chap. xl.—*Genesis.*

"If, therefore, it can be shown that mind and reason created all things, it follows that those things which come after are also managed by reason and providence. But if un-intelligent and blind nature produces all things, the reason of judgment is undoubtedly overthrown ; and there is no ground to expect either punishment of sin or reward of well-doing where there is no judge. Since, then, the whole matter depends upon this, and hangs by this head, do not take it amiss if I wish this to be discussed and handled somewhat more fully. For in this the first gate, as it were, is shut towards all things which are propounded, and therefore I wish first of all to have it opened to me. Now therefore hear what my doctrine is ; and if any one of you pleases, let him reply to me : for I shall not be ashamed to learn, if I hear that which is true, and to assent to him who speaks rightly. The discourse, then, which you delivered yesterday, which asserted that all things consist by art, and measure, and reason, does not fully persuade me that it is mind and reason that has made the world ; for I have many things which I can show to consist by competent measure, and form, and species, and which yet were not made by mind and reason. Then, besides, I see that many things are done in the world without arrangement, consequence, or justice, and that nothing can be done without the course of *genesis*. This I shall in the sequel prove most clearly from my own case."

Chap. xli.—*The rainbow.*

When the old man had thus spoken, Aquila answered: "As you yourself proposed that any one who pleased should have an opportunity of answering to what you might say, my brother Niceta permits me to conduct the argument to-day." Then the old man: "Go on, my son, as you please." And Aquila answered: "You promised that you would show that there are many things in the world which have a form and species arranged by equal reason, which yet it is evident were not effected by God as their Creator. Now, then, as you have promised, point out these things." Then said the old man: "Behold, we see the bow in the heaven assume a circular shape, completed in all proportion, and have an appearance of reality, which perhaps neither mind could have constructed nor reason described; and yet it is not made by any mind. Behold, I have set forth the whole in a word: now answer me."

Chap. xlii.—*Types and forms.*

Then said Aquila: "If anything is expressed from a type and form, it is at once understood that it is from reason, and that it could not be made without mind; since the type itself, which expresses figures and forms, was not made without mind. For example, if wax be applied to an engraved ring, it takes the stamp and figure from the ring, which undoubtedly is without sense; but then the ring, which expresses the figure, was engraven by the hand of a workman, and it was mind and reason that gave the type to the ring. So then the bow also is expressed in the air; for the sun, impressing its rays on the clouds in the process of rarefaction, and affixing the type of its circularity to the cloudy moisture, as it were to soft wax, produces the appearance of a bow; and this, as I have said, is effected by the reflection of the

sun's brightness upon the clouds, and reproducing the brightness of its circle from them.   Now this does not always take
place, but only when the opportunity is presented by the
rarefaction of moistened clouds.   And consequently, when
the clouds again are condensed and unite, the form of the
bow is dissolved and vanishes.   Finally, the bow never is
seen without sun and clouds, just as the image is not produced, unless there be the type, and wax, or some other
material.   Nor is it wonderful if God the Creator in the beginning made types, from which forms and species may now
be expressed.   But this is similar to that, that in the beginning God created insensible elements, which He might use
for forming and developing all other things.   But even those
who form statues, first make a mould of clay or wax, and
from it the figure of the statue is produced.   And then afterwards a shadow is also produced from the statue, which
shadow always bears the form and likeness of the statue.
What shall we say then?   That the insensible statue forms
a shadow finished with as diligent care as the statue itself?
Or shall the finishing of the shadow be unhesitatingly ascribed
to him who has also fashioned the statue?

CHAP. XLIII.—*Things apparently useless and vile made by
God.*

"If, then, it seems to you that this is so, and what has
been said on this subject is enough, let us come to inquire
into other matters; or if you think that something is still
wanting, let us go over it again."   And the old man said: "I
wish you would go over this again, since there are many other
things which I see to be made in like manner: for both the
fruits of trees are produced in like manner, beautifully formed
and wonderfully rounded; and the appearance of the leaves
is formed with immense gracefulness, and the green membrane is woven with exquisite art: then, moreover, fleas, mice,
lizards, and such like, shall we say that these are made by
God?   Hence, from these vile objects a conjecture is derived
concerning the superior, that they are by no means formed
by the art of mind."   "You infer well," said Aquila, "con-

cerning the texture of leaves, and concerning small animals, that from these belief is withdrawn from the superior creatures; but let not these things deceive you, that you should think that God, working as it were only with two hands, could not complete all things that are made; but remember how my brother Niceta answered you yesterday, and truly disclosed the mystery before the time, as a son speaking with his father, and explained why and how things are made which seem to be useless."

CHAP. XLIV.—*Ordinate and inordinate.*

Then the old man: "I should like to hear from you why those useless things are made by the will of that supreme mind?" "If," said he, "it is fully manifest to you that there is in them the work of mind and reason, then you will not hesitate to say also why they were made, and to declare that they have been rightly made." To this the old man answered: "I am not able, my son, to say that those things which seem formed by art are made by mind, by reason of other things which we see to be done unjustly and disorderly in the world." "If," says Aquila, "those things which are done disorderly do not allow you to say that they are done by the providence of God, why do not those things which are done orderly compel you to say that they are done by God, and that irrational nature cannot produce a rational work? For it is certain, nor do we at all deny, that in this world some things are done orderly, and some disorderly. Those things, therefore, that are done rationally, believe that they are done by providence; but those that are done irrationally and inordinately, that they befall naturally, and happen accidentally. But I wonder that men do not perceive, that where there is sense things may be done ordinately and inordinately, but where there is no sense neither the one nor the other can be done; for reason makes order, and the course of order necessarily produces something inordinate, if anything contrary happen to disturb order." Then the old man: "This very thing I wish you to show me."

Chap. XLV.—*Motions of the sun and moon.*

Says Aquila: " I shall do so without delay. Two visible signs are shown in heaven—one of the sun, the other of the moon; and these are followed by five other stars, each describing its own separate orbit. These, therefore, God has placed in the heaven, by which the temperature of the air may be regulated according to the seasons, and the order of vicissitudes and alternations may be kept. But by means of the very same [signs], if at any time plague and corruption is sent upon the earth for the sins of men, the air is disturbed, pestilence is brought upon animals, blight upon crops, and a destructive year in every way upon men; and thus it is that by one and the same means order is both kept and destroyed. For it is manifest even to the unbelieving and unskilful, that the course of the sun, which is useful and necessary to the world, and which is assigned by providence, is always kept orderly; but the courses of the moon, in comparison of the course of the sun, seem to the unskilful to be inordinate and unsettled in her waxings and wanings. For the sun moves in fixed and orderly periods: for from him are hours, from him the day when he rises, from him also the night when he sets; from him months and years are reckoned, from him the variations of seasons are produced; while, rising to the higher regions, he tempers the spring; but when he reaches the top of the heaven, he kindles the summer's heats: again, sinking, he produces the temper of autumn; and when he returns to his lowest circle, he bequeaths to us the rigour of winter's cold from the icy binding of heaven.

Chap. XLVI.—*Sun and moon ministers both of good and evil.*

" But we shall discourse at greater length on these subjects at another time. Now, meantime, [we remark that] though he is that good servant for regulating the changes of the seasons, yet, when chastisement is inflicted upon men according to the will of God, he glows more fiercely, and burns up the world with more vehement fires. In like manner also the course of the moon, and that changing which seems to the unskilful to be disorderly, is adapted to the growth of crops, and cattle, and all living creatures; for by her waxings and wanings, by a certain wonderful contrivance of providence, everything that is born is nourished and grows; concerning which we could speak more at length and unfold the matter in detail, but that the method of the question proposed recalls us. Yet, by the very same appliances by which they are produced, all things are nourished and increased; but when, from any just cause, the regulation of the appointed order is changed, corruption and distemper arises, so that chastisement may come upon men by the will of God, as we have said above.

Chap. xlvii.—*Chastisements on the righteous and the wicked.*

" But perhaps you will say, What of the fact that, in that common chastisement, like things befall the pious and the impious? It is true, and we confess it; but the chastisement turns to the advantage of the pious, that, being afflicted in the present life, they may come more purified to the future, in which perpetual rest is prepared for them, and that at the same time even the impious may somewhat profit from their chastisement, or else that the just sentence of the future judgment may be passed upon them; since in the same chastisements the righteous give thanks to God, while the unrighteous blaspheme. Therefore, since the opinion of things is divided into two parts, that some things are done by order and others against order, it ought, from those things which are done according to order, to be believed that there is a providence; but with respect to those things which are done against order, we should inquire their causes from those who have learned them by prophetic teaching: for those who have become acquainted with prophetic discourse know when, and for what reason, blight, hail, and pestilence, and such like, have occurred in every generation, and for what sins these have been sent as a punishment; whence causes of sadness, lamentations, and griefs have befallen the human race; whence also trembling sickness has ensued, and that this has been from the beginning the punishment of parricide.[1]

[1] Gen. iv. 12, in LXX.

CHAP. XLVIII.—*Chastisements for sins.*

"For in the beginning of the world there were none of these evils, but they took their rise from the impiety of men; and thence, with the constant increase of iniquities, the number of evils has also increased. But for this reason divine providence has decreed a judgment with respect to all men, because the present life was not such that every one could be dealt with according to his deservings. Those things, therefore, which were well and orderly appointed from the beginning, when no causes of evil existed, are not to be judged of from the evils which have befallen the world by reason of the sins of men. In short, as an indication of the things which were from the beginning, some nations are found which are strangers to these evils. For the Seres, because they live chastely, are kept free from them all; for with them it is unlawful to come at a woman after she has conceived, or while she is being purified. No one there eats unclean flesh, no one knows aught of sacrifices; all are judges to themselves according to justice. For this reason they are not chastened with those plagues which we have spoken of; they live to extreme old age, and die without sickness. But we, miserable as we are, dwelling as it were with deadly serpents[1]—I mean with wicked men—necessarily suffer with them the plagues of afflictions in this world, but we cherish hope from the comfort of good things to come."

CHAP. XLIX.—*God's precepts despised.*

"If," said the old man, "even the righteous are tormented on account of the iniquities of others, God ought, as foreseeing this, to have commanded men not to do those things from which it should be necessary that the righteous be afflicted with the unrighteous; or if they did them, He ought to have applied some correction or purification to the world."[2] "God," said Aquila, "did so command, and gave precepts by the prophets how men ought to live; but even these pre-

---

[1] Ezek. ii. 6.

[2] This rendering is according to a marginal reading.

cepts they despised : yea, if any desired to observe them, them they afflicted with various injuries, until they drove them from their purposed observance, and turned them to the rabble of infidelity, and made them like unto themselves.

Chap. l.—*The flood.*

" Wherefore, in short, at the first, when all the earth had been stained with sins, God brought a flood upon the world, which you say happened under Deucalion; and at that time He saved a certain righteous man, with his sons, in an ark, and with him the race of all plants and animals. And yet even those who sprang from them, after a time, again did deeds like to those of their predecessors; for those things that had befallen them were forgotten, so that their descendants did not even believe that the flood had taken place. Wherefore God also decreed that there should not be another flood in the present world, else there should have been one in every generation, according to the account of their sins by reason of their unbelief; but He rather granted that certain angels who delight in evil should bear sway over the several nations —and to them was given power over individual men, yet only on this condition, if any one first had made himself subject to them by sinning—until He should come who delights in good, and by Him the number of the righteous should be completed, and by the increase of the number of pious men all over the world impiety should be in some measure repressed, and it should be known to all that all that is good is done by God.

Chap. li.—*Evils brought in by sin.*

" But by the freedom of the will, every man, while he is unbelieving in regard to things to come, by evil deeds runs into evils. And these are the things in the world which seem to be done contrary to order, which owe their existence to unbelief. Therefore the dispensation of divine providence is withal to be admired, which granted to those men in the beginning, walking in the good way of life, to enjoy incorruptible good things; but when they sinned, they gave birth to evil by sin. And to every good thing evil is joined as by a certain covenant of alliance on the part of sin, since indeed the earth has been polluted with human blood, and altars have been lighted to demons, and they have polluted the very air by the filthy smoke of sacrifices; and so at length the elements, being first corrupted, have handed over to men the fault of their corruption, as roots [communicate their qualities] to the branches and the fruit.

Chap. lii.—*"No rose without its thorn."*

" Observe therefore in this, as I have said, how justly divine providence comes to the help of things vitiated; that, inasmuch as evils which had derived their origin from sin were associated with the good things of God, He should assign two chiefs to these two departments. And [accordingly] to Him who rejoices in good He has appointed the ordering of good things, that He might bring those who believe [in Him] to the faith of His providence; but to him who rejoices in evil, He has given over those things which are done without order and uselessly, from which of course the faith of His providence comes into doubt; and thus a just division has been made by a just God. Hence therefore it is, that whereas the orderly course of the stars produces faith that the world was made by the hand of a designer, on the other hand, the disturbance of the air, the pestilent breeze, the uncontrolled fire of the lightning, cast doubt upon the work of providence. For, as we have said, every good thing has its corresponding contrary evil thing joined with it; as hail is opposite to the fertilizing showers, the corruption of mildew is associated with the gentle dew, the whirlwinds of storms are joined with the soft winds, unfruitful trees with fruitful, noxious herbs with useful, wild and destructive animals with gentle ones. But all these things are arranged by God, because that the choice of men's will has departed from the purpose of good, and fallen away to evil.

Chap. liii.—*Everything has its corresponding contrary.*

" Therefore this division holds in all the things of the world;

and as there are pious men, so there are also impious ; as there are prophets, so also there are false prophets; and amongst the Gentiles there are philosophers and false philosophers. Also the Arabian nations, and many others, have imitated the circumcision of the Jews for the service of their impiety. So also the worship of demons is contrary to the divine worship, baptism to baptism, laws to the law, false apostles to apostles, and false teachers to teachers. And hence it is that among the philosophers some assert providence, others deny it; some maintain that there is one God, others that there are more than one : in short, the matter has come to this, that whereas demons are expelled by the word of God, by which it is declared that there is a providence, the magical art, for the confirmation of infidelity, has found out ways of imitating this by contraries. Thus has been discovered the method of counteracting the poison of serpents by incantations, and the effecting of cures contrary to the word and power of God. The magic art has also found out ministries contrary to the angels of God, placing the calling up of souls and the figments of demons in opposition to these. And, not to prolong the discourse by a further enumeration, there is nothing whatever that makes for the belief of providence, which has not something, on the other hand, prepared for unbelief ; and therefore they who do not know that division of things, think that there is no providence, by reason of those things in the world which are discordant from themselves. But do you, my father, as a wise man, choose from that division the part which preserves order and makes for the belief of providence, and do not only follow that part which runs against order and neutralizes the belief of providence."

CHAP. LIV.—*An illustration.*

To this the old man answered : " Show me a way, my son, by which I may establish in my mind one or other of these two orders, the one of which asserts, and the other denies, providence." " To one having a right judgment," says Aquila, " the decision is easy. For this very thing that you say, order and disorder, may be produced by a contriver, but not by insensible nature. For let us suppose, by way of illustration, that a great mass were torn from a high rock, and cast down headlong, and when dashed upon the ground were broken into many pieces, could it in any way happen that, amongst that multitude of fragments, there should be found even one which should have any perfect figure and shape?" The old man answered: "It is impossible." "But," said Aquila, "if there be present a statuary, he can by his skilful hand and reasonable mind form the stone cut from the mountain into whatever figure he pleases." The old man said: "That is true." "Therefore," says Aquila, "when there is not a rational mind, no figure can be formed out of the mass; but when there is a designing mind, there may be both form and deformity: for example, if a workman cuts from the mountain a block to which he wishes to give a form, he must first cut it out unformed and rough; then, by degrees hammering and hewing it by the rule of his art, he expresses the form which he has conceived in his mind. Thus, therefore, from informity or deformity, by the hand of the workman form is attained, and both proceed from the workman. In like manner, therefore, the things which are done in the world are accomplished by the providence of a contriver, although they may seem not quite orderly. And therefore, because these two ways have been made known to you, and you have heard the divisions of them, flee from the way of unbelief, lest haply it lead you to that prince who delights in evils; but follow the way of faith, that you may come to that King who delighteth in good men."

Chap. lv.—*The two kingdoms.*

To this the old man answered: "But why was that prince made who delights in evil? And from what was he made? Or was he not made?" Aquila said: "The treatment of that subject belongs to another time; but that you may not go away altogether without an answer to this, I shall give a few hints on this subject also. God, foreseeing all things before the creation of the world, knowing that the men who were to be would some of them indeed incline to good, but others to the opposite, assigned those who should choose the good to His own government and His own care, and called them His peculiar inheritance;[1] but He gave over the government of those who should turn to evil to those angels who, not by their substance, but by opposition, were unwilling to remain with God, being corrupted by the vice of envy and pride. Those, therefore, he made worthy princes of worthy subjects; yet he so delivered them over to those angels, that they have not the power of doing what they will against them, unless they transgress the bounds assigned to them from the beginning. And this is the bound assigned, that unless one first do the will of the demons, the demons have no power over him."

Chap. LVI.—*Origin of evil.*

Then the old man said: "You have stated it excellently, my son. It now remains only that you tell me whence is the substance of evil: for if it was made by God, the evil fruit shows that the root is in fault; for it appears that it also is of an evil nature. But if this substance was co-eternal with God, how can that which was equally unproduced and co-eternal be subject to the other?" "It was not always," said Aquila; "but neither does it necessarily follow, if it was made by God, that its Creator should be thought to be such as is that which has been made by Him. For indeed God made the substance of all things; but if a reasonable mind, which has been made· by God, do not acquiesce in the laws of its Creator, and go beyond the bounds of the temperance prescribed to it, how does this reflect on the Creator? Or if there is any reason higher than this, we do not know it; for we cannot know anything perfectly, and especially concerning those things for our ignorance of which we are not to be judged. But those things for which we are to be judged are most easy to be understood, and are despatched almost in a word. For almost the whole rule of our actions is summed up in this, that what we are unwilling to suffer we should not do to others. For as you would not be killed, you must

[1] Deut. xxxii. 8, in LXX.

beware of killing another; and as you would not have your own marriage violated, you must not defile another's bed; you would not be stolen from, neither must you steal; and every matter of men's actions is comprehended within this rule."

Chap. LVII.—*The old man unconvinced.*

Then the old man: "Do not take amiss, my son, what I am going to say. Though your words are powerful, yet they cannot lead me to believe that anything can be done apart from *genesis*. For I know that all things have happened to me by the necessity of *genesis*, and therefore I cannot be persuaded that either to do well or to do ill is in our power; and if we have not our actions in our power, it cannot be believed that there is a judgment to come, by which either punishments may be inflicted on the evil, or rewards bestowed on the good. In short, since I see that you are initiated in this sort of learning, I shall lay before you a few things from the art itself." "If," says Aquila, "you wish to add anything from that science, my brother Clement will answer you with all care, since he has attended more fully to the science of mathematics. For I can maintain in other ways that our actions are in our own power; but I ought not to presume upon those things which I have not learned."

Chap. LVIII.—*Sitting in judgment upon God.*

When Aquila had thus spoken, then I Clement said: "To-morrow, my father, you shall speak as you please, and we will gladly hear you; for I suppose it will also be gratifying to you that you have to do with those who are not ignorant of the science which you profess." When, therefore, it had been settled between the old man and me, that on the following day we should hold a discussion on the subject of *genesis*—whether all things are done under its influence, or there be anything in us which is not done by *genesis*, but by the judgment of the mind—Peter rose up, and began to speak to the following effect: "To me it is exceedingly wonderful, that things which can easily be found out men make difficult by recondite thoughts and words; and those especially who think themselves wise, and who, wishing to comprehend the will of God, treat God as if He were a man, yea, as if He were something less than a man : for no one can know the purpose or mind of a man unless he himself reveal his thoughts ; and neither can any one learn a profession unless he be for a long time instructed by a master. How much more must it be, that no one can know the mind or the work of the invisible and incomprehensible God, unless He Himself send a prophet to declare His purpose, and expound the way of His creation, so far as it is lawful for men to learn it! Hence I think it ridiculous when men judge of the power of God in natural ways, and think that this is possible and that impossible to Him, or this greater and that less, while they are ignorant of everything; who, being unrighteous men, judge the righteous God; unskilled, judge the contriver ; corrupt, judge the incorruptible ; creatures, judge the Creator.

CHAP. LIX.—*The true Prophet.*

" But I would not have you think, that in saying this I take away the power of judging concerning things ; but I give counsel that no one walk through devious places, and rush into errors without end. And therefore I advise not only wise men, but indeed all men who have a desire of knowing what is advantageous to them, that they seek after the true Prophet; for it is He alone who knoweth all things, and who knoweth what and how every man is seeking. For He is within the mind of every one of us, but in those who have no desire of the knowledge of God and His righteousness, He is inoperative ; but He works in those who seek after that which is profitable to their souls, and kindles in them the light of knowledge. Wherefore seek Him first of all ; and if you do not find Him, expect not that you shall learn anything from any other. But He is soon found by those who diligently seek Him through love of the truth, and whose souls are not taken possession of by wickedness. For He is present with those who desire Him in the innocency of their spirits, who bear patiently, and draw sighs from the bottom of their hearts through love of the truth ; but He deserts malevolent minds,[1] because as a prophet He knows the thoughts of every one. And therefore let no one think that he can find Him by his own wisdom, unless, as we have said, he empty his mind of all wickedness, and conceive a pure and faithful desire to know Him. For when any one has so prepared himself, He Himself as a prophet, seeing a mind prepared for Him, of His own accord offers Himself to his knowledge.

CHAP. LX.—*His deliverances not to be questioned.*

"Therefore, if any one wishes to learn all things, [he cannot do it by] discussing them one by one; for, being mortal, he shall not be able to trace the counsel of God, and to scan immensity itself. But if, as we have said, he desires to learn all things, let him seek after the true Prophet; and when he has found Him, let him not treat with Him by questions and disputations and arguments; but if He has given any response, or pronounced any judgment, it cannot be doubted that this is certain. And therefore, before all things, let the true Prophet be sought, and His words be laid hold of. In respect to these this only should be discussed by every one, that he may satisfy himself if they are truly His prophetic words ; that is, if they contain undoubted faith of things to come, if they mark out definite times, if they preserve the order of things, if they do not relate as last those things which are first, nor as first those things which were done last, if they contain nothing subtle, nothing composed by magic art to deceive, or if they have not transferred to themselves things which were revealed to others, and have mixed them with falsehoods. And when, all these things having been discussed by right judgment, it is established that they are prophetic words, so they ought to be at once believed concerning all things on which they have spoken and answered.

CHAP. LXI.—*Ignorance of the philosophers.*

"For let us consider carefully the work of divine providence. For whereas the philosophers have introduced certain

[1] Wisd. i. 4.

subtile and difficult words, so that not even the terms that they use in their discourses can be known and understood by all, God has shown that those who thought themselves word-farmers are altogether unskilful as respects the knowledge of the truth. For the knowledge of things which is imparted by the true Prophet is simple, and plain, and brief; which those men walking through devious places, and through the stony difficulties of words, are wholly ignorant of. Therefore, to modest and simple minds, when they see things come to pass which have been foretold, it is enough, and more than enough, that they may receive most certain knowledge from most certain prescience; and for the rest may be at peace, having received evident knowledge of the truth. For all other things are treated by opinion, in which there can be nothing firm. For what speech is there which may not be contradicted? And what argument is there that may not be overthrown by another argument? And hence it is, that by disputation of this sort men can never come to any end of knowledge and learning, but find the end of their life sooner than the end of their questions.

CHAP. LXII.—*End of the conference.*

"And, therefore, since amongst these [philosophers] are things uncertain, we must come to the true Prophet. Him God the Father wished to be loved by all, and accordingly He has been pleased wholly to extinguish those opinions which have originated with men, and in regard to which there is nothing like certainty—that He [the true Prophet] might be the more sought after, and that He whom[1] they had obscured should show to men the way of truth. For on this account also God made the world, and by Him the world is filled; whence also He is everywhere near to them who seek Him, though He be sought in the remotest ends of the earth. But if any one seek Him not purely, nor holily, nor faithfully, He is indeed within him, because He is everywhere, and is

---

[1] If we were to read *quam* instead of *quem*, the sense would be: that He might lay open to men the way of truth which they had blocked up. So Whiston.

found within the minds of all men; but, as we have said before, He is dormant to the unbelieving, and is held to be absent from those by whom His existence is not believed." And when Peter had said this, and more to the same effect, concerning the true Prophet, he dismissed the crowds; and when he very earnestly entreated the old man to remain with us, he could prevail nothing; but he also departed, to return next day, as had been agreed upon. And after this, we also, with Peter, went to our lodging, and enjoyed our accustomed food and rest.

RECOGNITIONS OF CLEMENT.

BOOK IX.

CHAP. I.—*An explanation.*

N the following day, Peter, along with us, hastened early to the place in which the discussion had been held the day before; and when he saw that great crowds had assembled there to hear, and saw the old man with them, he said to him: "Old man, it was agreed yesterday that you should confer to-day with Clement; and that you should either show that nothing takes place apart from *genesis,* or that Clement should prove that there is no such thing as *genesis,* but that what we do is in our own power." To this the old man answered: "I both remember what was agreed upon, and I keep in memory the words which you spoke after the agreement was made, in which you taught that it is impossible for man to know anything, unless he learn from the true Prophet." Then Peter said: "You do not know what I meant; but I shall now explain to you. I spoke of the will and purpose of God, which He had before the world was, and by which purpose He made the world, appointed times, gave the law, promised a world to come to the righteous for the rewarding of their good deeds, and decreed punishments to the unjust according to a judicial sentence. I said that this counsel and this will of God cannot be found out by men, because no man can gather the mind of God from conjectures and opinion, unless a prophet sent by Him declare it. I did not therefore speak of any doctrines or studies, that they cannot be found out or known without a prophet; for I know that both arts and sciences can be known and practised by men, which they have learned, not from the true Prophet, but from human instructors.

Chap. ii.—*Preliminaries.*

"Since, therefore, you profess to be conversant with the position of the stars and the courses of the heavenly bodies, and that from these you can convince Clement that all things are subject to *genesis*, or that you will learn from him that all things are governed by providence, and that we have something in our own power, it is now the time for you two to set about this." To this the old man answered: "Now indeed it was not necessary to raise questions of this kind, if it were possible for us to learn from the true Prophet, and to hear in a definite proposition, that anything depends on us and on the freedom of our will; for your yesterday's discourse affected me greatly, in which you disputed concerning the prophetic power. Whence also I assent to and confirm your judgment, that nothing can be known by man with certainty, and without doubt, seeing that he has but a short period of life, and a brief and slender breath, by which he seems to be kept in life. However, since I am understood to have promised to Clement, before I heard anything of the prophetic power, that I should show that all things are subject to *genesis*, or that I should learn from him that there is something in ourselves, let him do me this favour, that he first begin, and propound and explain what may be objected: for I, ever since I heard from you a few words concerning the power of prophecy, have, I confess, been confounded, considering the greatness of prescience; nor do I think that anything ought to be received which is collected from conjectures and opinion."

Chap. iii.—*Beginning of the discussion.*

When the old man had said this, I Clement began to speak as follows: "God by His Son created the world as a double house, separated by the interposition of this firmament, which is called heaven; and appointed angelic powers to dwell in the higher, and a multitude of men to be born in this visible world, from amongst whom He might choose friends for His Son, with whom He might rejoice, and who might be prepared for Him as a beloved bride for a bridegroom. But even till the time of the marriage, which is the manifestation of the world to come, He has appointed a certain power, to choose out and watch over the good ones of those who are born in this world, and to preserve them for His Son, set apart in a certain place of the world, which is without sin; in which there are already some, who are there being prepared, as I said, as a bride adorned for the coming of the bridegroom. For the prince of this world and of the present age is like an adulterer, who corrupts and violates the minds of men, and, seducing them from the love of the true bridegroom, allures them to strange lovers.

Chap. iv.—*Why the evil prince was made.*

"But some one will say, How then was it necessary that that prince should be made, who was to turn away the minds of men from the true prince? Because God, who, as I have said, wished to prepare friends for His Son, did not wish them to be such as by necessity of nature could not be aught else, but such as should desire of their own choice and will to be good; because neither is that praiseworthy which is not desirable, nor is that judged to be good which is not sought for with purpose. For there is no credit in being that from which the necessity of your nature does not admit of your changing. Therefore the providence of God has willed that a multitude of men should be born in this world, that those who should choose a good life might be selected from many. And because He foresaw that the present world could not consist except by variety and inequality, He gave to each mind freedom of motions, according to the diversities of present things, and appointed this prince, through his suggestion of those things which run contrary, that the choice of better things might depend upon the exercise of virtue.

Chap. v.—*Necessity of inequality.*

"But to make our meaning plainer, we shall explain it by particulars. Was it proper, for example, that all men in this world should be kings, or princes, or lords, or teachers, or lawyers, or geometers, or goldsmiths, or bakers, or smiths, or grammarians, or rich men, or farmers, or perfumers, or fishermen, or poor men? It is certain that all could not be these. Yet all these professions, and many more, the life of men requires, and without these it cannot be passed; therefore inequality is necessary in this world. For there cannot be a king, unless he has subjects over whom he may rule and reign; nor can there be a master, unless he has one over whom he may bear sway; and in like manner of the rest.

CHAP. VI.—*Arrangements of the world for the exercise of virtue.*

"Therefore the Creator, knowing that no one would come to the contest of his own accord, while labour is shunned,— that is, to the practice of those professions which we have mentioned, by means of which either the justice or the mercy of every one can be manifested,—made for men a body susceptible of hunger, and thirst, and cold, in order that men, being compelled for the sake of supporting their bodies, might come down to all the professions which we have mentioned, by the necessity of livelihood. For we are taught to cultivate every one of these arts, for the sake of food, and drink, and clothing. And in this the purpose of each one's mind is shown, whether he will supply the demands of hunger and cold by means of thefts, and murders, and perjuries, and other crimes of that sort; or whether, keeping justice and mercy and continence, he will fulfil the service of imminent necessity by the practice of a profession and the labour of his hands. For if he supply his bodily wants with justice, and piety, and mercy, he comes forth as a victor in the contest set before him, and is chosen as a friend of the Son of God. But if he serve carnal lusts, by frauds, iniquities, and crimes, he becomes a friend of the prince of this world, and of all demons; by whom he is also taught this, to ascribe to the courses of the stars the errors of his own evil doings, although he chose them of purpose, and willingly. For arts are learned and practised, as we have said, under the compulsion of the desire of food and drink; which desire, when the knowledge of the truth comes to any one, becomes weaker, and frugality takes its place. For what expense have those who use water and bread, and who expect it from God?

Chap. vii.—*The old and the new birth.*

" There is therefore, as we have said, a certain necessary inequality in the dispensation of the world. Since indeed all men cannot know all things, and accomplish all works, yet all need the use and service of almost all. And on this account it is necessary that one work, and another pay him for his work; that one be servant, and another be master; that one be subject, another be king. But this inequality, which is a necessary provision for the life of men, divine providence has turned into an occasion of justice, mercy, and humanity: that while these things are transacted between man and man, every one may have an opportunity of acting justly with him to whom he has to pay wages for his work; and of acting mercifully to him who, perhaps through sickness or poverty, cannot pay his debt; and of acting humanely towards those who by their creation seem to be subject to him; also of maintaining gentleness towards subjects, and of doing all things according to the law of God. For He has given a law, thereby aiding the minds of men, that they may the more easily perceive how they ought to act with respect to everything, in what way they may escape evil, and in what way tend to future blessings; and how, being regenerate in water, they may by good works extinguish the fire of their old birth. For our first birth descends through the fire of lust, and therefore, by the divine appointment, this second birth is introduced by water, which may extinguish the nature of fire; and that the soul, enlightened by the heavenly Spirit, may cast away the fear of the first birth: provided, however, it so live for the time to come, that it do not at all seek after any of the pleasures of this world, but be, as it were, a pilgrim and a stranger,[1] and a citizen of another city.

[1] Ps. xxxix. 12.

CHAP. VIII.—*Uses of evils.*

"But perhaps you will say, that in those things indeed in which the necessity of nature demands the service of arts and works, any one may have it in his power to maintain justice, and to put what restraint he pleases either upon his desires or his actions; but what shall we say of the sicknesses and infirmities which befall men, and of some being harassed with demons, and fevers, and cold fits, and some being attacked with madness, or losing their reason, and all those things which overwhelm the race of man with innumerable misfortunes? To this we say, that if any one consider the reason of the whole mystery, he will pronounce these things to be more just than those that we have already explained. For God has given a nature to men, by which they may be taught concerning what is good, and to resist evil; that is, they may learn arts, and to resist pleasures, and to set the law of God before them in all things. And for this end He has permitted certain contrary powers to wander up and down in the world, and to strive against us, for the reasons which have been stated before, that by striving with them the palm of victory and the merit of rewards may accrue to the righteous.

CHAP. IX.—" *Conceived in sin.*"

"From this, therefore, it sometimes happens, that if any persons have acted incontinently, and have been willing not so much to resist as to yield, and to give harbour to these [demons] in themselves, by their noxious breath an intemperate, ill-conditioned, and diseased progeny is begotten. For while lust is wholly gratified, and no care is taken in the copulation, undoubtedly a weak generation is affected with the defects and frailties of those demons by whose instigation these things are done. And therefore parents are responsible for their children's defects of this sort, because they have not observed the law of intercourse. Though there are also more secret causes, by which souls are made subject to these evils, which it is not to our present purpose to state, yet it behoves every one to acknowledge the law of God, that he may learn from it the observance of generation, and avoid causes of impurity, that that which is begotten may be pure. For it is not right, while in the planting of shrubs and the sowing of crops a suitable season is sought for, and the land is cleaned, and all things are suitably prepared, lest haply the seed which is sown be injured and perish, that in the case of man only, who is over all these things, there should be no attention or caution in sowing his seed.

CHAP. X.—*Tow smeared with pitch.*

" But what, it is said, of the fact that some who in their childhood are free from any bodily defect, yet in process of time fall into those evils, so that some are even violently hurried on to death ?   Concerning these also the account is at hand, and is almost the same : for those powers which we have said to be contrary to the human race, are in some way invited into the heart of every one by many and diverse lusts, and find a way of entrance; and they have in them such influence and power as can only encourage and incite, but cannot compel or accomplish.   If, therefore, any one consents to them, so as to do those things which he wickedly desires, his consent and deed shall find the reward of destruction and the worst kind of death.   But if, thinking of the future judgment, he be checked by fear, and reclaim himself, so that he do not accomplish in action what he has conceived in his evil thought, he shall not only escape present destruction, but also future punishments.   For every cause of sin seems to be like tow smeared over with pitch, which immediately breaks into flame as soon as it receives the heat of fire; and the kindling of this fire is understood to be the work of demons.   If, therefore, any one be found smeared with sins and lusts as with pitch, the fire easily gets the mastery of him.   But if the tow be not steeped in the pitch of sin, but in the water of purification and regeneration, the fire of the demons shall not be able to be kindled in it.

CHAP. XI.—*Fear.*

"But some one will say, And what shall we do now,

whom it has already happened to us to be smeared with sins as with pitch? I answer: Nothing; but hasten to be washed, that the fuel of the fire may be cleansed out of you by the invocation of the holy name, and that for the future you may bridle your lusts by fear of the judgment to come, and with all constancy beat back the hostile powers whenever they approach your senses. But you say, If any one fall into love, how shall he be able to contain himself, though he see before his eyes even that river of fire which they call Pyriphlegethon? This is the excuse of those who will not be converted to repentance. But now I would not have you talk of Pyriphlegethon. Place before you human punishments, and see what influence fear has. When any one is brought to punishment for the crime of love, and is bound to the stake to be burned, can he at that time conceive any desire of her whom he loved, or place her image before his eyes? By no means, you will say. You see, then, that present fear cuts off unrighteous desires. But if those who believe in God, and who confess the judgment to come, and the penalty of eternal fire,—if they do not refrain from sin, it is certain that they do not believe with full faith: for if faith is certain, fear also becomes certain; but if there be any defect in faith, fear also is weakened, and then the contrary powers find opportunity of entering. And when they have consented to their persuasions, they necessarily become subject also to their power, and by their instigation are driven to the precipices of sin.

Chap. XII.—*Astrologers.*

"Therefore the astrologers, being ignorant of such mysteries, think that these things happen by the courses of the heavenly bodies: hence also, in their answers to those who go to them to consult them as to future things, they are deceived in very many instances. Nor is it to be wondered at, for they are not prophets; but by long practice, the authors of errors find a sort of refuge in those things by which they were deceived, and introduce certain *climacteric periods,* that they may pretend a knowledge of uncertain things. For they represent these *climacterics* as times of danger, in which one sometimes is destroyed, sometimes is not destroyed, not knowing that it is not the course of the stars, but the operation of demons, that regulates these things; and those demons, being anxious to confirm the error of astrology, deceive men to sin by mathematical calculations, so that when they suffer the punishment of sin, either by the permission of God or by legal sentence, the astrologer may seem to have spoken truth. And yet they are deceived even in this; for if men be quickly turned to repentance, and remember and fear the future judgment, the punishment of death is remitted to those who are converted to God by the grace of baptism.

Chap. XIII.—*Retribution here or hereafter.*

"But some one will say, Many have committed even murder, and adultery, and other crimes, and have suffered no evil. This indeed rarely happens to men, but to those who know not the counsel of God it frequently seems to happen. But God, who knows all things, knows how and why he who sins does sin, and what cause leads each one to sin. This, however, is in general to be noticed, that if any are evil, not so much in their mind as in their doings, and are not borne to sin under the incitement of purpose, upon them punishment is inflicted more speedily, and more in the present life; for everywhere and always God renders to every one according to his deeds, as He judges to be expedient. But those who practise wickedness of purpose, so that they sometimes even rage against those from whom they have received benefits, and who take no thought for repentance—their punishment He defers to the future. For these men do not, like those of whom we spoke before, deserve to end the punishment of their crimes in the present life; but it is allowed them to occupy the present time as they will, because their correction is not such as to need temporal chastisements, but such as to demand the punishment of eternal fire in hell; and there their souls shall seek repentance, where they shall not be able to find it.

Chap. xiv.—*Knowledge deadens lusts.*

"But if, while in this life, they had placed before their eyes the punishments which they shall then suffer, they would certainly have bridled their lusts, and would in nowise have fallen into sin. For the understanding in the soul has much power for cutting off all its desires, especially when it has acquired the knowledge of heavenly things, by means of which, having received the light of truth, it will turn away from all darkness of evil actions. For as the sun obscures and conceals all the stars by the brightness of his shining, so also the mind, by the light of knowledge, renders all the lusts of the soul ineffective and inactive, sending out upon them the thought of the judgment to come as its rays, so that they can no longer appear in the soul.

Chap. xv.—*Fear of men and of God.*

"But as a proof that the fear of God has much efficacy for the repressing of lusts, take the example of human fear. Who is there among men that does not covet his neighbour's goods? And yet they are restrained, and act honestly, through fear of the punishment which is prescribed by the laws. Through fear, nations are subject to their kings, and armies obey with arms in their hands. Slaves, although they are stronger than their masters, yet through fear submit to their masters' rule. Even wild beasts are tamed by fear; the strongest bulls submit their necks to the yoke, and huge elephants obey their masters, through fear. But why do we use human examples, when even divine are not wanting? Does not the earth itself remain under the fear of precept, which it testifies by its motion and quaking? The sea keeps its prescribed bounds; the angels maintain peace; the stars keep their order, and the rivers their channels: it is certain also that demons are put to flight by fear. And not to lengthen the discourse by too many particulars, see how the fear of God, restraining everything, keeps all things in proper harmony, and in their fixed order. How much more, then, may you be sure that the lusts of demons which arise in your hearts may be extinguished and wholly abolished by the admonition of the fear of God, when even the inciters of lust are themselves put to flight by the influence of fear? You know that these things are so; but if you have anything to answer, proceed."

Chap. xvi.—*Imperfect conviction.*

Then said the old man: "My son Clement has wisely framed his argument, so that he has left us nothing to say to these things; but all his discourse which he has delivered on the nature of men has this bearing, that along with the fact that freedom of will is in man, there is also some cause of evil without him, whereby men are indeed incited by various lusts, yet are not compelled to sin; and that for this reason, he said, because fear is much more powerful than they, and it resists and checks the violence of desires, so that, although natural emotions may arise, yet sin may not be committed, those demons being put to flight who incite and inflame these emotions. But these things do not convince me; for I am conscious of certain things from which I know well, that by the arrangement of the heavenly bodies men become murderers or adulterers, and perpetrate other evils; and in like manner honourable and modest women are compelled to act well.

Chap. xvii.—*Astrological lore.*[1]

"In short, when Mars, holding the centre in his house, regards Saturn quarterly, with Mercury towards the centre, the full moon coming upon him, in the daily *genesis*, he produces murderers, and those who are to fall by the sword,[2] bloody, drunken, lustful, devilish men, inquirers into secrets,[3] malefactors, sacrilegious persons, and such like; especially when there was no one of the good stars looking on. But

---

[1] Ch. xvii. and ch. xix.–xxix. are taken in an altered form from the writing ascribed to Bardesanes, *De Fato.*

[2] Conjectural reading, "to kill with the sword."

[3] That is, violators of the sacred mysteries, which was regarded as one of the most horrid of crimes.

again Mars himself, having a quarterly position with respect
to Venus, in a direction toward the centre, while no good
star looks on, produces adulterers and incestuous persons.
Venus with the Moon, in the borders and houses of Saturn,
if she was with Saturn, and Mars looking on, produces
women that are viragos, ready for agriculture, building,
and every manly work, to commit adultery with whom they
please, and not to be convicted by their husbands, to use no
delicacy, no ointments, nor feminine robes and shoes, but to
live after the fashion of men. But the unpropitious Venus
makes men to be as women, and not to act in any respect as
men, if she is with Mars in Aries; on the contrary, she produces women if she is in Capricorn or Aquarius."

Chap. xviii.—*The reply.*

And when the old man had pursued this subject at great
length, and had enumerated every kind of mathematical figure,
and also the position of the heavenly bodies, wishing thereby
to show that fear is not sufficient to restrain lusts, I answered
again: "Truly, my father, you have argued most learnedly
and skilfully; and reason herself invites me to say something
in answer to your discourse, since indeed I am acquainted
with the science of mathematics, and gladly hold a conference
with so learned a man. Listen, therefore, while I reply to
what you have said, that you may learn distinctly that *genesis*
is not at all from the stars, and that it is possible for those
to resist the assault of demons who have recourse to God;
and, as I said before, that not only by the fear of God can
natural lusts be restrained, but even by the fear of men, as
we shall now instruct you.

Chap. xix.—*Refutation of astrology.*

"There are, in every country or kingdom, laws imposed by
men, enduring either by writing or simply through custom,
which no one easily transgresses. In short, the first Seres,
who dwell at the beginning of the world,[1] have a law not to

---

[1] That is, the farthest east, not, as some of the annotators suppose,
from the beginning of the world.

know murder, nor adultery, nor whoredom, and not to commit theft, and not to worship idols ; and in all that country, which is very large, there is neither temple, nor image, nor harlot, nor adulteress, nor is any thief brought to trial. But neither is any man ever slain there ; and no man's liberty of will is compelled, according to your doctrine, by the fiery star of Mars, to use the sword for the murder of man ; nor does Venus in conjunction with Mars compel to adultery, although of course with them Mars occupies the middle circle of heaven every day. But amongst the Seres the fear of laws is more powerful than the configuration of *genesis*.

Chap. xx.—*Brahmans.*

" There are likewise amongst the Bactrians, in the Indian countries, immense multitudes of Brahmans, who also themselves, from the tradition of their ancestors, and peaceful customs and laws, neither commit murder nor adultery, nor worship idols, nor have the practice of eating animal food, are never drunk, never do anything maliciously, but always fear God. And these things indeed they do, though the rest of the Indians commit both murders and adulteries, and worship idols, and are drunken, and practise other wickednesses of this sort. Yea, in the western parts of India itself there is a certain country, where strangers, when they enter it, are taken and slaughtered and eaten ; and neither have good stars prevented these men from such wickednesses and from accursed food, nor have malign stars compelled the Brahmans to do any evil. Again, there is a custom among the Persians to marry mothers, and sisters, and daughters. In all that district the Persians contract incestuous marriages.

Chap. xxi.—*Districts of heaven.*

" And that those who study mathematics may not have it in their power to use that subterfuge by which they say that there are certain districts of heaven to which it is granted to have some things peculiar to themselves, some of that nation of Persians have gone to foreign countries, who are called Magusæi, of whom there are some to this day in Media, others in Parthia, some also in Egypt, and a considerable number in Galatia and Phrygia, all of whom maintain the form of this incestuous tradition without variation, and hand it down to their posterity to be observed, even although they have changed their district of heaven ; nor has Venus with the Moon in the confines and houses of Saturn, with Saturn also and Mars looking on, compelled them to have a *genesis* among other men.[1]

Chap. xxii.—*Customs of the Gelones.*

"Amongst the Geli also there is a custom, that women cultivate the fields, build, and do every manly work ; and they are also allowed to have intercourse with whom they please, and are not found fault with by their husbands, or called adulteresses : for they have promiscuous intercourse everywhere, and especially with strangers ; they do not use ointments ; they do not wear dyed garments, nor shoes. On the other hand, the men of the Gelones are adorned, combed, clothed in soft and various-coloured garments, decked with gold, and besmeared with ointments, and that not through lack of manliness, for they are most warlike, and most keen hunters. Yet the whole women of the Gelones had not at their birth the unfavourable Venus in Capricornus or Aquarius ; nor had all their men Venus placed with Mars in Aries, by which configuration the Chaldean science asserts that men are born effeminate and dissolute.

Chap. xxiii.—*Manners of the Susidæ.*

"But, further, in Susæ the women use ointments, and indeed of the best sort, being decked with ornaments and precious stones ; also they go abroad supported by the aid of their maid-servants, with much greater ambition than the men. They do not, however, cultivate modesty, but have intercourse indifferently with whomsoever they please, with slaves and

[1] This is a literal translation of text. If we read *genesi* for *genesim*, we get : " nor has Venus, etc., compelled them to keep up this custom in the midst of others through the force of *genesis*." Eusebius reads : " And assuredly Venus, etc., is not found in the *genesis* of all of them."

guests, such liberty being allowed them by their husbands;
and not only are they not blamed for this, but they also rule
over their husbands. And yet the *genesis* of all the Susian
women has not Venus with Jupiter and Mars in the middle
of the heaven in the houses of Jupiter. In the remoter parts
of the East, if a boy be treated unnaturally, when it is discovered, he is killed by his brothers, or his parents, or any of
his relations, and is left unburied. And again, among the
Gauls, an old law allows boys to be thus treated publicly;
and no disgrace is thought to attach to it. And is it
possible, that all those who are so basely treated among the
Gauls, have had Lucifer with Mercury in the houses of
Saturn and the confines of Mars?

Chap. xxiv.—*Different customs of different countries.*

"In the regions of Britain several men have one wife; in
Parthia many women have one husband; and each part of the
world adheres to its own manners and institutions. None of
the Amazons have husbands, but, like animals, they go out
from their own territories once a year about the vernal
equinox, and live with the men of the neighbouring nation,
observing a sort of solemnity the while, and when they have
conceived by them they return; and if they bring forth
a male child, they cast him away, and rear only females.
Now, since the birth of all is at one season, it is absurd to
suppose that in the case of males Mars is at the time in equal
portions with Saturn, but never in the *genesis* of females;
and that they have not Mercury placed with Venus in his
own houses, so as to produce either painters, or sculptors,
or money-changers; or in the houses of Venus, so that perfumers, or singers, or poets might be produced. Among the
Saracens, and Upper Libyans, and Moors, and the dwellers
about the mouths of the ocean, and also in the remote districts of Germany, and among the Sarmatians and Scythians,
and all the nations who dwell in the regions of the Pontic
shore, and in the island Chrysea, there is never found a
money-changer, nor a sculptor, nor a painter, nor an architect,
nor a geometrician, nor a tragedian, nor a poet. Therefore

the influence of Mercury and Venus must be wanting among them.

Chap. xxv.—*Not genesis, but free-will.*

" The Medes alone in all the world, with the greatest care, throw men still breathing to be devoured by dogs; yet they have not Mars with the Moon placed in Cancer all through their daily *genesis*. The Indians burn their dead, and the wives of the dead voluntarily offer themselves, and are burned with them.   But all the Indian women who are burned alive have not the Sun under the earth in nightly *genesis*, with Mars in the regions of Mars. Very many of the Germans end their lives by the halter; but all have not therefore the Moon with Hora begirt by Saturn and Mars. From all this it appears that the fear of the laws bears sway in every country, and the freedom of will which is implanted in man by the Spirit complies with the laws; and *genesis* can neither compel the Seres to commit murder, nor the Brahmans to eat flesh, nor the Persians to shun incest, nor the Indians to refrain from burning, nor the Medes from being devoured by dogs, nor the Parthians from having many wives, nor the women of Mesopotamia from preserving their chastity, nor the Greeks from athletic exercises, nor the Gallic boys from being abused; nor can it compel the barbarous nations to be instructed in the studies of the Greeks; but, as we have said, each nation observes its own laws according to free-will, and annuls the decrees of *genesis* by the strictness of laws.

Chap. xxvi.—*Climates.*

" But some one skilled in the science of mathematics will say that *genesis* is divided into seven parts, which they call climates, and that over each climate one of the seven heavenly bodies bears rule; and that those diverse laws to which we have referred are not given by men, but by those dominant stars according to their will, and that that which pleases the star is observed by men as a law. To this we shall answer, in the first place, that the world is not divided into seven parts; and in the second place, that if it were so, we find many different laws in one part and one country; and therefore there are neither seven [laws] according to the number of the heavenly bodies, nor twelve according to the number of the signs, nor thirty-six according to that of the divisions of ten degrees; but they are innumerable.

Chap. XXVII.—*Doctrine of " climates" untenable.*

"Moreover, we ought to remember the things which have been mentioned, that in the one country of India there are both persons who feed on human flesh, and persons who abstain even from the flesh of sheep, and birds, and all living creatures; and that the Magusæi marry their mothers and daughters not only in Persia, but that in every nation where they dwell they keep up their incestuous customs.[1] Then, besides, we have mentioned also innumerable nations, which are wholly ignorant of the studies of literature, and also some wise men have changed the laws themselves in several places; and some laws have been voluntarily abandoned, on account of the impossibility of observing them, or on account of their baseness. Assuredly we can easily ascertain how many rulers have changed the laws and customs of nations which they have conquered, and subjected them to their own laws. This is manifestly done by the Romans, who have brought under the Roman law and the civil decrees almost the whole world, and all nations who formerly lived under various laws and customs of their own. It follows, therefore, that the stars of the nations which have been conquered by the Romans have lost their climates and their portions.

Chap. XXVIII.—*Jewish customs.*

"I shall add another thing which may satisfy even the most incredulous. All the Jews who live under the law of Moses circumcise their sons on the eighth day without fail, and shed

---

[1] The text reads: "the incestuous customs of their evils, or of their evil persons." Hilgenfeld (*Bardesanes*, p. 113) notices that it should be, " of their ancestors."

the blood of the tender infant. But no one of the Gentiles has ever submitted to this on the eighth day; and, on the other hand, no one of the Jews has ever omitted it. How then shall the account of *genesis* stand with this, since Jews live in all parts of the world, mixed with Gentiles, and on the eighth day suffer the cutting of a member? And no one of the Gentiles, but only they themselves, as I have said, do this, induced to it not by the compulsion of any star, nor by the perfusion[1] of blood, but by the law of their religion; and in whatever part of the world they are, this sign is familiar to them. But also the fact that one name is among them all, wheresoever they are, does this also come through *genesis?* And also that no child born among them is ever exposed, and that on every seventh day they all rest, wherever they may be, and do not go upon a journey, and do not use fire?[2] Why is it, then, that no one of the Jews is compelled by *genesis* to go on a journey, or to build, or to sell or buy anything on that day?

CHAP. XXIX.—*The gospel more powerful than "genesis."*

"But I shall give a still stronger proof of the matters in hand. For, behold, scarcely seven years have yet passed since the advent of the righteous and true Prophet; and in the course of these, men of all nations coming to Judea, and moved both by the signs and miracles which they saw, and by the grandeur of His doctrine, received His faith; and then going back to their own countries, they rejected the lawless rites of the Gentiles, and their incestuous marriages. In short, among the Parthians—as Thomas, who is preaching the gospel amongst them, has written to us—not many now are addicted to polygamy; nor among the Medes do many throw their dead to dogs; nor are the Persians pleased with intercourse with their mothers, or incestuous marriages with their daughters; nor do the Susian women practise the adulteries that were

---

[1] Probably we should read *perfusionem* instead of *perfusione*, and then the translation would be: " no star compelling, or even urging on them the shedding of blood." So Whiston translates.

[2] Ex. xxxv. 3.

allowed them ; nor has *genesis* been able to force those into crimes whom the teaching of religion restrained.

CHAP. XXX.—" *Genesis*" *inconsistent with God's justice.*

" Behold, from the very matter in which we are now engaged, draw an inference, and from the circumstances in which we are now placed deduce a conclusion, how, through a rumour only reaching the ears of men that a Prophet had appeared in Judea to teach men with signs and miracles to worship one God, all were expecting with prepared and eager minds, even before the coming of my lord Peter, that some one would announce to them what He taught who had appeared. But lest I should seem to carry the enumeration too far, I shall tell you what conclusion ought to be drawn from the whole. Since God is righteous, and since He Himself made the nature of men, how could it be that He should place *genesis* in opposition to us, which should compel us to sin, and then that He should punish us when we do sin ? Whence it is certain that God punishes no sinner either in the present life or in that to come, except because He knows that He could have conquered, but neglected victory. For even in the present world He takes vengeance upon men, as He did upon those who perished in the deluge, who were all destroyed in one day, yea, in one hour, although it is certain that they were not all born in one hour according to the order of *genesis*. But it is most absurd to say that it befalls us by nature to suffer evils, if sins had not gone before.

CHAP. XXXI.—*Value of knowledge.*

"And therefore, if we desire salvation, we ought above all to seek after knowledge, being sure that if our mind remain in ignorance, we shall endure not only the evils of *genesis*, but also whatever other evils from without the demons may please, unless fear of laws and of the judgment to come resist all our desires, and check the violence of sinning. For even human fear does much good, and also much evil, unknown to *genesis*, as we have shown above. Therefore our mind is subject to errors in a threefold manner: from those things which

come to us through evil custom; or from those lusts which
the body naturally stirs up in us; or from those which hostile
powers compel us to. But the mind has it in its own nature to
oppose and fight against these, when the knowledge of truth
shines upon it, by which knowledge is imparted fear of the
judgment to come, which is a fit governor of the mind, and
which can recall it from the precipices of lusts. That these
things, therefore, are in our power, has been sufficiently
stated.

Chap. xxxii.—*Stubborn facts.*

"Now, old man, if you have anything to say in answer to
these things, say on." Then said the old man: "You have
most fully argued, my son; but I, as I said at the first, am
prevented by my own consciousness from according assent to
all this incomparable statement of yours. For I know both
my own *genesis* and that of my wife, and I know that those
things have happened which our *genesis* prescribed to each of
us; and I cannot now be withdrawn by words from those
things which I have ascertained by facts and deeds. In
short, since I perceive that you are excellently skilled in this
sort of learning, hear the horoscope of my wife, and you shall
find the configuration whose issue has occurred. For she
had Mars with Venus above the centre, and the Moon setting
in the houses of Mars and the confines of Saturn. Now this
configuration leads women to be adulteresses, and to love
their own slaves, and to end their days in foreign travel and
in waters. And this has so come to pass. For she fell in
love with her slave, and fearing at once danger and reproach,
she fled with him, and going abroad, where she satisfied her
love, she perished in the sea."

Chap. xxxiii.—*An approaching Recognition.*

Then I answered: "How know you that she cohabited
with her slave abroad, and died in his society?" Then the
old man said: "I know it with perfect certainty; not indeed
that she was married to the slave, as indeed I had not even
discovered that she loved him. But after she was gone, my

brother gave me the whole story, telling me that first she had loved himself ; but he, being honourable as a brother, would not pollute his brother's bed with the stain of incest.   But she, being both afraid of me, and unable to bear the unhappy reproaches (and yet she should not be blamed for that to which her *genesis* compelled her), pretended a dream, and said to me : 'Some one stood by me in a vision, who ordered me to leave the city without delay with my two twins.'   When I heard this, being anxious for her safety and that of my sons, I immediately sent away her and the children, retaining with myself one who was younger.   For this she said that he had permitted who had given her warning in her sleep."

Chap. xxxiv.—*The other side of the story.*

Then I Clement, understanding that he perchance was my father, was drowned in tears, and my brothers also were ready to rush forward and to disclose the matter; but Peter restrained them, saying: "Be quiet, until I give you permission."   Therefore Peter, answering, said to the old man : "What was the name of your younger son ?"   And he said : "Clement."   Then Peter : "If I shall this day restore to you your most chaste wife and your three sons, will you believe that a modest mind can overcome unreasonable impulses, and that all things that have been spoken by us are true, and that *genesis* is nothing?"   Then said the old man : "As it is impossible for you to perform what you have promised, so it is impossible that anything can take place apart from *genesis.*"   Then says Peter : "I wish to have all who are here present as witnesses that I shall this day hand over to you your wife, who is living most chastely, with your three sons.   And now take a token of these things from this, that I know the whole story much more accurately than you do; and I shall relate the whole occurrences in order, both that you may know them, and that those who are present may learn."

Chap. xxxv.—*Revelations.*

When he had said this, he turned to the crowds, and thus

began : "This person whom you see, O men, in this poor
garb, is a citizen of the city Rome, descended of the stock
of Cæsar himself. His name is Faustinianus. He obtained
as his wife a woman of the highest rank, Matthidia by name.
By her he had three sons, two of whom were twins; and
the one who was the younger, whose name was Clement, is
this man !" When he said this, he pointed to me with
his finger. "And his twin sons are these men, Niceta and
Aquila, the one of whom was formerly called Faustinus and
the other Faustus." But as soon as Peter pronounced our
names, all the old man's limbs were weakened, and he fell
down in a swoon. But we his sons rushed to him, and
embraced and kissed him, fearing that we might not be able
to recall his spirit. And while these things were going on,
the people were confounded with very wonder.

Chap. xxxvi.—*New revelations.*

But Peter ordered us to rise from embracing our father,
lest we should kill him ; and he himself, laying hold of his
hand, and lifting him up as from a deep sleep, and gradually
reviving him, began to set forth to him the whole transactions
as they had really happened : how his brother had fallen in
love with Matthidia, and how she, being very modest, had
been unwilling to inform her husband of his brother's lawless
love, lest she should stir up hostility between the brothers,
and bring disgrace upon the family; and how she had wisely
pretended a dream, by which she was ordered to depart from
the city with her twin sons, leaving the younger one with his
father ; and how on their voyage they had suffered shipwreck
through the violence of a storm ; and how, when they were
cast upon an island called Antaradus, Matthidia was thrown
by a wave upon a rock, but her twin children were seized by
pirates and carried to Cæsarea, and there sold to a pious
woman, who treated them as sons, and brought them up, and
caused them to be educated as gentlemen ; and how the pirates
had changed their names, and called the one Niceta and
the other Aquila ; and how afterwards, through [common]
studies and acquaintanceship, they had adhered to Simon ;

and how they had turned away from him when they saw
him to be a magician and a deceiver, and had come to
Zaccheus; and how subsequently they had been associated
with himself; and how Clement also, setting out from the
city for the sake of learning the truth, had, through his
acquaintance with Barnabas, come to Cæsarea, and had
become known to him, and had adhered to him, and how he
had been taught by him the faith of his religion; and also
how he had found and recognised his mother begging at
Antaradus, and how the whole island rejoiced at his recognition of her; and also concerning her sojourn with her most
chaste hostess, and the cure that he had wrought upon her,
and concerning the liberality of Clement to those who had been
kind to his mother; and how afterwards, when Niceta and
Aquila asked who the strange woman was, and had heard
the whole story from Clement, they cried out that they were
her twin sons Faustinus and Faustus; and how they had unfolded the whole history of what had befallen them; and how
afterwards, by the persuasion of Peter himself, they were
presented to their mother with caution, lest she should be
cut off by the sudden joy.

Chap. xxxvii.—*Another Recognition.*

But while Peter was detailing these things in the hearing
of the old man, in a narrative which was most pleasing to the
crowd, so that the hearers wept through wonder at the events,
and through compassion for sufferings incident to humanity,[1]
my mother, hearing (I know not how) of the recognition of
my father, rushed into the middle of us in breathless haste,
crying out, and saying: " Where is my husband, my lord
Faustinianus, who has been so long afflicted, wandering from
city to city in search of me?"   While she shouted thus like
one demented, and gazed around, the old man, running up,
began to embrace and hug her with many tears.   And while
these things were going on, Peter requested the crowds to
disperse, saying that it was unseemly to remain longer; but
that opportunity must be afforded them of seeing one another

---

[1] Lit. " through pity of humanity."

more privately. "But to-morrow," said he, "if any of you wish it, let them assemble to hear the word."

Chap. xxxviii.—"*Angels unawares.*"

When Peter had said this, the crowds dispersed ; and when we also were intending to go to our lodging, the master of the house said to us : "It is base and wicked that such and so great men should stay in a hostelry, when I have almost my whole house empty, and very many beds spread, and all necessary things provided." But when Peter refused, the wife of the householder prostrated herself before him with her children, and besought him, saying, "I entreat you, stay with us." But not even so did Peter consent, until the daughter of those people who asked him, who had been for a long time vexed with an unclean spirit, and bound with chains, who had been shut up in a closet, having had the demon expelled from her, and the door of the closet opened, came with her chains and fell down at Peter's feet, saying : "It is right, my lord, that you keep my deliverance-feast here to-day, and not sadden me or my parents." But when Peter asked what was the meaning of her chains and of her words, her parents, gladdened beyond hope by the recovery of their daughter, were, as it were, thunderstruck with astonishment, and could not speak ; but the servants who were in attendance said : "This girl has been possessed of a demon from her seventh year, and used to cut, and bite, and even to tear in pieces, all who attempted to approach her, and this she has never ceased to do for twenty years till the present time. Nor could any one cure her, or even approach her, for she rendered many helpless, and even destroyed some ; for she was stronger than any man, being doubtless strengthened by the power of the demon. But now, as you see, the demon has fled from your presence, and the doors which were shut with the greatest strength have been opened, and she herself stands before you in her sound mind, asking of you to make the day of her recovery gladsome both to herself and her parents, and to remain with them." When one of the servants had made this statement, and the chains of their own accord were loosened from her hands and feet, Peter, being sure that it was by his means that soundness was restored to the girl, consented to remain with them.   And he ordered those also who had remained in the lodging, with his wife, to come over ; and every one of us having got a separate bed-chamber, we remained ; and having taken food in the usual manner, and given praises to God, we went to sleep in our several apartments.

RECOGNITIONS OF CLEMENT.

BOOK X.

Chap. i.—*Probation.*

UT in the morning, after sunrise, I Clement, and Niceta and Aquila, along with Peter, came to the apartment in which my father and mother were sleeping; and finding them still asleep, we sat down before the door, when Peter addressed us in such terms as these: "Listen to me, most beloved fellow-servants: I know that you have a great affection for your father; therefore I am afraid that you will urge him too soon to take upon himself the yoke of religion, while he is not yet prepared for it; and to this he may perhaps consent, through his affection for you. But this is not to be depended on; for what is done for the sake of men is not worthy of approbation, and soon falls to pieces. Therefore it seems to me, that you should permit him to live for a year according to his own judgment; and during that time he may travel with us, and while we are instructing others he may hear with simplicity; and as he hears, if he has any right purpose of acknowledging the truth, he will himself request that he may take up the yoke of religion; or if he do not please to take it, he may remain a friend. For those who do not take it up heartily, when they begin not to be able to bear it, not only cast off that which they had taken up, but by way of excuse, as it were, for their weakness, they begin to speak evil of the way of religion, and to malign those whom they have not been able to follow or to imitate."

Chap. ii.—*A difficulty.*

To this Niceta answered: "My lord Peter, I say nothing against your right and good counsels; but I wish to say one thing, that thereby I may learn something that I do not know. What if my father should die within the year during which you recommend that he should be put off? He will go down to hell helpless, and so be tormented for ever." Then said Peter: "I embrace your kindly purpose towards your father, and I forgive you in respect of things of which you are ignorant. For do you suppose that, if any one is thought to have lived righteously, he shall forthwith be saved? Do you not think that he must be examined by Him who knows the secrets of men, as to how he has lived righteously, whether perchance according to the rule of the Gentiles, obeying their institutions and laws; or for the sake of the friendship of men; or merely from custom, or any other cause; or from necessity, and not on account of righteousness itself, and for the sake of God? For those who have lived righteously, for the sake of God alone and His righteousness, they shall come to eternal rest, and shall receive the perpetuity of the heavenly kingdom. For salvation is not attained by force, but by liberty; and not through the favour of men, but by the faith of God. Then, besides, you ought to consider that God is prescient, and knows whether this man is one of His. But if He knows that he is not, what shall we do with respect to those things which have been determined by Him from the beginning? But wherein I can, I give counsel: when he is awake, and we sit down together, then do you, as if you wished to learn something, ask a question about those matters which it is fitting for him to learn; and while we speak to one another, he will gain instruction. But yet wait first to see if he himself ask anything; for if he do so, the occasion of discourse will be the fitter. But if he do not ask anything, let us by turns put questions to one another, wishing to learn something, as I have said. Such is my judgment, state what is yours."

Chap. III.—*A suggestion.*

And when we had commended his right counsel, I Clement said: "In all things, the end for the most part looks back upon the beginning, and the issue of things is similar to their commencement. I hope, therefore, with respect to our father also, since God by your means has given a good beginning, that He will bestow also an ending suitable to the beginning, and worthy of Himself. However, I make this suggestion, that if, as you have said, we begin to speak, in presence of my father, as if for the purpose of discussing some subject, or learning something from one another, you, my lord Peter, ought not to occupy the place of one who has anything to learn; for if he see this, he will rather be offended. For he is convinced that you fully know all things, as indeed you do. How then will it be, if he see you pretending ignorance? This, as I have said, will rather hurt him, being ignorant of your design. But if we brothers, while we converse among ourselves, are in any doubt, let a fitting solution be given by you to our inquiry. For if he see even you hesitating and doubting, then truly he will think that no one has knowledge of the truth."

Chap. IV.—*Free inquiry.*

To this Peter answered: "Let us not concern ourselves about this; and if indeed it is fitting that he enter the gate of life, God will afford a fitting opportunity; and there shall be a beginning from God, and not from man. And therefore, as I have said, let him journey with us, and hear our discussions; but because I saw you in haste, therefore I said that opportunity must be sought; and when God shall give it, do you comply with my advice in what I shall say." While we were thus talking, a boy came to tell us that our father was now awake; and when we were intending to go in to him, he himself came to us, and saluting us with a kiss, after we had sat down again, he said: "Is it permitted to one to ask a question, if he wishes it; or is silence enforced, after the manner of the Pythagoreans?" Then said Peter: "We do not compel those who come to us either to keep silence continually, or to ask questions; but we leave them free to do as they will, knowing that he who is anxious about his salvation, if he feels pain in any part of his soul, does not suffer it to be silent. But he who neglects his salvation, no advantage is conferred upon him if he is compelled to ask, excepting this only, that he may seem to be earnest and diligent. Wherefore, if you wish to get any information, ask on."

Chap. v.—*Good and evil.*

Then the old man said : "There is a saying very prevalent among the Greek philosophers, to the effect that there is in reality neither good nor evil in the life of man; but that men call things good or evil as they appear to them, prejudiced by the use and custom of life. For not even murder is really an evil, because it sets the soul free from the bonds of the flesh. Further, they say that even just judges put to death those who commit crimes; but if they knew homicide to be an evil, just men would not do that. Neither do they say that adultery is an evil; for if the husband does not know, or does not care, there is, they say, no evil in it. But neither, say they, is theft an evil; for it takes away what one does not possess from another who has it. And, indeed, it ought to be taken freely and openly; but in that it is done secretly, that is rather a reproof of his inhumanity from whom it is secretly taken. For all men ought to have the common use of all things that are in this world; but through injustice one says that this is his, and another that that is his, and so division is caused among men. In short, a certain man, the wisest among the Greeks,[1] knowing that these things are so, says that friends should have all things common. Now, in *all things* unquestionably wives are included. He says also that, as the air and the sunshine cannot be divided, so neither ought other things to be divided, which are given in this world to all to be possessed in common, but should be so possessed. But I wished to say this, because I am desirous to turn to well-

---

[1] Allusion is made to Socrates and community of wives, as stated in the *Republic* of Plato.

doing, and I cannot act well unless I first learn what is good; and if I can understand that, I shall thereby perceive what is evil, that is, opposite to good.

CHAP. VI.—*Peter's authority.*

"But I should like that one of you, and not Peter, should answer what I have said; for it is not fitting to take words and instruction at his hand, with questions; but when he gives a deliverance on any subject, that should be held without answering again. And therefore let us keep him as an umpire; so that if at any time our discussion does not come to an issue, he may declare what seems good to him, and so give an undoubted end to doubtful matters. And now therefore I could believe, content with his sole opinion, if he expressed any opinion; and this is what I shall do at last. Yet I wish first to see if it is possible by discussion to find what is sought. My wish therefore is, that Clement should begin first, and should show if there is any good or evil in substance or in actions."

CHAP. VII.—*Clement's argument.*

To this I answered: " Since indeed you wish to learn from me if there is any good or evil in nature or in act, or whether it is not rather that men, prejudiced by custom, think some things to be good, and others to be evil, forasmuch as they have made a division among themselves of common things, which ought, as you say, to be as common as the air and the sunshine; I think that I ought not to bring before you any statements from any other quarter than from those studies in which you are well versed, and which you support, so that what I say you will receive without hesitation. You assign certain boundaries of all the elements and the heavenly bodies, and these, you say, meet in some without hurt, as in marriages; but in others they are hurtfully united, as in adulteries. And you say that some things are general to all, but other things do not belong to all, and are not general. But not to make a long discussion, I shall speak briefly of the matter. The earth which is dry is in need of the addition and admixture of water, that it may be able to produce fruits, without which man cannot live : this is therefore a legitimate conjunction. On the contrary, if the cold of hoar-frost be mixed with the earth, or heat with the water, a conjunction of this sort produces corruption ; and this, in such things, is adultery."

CHAP. VIII.—*Admitted evils.*

Then my father answered : " But as the harmfulness of an inharmonious conjunction of elements or stars is immediately betrayed, so ought also adultery to be immediately shown that it is an evil." Then I : " First tell me this, whether, as you yourself have confessed, evils are produced from incongruous and inharmonious mixture ; and then after that we shall inquire into the other matter." Then my father said : " The nature of things is as you say, my son." Then I answered : " Since, then, you wish to learn of these things, see how many things there are which no one doubts to be evils. Do you not think that a fever, a fire, sedition, the fall of a house, murder, bonds, racks, pains, mournings, and such like, are evils ? " Then said my father : " It is true, my son, that these things are evil, and very evil ; or, at all events, whoever denies that they are evil, let him suffer them !"

CHAP. IX.—*Existence of evil on astrological principles.*

Then I answered : " Since, therefore, I have to deal with one who is skilled in astrological science, I shall treat the matter with you according to that science, that, taking my method from those things with which you are familiar, you may the more readily acquiesce. Listen now, therefore : you confess that those things which we have mentioned are evils, such as fevers, conflagrations, and such like. Now these, according to you, are said to be produced by malignant stars, such as the humid Saturn and the hot Mars ; but things contrary to these are produced by benignant stars, such as the temperate Jupiter and the humid Venus. Is it not so ? " My father answered : " It is so, my son ; and it cannot be otherwise." Then said I : " Since you say, therefore, that good things are produced by good stars—by Jupiter and Venus, for example—let us see what is the product where any one of the

evil stars is mixed with the good, and let us understand that
that is evil. For you lay it down that Venus makes marriages, and if she have Jupiter in her configuration she makes
the marriages chaste; but if Jupiter be not regarding, and
Mars be present, then you pronounce that the marriages
are corrupted by adultery." Then said my father: "It is
even so." Then I answered: "Therefore adultery is an evil,
seeing that it is committed through the admixture of evil
stars; and, to state it in a word, all things that you say that
the good stars suffer from the mixture of evil stars, are undoubtedly to be pronounced to be evil. Those stars, therefore,
by whose admixture we have said that fevers, conflagrations,
and other such like evils are produced,—those, according to
you, work also murders, adulteries, thefts, and also produce
haughty and stolid men."

CHAP. X.—*How to make progress.*

Then my father said: "Truly you have shown briefly
and incomparably that there are evils in actions; but still I
should wish to learn this, how God justly judges those who
sin, as you say, if *genesis* compels them to sin?" Then I
answered: "I am afraid to speak anything to you, my
father, because it becomes me to hold you in all honour;
else I have an answer to give you, if it were becoming."
Then says my father: "Speak what occurs to you, my son;
for it is not you, but the method of inquiry, that does the
wrong, as a modest woman to an incontinent man, if she is
indignant for her safety and her honour." Then I answered:
"If we do not hold by the principles that we have acknowledged and confessed, but if those things which have been
defined are always loosened by forgetfulness, we shall seem
to be weaving Penelope's web, undoing what we have done.
And therefore we ought either not to acquiesce too easily,
before we have diligently examined the doctrine propounded;
or if we have once acquiesced, and the proposition has been
agreed to, then we ought to keep by what has been once determined, that we may go on with our inquiries respecting
other matters." And my father said: "You say well, my

son ; and I know why you say this : it is because in the discussion yesterday on natural causes, you showed that some
malignant power, transferring itself into the order of the
stars, excites the lusts of men, provoking them in various
ways to sin, yet not compelling or producing sins." To this I
answered : " It is well that you remember it ; and yet, though
you do remember it, you have fallen into error." Then said
my father : " Pardon me, my son ; for I have not yet much
practice in these things : for indeed your discourses yesterday, by their truth, shut me up to agree with you ; yet in my
consciousness there are, as it were, some remains of fevers,
which for a little hold me back from faith, as from health.
For I am distracted, because I know that many things, yea,
almost all things, have befallen me according to *genesis.*"

CHAP. XI.—*Test of astrology.*

Then I answered : " I shall therefore tell you, my father,
what is the nature of mathematics, and do you act according
to what I tell you. Go to a mathematician, and tell him first
that such and such evils have befallen you at such a time, and
that you wish to learn of him whence, or how, or through
what stars they have befallen you. He will no doubt answer
you that a malignant Mars or Saturn has ruled your times,
or that some one of them has been periodic ; or that some
one has regarded you diametrically, or in conjunction, or
centrally ; or some such answer will he give, adding that in
all these some one was not in harmony with the malignant
one, or was invisible, or was in the figure, or was beyond the
division, or was eclipsed, or was not in contact, or was among
the dark stars ; and many other like things will he answer,
according to his own reasons, and will condescend upon particulars. After him go to another mathematician, and tell
him the opposite, that such and such good happened to you
at that time, mentioning to him the same time, and ask him
from what parts of your *genesis* this good has come to you,
and take care, as I said, that the times are the same with
those about which you asked concerning evils. And when
you have deceived him concerning the times, see what figures

he will invent for you, by which to show that good things ought to have befallen you at those very times. For it is impossible for those treating of the *genesis* of men not to find in every quarter, as they call it, of the heavenly bodies, some stars favourably placed, and some unfavourably; for the circle is equally complete in every part, according to mathematics, admitting of diverse and various causes, from which they can take occasion of saying whatever they please.

Chap. XII.—*Astrology baffled by free-will.*

"For, as usually happens when men see unfavourable dreams, and can make nothing certain out of them, when any event occurs, then they adapt what they saw in the dream to what has occurred; so also is mathematics. For before anything happens, nothing is declared with certainty; but after something has happened, they gather the causes of the event. And thus often, when they have been at fault, and the thing has fallen out otherwise, they take the blame to themselves, saying that it was such and such a star which opposed, and that they did not see it; not knowing that their error does not proceed from their unskilfulness in their art, but from the inconsistency of the whole system. For they do not know what those things are which we indeed desire to do, but in regard to which we do not indulge our desires. But we who have learned the reason of this mystery know the cause, since, having freedom of will, we sometimes oppose our desires, and sometimes yield to them. And therefore the issue of human doings is uncertain, because it depends upon freedom of will. For a mathematician can indeed indicate the desire which a malignant power produces; but whether the acting or the issue of this desire shall be fulfilled or not, no one can know before the accomplishment of the thing, because it depends upon freedom of will. And this is why ignorant astrologers have invented to themselves the talk about climacterics as their refuge in uncertainties, as we showed fully yesterday.

Chap. XIII.—*People admitted.*

"If you have anything that you wish to say to this, say on."

Then my father : " Nothing can be more true, my son, than what you have stated." And while we were thus speaking among ourselves, some one informed us that a great multitude of people were standing outside, having assembled for the purpose of hearing. Then Peter ordered them to be admitted, for the place was large and convenient. And when they had come in, Peter said to us : " If any one of you wishes, let him address the people, and discourse concerning idolatry." To whom I Clement answered : " Your great benignity and gentleness and patience towards all encourages us, so that we dare speak in your presence, and ask what we please ; and therefore, as I said, the gentleness of your disposition invites and encourages all to undertake the precepts of saving doctrine. This I never saw before in any one else, but in you only, with whom there is neither envy nor indignation. Or what do you think ? "

Chap. xiv.—*No man has universal knowledge.*

Then Peter said : " These things come not only from envy or indignation ; but sometimes there is a bashfulness in some persons, lest haply they may not be able to answer fully the questions that may be proposed, and so they avoid the discovery of their want of skill. But no one ought to be ashamed of this, because there is no man who ought to profess that he knows all things; for there is only One who knows all things, even He who also made all things. For if our Master declared that He knew not the day and the hour whose signs even He foretold, and referred the whole to the Father, how shall we account it disgraceful to confess that we are ignorant of some things, since in this we have the example of our Master ? But this only we profess, that we know those things which we have learned from the true Prophet ; and that those things have been delivered to us by the true Prophet, which He judged to be sufficient for human knowledge."

Chap. xv.—*Clement's discourse.*

Then I Clement went on to speak thus : " At Tripolis, when you were disputing against the Gentiles, my lord

Peter, I greatly wondered at you, that although you were instructed by your father according to the fashion of the Hebrews and in observances of your own law, and were never polluted by the studies of Greek learning, you argued so magnificently and so incomparably; and that you even touched upon some things concerning the histories of the gods, which are usually declaimed in the theatres. But as I perceived that their fables and blasphemies are not so well known to you, I shall discourse upon these in your hearing, repeating them from the very beginning, if it please you." Then says Peter: "Say on; you do well to assist my preaching." Then said I: "I shall speak, therefore, because you order me, not by way of teaching you, but of making public what foolish opinions the Gentiles entertain of the gods."

CHAP. XVI.—"*Would that all God's people were prophets.*"

But when I was about to speak, Niceta, biting his lip, beckoned to me to be silent. And when Peter saw him, he said: "Why would you repress his liberal disposition and noble nature, that you would have him be silent for my honour, which is nothing? Or do you not know, that if all nations, after they have heard from me the preaching of the truth, and have believed, would betake themselves to teaching, they would gain the greater glory for me, if indeed you think me desirous of glory? For what so glorious as to prepare disciples for Christ, not who shall be silent, and shall be saved alone, but who shall speak what they have learned, and shall do good to others? I wish indeed that both you, Niceta, and you, beloved Aquila, would aid me in preaching the word of God, and the rather because those things in which the Gentiles err are well known to you; and not you only, but all who hear me, I wish, as I have said, so to hear and to learn, that they may be able also to teach: for the world needs many helpers, by whom men may be recalled from error." When he had spoken thus, he said to me: "Go on then, Clement, with what you have begun."

Chap. xvii.—*Gentile cosmogony.*

And I immediately rejoined: " Seeing that when you were disputing at Tripolis, as I said, you discoursed much concerning the gods of the Gentiles profitably and convincingly, I desire to set forth in your presence the ridiculous legends concerning their origin, both that you may not be unacquainted with the falsehood of this vain superstition, and that the hearers who are present may know the disgraceful character of their error. The wise men, then, who are among the Gentiles, say that first of all things was chaos; that this, through a long time solidifying its outer parts, made bounds to itself and a sort of foundation, being gathered, as it were, into the manner and form of a huge egg, within which, in the course of a long time, as within the shell of the egg, there was cherished and vivified a certain animal; and that afterwards, that huge globe being broken, there came forth a certain kind of man of double sex, which they call masculo-feminine. This they called Phanetas, from appearing, because when it appeared, they say, then also light shone forth. And from this, they say that there were produced substance, prudence, motion, and coition, and from these the heavens and the earth were made. From the heaven they say that six males were produced, whom they call Titans ; and in like manner, from the earth six females, whom they called Titanides. And these are the names of the males who sprang from the heaven: Oceanus, Cœus, Crios, Hyperion, Iapetus, Chronos, who amongst us is called Saturn. In like manner, the names of the females who sprang from the earth are these: Theia, Rhea, Themis, Mnemosyne, Tethys, Hebe.

Chap. xviii.—*Family of Saturn.*

" Of all these, the first-born of the heaven took to wife the first-born of earth ; the second the second, and in like manner all the rest. The first male, therefore, who had married the first female, was on her account drawn downwards ; but the second female rose upwards, by reason of him to whom she was married ; and so each doing in their order, remained in

those places which fell to their share by the nuptial lot.
From their intercourse they assert that innumerable others
sprang. But of these six males, the one who is called Saturn
received in marriage Rhea, and having been warned by a
certain oracle that he who should be born of her should be
more powerful than himself, and should drive him from his
kingdom, he determined to devour all the sons that should
be born to him. First, then, there is born to him a son called
Aides, who amongst us is called Orcus; and him, for the
reason we have just stated, he took and devoured. After
him he begot a second son, called Neptune; and him he
devoured in like manner. Last of all, he begot him whom
they call Jupiter; but him his mother Rhea pitying, by
stratagem withdrew from his father when he was about to
devour him. And first, indeed, that the crying of the child
might not be noticed, she made certain Corybantes strike
cymbals and drums, that by the deafening sound the crying
of the infant might not be heard.

Chap. xix.—*Their destinies.*

" But when he understood from the lessening of her belly
that her child was born, he demanded it, that he might
devour it; then Rhea presented him with a large stone, and
told him that that was what she had brought forth. And
he took it, and swallowed it; and the stone, when it was
devoured, pushed and drove forth those sons whom he had
formerly swallowed. Therefore Orcus, coming forth first,
descended, and occupies the lower, that is, the infernal
regions. The second, being above him—he whom they call
Neptune—is thrust forth upon the waters. The third, who
survived by the artifice of his mother Rhea, she put upon a
she-goat and sent into heaven.

Chap. xx.—*Doings of Jupiter.*

" But enough of the old wife's fables and genealogy of the
Gentiles; for it were endless if I should set forth all the genera-
tions of those whom they call gods, and their wicked doings.
But by way of example, omitting the rest, I shall detail the

wicked deeds of him only whom they hold to be the greatest
and the chief, and whom they call Jupiter. For they say
that he possesses heaven, as being superior to the rest; and
he, as soon as he grew up, married his own sister, whom
they call Juno, in which truly he at once becomes like
a beast. Juno bears Vulcan; but, as they relate, Jupiter
was not his father. However, by Jupiter himself she became
mother of Medea; and Jupiter having received a response
that one who should be born of her should be more powerful
than himself, and should expel him from his kingdom, took
her and devoured her. Again Jupiter produced Minerva
from his brain, and Bacchus from his thigh. After this,
when he had fallen in love with Thetis, they say that Prometheus informed him that, if he lay with her, he who should
be born of her should be more powerful than his father; and
for fear of this, he gave her in marriage to one Peleus.
Subsequently he had intercourse with Persephone, who was
his own daughter by Ceres; and by her he begot Dionysius,[1]
who was torn in pieces by the Titans. But calling to mind,
it is said, that perhaps his own father Saturn might beget
another son, who might be more powerful than himself, and
might expel him from the kingdom, he went to war with
his father, along with his brothers the Titans; and having
beaten them, he at last threw his father into prison, and cut
off his genitals, and threw them into the sea. But the blood
which flowed from the wound, being mixed with the waves,
and turned into foam by the constant churning, produced
her whom they call Aphrodite, and whom with us they call
Venus. From his intercourse with her who was thus his
own sister, they say that this same Jupiter begot Cypris,
who, they say, was the mother of Cupid.

Chap. xxi.—*A black catalogue.*

"Thus much of his incests; I shall now speak of his
adulteries. He defiled Europa, the wife of Oceanus, of

---

[1] Dionysius appears here and subsequently in the text for Dionysus,
the Greek god corresponding to the Latin Bacchus. Some of the other
names are more or less corrupt forms.

whom was born Dodonæus ; Helen, the wife of Pandion,
of whom Musæus; Eurynome, the wife of Asopus, of whom
Ogygias; Hermione, the wife of Oceanus, of whom the
Graces, Thalia, Euphrosyne, Aglaia ; Themis, his own sister,
of whom the Hours, Eurynomia, Dice, Irene ; Themisto, the
daughter of Inachus, of whom Arcas : Idæa, the daughter of
Minos, of whom Asterion ; Phœnissa, the daughter of Al-
phion, of whom Endymion ; Io, the daughter of Inachus,
of whom Epaphus ; Hippodamia and Isione, daughters of
Danaus, of whom Hippodamia was the wife of Olenus, and
Isione of Orchomenus or Chryses ; Carme, the daughter of
Phœnix, of whom was born Britomartis, who was an attendant of Diana ; Callisto, the daughter of Lycaon, of whom
Orcas ; Lybee, the daughter of Munantius, of whom Belus ;
Latona, of whom Apollo and Diana ; Leandia, the daughter
of Eurymedon, of whom Coron ; Lysithea, the daughter of
Evenus, of whom Helenus ; Hippodamia, the daughter of
Bellerophon, of whom Sarpedon ; Megaclite, the daughter
of Macarius, of whom Thebe and Locrus ; Niobe, the daughter of Phoroneus, of whom Argus and Pelasgus ; Olympias,
the daughter of Neoptolemus, of whom Alexander ; Pyrrha,
the daughter of Prometheus, of whom Helmetheus ; Protogenia
and Pandora, daughters of Deucalion, of whom he begot
Æthelius, and Dorus, and Melera, and Pandorus ; Thai-
crucia, the daughter of Proteus, of whom was born Nym-
pheus ; Salamis, the daughter of Asopus, of whom Saracon ;
Taygete, Electra, Maia, Plutide, daughters of Atlas, of
whom respectively he begot Lacedæmon, Dardanus, Mercury, and Tantalus ; Phthia, the daughter of Phoroneus, of
whom he begot Achæus ; Chonia, the daughter of Aramnus,
of whom he begot Lacon ; Chalcea, a nymph, of whom was
born Olympus ; Charidia, a nymph, of whom Alcanus ;
Chloris, who was the wife of Ampycus, of whom Mopsus was
born ; Cotonia, the daughter of Lesbus, of whom Polymedes ;
Hippodamia, the daughter of Anicetus ; Chrysogenia, the
daughter of Peneus, of whom was born Thissæus.

Chap. XXII.—*Vile transformations of Jupiter.*

" There are also innumerable adulteries of his, of which no offspring was the result, which it were tedious to enumerate. But amongst those whom we have mentioned, he violated some being transformed, like a magician. In short, he seduced Antiope, the daughter of Nycteus, when turned into a satyr, and of her were born Amphion and Zethus ; Alcmene, when changed into her husband Amphitryon, and of her was born Hercules ; Ægina, the daughter of Asopus, when changed into an eagle, of whom Æacus was born. So also he defiled Ganymede, the son of Dardanus, being changed into an eagle ; Manthea, the daughter of Phocus, when changed into a bear, of whom was born Arctos ; Danaë, the daughter of Acrisius, being changed into gold, of whom Perseus ; Europa, the daughter of Phœnix, changed into a bull, of whom were born Minos, Rhadamanthus, and Sarpedon ; Eurymedusa, the daughter of Achelaus, being changed into an ant, of whom Myrmidon ; Thalia, the nymph, being changed into a vulture, of whom were born the Palisci, in Sicily ; Imandra, the daughter of Geneanus, at Rhodes, being changed into a shower ; Cassiopeia, being changed into her husband Phœnix, and of her was born Anchinos ; Leda, the daughter of Thestius, being changed into a swan, of whom was born Helen ; and again the same, being changed into a star, and of her were born Castor and Pollux ; Lamia, being changed into a lapwing ; Mnemosyne, being changed into a shepherd, of whom were born the nine Muses ; Nemesis, being changed into a goose ; the Cadmian Semele, being changed into fire, and of her was born Dionysius. By his own daughter Ceres he begot Persephone, whom also himself he defiled, being changed into a dragon.

Chap. XXIII.—*Why a god ?*

" He also committed adultery with Europa, the wife of his own uncle Oceanus, and with her sister Eurynome, and punished their father ; and he committed adultery with Plute, the daughter of his own son Atlas, and condemned Tantalus,

whom she bore to him.   Of Larisse, the daughter of Orchomenus, he begot Tityon, whom also he consigned to punishment.   He carried off Dia, the wife of his own son Ixion,
and subjected him to perpetual punishment ; and almost all
the sons who sprang from his adulteries he put to violent
deaths ; and indeed the sepulchres of almost all of them are
well known.   Yea, the sepulchre of this parricide himself,
who destroyed his uncles and defiled their wives, who committed whoredom with his sisters, this magician of many
transformations, is shown among the Cretans, who, although
they know and acknowledge his horrid and incestuous deeds,
and tell them to all, yet are not ashamed to confess him to
be a god.   Whence it seems to me to be wonderful, yea,
exceeding wonderful, how he who exceeds all men in wickedness and crimes, has received that holy and good name which
is above every name, being called the father of gods and men ;
unless perhaps he who rejoices in the evils of men has persuaded unhappy souls to confer honour above all others upon
him whom he saw to excel all others in crimes, in order that
he might allure all to the imitation of his evil deeds.

CHAP. XXIV.—*Folly of polytheism.*

" But also the sepulchres of his sons, who are regarded
amongst these [the Gentiles] as gods, are openly pointed out,
one in one place, and another in another : that of Mercury
at Hermopolis ; that of the Cyprian Venus at Cyprus ; that
of Mars in Thrace ; that of Bacchus at Thebes, where he is
said to have been torn in pieces ; that of Hercules at Tyre,
where he was burnt with fire ; that of Æsculapius in Epi-
daurus.   And all these are spoken of, not only as men who
have died, but as wicked men who have been punished for
their crimes ; and yet they are adored as gods by foolish men.

CHAP. XXV.—*Dead men deified.*

" But if they choose to argue, and affirm that these are
rather the places of their birth than of their burial or death,
the former and ancient doings shall be convicted from those
at hand and still recent, since we have shown that they wor-

ship those whom they themselves confess to have been men, and to have died, or rather to have been punished; as the Syrians worship Adonis, and the Egyptians Osiris; the Trojans, Hector; Achilles is worshipped at Leuconesus, Patroclus at Pontus, Alexander the Macedonian at Rhodes; and many others are worshipped, one in one place and another in another, whom they do not doubt to have been dead men. Whence it follows that their predecessors also, falling into a like error, conferred divine honour upon dead men, who perhaps had had some power or some skill, and especially if they had stupified stolid men by magical phantasies.

Chap. XXVI.—*Metamorphoses.*

"Hence there has now been added, that the poets also adorn the falsehoods of error by elegance of words, and by sweetness of speech persuade that mortals have been made immortal; yea more, they say that men are changed into stars, and trees, and animals, and flowers, and birds, and fountains, and rivers. And but that it might seem to be a waste of words, I could even enumerate almost all the stars, and trees, and fountains, and rivers, which they assert to have been made of men; yet, by way of example, I shall mention at least one of each class. They say that Andromeda, the daughter of Cepheus, was turned into a star; Daphne, the daughter of the river Lado, into a tree; Hyacinthus, beloved of Apollo, into a flower; Callisto into the constellation which they call Arctos; Progne and Philomela, with Tereus, into birds; that Thysbe in Cilicia was dissolved into a fountain; and Pyramus, at the same place, into a river. And they assert that almost all the stars, trees, fountains, and rivers, flowers, animals, and birds, were at one time human beings."

Chap. XXVII.—*Inconsistency of polytheists.*

But Peter, when he heard this, said: "According to them, then, before men were changed into stars, and the other things which you mention, the heaven was without stars, and the earth without trees and animals; and there were neither fountains, nor rivers, nor birds. And without these, how did those men themselves live, who afterwards were changed into them, since it is evident that, without these things, men could not live upon the earth?" Then I answered: "But they are not even able to observe the worship of their own gods consistently; for every one of those whom they worship has something dedicated to himself, from which his worshippers ought to abstain: as they say the olive is dedicated to Minerva, the she-goat to Jupiter, seeds to Ceres, wine to Bacchus,.water to Osiris, the ram to Hammon, the stag to Diana, the fish and the dove to the demon of the Syrians, fire to Vulcan; and to each one, as I have said, is there something specially consecrated, from which the worshippers are bound to abstain, for the honour of those to whom they are consecrated. But were one abstaining from one thing, and another from another, by doing honour to one of the gods, they incur the anger of all the rest; and therefore, if they would conciliate them all, they must abstain from all things for the honour of all, so that, being self-condemned by a just sentence before the day of judgment, they should perish by a most wretched death through starvation.

CHAP. XXVIII.—*Buttresses of Gentilism.*

"But let us return to our purpose. What reason is there, yea, rather, what madness possesses the minds of men, that they worship and adore as a god, a man whom they not only know to be impious, wicked, profane—I mean Jupiter—incestuous, a parricide, an adulterer, but even proclaim him publicly as such in their songs in the theatres? Or if by means of these deeds he has deserved to be a god, then also, when they hear of any murderers, adulterers, parricides, incestuous persons, they ought to worship them also as gods. But I cannot understand why they venerate in him what they execrate in others." Then Peter answered: "Since you say that you cannot understand it, learn of me why they venerate wickedness in him. In the first place, it is that, when they themselves do like deeds, they may know that they shall

be acceptable to him, inasmuch as they have but imitated him
in his wickedness.   In the second place, because the ancients
have left these things skilfully composed in their writings,
and elegantly engrafted in their verses.   And now, by the
aid of youthful education, since the knowledge of these things
adheres to their tender and simple minds, it cannot without
difficulty be torn from them and cast away."

Chap. xxix.—*Allegories.*

When Peter had said this, Niceta answered: "Do not
suppose, my lord Peter, but that the learned men of the Gentiles have certain plausible arguments, by which they support
those things which seem to be blameworthy and disgraceful.
And this I state, not as wishing to confirm their error (for
far be it from me that such a thing should ever come into
my thought); but yet I know that there are amongst the
more intelligent of them certain defences, by which they are
accustomed to support and colour over those things which
seem to be absurd.   And if it please you that I should state
some of them—for I am to some extent acquainted with them
—I shall do as you order me."   And when Peter had given
him leave, Niceta proceeded as follows.

Chap. xxx.—*Cosmogony of Orpheus.*

" All the literature among the Greeks which is written on
the subject of the origin of antiquity, is based upon many
authorities, but especially two, Orpheus and Hesiod.   Now
their writings are divided into two parts, in respect of their
meaning,—that is, the literal and the allegorical; and the
vulgar crowd has flocked to the literal, but all the eloquence of
the philosophers and learned men is expended in admiration of
the allegorical.   It is Orpheus, then, who says that at first there
was chaos, eternal, unbounded, unproduced, and that from it
all things were made.   He says that this chaos was neither
darkness nor light, neither moist nor dry, neither hot nor cold,
but that it was all things mixed together, and was always one
unformed mass; yet that at length, as it were after the
manner of a huge egg, it brought forth and produced from

itself a certain double form, which had been wrought through
immense periods of time, and which they call masculo-feminine, a form concrete from the contrary admixture of such
diversity; and that this is the principle of all things, which
came of pure matter, and which, coming forth, effected a
separation of the four elements, and made heaven of the two
elements which are first [fire and air], and earth of the others
[earth and water]; and of these he says that all things now
are born and produced by a mutual participation of them. So
far Orpheus.

Chap. xxxi.—*Hesiod's cosmogony.*

" But to this Hesiod adds, that after chaos the heaven and
the earth were made immediately, from which he says that
those eleven were produced (and sometimes also he speaks of
them as twelve) of whom he makes six males and five females.
And these are the names that he gives to the males:
Oceanus, Cœus, Crius, Hyperion, Iapetus, Chronos, who is
also called Saturn. Also the names of the females are:
Theia, Rhea, Themis, Mnemosyne, Tethys. And these names
they thus interpret allegorically. They say that the number
is eleven or twelve: that the first is nature itself, which also
they would have to be called Rhea, from *flowing;* and they
say that the other ten are her accidents, which also they call
qualities; yet they add a twelfth, namely Chronos, who with
us is called Saturn, and him they take to be time. Therefore
they assert that Saturn and Rhea are time and matter; and
these, when they are mixed with moisture and dryness, heat
and cold, produce all things.

Chap. xxxii.—*Allegorical interpretation.*

" She therefore (Rhea, or nature), it is said, produced, as it
were, a certain bubble which had been collecting for a long
time; and it being gradually collected from the spirit which
was in the waters, swelled, and being for some time driven over
the surface of matter, from which it had come forth as from
a womb, and being hardened by the rigour of cold, and always
increasing by additions of ice, at length was broken off and

sunk into the deep, and drawn by its own weight, went down
to the infernal regions; and because it became invisible it was
called Aides, and is also named Orcus or Pluto. And since
it was sunk from the top to the bottom, it gave place to the
moist element to flow together; and the grosser part, which
is the earth, was laid bare by the retirement of the waters.
They say, therefore, that this freedom of the waters, which
was formerly restrained by the presence of the bubble, was
called Neptune after the bubble attained the lowest place.
After this, when the cold element had been sucked down to
the lower regions by the concretion of the icy bubble, and the
dry and the moist element had been separated, there being
now no hindrance, the warm element rushed by its force and
lightness to the upper regions of the air, being borne up by
wind and storm. This storm, therefore, which in Greek is
called καταιγίς, they called *ægis*—that is, a she-goat; and the
fire which ascended to the upper regions they called Jupiter;
wherefore they say that he ascended to Olympus riding on a
she-goat.

CHAP. XXXIII.—*Allegory of Jupiter, etc.*

" Now this Jupiter the Greeks would have to be called
from his living, or giving life, but our people from his giving
succour. They say, therefore, that this is the living substance, which, placed in the upper regions, and drawing all
things to itself by the influence of heat, as by the convolution
of the brain, and arranging them by the moderation of a
certain tempering, is said from his head to have produced
wisdom, whom they call Minerva, who was called ʼΑθήνη by
the Greeks on account of her immortality; who, because the
father of all created all things by his wisdom, is also said to
have been produced from his head, and from the principal
place of all, and is represented as having formed and adorned
the whole world by the regulated admixture of the elements.
Therefore the forms which were impressed upon matter, that
the world might be made, because they are constrained by
the force of heat, are said to be held together by the energy
of Jupiter. And since there are enough of these, and they

do not need anything new to be added to them, but each
thing is repaired by the produce of its own seed, the hands
of Saturn are said to be bound by Jupiter; because, as I
have said, time now produces from matter nothing new: but
the warmth of seeds restores all things according to their
kinds; and no birth of Rhea—that is, no increase of flowing
matter—ascends further. And therefore they call that first
division of the elements the mutilation of Saturn, because he
cannot any more produce a world.

Chap. xxxiv.—*Other allegories.*

"And of Venus they give forth an allegory to this effect.
When, say they, the sea was put under the air, and when
the brightness of the heavens shone more pleasantly, being
reflected from the waters, the loveliness of things, which
appeared fairer from the waters, was called Venus; and she
[it] being united with the air as with her [its] own brother,
so as to produce beauty, which might be the object of
desire, is said to have given birth to Cupid. In this way,
therefore, as we have said, they teach that Chronos, who is
Saturn, is allegorically time; Rhea is matter; Aides—that is,
Orcus—is the depth of the infernal regions; Neptune is water;
Jupiter is air—that is, the element of heat; Venus is the
loveliness of things; Cupid is desire, which is in all things, and
by which posterity is propagated, or even the reason of things,
which gives delight when wisely looked into. Hera—that is,
Juno—is said to be that middle air which descends from
heaven to earth. To Diana, whom they call Proserpine, they
hand over the air below. They say that Apollo is the Sun
himself, which goes round the heaven; that Mercury is
speech, by which a reason is rendered for everything; that
Mars is unrestrained fire, which consumes all things. But
not to delay you by enumerating everything, those who have
the more abstruse intelligence concerning such things think
that they give fair and just reasons, by applying this sort of
allegory to every one of their objects of worship."

Chap. xxxv.—*Uselessness of these allegories.*

When Niceta had thus spoken, Aquila answered : "Whoever he was that was the author and inventor of these things, he seems to me to have been very impious, since he covered over those things which seem to be pleasant and seemly, and made the ritual of his superstition to consist in base and shameful observances, since those things which are written according to the letter are manifestly unseemly and base ; and the whole observance of their religion consists in these, that by such crimes and impieties they may teach men to imitate their gods whom they worship. For in these allegories what profit can there be to them ? For although they are framed so as to be decent, yet no use is derived from them for worship, nor for amendment of morals.

Chap. xxxvi.—*The allegories an after-thought.*

" Whence it is the more evident that prudent men, when they saw that the common superstition was so disgraceful, so base, and yet they had not learned any way of correcting it, or any knowledge, endeavoured with what arguments and interpretations they could to veil unseemly things under seemly speech, and not, as they say, to conceal seemly reasons under unseemly fables. For if this were the case, surely their statues and their pictures would never be made with [representations of] their vices and crimes. The swan, which committed adultery with Leda, would not be represented, nor the bull which committed adultery with Europa ; nor would they turn into a thousand monstrous shapes, him whom they think better than all. And assuredly, if the great and wise men who are amongst them knew that all this is fiction and not truth, would not they charge with impiety and sacrilege those who should exhibit a picture or carve an image of this sort, to the injury of the gods ? In short, let them present a king of their own time in the form of an ox, or a goose, or an ant, or a vulture, and let them write the name of their king upon it, and set up such a statue or figure in a public place, and they will soon be made to feel the wrong of their deed, and the greatness of its punishment.

CHAP. XXXVII.—*Like gods, like worshippers.*

"But since those things rather are true which the public baseness testifies, and concealments have been sought and fabricated by prudent men to excuse them by seemly speeches, therefore are they not only not prohibited, but even in the very mysteries figures are produced of Saturn devouring his sons, and of the boy hidden by the cymbals and drums of the Corybantes; and with respect to the mutilation of Saturn, what better proof of its truth could there be, than that even his worshippers are mutilated, by a like miserable fate, in honour of their god? Since then these things are manifestly seen, who shall be found of so little sense, yea, of such stolidity, that he does not perceive that those things are true concerning the unfortunate gods, which their more unfortunate worshippers attest by the wounding and mutilation of their bodies?

CHAP. XXXVIII.—*Writings of the poets.*

"But if, as they say, these things, so creditably and piously done, are dispensed by so discreditable and impious a ritual, assuredly he is sacrilegious, whoever either gave forth these things at first, or persists in fulfilling them, now that they have unhappily been given forth. And what shall we say of the books of the poets? Ought not they, if they have debased the honourable and pious deeds of the gods with base fables, to be forthwith cast away and thrown into the fire, that they may not persuade the still tender age of boys that Jupiter himself, the chief of the gods, was a parricide towards his parents, incestuous towards his sisters and his daughters, and even impure towards boys; that Venus and Mars were adulterers, and all those things which have been spoken of above? What do you think of this matter, my lord Peter?"

CHAP. XXXIX.—*All for the best.*

Then he answered: "Be sure, beloved Aquila, that all things are done by the good providence of God, that the cause which was to be contrary to the truth should not only be infirm and weak, but also base.   For if the assertion of error had been stronger and more truth-like, any one who had been deceived by it would not easily return to the path of truth. If even now, when so many wicked and disgraceful things are related concerning the gods of the Gentiles, scarce any one forsakes the base error, how much more if there had been in it anything seemly and truth-like?   For the mind is with difficulty transferred from those things with which it has been imbued in early youth ; and on this account, as I said, it has been effected by divine providence, that the substance of error should be both weak and base.   But all other things also divine providence dispenses fitly and advantageously, although the method of the divine dispensation, as good, and the best possible, is not clear to us who are ignorant of the causes of things."

Chap. xl.—*Further information sought.*

When Peter had thus said, I Clement asked Niceta that he would explain to us, for the sake of instruction, some things concerning the allegories of the Gentiles, which he had carefully studied; "for," said I, "it is useful that when we dispute with the Gentiles, we should not be unacquainted with these things."   Then said Niceta : "If my lord Peter permits me, I can do as you ask me."   Then said Peter : "To-day I have given you leave to speak in opposition to the Gentiles, as you know."   And Niceta said : "Tell me then, Clement, what you would have me speak about."   And I said to him : "Inform us how the Gentiles represent matters concerning the supper of the gods, which they had at the marriage of Peleus and Thetis.   What do they make of the shepherd Paris, and what of Juno, Minerva, and Venus, between whom he acted as judge?   What of Mercury? and what of the apple, and the other things which follow in order?"

Chap. xli.—*Explanation of mythology.*

Then Niceta : "The affair of the supper of the gods stands in this wise.   They say that the banquet is the world, that the order of the gods sitting at table is the position of the heavenly bodies. Those whom Hesiod calls the first children of heaven and earth, of whom six were males and six females, they refer to the number of the twelve signs, which go round all the world. They say that the dishes of the banquet are the reasons and causes of things, sweet and desirable, which in the shape of inferences from the positions of the signs and the courses of the stars, explain how the world is ruled and governed. Yet they say that these things exist after the free manner of a banquet, inasmuch as the mind of every one has the option whether he shall taste aught of this sort of knowledge, or whether he shall refrain; and as in a banquet no one is compelled, but every one is at liberty to eat, so also the manner of philosophizing depends upon the choice of the will. They say that discord is the lust of the flesh, which rises up against the purpose of the mind, and hinders the desire of philosophizing; and therefore they say that the time was that in which the marriage was celebrated. Thus they make Peleus and the nymph Thetis to be the dry and the moist element, by the admixture of which the substance of bodies is composed. They hold that Mercury is speech, by which instruction is conveyed to the mind; that Juno is chastity, Minerva courage, Venus lust, Paris the understanding. If therefore, say they, it happens that there is in a man a barbarous and uncultivated understanding, and ignorant of right judgment, he will despise chastity and courage, and will give the prize, which is the apple, to lust; and thereby ruin and destruction will come not only upon himself, but also upon his countrymen and the whole race. These things, therefore, it is in their power to compose from whatever matter they please; yet they can be adapted to every man; because if any one has a pastoral and rustic and uncultivated understanding, and does not wish to be instructed, when the heat of his body shall make suggestions concerning the pleasure of lust, straightway he despises the virtues of studies and the blessings of knowledge, and turns his mind to bodily pleasures. And hence it is that implacable wars arise, cities are destroyed, countries fall, even as Paris, by the abduction of Helen, armed the Greeks and the barbarians to their mutual destruction."

CHAP. XLII.—*Interpretation of Scripture.*

Then Peter, commending his statement, said : " Ingenious men, as I perceive, take many verisimilitudes from the things which they read ; and therefore great care is to be taken, that when the law of God is read, it be not read according to the understanding of our own mind. For there are many sayings in the divine Scriptures which can be drawn to that sense which every one has preconceived for himself; and this ought not to be done. For you ought not to seek a foreign and extraneous sense, which you have brought from without, which you may confirm from the authority of the Scriptures, but to take the sense of truth from the Scriptures themselves ; and therefore it behoves you to learn the meaning of the Scriptures from him who keeps it according to the truth handed down to him from his fathers, so that he can authoritatively declare what he has rightly received. But when one has received an entire and firm rule of truth from the Scriptures, it will not be improper if he contribute to the establishment of true doctrine anything from common education and from liberal studies, which, it may be, he has attached himself to in his boyhood ; yet so that, when he has learned the truth, he renounce falsehood and pretence."

CHAP. XLIII.—*A word of exhortation.*

And when he had said this, he looked to our father, and said : " You therefore, old man, if indeed you care for your soul's safety, that when you desire it to be separated from the body, it may, in consequence of this short conversion, find eternal rest, ask about whatever you please, and seek counsel, that you may be able to cast off any doubt that remains in you. For even to young men the time of life is uncertain ; but to old men it is not even uncertain, for there is no doubt that there is but little time remaining to them. And therefore both young and old ought to be very earnest about their conversion and repentance, and to be

taken up with the adornment of their souls for the future
with the worthiest ornaments, such as the doctrines of truth,
the grace of chastity, the splendour of righteousness, the
fairness of piety, and all other things with which it becomes
a reasonable mind to be adorned.   Then, besides, they should
break off from unseemly and unbelieving companions, and
keep company with the faithful, and frequent those assemblies
in which subjects are handled relating to chastity, righteousness, and piety; to pray to God always heartily, and to ask
of Him those things which ought to be asked of God; to
give thanks to Him ; to repent truly of their past doings ; in
some measure also, if possible, by deeds of mercy towards the
poor, to help their penitence : for by these means pardon will
be more easily bestowed, and mercy will be sooner shown to
the merciful.

Chap. XLIV.—*Earnestness.*

" But if he who comes to repentance is of more advanced
age, he ought the more to give thanks to God, because,
having received the knowledge of the truth, after all the
violence of carnal lust has been broken, there awaits him no
fight of contest, by which to repress the pleasures of the
body rising against the mind.   It remains, therefore, that he
be exercised in the learning of the truth, and in works of
mercy, that he may bring forth fruits worthy of repentance ;
and that he do not suppose that the proof of conversion is
shown by length of time, but by strength of devotion and of
purpose.   For minds are manifest to God ; and He does not
take account of times, but of hearts.   For He approves if
any one, on hearing the preaching of the truth, does not
delay, nor spend time in negligence, but immediately, and
if I may say so, in the same moment, abhorring the past,
begins to desire things to come, and burns with love of the
heavenly kingdom.

Chap. XLV.—*All ought to repent.*

" Wherefore, let no one of you longer dissemble nor look
backwards, but willingly approach to the gospel of the king-

dom of God. Let not the poor man say, When I shall become rich, then I shall be converted. God does not ask money of you, but a merciful heart and a pious mind. Nor let the rich man delay his conversion by reason of worldly care, while he thinks how he may dispose the abundance of his fruits ; nor say within himself, 'What shall I do ? where shall I bestow my fruits ?' Nor say to his soul, 'Thou hast much goods laid up for many years ; feast and rejoice.' For it shall be said to him, 'Thou fool, this night thy soul shall be taken from thee, and whose shall those things be which thou hast provided ?'[1] Therefore let every age, every sex, every condition, haste to repentance, that they may obtain eternal life. Let the young be thankful that they put their necks under the yoke of discipline in the very violence of their desires. The old also are themselves praiseworthy, because they change for the fear of God, the custom of a long time in which they have been unhappily occupied.

Chap. XLVI.—*The sure word of prophecy.*

"Let no one therefore put off. Let no one delay. For what occasion is there for delaying to do well? Or are you afraid, lest, when you have done well, you do not find the reward as you supposed? And what loss will you sustain if you do well without reward? Would not conscience alone be sufficient in this? But if you find as you anticipate, shall you not receive great things for small, and eternal for temporal? But I say this for the sake of the unbelieving. For the things which we preach are as we preach them ; because they cannot be otherwise, since they have been promised by the prophetic word.

Chap. XLVII.—"*A faithful saying, and worthy of all acceptation.*"

"But if any one desires to learn exactly the truth of our preaching, let him come to hear, and let him ascertain what the true Prophet is ; and then at length all doubtfulness will cease in him, unless with obstinate mind he resist those things

[1] Luke xii. 17, 19, 20.

which he finds to be true. For there are some whose only object it is to gain the victory in any way whatever, and who seek praise for this rather than their salvation. These ought not to have a single word addressed to them, lest both the noble word suffer injury, and condemn to eternal death him who is guilty of the wrong done to it. For what is there in respect of which any one ought to oppose our preaching? or in respect of which the word of our preaching is found to be contrary to the belief of what is true and honourable? It says that the God the Father, the Creator of all, is to be honoured, as also His Son, who alone knows Him and His will, and who alone is to be believed concerning all things which He has enjoined. For He alone is the law and the Lawgiver, and the righteous Judge, whose law decrees that God, the Lord of all, is to be honoured by a sober, chaste, just, and merciful life, and that all hope is to be placed in Him alone.

Chap. xlviii.—*Errors of the philosophers.*

" But some one will say that precepts of this sort are given by the philosophers also. Nothing of the kind : for they do indeed give commandments concerning justice and sobriety, but they are ignorant that God is the recompenser of good and evil deeds; and therefore their laws and precepts only shun a public accuser, but cannot purify the conscience. For why should one fear to sin in secret, who does not know that there is a witness and a judge of secret things? Besides, the philosophers in their precepts add that even the gods, who are demons, are to be honoured; and this alone, even if in other respects they seemed worthy of approbation, is sufficient to convict them of the most dreadful impiety, and condemn them by their own sentence, since they declare indeed that there is one God, yet command that many be worshipped, by way of humouring human error. But also the philosophers say that God is not angry, not knowing what they say. For anger is evil, when it disturbs the mind, so that it loses right counsel. But that anger which punishes the wicked does not bring disturbance to the mind; but it is one and the same affection, so to speak, which assigned rewards to the good and punishment to the evil; for if He should bestow blessings upon the good and the evil, and confer equal rewards upon the pious and the impious, He would appear to be unjust rather than good.

Chap. xlix.—*God's long-suffering.*

"But you say, Neither ought God to do evil. You say truly; nor does He. But those who have been created by Him, while they do not believe that they are to be judged, indulging their pleasures, have fallen away from piety and righteousness. But you will say, If it is right to punish the wicked, they ought to be punished immediately when they do wickedly. You indeed do well to make haste; but He who is eternal, and from whom nothing is secret, inasmuch as He is without end, in the same proportion is His patience extended, and He regards not the swiftness of vengeance, but the causes of salvation. For He is not so much pleased with the death as with the conversion of a sinner.[1] Therefore, in short, He has bestowed upon men holy baptism, to which, if any one makes haste to come, and for the future remains without stain, all his sins are thenceforth blotted out, which were committed in the time of his ignorance.

Chap. l.—*Philosophers not benefactors of men.*

"For what have the philosophers contributed to the life of man, by saying that God is not angry with men? Only to teach them to have no fear of any punishment or judgment, and thereby to take away all restraint from sinners. Or what have they benefited the human race, who have said that there is no God, but that all things happen by chance and accident? What but that men, hearing this, and thinking that there is no judge, no guardian of things, are driven headlong, without fear of any one, to every deed which either rage, or avarice, or lust may dictate. For they truly have much benefited the life of man who have said that nothing can be done apart from *genesis;* that is, that every one,

[1] Ezek. xviii. 33.

ascribing the cause of his sin to *genesis*, might in the midst of his crimes declare himself innocent, while he does not wash out his guilt by repentance, but doubles it by laying the blame upon fate. And what shall I say of those philosophers who have maintained that the gods are to be worshipped, and such gods as were described to you a little while ago? What else was this but to decree that vices, crimes, and base deeds should be worshipped? I am ashamed of you, and I pity you, if you have not yet discovered that these things were unworthy of belief, and impious, and execrable, or if, having discovered and ascertained them to be evil, ye have nevertheless worshipped them as if they were good, yea, even the best.

CHAP. LI.—*Christ the true Prophet.*

"Then, besides, of what sort is that which some of the philosophers have presumed to speak even concerning God, though they are mortal, and can only speak by opinion concerning invisible things, or concerning the origin of the world, since they were not present when it was made, or concerning the end of it, or concerning the treatment and judgment of souls in the infernal regions, forgetting that it belongs indeed to a reasonable man to know things present and visible, but that it is the part of prophetic prescience alone to know things past, and things future, and things invisible? These things, therefore, are not to be gathered from conjectures and opinions, in which men are greatly deceived, but from faith in prophetic truth, as this doctrine of ours is. For we speak nothing of ourselves, nor announce things gathered by human judgment; for this were to deceive our hearers. But we preach the things which have been committed and revealed to us by the true Prophet. And concerning His prophetic prescience and power, if any one, as I have said, wishes to receive clear proofs, let him come instantly and be alert to hear, and we shall give evident proofs by which he shall seem not only to hear the power of prophetic prescience with his ears, but even to see it with his eyes and handle it with his hand; and when he has entertained a sure faith concerning Him, he will without any labour take upon him the yoke of righteousness and piety;[1] and so great sweetness will he perceive in it, that not only will he not find fault with any labour being in it, but will even desire something further to be added and imposed upon him."

Chap. lii.—*Appion and Anubion.*

And when he had said this, and more to the same purpose, and had cured some who were present who were infirm and possessed of demons, he dismissed the crowds, while they gave thanks and praised God, charging them to come to the same place on the following days also for the sake of hearing. And when we were together at home, and were preparing to eat, one entering told us that Appion Pleistonices,[1] with Anubion, were lately come from Antioch, and were lodging with Simon. Then my father, when he heard this, rejoiced, and said to Peter: "If you permit me, I should like to go and salute Appion and Anubion, for they are great friends of mine; and perhaps I shall be able to persuade Anubion to dispute with Clement on the subject of *genesis*." Then Peter said: "I consent; and I commend you, because you respect your friends. But consider how all things occur to you according to your wish by God's providence; for, behold, not only have [the objects of] proper affection been restored to you by the appointment of God, but also the presence of your friends is arranged for you." Then said my father: "Truly I consider that it is so as you say." And when he had said this, he went away to Anubion.

Chap. liii.—*A transformation.*

But we, sitting with Peter the whole night, asking questions, and learning of him on many subjects, remained awake through very delight in his teaching and the sweetness of

---

[1] Matt. xi. 30.

[2] The name is generally written Apion. The meaning of Pleistonices is doubtful, some supposing that it indicates his birthplace, some his father; but generally it is taken as an epithet, and it will then refer to his frequent victories in literary contests.

his words; and when it was daybreak, Peter, looking at me and my brothers, said: "I wonder what has befallen your father." And while he was speaking my father came in, and found Peter speaking to us about him. And when he had saluted he began to apologize, and to explain the reason why he had remained abroad. But we, looking at him, were horrified; for we saw on him the face of Simon, yet we heard the voice of our father. And when we shrank from him, and cursed him, my father was astonished at our treating him so harshly and barbarously. Yet Peter was the only one who saw his natural countenance; and he said to us: "Why do you curse your father?" And we, along with our mother, answered him: "He appears to us to be Simon, though he has our father's voice." Then Peter: "You indeed know only his voice, which has not been changed by the sorceries; but to me also his face, which to others appears changed by Simon's art, is known to be that of your father Faustinianus." And looking at my father, he said: "The cause of the dismay of your wife and your sons is this,—the appearance of your countenance does not seem to be as it was, but the face of the detestable Simon appears in you."

Chap. liv.—*Excitement in Antioch.*

And while he was thus speaking, one of those returned who had gone before to Antioch, and said to Peter: "I wish you to know, my lord Peter, that Simon at Antioch, doing many signs and prodigies in public, has inculcated upon the people nothing but what tends to excite hatred against you, calling you a magician, a sorcerer, a murderer; and to such an extent has he stirred up hatred against you, that they greatly desire, if they can find you anywhere, even to devour your flesh. And therefore we who were sent before, seeing the city greatly moved against you, met together in secret, and considered what ought to be done.

Chap. lv.—*A stratagem.*

"And when we saw no way of getting out of the difficulty, there came Cornelius the centurion, being sent by Cæsar to

the president of Cæsarea on public business. Him we sent
for alone, and told him the reason why we were sorrowful, and
entreated him that, if he could do anything, he should help
us. Then he most readily promised that he would straightway
put him to flight, if only we would aid his plans. And when
we promised that we would be active in doing everything,
he said, ' Cæsar has ordered sorcerers to be sought out and
destroyed in the city of Rome and through the provinces,
and a great number of them have been already destroyed.
I shall therefore give out, through my friends, that I am
come to apprehend that magician, and that I am sent by
Cæsar for this purpose, that he may be punished with the
rest of his fraternity. Let your people, therefore, who are
with him in disguise, intimate to him, as if they had heard it
from some quarter, that I am sent to apprehend him; and
when he hears this, he is sure to take to flight. Or if you
think of anything better, tell me. Why need I say more?'
It was so done by those of ours who were with him, disguised
for the purpose of acting as spies on him. And when Simon
learned that this was come upon him, he received the information as a great kindness conferred upon him by them, and
took to flight. He therefore departed from Antioch, and, as
we have heard, came hither with Athenodorus.

Chap. LVI.—*Simon's design in the transformation.*

" All we, therefore, who went before you, considered that
in the meantime you should not go up to Antioch, till we see
if the hatred of you which he has sown among the people be
in any degree lessened by his departure." When he who had
come from Antioch had imparted this information, Peter,
looking to our father, said, " Faustinianus, your countenance
has been transformed by Simon Magus, as is evident; for
he, thinking that he was being sought for by Cæsar for
punishment, has fled in terror, and has placed his own
countenance upon you, if haply you might be apprehended
instead of him, and put to death, that so he might cause
sorrow to your sons." But my father, when he heard this,
crying out, said with tears: " You have judged rightly, O

Peter: for Anubion also, who is very friendly with me, began to inform me in a certain mysterious way of his plots; but unhappily I did not believe him, because I had done him no harm."

Chap. LVII.—*Great grief.*

And when all of us, along with my father, were agitated with sorrow and weeping, meantime Anubion came to us, intimating to us that Simon had fled during the night, making for Judæa. But seeing our father lamenting and bewailing himself, and saying, "Wretch that I am, not to believe when I heard that he is a magician! What has befallen wretched me, that on one day, being recognised by my wife and my sons, I have not been able to rejoice with them, but have been rolled back to the former miseries which I endured in my wandering!"—but my mother, tearing her dishevelled hair, bewailed much more bitterly,—we also, confounded at the change of our father's countenance, were, as it were, thunder-struck and beside ourselves, and could not understand what was the matter. But Anubion, seeing us all thus afflicted, stood like one dumb. Then Peter, looking at us his sons, said: "Believe me that this is your very father; wherefore also I charge you that you respect him as your father. For God will afford some opportunity on which he shall be able to put off the countenance of Simon, and to recover the manifest figure of your father—that is, his own."

Chap. LVIII.—*How it all happened.*

Then, turning to my father, he said: "I gave you leave to salute Appion and Anubion, who, you said, were your friends from boyhood, but not that you should speak with Simon." Then my father said: "I confess I have sinned." Then said Anubion: "I also with him beg and entreat of you to pardon the old man—good and noble man as he is. He was unhappily seduced and imposed upon by the magician in question; for I will tell you how the thing was done. When he came to salute us, it happened that at that very time we were standing around him, hearing him tell that he

intended to flee away that night, for that he had heard that
some persons had come even to this city of Laodicea to
apprehend him by command of the emperor, but that he
wished to turn all their rage against this Faustinianus, who
has lately come hither. And he said to us : ' Only you make
him sup with us, and I shall compound a certain ointment,
with which, when he has supped, he shall anoint his face,
and from that time he shall seem to all to have my countenance. But you first anoint your faces with the juice of a
certain herb, that you may not be deceived as to the change
of his countenance, so that to all except you he shall seem
to be Simon.'

CHAP. LIX.—*A scene of mourning.*

" And when he said this, I said to him, ' And what advantage will you gain from this deed ?' Then Simon said : ' In
the first place, that those who are seeking me may lay hold
on him, and so give over the search for me. But if he be
punished by Cæsar, that his sons may have much sorrow,
who forsook me, and fled to Peter, and are now his assistants.'
Now I confess to you, Peter, what is true. I did not dare
then tell Faustinianus; but neither did Simon give us opportunity of speaking with him in private, and disclosing to
him fully Simon's design. Meantime, about the middle of
the night, Simon has fled away, making for Judæa. And
Athenodorus and Appion have gone to convoy him ; but I
pretended bodily indisposition, that I might remain at home,
and make him return quickly to you, if haply he may in any
way be concealed with you, lest, being seized by those who
are in quest of Simon, he be brought before Cæsar, and
perish without cause. And now, in my anxiety about him, I
have come to see him, and to return before those who have
gone to convoy Simon come back." And turning to us,
Anubion said : "I, Anubion, indeed see the true countenance
of your father, because I was previously anointed by Simon
himself, as I have told you, that the real face of Faustinianus
might appear to my eyes; whence I am astonished and
wonder at the art of Simon Magus, because you standing

here do not recognise your father." And while my father and mother, and all of us, wept for the things which had befallen, Anubion, moved with compassion, also wept.

Chap. lx.—*A counterplot.*

Then Peter, moved with compassion, promised that he would restore the face of our father, saying to him: "Listen, Faustinianus: As soon as the error of your transformed countenance shall have conferred some advantage on us, and shall have subserved the designs which we have in view, then I shall restore to you the true form of your countenance; on condition, however, that you first despatch what I shall command you." And when my father promised that he would with all his might fulfil everything that he might charge him with, provided only that he might recover his own countenance, Peter thus began: "You have heard with your own ears, that one of those who had been sent before has returned from Antioch, and told us how Simon, while he was there, stirred up the multitudes against me, and inflamed the whole city into hatred of me, declaring that I am a magician, and a murderer, and a deceiver, so that they are eager, if they see me, even to eat my flesh. Do therefore what I tell you: leave Clement with me, and go before us to Antioch, with your wife, and your sons Faustus and Faustinus. And I shall also send others with you, whom I think fit, who shall observe whatsoever I command them.

Chap. lxi.—*A mine dug.*

"When therefore you come with them to Antioch, as you will be thought to be Simon, stand in a public place, and proclaim your repentance, and say: 'I Simon declare to you, and confess that all that I said concerning Peter was false: for he is neither a seducer, nor a magician, nor a murderer, nor any of the things that I spoke against him; but I said all these things under the instigation of madness. I therefore entreat you, even I myself, who erewhile gave you causes of hatred against him, that you think no such thing concerning him. But lay aside your hatred; cease from your indignation; because he is truly sent by God for the salvation of the world—a disciple and apostle of the true Prophet. Wherefore I advise, exhort, and charge you that you hear him, and believe him when he preaches to you the truth, lest haply, if you despise him, your very city suddenly perish. But I will tell you why I now make this confession to you. This night an angel of God rebuked me for my wickedness, and scourged me terribly, because I was an enemy to the herald of the truth. Therefore I entreat you, that even if I myself should ever again come to you, and attempt to say anything against Peter, you will not receive nor believe me. For I confess to you, I was a magician, a seducer, a deceiver; but I repent, for it is possible by repentance to blot out former evil deeds.'"

CHAP. LXII.—*A case of conscience.*

When Peter made this intimation to my father, he answered: "I know what you wish; do not trouble yourself further: for I understand and know what I am to undertake when I come to the place." And Peter gave him further instruction, saying: "When therefore you come to the place, and see the people turned by your discourse, and laying aside their hatred, and returning to their longing for me, send and tell me, and I shall come immediately; and when I come, I shall without delay set you free from this strange countenance, and restore to you your own, which is known to all your friends." And having said this, he ordered my brothers to go with him, and at the same time our mother Matthidia, and some of our friends. But my mother refused to go along with him, and said: "It seems as if I should be an adulteress if I were to associate with the countenance of Simon; but if I be compelled to go along with him, it is at all events impossible that I can lie in the same bed with him; but I do not know if I can consent even to go with him." And when she stoutly refused, Anubion began to exhort her, saying: "Believe me and Peter. But does not even his voice persuade you that he is your husband Faustinianus, whom truly I love not less than you do? And, in short, I also myself

2 G

shall come with you." And when Anubion had said this, my mother promised that she would go with him.

Chap. LXIII.—*A pious fraud.*

Then said I : " God arranges our affairs to our liking; for we have with us Anubion an astrologer, with whom, if we come to Antioch, we shall dispute with all earnestness on the subject of *genesis*." And when our father had set out, after the middle of the night, with those whom Peter had ordered to accompany him, and with Anubion ; in the morning, before Peter went to the discussion, those men returned who had convoyed Simon, namely Appion and Athenodorus, and came to us inquiring after my father. But Peter, when he was informed of their coming, ordered them to enter. And when they were seated, they asked, " Where is Faustinianus ? " Peter answered : " We do not know; for since the evening that he went to you, no one of his friends has seen him. But yesterday morning Simon came inquiring for him ; and because we gave him no answer, I know not what he meant, but he said that he was Faustinianus. But when nobody believed him, he wept and lamented, and threatened that he would destroy himself; and afterwards he went away towards the sea."

Chap. LXIV.—*A competition in lying.*

When Appion heard this, and those who were with him, they raised a great howling, saying : " Why have you done this ? Why did you not receive him ? " And when Athenodorus was going to tell me that it was my father Faustinianus himself, Appion prevented him, and said : " We have learned from some one that he has gone with Simon, and that at the entreaty of Faustinianus himself, being unwilling to see his sons, because they are Jews. When therefore we heard this, we came to inquire after him here; but since he is not here, it appears that he must have spoken truly who told us that he has gone with Simon. This, therefore, we tell you." But I Clement, when I understood the designs of Peter, that he wished to make them suppose that the old man would be required at their hands, so that they might be afraid and flee away, I began to aid his design, and said to Appion : " Listen, dear Appion : what we believe to be good, we wish to deliver to our father also ; but if he will not receive it, but rather, as you say, flees away through abhorrence of us—it may perhaps be harsh to say so—we care nothing about him." And when I had said this, they departed, cursing my cruelty, and followed the track of Simon, as we learned on the following day.

CHAP. LXV.—*Success of the plot.*

Meantime, while Peter was daily, according to his custom, teaching the people, and working many miracles and cures, after ten days came one of our people from Antioch, sent by my father, informing us how my father stood in public, accusing Simon, whose face indeed he seemed to wear, and extolling Peter with unmeasured praises, and commending him to all the people, and making them long for him, so that all were changed by his speech, and longed to see him ; and that many had come to love Peter so much, that they raged against my father in his character of Simon, and thought of laying hands on him, because he had done such wrong to Peter! " Wherefore," said he, " make haste, lest haply he be murdered ; for he sent me with speed to you, being in great fear, to ask you to come without delay, that you may find him alive, and also that you may appear at the favourable moment, when the city is growing in affection towards you." He also told us how, as soon as my father entered the city of Antioch, the whole people were gathered to him, supposing him to be Simon ; and he began to make public confession to them all, according to what the restoration of the people demanded : for all, as many as came, both noble and common, both rich and poor, hoping that some prodigies would be wrought by him in his usual way, he addressed thus :

CHAP. LXVI.—*Truth told by lying lips.*

" It is long that the divine patience bears with me, Simon, the most unhappy of men ; for whatever you have wondered at in me was done, not by means of truth, but by the lies and tricks of demons, that I might subvert your faith and condemn my own soul. I confess that all things that I said about Peter were lies; for he never was either a magician or a murderer, but has been sent by God for the salvation of you all; and if from this hour you think that he is to be despised, be assured that your very city may suddenly be destroyed. But, [you will ask,] what is the reason that I make this confession to you of my own accord? I was vehemently rebuked by an angel of God this night, and most severely scourged, because I was his enemy. I therefore entreat you, that if from this hour even I myself shall ever open my mouth against him, you will drive me from your sight; for that foul demon, who is an enemy to the salvation of men, speaks against him through my mouth, that you may not attain to life by his means. For what miracle could the magic art show you through me? I made brazen dogs bark, and statues move, men change their appearances, and suddenly vanish from men's sight; and for these things you ought to have cursed the magic art, which bound your souls with devilish fetters, that I might show you a vain miracle, that you might not believe Peter, who cures the sick in the name of Him by whom he is sent, and expels demons, and gives sight to the blind, and restores health to the palsied, and raises the dead."

Chap. lxvii.—*Faustinianus is himself again.*

Whilst he made these and similar statements, the people began to curse him, and to weep and lament because they had sinned against Peter, believing him to be a magician or wicked man. But the same day, at evening, Faustinianus had his own face restored to him, and the appearance of Simon Magus left him. Now Simon, hearing that his face on Faustinianus had contributed to the glory of Peter, came in haste to anticipate Peter, and intending to cause by his art that his likeness should be taken from Faustinianus, when Christ had already accomplished this according to the word of His apostle. But Niceta and Aquila, seeing their father's face restored after the necessary proclamation, gave thanks

to God, and would not suffer him to address the people any
more.

Chap. LXVIII.—*Peter's entry into Antioch.*

But Simon began, though secretly, to go amongst his
friends and acquaintances, and to malign Peter more than
before.   Then all spat in his face, and drove him from the
city, saying: "You will be chargeable with your own death,
if you think of coming hither again, speaking against Peter."
These things being known [at Laodicea], Peter ordered the
people to meet on the following day; and having ordained one
of those who followed him as bishop over them, and others
as presbyters, and having baptized multitudes, and restored
to health all who were troubled with sicknesses or demons, he
stayed there three days longer; and all things being properly
arranged, he bade them farewell, and set out from Laodicea,
being much longed for by the people of Antioch.   And the
whole city began to hear, through Niceta and Aquila, that
Peter was coming. Then all the people of the city of
Antioch, hearing of Peter's arrival, went to meet him, and
almost all the old men and the nobles came with ashes
sprinkled on their heads, in this way testifying their repentance, because they had listened to the magician Simon, in
opposition to his preaching.

Chap. LXIX.—*Peter's thanksgiving.*

Stating these and such like things, they bring to him those
distressed with sicknesses, and tormented with demons, paralytics also, and those suffering diverse perils; and there was
an infinite number of sick people collected.   And when
Peter saw that they not only repented of the evil thoughts
they had entertained of him through means of Simon, but
also that they showed so entire faith in God, that they believed that all who suffered from every sort of ailment could
be healed by him, he spread out his hands towards heaven,
pouring out prayers with tears, and gave thanks to God,
saying: "I bless thee, O Father, worthy of all praise, who
hast deigned to fulfil every word and promise of Thy Son,

that every creature may know that Thou alone art God in heaven and in earth."

Chap. lxx.—*Miracles.*

With such sayings, he went up on a height, and ordered all the multitude of sick people to be ranged before him, and addressed them all in these words : " As you see me to be a man like to yourselves, do not suppose that you can recover your health from me, but through Him who, coming down from heaven, has shown to those who believe in Him a perfect medicine for body and soul. Hence let all this people be witnesses to your declaration, that with your whole heart you believe in the Lord Jesus Christ, that they may know that themselves also may be saved by Him." And when all the multitude of the sick with one voice cried out that He is the true God whom Peter preaches, suddenly an overpowering light of the grace of God appeared in the midst of the people ; and the paralytics being cured, began to run to Peter's feet, the blind to shout on the recovery of their sight, the lame to give thanks on regaining the power of walking, the sick to rejoice in restored health ; some even who were barely alive, being already without consciousness or the power of speech, were raised up ; and all the lunatics, and those possessed of demons, were set free.

Chap. lxxi.—*Success.*

So great grace of His power did the Holy Spirit show on that day, that all, from the least to the greatest, with one voice confessed the Lord ; and not to delay you with many words, within seven days, more than ten thousand men, believing in God, were baptized and consecrated by sanctification : so that Theophilus, who was more exalted than all the men of power in that city, with all eagerness of desire consecrated the great palace of his house under the name of a church, and a chair was placed in it for the Apostle Peter by all the people ; and the whole multitude assembling daily to hear the word, believed in the healthful doctrine which was avouched by the efficacy of cures.

CHAP. LXXII.—*Happy ending.*

Then I Clement, with my brothers and our mother, spoke to our father, asking him whether any remnants of unbelief remained in him. And he said : " Come, and you shall see, in the presence of Peter, what an increase of faith has grown in me." Then Faustinianus approached, and fell down at Peter's feet, saying : " The seeds of your word, which the field of my mind has received, are now sprung up, and have so advanced to fruitful maturity, that nothing is wanting but that you separate me from the chaff by that spiritual reaping-hook of yours, and place me in the garner of the Lord, making me partaker of the divine table." Then Peter, with all alacrity grasping his hand, presented him to me Clement, and my brothers, saying : " As God has restored your sons to you, their father, so also your sons restore their father to God." And he proclaimed a fast to all the people, and on the next Lord's day he baptized him ; and in the midst of the people, taking occasion from his conversion, he related all his fortunes, so that the whole city received him as an angel, and paid him no less honour than they did to the apostle. [And these things being known, Peter ordered the people to meet on the following day ; and having ordained one of his followers as bishop, and others as presbyters, he baptized also a great number of people, and restored to health all who had been distressed with sicknesses.[1]]

[1] This sentence occurs only in one MS.

INDEXES.

I.

PASSAGES OF SCRIPTURE.

473

II.

INDEX OF SUBJECTS.

MURRAY AND GIBB, EDINBURGH,

PRINTERS TO HER MAJESTY'S STATIONERY OFFICE.

Books for the Library of Clergymen and Educated Laymen.

Clark's Foreign Theological Library.

ANNUAL SUBSCRIPTION, ONE GUINEA (PAYABLE IN ADVANCE) FOR FOUR
VOLUMES, DEMY 8VO.

₊ *When not paid in advance, the retail bookseller is entitled to charge* 24s.

THE following are the Contents of each of the Series. Each Work may be had separately at the price within parentheses.

₊ A SELECTION of Twelve Volumes from First Series will be supplied at the Subscription Price of Three Guineas ; or Twenty Volumes from First and Second Series at the Subscription Price of Five Guineas; or of Thirty-two Volumes from First, Second, and Third Series for Eight Guineas (or a larger number at same ratio).

The following may be added to, or substituted for the same number of Volumes in, such a selection :—

> Macdonald's Introduction to the Pentateuch. 2 Volumes.
> Hengstenberg's Egypt and the Books of Moses. 1 Volume.
> Ackerman on the Christian Element in Plato. 1 Volume.
> Robinson's Greek Lexicon of the New Testament. 1 Volume.

FIRST SERIES.

Twenty-nine Volumes. Subscription Price, £7, 12s. 6d.

Hengstenberg's Commentary on the Psalms. 3 Volumes. (£1, 13s.)
Shedd's History of Christian Doctrine. 2 Volumes. (£1, 1s.)
Gieseler's Compendium of Ecclesiastical History. 5 Volumes. (£2, 12s. 6d.)
Neander's General Church History. 9 Volumes. (£2, 11s. 6d.)
Olshausen on the Gospels and Acts. 4 Volumes. (£2, 2s.)
Olshausen on the Romans. (10s. 6d.)
Olshausen on the Corinthians. (9s.)
Olshausen on the Galatians, Ephesians, Colossians, and Thessalonians. (10s. 6d.)
Olshausen on Philippians, Titus, and Timothy. (10s. 6d.)
Olshausen and Ebrard on the Hebrews. (10s. 6d.)
Havernick's General Introduction to the Old Testament. (10s. 6d.)

SECOND SERIES.

Twenty Volumes. Subscription Price, £5, 5s.

Stier on the Words of the Lord Jesus. 8 Volumes. (£4, 4s.)
Hengstenberg's Christology of the Old Testament. 4 Volumes. (£2, 2s.)
Ullmann's Reformers before the Reformation. 2 Volumes. (£1, 1s.)
Gerlach's Commentary on the Pentateuch. 1 Volume. (10s. 6d.)
Baumgarten's Apostolic History. 3 Volumes. (£1, 7s.)
₊ Müller on the Doctrine of Sin. 2 Volumes. (£1, 1s.)

₊ A new translation of this important work has been carefully prepared, and will be supplied to regular Subscribers who may wish it, at subscription price (10s. 6d.).

[Over.

Foreign Theological Library—*continued.*

THIRD SERIES.

Twenty Volumes (1859–60–61–62–63).   Subscription Price, £5, 5s.

N.B.—A single Year's Books (except in the case of the current Year) cannot be supplied separately.   Non-subscribers, price 10s. 6d. each Volume, with exceptions marked.

*** The following is the order of Publication, but any Two Years or more can be had at Subscription Price :—

1st Year (1859).

Kurtz on Old Covenant Dispensation.   3 Volumes.
Stier on the Words of the Risen Saviour, and on the Epistle of St. James.   1 Vol.

2d Year (1860).

Hengstenberg on Ecclesiastes.   1 Volume.   (9s.)
Tholuck on St. John.   1 Volume.   (9s.)
Tholuck on the Sermon on the Mount.   1 Volume.
Ebrard on Epistles of John.   1 Volume.

3d Year (1861).

Lange on St. Matthew's Gospel.   Volumes I. and II.
Dorner on Person of Christ.   Division I., Vol. I. ; and Division II., Vol. I.

4th Year (1862).

Dorner on Person of Christ.   Division I., Volume II.
Dorner on Person of Christ.   Division II., Volume II.
Lange on Matthew and Mark.   Volume III.
Oosterzee on St. Luke.   Edited by Dr. Lange.   Volume I.   (9s.)

5th Year (1863).

Oosterzee on St. Luke.   Edited by Dr. Lange.   Vol. II.   (Completion.)   (9s.)
Dorner on Person of Christ.   Division II., Volume III.
Kurtz on the Old Testament Sacrifices.
Ebrard on the Gospel History.

FOURTH SERIES.

1st Year (1864).

Lange, Commentary on the Acts of the Apostles.   2 Volumes.
Keil and Delitzsch, Commentary on the Pentateuch.   Volumes I. and II.

2d Year (1865).

Hengstenberg on the Gospel of St. John.   2 Volumes.
Keil and Delitzsch on the Pentateuch.   Volume III.
Keil and Delitzsch on Joshua, Judges, and Ruth.

3d Year (1866).

Keil and Delitzsch on Samuel.   1 Volume.
Keil and Delitzsch on Job.   2 Volumes.
Martensen's System of Christian Doctrine.   1 Volume.

4th Year (1867).

Delitzsch's System of Biblical Psychology.   (12s.)
Delitzsch's Commentary on Isaiah.   2 Volumes.
Auberlen on the Divine Revelation.

5th Year (1868).

First Issue—
Keil and Delitzsch's Commentary on the Minor Prophets.   2 Volumes.

Subscribers' Names received by all Booksellers.

EDINBURGH: T. AND T. CLARK.

LONDON (for Non-subscribers only): HAMILTON, ADAMS, AND Co.